STELLIFORM PRESS

Earth-focused fiction. Stellar stories.
Stelliform.press.

Stelliform Press is shaping conversations about nature and our place within it. We invite you to join the conversation by leaving a comment or review on your favorite social media platform. Find us on the web at www.stelliform.press and on Twitter, Instagram and Facebook @StelliformPress.

The Cambridge Companion to
Winston Churchill

Viewed by some as the saviour of his nation, and by others as a racist imperialist, who was Winston Churchill really, and how has he become such a controversial figure? Combining the best of established scholarship with important new perspectives, this Companion places Churchill's life and legacy in a broader context. It highlights different aspects of his life and personality, examining his core beliefs, working practices, key relationships and the political issues and campaigns that he helped shape, and which in turn shaped him. Controversial subjects, such as area bombing, Ireland, India and Empire are addressed in full, to try and explain how Churchill has become such a deeply divisive figure. Through careful analysis, this book presents a full and rounded picture of Winston Churchill, providing much needed nuance and context to the debates about his life and legacy.

ALLEN PACKWOOD BA, MPhil (Cantab), is a Fellow of Churchill College at the University of Cambridge, and the Director of the Churchill Archives Centre. He is a Fellow of the Royal Historical Society and was awarded an OBE for services to archives and scholarship in the 2016 Queen's Birthday Honours. His book, *How Churchill Waged War*, was published in 2018.

The Cambridge Companion to
Winston Churchill

Edited by
ALLEN PACKWOOD
Churchill College, Cambridge

CAMBRIDGE
UNIVERSITY PRESS

CAMBRIDGE
UNIVERSITY PRESS

Shaftesbury Road, Cambridge CB2 8EA, United Kingdom

One Liberty Plaza, 20th Floor, New York, NY 10006, USA

477 Williamstown Road, Port Melbourne, VIC 3207, Australia

314–321, 3rd Floor, Plot 3, Splendor Forum, Jasola District Centre, New Delhi – 110025, India

103 Penang Road, #05–06/07, Visioncrest Commercial, Singapore 238467

Cambridge University Press is part of Cambridge University Press & Assessment, a department of the University of Cambridge.

We share the University's mission to contribute to society through the pursuit of education, learning and research at the highest international levels of excellence.

www.cambridge.org
Information on this title: www.cambridge.org/9781108840231
DOI: 10.1017/9781108879255

First published 2023

A catalogue record for this publication is available from the British Library.

ISBN 978-1-108-84023-1 Hardback
ISBN 978-1-108-79416-9 Paperback

Contents

Figures

Contributors

PIERS BRENDON was Keeper of the Churchill Archives Centre from 1995 to 2001. He is the author of sixteen books, including *Winston Churchill: A Brief Life* (1984) and *Churchill's Bestiary: His Life Through Animals* (2018). He is Fellow of Churchill College, Cambridge and Fellow of the Royal Society of Literature.

PETER CLARKE is Emeritus Professor of Modern British History at the University of Cambridge. Over the last fifty years he has engaged with different aspects of Churchill's career in many of his books, most specifically in *Mr Churchill's Profession* (2015). This focussed on the importance of Churchill's career as a well-paid writer and on the way in which he wrote about the English-speaking peoples.

MARTIN DAUNTON is Emeritus Professor of Economic History at the University of Cambridge and Visiting Professor of Economic History at Gresham College. He has covered Churchill's economics in *Trusting Leviathan: The Politics of Taxation in Britain, 1799–1914* (2001) and *Just Taxes: The Politics of Taxation in Britain, 1914–1979* (2002), and has also written on welfare policy. He has recently completed a book on the economic governance of the world since 1933 and is currently working on intergenerational equity.

WARREN DOCKTER is a graduate of the University of Tennessee and gained his PhD at the University of Nottingham in July 2012. He is the author of *Winston Churchill and the Islamic World: Orientalism, Empire and Diplomacy in the Middle East* (2015). Warren has been Archives By-Fellow at Churchill College, Cambridge; Junior Research Fellow at Clare Hall, Cambridge; and a lecturer at Exeter University, Royal Holloway, University of London and Aberystwyth University. He has recently returned to Tennessee to become President of the East Tennessee Historical Society. He holds an Honorary Lectureship in International Politics at Aberystwyth University.

NIAMH GALLAGHER is Lecturer in Modern British and Irish History and Fellow of St Catharine's College at the University of Cambridge. Her debut monograph, *Ireland and the Great War: A Social and Political History* (2019), is the first work of Irish history to win the Royal Historical Society's Whitfield Prize. Her research spans the First World War, the Irish Revolutionary period, and Ireland and the British Empire. She co-convenes the *Future of the Island of Ireland* series and makes regular media appearances.

GAYNOR JOHNSON is Professor of International History at the University of Kent. Her most recent publications relate to the history and operation of the British Foreign Office and the use of prosopography as a research tool for international historians. She has also published widely on twentieth-century British foreign policy. Her most recent book is *Politician and Internationalist: Lord Robert Cecil* (2013). She is currently writing two books: one on British ambassadors to Paris during the era between the two world wars and another on the institutional history of the Foreign Office.

H. KUMARASINGHAM is Senior Lecturer in British Politics at the University of Edinburgh. He is a political historian of the United Kingdom, the Commonwealth and the British Empire. His work covers the high politics of the post-war period, especially concerning constitutional and imperial issues. He is currently co-editing *The Cambridge Constitutional History of the United Kingdom* and is Co-Editor of *The Transactions of the Royal Historical Society.*

SEAN LANG is Senior Lecturer in History at Anglia Ruskin University, where he lectures on the British Empire and modern Europe. He also lectures regularly for the Cambridge University Institute of Continuing Education. He broadcasts regularly on radio and television on history and politics and devised and helped present the series *Acts and Facts* for BBC Parliament. His most recent work is a chapter on how the 1919 Peace Settlement was received by young people around the Empire in *1918: Tourner la Page?* (2021).

DAVID LOUGH is a historian and author. He used the experience of his private banking career to research the previously untold story of Winston Churchill's precarious personal finances, thus illuminating a new human side of the figure who has often been treated as an icon. The result was the much-acclaimed *No More Champagne: Churchill and His Money*

(2015). His second book was *Darling Winston: Forty Years of Letters between Winston Churchill and His Mother* (2018).

ALLEN PACKWOOD is Director of the Churchill Archives Centre and Fellow of Churchill College, Cambridge. He has organised international conferences and co-curated several major exhibitions on the life of Winston Churchill and is the author of *How Churchill Waged War* (2018).

BARRY PHIPPS is Director of Studies in the History of Art at Churchill College, Cambridge. He specialises in modern and contemporary art, often in relation to the sciences. His academic background is rooted in fine art as an undergraduate and lecturer, with research degrees in continental philosophy (Warwick), the history of art (Oxford) and the history and philosophy of architecture (Cambridge). In keeping with this multi-disciplinary background, he has written and lectured on a broad range of topics, from post-war architecture to modern British sculpture, and from new Nordic art to contemporary European photography.

SONIA PURNELL is a journalist and bestselling author known for her lively writing style and meticulous research, with a growing readership across the world. Her first book – the unauthorised biography of Boris Johnson, *Just Boris: A Tale of Blond Ambition* – was long-listed for the Orwell Prize in 2011. Her second book, *First Lady* in the UK and *Clementine* in the USA (a finalist for the Plutarch Prize), revealed for the first time the vital role played in Winston Churchill's career by his wife Clementine and has been optioned for a Hollywood movie. Her new work, *A Woman of No Importance*, is the astonishing but true-life tale of a female spy in the Second World War, Virginia Hall, a young American socialite with a wooden leg who helped fan the flames of French resistance. It won the Plutarch Prize in 2020.

KISHAN S. RANA was educated at St Stephens College, Delhi University before joining the Indian Foreign Service in 1960. He served for thirty-five years in China, Geneva and Delhi, and then as Ambassador or High Commissioner to Algeria, Czechoslovakia and Kenya (and Consul General, San Francisco, 1986–9), then to Mauritius and Germany. In 1981–3 he served as a joint secretary in Prime Minister Indira Gandhi's office for a year, and directly after that he headed personnel administration in the Ministry of External Affairs. Since 2000 he has focussed on teaching and writing and is currently Professor Emeritus and a part-time e-learning teaching faculty member at DiploFoundation, Malta and Geneva. He has recently written *Churchill and India: Manipulation or Betrayal?* (2022).

DAVID REYNOLDS is Professor Emeritus of International History at Cambridge University and Fellow of Christ's College, Cambridge. He was elected Fellow of the British Academy in 2005. His books on Churchill include *In Command of History: Churchill Fighting and Writing the Second World War* (Wolfson Prize) and, with Vladimir Pechatnov, *The Kremlin Letters: Stalin's Wartime Correspondence with Churchill and Roosevelt* (Link-Kuehl Prize). Among his works on broader themes are *The Long Shadow: The Great War and the 20th Century* and *Island Stories: An Unconventional History of Britain*. He has also written and presented several television documentaries on Churchill and the two world wars.

PETER SLOMAN is Professor of British Politics at the University of Cambridge and Fellow of Churchill College, Cambridge. He is the author of two books, *The Liberal Party and the Economy, 1929–1964* (2015) and *Transfer State: The Idea of a Guaranteed Income and the Politics of Redistribution in Modern Britain* (2019), together with a number of articles on British party politics and economic and social policy.

VICTORIA TAYLOR is an aviation historian based at the University of Hull and Sheffield Hallam University, where she completed her PhD thesis on the Luftwaffe and National Socialism in 2022. In recognition of this research, she was awarded the 2020 Royal Air Force Museum Doctoral Academic Prize in 2021. She also completed her Master's in Historical Research (MRes) thesis on Britain's wartime and post-war mythologisation of Operation Chastise at Hull, for which she was awarded the Royal Air Force Museum's RAF Centenary Master's Academic Prize in 2019. Victoria specialises in the history of airpower, aviation and the public imagination in Britain and Germany.

RICHARD TOYE is Professor of Modern History at the University of Exeter. He has written widely on British and international history and in particular on the life and career of Winston Churchill. His books include *The Roar of the Lion: The Untold Story of Churchill's World War II Speeches* (2013) and *Winston Churchill: A Life in the News* (2020).

DAVID B. WOOLNER is Professor of History, Marist College; Senior Fellow and Resident Historian of the Roosevelt Institute; and Senior Fellow of the Center for Civic Engagement at Bard College. He is the author of *The Last 100 Days: FDR at War and at Peace* (2017) and editor/co-editor of five books, including *Progressivism in America: Past, Present and Future* (2016), *FDR's World: War, Peace and Legacies* (2008) and *FDR, the Vatican, and the Roman Catholic Church in America* (2003). He is a member of the Scholarly Advisory Board of the Gilder Lehrman Institute of American History and was recently named a Fulbright Specialist by the U. S. Department of State's Bureau of Educational and Cultural Affairs. He served as a historical consultant to the Ken Burns films *The Roosevelts: An Intimate History* and *The U.S. and the Holocaust,* and to numerous special exhibitions at the FDR Presidential Library and Museum.

Foreword

THE RT HON THE LORD BOATENG PC DL, CHAIR OF THE SIR
WINSTON CHURCHILL ARCHIVE TRUST

No single individual in modern times has captured the imagination
and interest of so many for so long and for such a variety of reasons as Sir
Winston Churchill. This reflects the strength of his personality and the
complexity of his character, as well as the significance of his achievements as
a wartime leader in mobilising the global effort against the evils of fascism.

He was certainly the first political figure of which I was aware, growing up in the Gold Coast and Ghana – apart, of course, from our own
national liberation hero, Dr Kwame Nkrumah. My father Kwaku
Boateng, a lawyer and Cabinet minister in post-independent Ghana,
treasured a collection of Churchill's works. My mother Peggy, who taught
English and what was then called elocution, though an implacable foe of
his peacetime policy, nevertheless delighted in his use of the English
language. The records of his speeches were therefore played frequently on
the family Grundig RadioGram, often and much to my annoyance in
preference to my own choice, *The Wizard of Oz*, *Pinocchio* or *Peter and the
Wolf*. They therefore formed part of the soundtrack of my childhood.

There is so much that has been written about Sir Winston Churchill in
so many languages – not least, of course, by Churchill himself. He was
acutely conscious of the importance of shaping the narrative around his
own life. There are a wide range of views about the man and his legacy. He
is rated from hero to zero. The nature of the debates about him has
inevitably shifted over time in response to new scholarship and changes
in societal values and interests. This important collection of essays reflects
some of the best of the contemporary thinking on its subject.

Britain is no longer an imperial power. The notion of racial hierarchy is
discredited and its promulgation in any form rightly no longer acceptable.

Class distinctions are disparaged and levelling up is seen as a political imperative. Ours is a very different world from the one into which Churchill was born and whose values and worldview he clung to all his life, even in the face of the more enlightened views of some of his contemporaries and sometimes of the clear evidence. And yet without his qualities of leadership and the moral heroism he inspired in the face of implacable evil, the freedoms we take for granted and the right of national self-determination the Atlantic Charter endorsed would arguably be non-existent.

I say 'arguably' because dissenting and contested views were the stuff of Churchill's long life, and controversy over his legacy has not abated over the many years since his death. It has, however, of late taken on an even more strident and polarised tone. There has been an attempt to weaponise Churchill in the current culture wars in a way that does neither him nor the cause of reasoned and respectful argument any justice. This makes this book of essays even more welcome, not just for its scholarship and erudition but also for its sense of balance and openness to the serious analysis of contested views.

Much of the scholarship in these essays draws on material contained in the Churchill Archives in Cambridge, which are held in trust for the nation. Meticulously and sensitively edited, this book brings together a range of authors, each with their own fresh and interesting perspective on Churchill's life and times. It deserves to be widely read.

The role of the Sir Winston Churchill Archive Trust that holds this material is not to be a protagonist in the ongoing controversies that surround Churchill but to preserve and promote access to the evidence of his writings and times. The papers held in the Archive are the raw material of history, and their dissemination across the generations and continents represents a contribution to a better understanding not only of a complex man but also of the making of the modern world. Holding those papers in safety while also creating a safe space for the exchange of sometimes conflicting views and ideas is both a responsibility and a privilege.

One of the lessons I draw from this book of essays and the life of this complex man is that the freedom to express contested ideas is not to be taken for granted and requires constant vigilance in its defence. The threats to such freedom globally and domestically are all too apparent. We still have need for the lessons history teaches us.

Acknowledgements

This book could not have been written without the support of its contributing authors, who gave freely of their time and expertise. Quotes from the speeches, works and writings of Winston S. Churchill are reproduced with permission of Curtis Brown, London on behalf of The Estate of Winston S. Churchill. © The Estate of Winston S. Churchill. The Royal Institution of Cornwall kindly gave permission for a quote from the estate of A. L. Rowse. Thanks are also due to Felicity Bryan Associates, Professor John Charmley, Leonie Gombrich, David Higham Associates, The Munnings Art Museum, The Franklin D. Roosevelt Presidential Library and Professor David Stafford. Images from the Broadwater Collection are reproduced with permission of Curtis Brown, London, while the image of Churchill's painting, *Tower of the Koutoubia Mosque* (Figure 8.1), is reproduced courtesy of Churchill Heritage Limited. In both cases, thanks are due to the late and much-missed Mrs Catherine Churchill.

The editor would like to express his gratitude to Elizabeth Friend-Smith and the team at Cambridge University Press and to his colleagues at Churchill College and the Churchill Archives Centre, especially Andrew Riley, who read the text and made enormously helpful suggestions. Thanks are due to Lord Boateng for providing the foreword and to Piers Brendon, Peter Clarke, Warren Dockter, David Reynolds and Richard Toye for offering additional advice, support and expertise.

Abbreviations

Abbreviations of Key Sources

The official biography of Winston Churchill begun by Randolph Churchill and completed by Martin Gilbert is cited in the notes as OB. The accompanying companion volumes are cited as CV. See note 7 in the Introduction for full publication details.

CAC denotes original documents from the Churchill Archives Centre at Churchill College, Cambridge.

The Complete Speeches of Winston Churchill edited by Robert Rhodes James is cited as Complete Speeches.

TNA denotes original documents from the UK National Archives at Kew in London.

Other Commonly Occurring Abbreviations

ANZAC	Australian and New Zealand Army Corps
BBC	British Broadcasting Corporation
ECHR	European Convention on Human Rights
EEC	European Economic Community
EU	European Union
FDR	President Franklin Delano Roosevelt
GATT	General Agreement on Tariff and Trade
GDP	gross domestic product
IPP	Irish Parliamentary Party
IRA	Irish Republican Army
MP	member of parliament
NATO	North Atlantic Treaty Organization

ONG	One Nation Group
PRA	President of the Royal Academy
RA	Royal Academy
RAF	Royal Air Force
RIC	Royal Irish Constabulary
RNAS	Royal Naval Air Service
SIS	Secret Intelligence Service
SOE	Special Operations Executive
TR	President Theodore Roosevelt
UN	United Nations
USA	United States of America
USSR	Union of Soviet Socialist Republics (Soviet Union)
UVF	Ulster Volunteer Force

Introduction
Who Was Winston Churchill?

Who was Winston Churchill? In 2017 he was portrayed both as an irascible, tub-thumping, cigar-chewing maverick by Gary Oldman in the film *Darkest Hour* and as a man on the edge of a nervous breakdown wracked by guilt over his role in the First World War by Brian Cox in the movie *Churchill*. Both films are perhaps revealing of what contemporary audiences want to see; a loner who defies the establishment and a leader who develops through a redemptive arc, suffering a crisis of conscience only to have his resolve stiffened through contact with ordinary people before re-finding his voice. It makes for great drama, but it is not history.

Add to this Churchill's presence in other movies, such as *The Gathering Storm* (2002) or *The King's Speech* (2010), not to mention popular television series like *The Crown* and even *Dr Who*, and it is obvious that he has become as much a dramatic personality as an historical one. He is an instantly recognisable and often seemingly omnipresent figure. His words have been quoted and misquoted by politicians, journalists and celebrities; his legacy is the subject of fierce debate. It is evident that his deliberately high-profile leadership as the British prime minister during the Second World War has established a level of interest and scrutiny that has not diminished since his death in 1965. Churchill was made for the big screen because he was a colourful and controversial character and the controversies about him have been amplified because of his role in 1940 and the enduring significance of that moment in narratives of modern British history.

Two of his most recent biographies illustrate the polarisation in current Churchill scholarship. To Andrew Roberts, author of *Churchill: Walking with Destiny* (2018), Churchill did better than either of his two heroes, John Churchill, 1st Duke of Marlborough, or Napoleon, because 'the battles he won saved liberty'.[1] Meanwhile, to Geoffrey Wheatcroft, author of *Churchill's Shadow* (2021), 'so far from being a universal oracle of wisdom and virtue, few great men have been wrong so often, have made so many mistakes, or have held so many opinions and prejudices which were repugnant even at the time'.[2]

One of the few areas where Roberts and Wheatcroft agree is on 'the sheer vastness of Churchill's life' and the huge amount of literature it has generated.[3] This volume therefore aims to serve as an introduction, overview and guide to the life of one of the most researched, debated and contested figures of our recent past.

Winston Spencer-Churchill (1874–1965) was undoubtedly an influential personage within Britain and the Empire for much of the first six decades of the twentieth century and a powerful voice on the world stage from 1940 onwards. He was unusual in the role he played not only in shaping events but also in chronicling them, establishing a lasting reputation as an orator and writer. The interplay between his words and actions forms a recurring theme within this volume.

Yet his actions were not always of his own choosing or preference. Prior to 1940, he exercised political office at the discretion of the prime minister of the day, and both in and out of office he was working within the constraints of existing political, social, cultural and economic systems, often responding to events and adapting to new realities while wrestling with human emotions and frailties. Over the course of his six decades in public life, he was not always consistent or predictable and changed party twice. Perhaps he put it best himself when he said: 'To improve is to change; so to be perfect is to have changed often.'[4] According to one of his wartime civil servants, he also said: 'In the course of my life I have often had to eat my words, and I must confess that I have always found it a wholesome diet.'[5]

The chapters that follow combine contributions from established writers in the field with new perspectives from academics working in related areas. They seek to synthesise, summarise and develop the latest research, tracing the formation and development of Churchill's character, political opinions, worldview, thoughts and actions over the course of his lifetime while placing these in their proper historical context. It is a volume that sets out to look at Churchill in the round, and not just at his wartime leadership, and to show the interrelationship between Churchill the prime minister and what came before and after. It aims to put the spotlight back on themes such as social policy, economics, party politics and his writing, all of which, at different points, occupied large swathes of his time. Areas of controversy, such as empire, India, Ireland and his support for aerial bombing, have been given their own chapters.

The Basic Chronology of Churchill's Life and Career

Winston Leonard Spencer-Churchill was born on 30 November 1874 at Blenheim Palace, the ancestral home of his grandfather, the 7th Duke of Marlborough. His father was Lord Randolph Churchill (1849–95), a younger son of the duke, who became a prominent Conservative member of parliament and government minister and who briefly held the office of chancellor of the exchequer. His mother was born Jennie Jerome (1854–1921) in Brooklyn, New York, and was the daughter of the American entrepreneur Leonard Jerome, from whom Churchill took his middle name. Churchill was born into the highest echelons of British society at a time when the Empire was at its zenith and was raised as the son of famous and extravagant parents who left him with a complex emotional and financial inheritance, which is explored by David Lough in Chapter 2.

Young Winston experienced an education typical of a Victorian aristocrat. He was sent to a strict boarding school in Ascot just before his eighth birthday, then to a more liberal establishment in Brighton, before taking up a place at Harrow School. He did not excel academically, although neither was his performance quite as bad as he subsequently painted it, and it was decided that he would go into the army rather than to university. Churchill only qualified for the officer training school at Sandhurst on his third attempt, but he graduated 20th from a class of 130. His father died on 24 January 1895 just before Winston was gazetted as a cavalry officer in the 4th Queen's Own Hussars.

The years 1895–1900 were formative ones. Churchill quickly decided that army life was not for him and that he wanted to take up his father's mantle and pursue a career in politics. When his regiment was sent to India, he mitigated the boredom of military routine in Bangalore by embarking on a campaign of self-improvement through reading and playing polo at the highest inter-regimental level. He sought out action, using his family's extensive political connections to undertake a trip to Cuba (1895), where he accompanied Spanish forces involved in suppressing a Cuban national uprising, and subsequently got himself temporarily transferred to active operations on the Afghan frontier (1897) and in the Sudan (1898). He wrote up his experiences as newspaper articles and books, thereby raising his profile and generating an income. In 1899 he stood unsuccessfully for parliament in Oldham before taking up a lucrative offer to cover the Second Boer War as a newspaper correspondent. His subsequent capture and escape ensured his international celebrity and guaranteed his election for Oldham in 1900. Warren Dockter (Chapter 3) sheds new light on the overlap between Churchill's military career and political development during this crucial period, highlighting his growing interest in intelligence, while Peter Clarke (Chapter 4) analyses Churchill's first career as a journalist and writer.

Churchill's political career was controversial from the beginning. He became a member of a small group of disruptive Conservative MPs called the *Hughligans* (named for Lord Hugh Cecil) before breaking with the party of his father over opposition to the introduction of tariffs. Churchill's vocal support for free trade led to his defection to the Liberal Party (1904). His timing was opportune as the political pendulum was clearly swinging towards the Liberals, who formed an administration and soon afterwards won a landslide election victory (1906). This necessitated a change of constituency, and Churchill moved down the road from Oldham to Manchester North-West, but it also brought him into government as the undersecretary of state at the colonial office (1905–8).

Churchill enjoyed the patronage of Prime Minister Herbert Asquith and established a close working relationship with the Welsh politician David Lloyd George. He entered the British Cabinet in 1908 at the age of just thirty-three and served as president of the Board of Trade (1908–10), home secretary (1910–11) and first lord of the admiralty (1911–15). Yet there were always limits to Churchill's radicalism, and he remained at heart a Victorian paternalist. The tensions between his support for the liberal agenda, his imperialism and his belief in the established order are a recurring and important theme in Churchill scholarship. Two issues that dominated the Edwardian political agenda were social policy and Ireland. They are tackled in this volume by Peter Sloman and Niamh Gallagher in Chapters 5 and 6.

As Sean Lang shows in Chapter 7, the First World War was a defining experience for Churchill and one that nearly destroyed his political career. Desperate to see the fleet playing a more prominent role, he was the leading advocate in the Cabinet for the disastrous attempt to force the Dardanelles Strait. Though originally intended as a purely naval operation, events escalated when a multi-national force failed to wrest the Gallipoli peninsula from Turkish control. Defeat heaped pressure on Asquith to restructure his government and bring in the Conservative opposition. Their price for coalition was Churchill's removal from the Admiralty. Clementine Churchill feared her husband would die of grief.

He served briefly as chancellor of the Duchy of Lancaster, an office without any real power, before resigning from government and taking up a military commission on the Western Front, where he commanded a battalion of Royal Scots Fusiliers (1916). It was at this low ebb that he also discovered a passion for painting, a preoccupation that was to become so much more than a simple hobby, as Barry Phipps illustrates in Chapter 8, revealing the serious and sustained engagement between Churchill, art and artists.

By the end of the war, Churchill was back in government as minister for munitions (1917–19) and then as secretary of state for war and air (1919–21) and secretary of state for the colonies (1921–2). It was a period that saw him involved in dealing with the aftermath of the global conflict, in Ireland, in the Middle East and in his visceral response to the Bolshevik revolution in Russia. He also re-fought the war through his multi-volume history *The World Crisis*, which devoted many pages to a defence of his actions over the Dardanelles. The defeat of Lloyd George's coalition government in 1922, a campaign during which he was struck down by illness, famously left him 'without an office, without a seat, without a party, and without an appendix'.[6] It took him just over two years to get back into parliament and shortly thereafter, in response to the rise of socialism at home and communism abroad, he rejoined the Conservative Party.

To Churchill's surprise, he was amply rewarded for this second defection when Prime Minister Stanley Baldwin made him chancellor of the exchequer. His time in that office between 1924 and 1929 is often dismissed as a failure, with Churchill's decision to return the country to the gold standard widely seen as contributing to the subsequent Great Depression. This volume contains a more detailed and nuanced analysis by Martin Daunton in Chapter 9.

The 1930s saw Churchill out of office and campaigning against the Conservative-dominated governments of Baldwin and then Neville Chamberlain, initially opposing greater independence for India and later promoting British rearmament and condemning the appeasement of Hitler's Germany. His two all-consuming political campaigns of this period, against Indian independence and German appeasement, are explored respectively by Kishan S. Rana (Chapter 11) and Gaynor Johnson (Chapter 12), while Piers Brendon (Chapter 10) compares Churchill's imperialism with that of Presidents Theodore and Franklin Roosevelt. It was the outbreak of war that brought Churchill back to the political front rank, returning to the office of first lord of the admiralty that he had held at the commencement of the First World War.

Then came his premiership. Churchill was not elected prime minister. He led a national coalition government for five years. It was during these years, and especially 1940–1, that his reputation as the 'greatest Briton' was formed. He is widely credited with leading from the front and is often both praised and criticised for his bellicosity. The Anglo-American alliance was certainly central to his thinking and worldview, but he also had to manage the relationship with the Soviet Union, the Empire and other allies. The later stages of the war found both Britain and Churchill struggling to cope with their declining world role. These themes are explored by Allen Packwood, David B. Woolner and David Reynolds in Chapters 13, 14 and 15, respectively, while Victoria Taylor (Chapter 16) looks in detail at Churchill's support for the bombing offensives against Germany, perhaps the most controversial element of his policy of waging war until victory.

The Conservative Party were comprehensively defeated in the 1945 General Election, but Churchill chose not to retire and stayed on as Leader of the Opposition. He wrote and published his multi-volume war memoirs and embarked on new political campaigns. In the face of the Soviet domination of Eastern Europe and the developing Cold War, he sought to maintain and strengthen the alliance with the United States while also promoting greater unity between the countries of Western Europe. Richard Toye gives the context of Churchill's European campaign in Chapter 18.

Churchill had stated in 1942 that he had not become the king's first minister to preside over the liquidation of the British Empire, but, out of power from 1945, he could only watch as India was partitioned and

Palestine abandoned. What is uncertain is whether, had he still been in office, he would have been able to ensure that events turned out differently.

Back in 10 Downing Street as elected prime minister between 1951 and 1955, Churchill's room for manoeuvre on the domestic and international front was limited, while his health was failing. His last great political campaign was an attempt to seek a summit meeting with the Soviets and in this he was ultimately frustrated by President Eisenhower. The failure of his remaining political ambitions was obscured by his international celebrity. He was awarded the Nobel Prize for Literature and made a Knight of the Garter by Elizabeth II in 1953. H. Kumarasingham (Chapter 19) gives us a different perspective, showing Churchill in old age but clinging to office and the problems faced by the Conservative Party in removing someone who was both an international icon and an increasing electoral liability.

On leaving office in 1955, Churchill dedicated himself to finishing and publishing his last multi-volume work, *A History of the English-Speaking Peoples*. He did not intervene publicly in politics but remained a major international figure. After his death on 24 January 1965, seventy years to the day after the death of his father, he was given a state funeral and was buried in Bladon churchyard, within sight of his birthplace at Blenheim Palace.

Winston Churchill married Clementine Hozier on 12 September 1908. She played a key role in supporting and at times managing him. They had five children, four of whom – Diana, Randolph, Sarah and Mary – survived into adulthood. Marigold died in infancy. Family was always central to Churchill and Sonia Purnell (Chapter 17) has researched the role played by Clementine Churchill at the heart of his inner circle.

Churchill played a key part in creating his own archive and his own history. His personal papers have been housed in the Churchill Archives Centre at Churchill College, Cambridge since the 1970s. They were purchased for the nation in 1995 and are now vested in the ownership of the Sir Winston Churchill Archive Trust. Churchill College was itself conceived as a national and commonwealth memorial to Sir Winston and in accordance with his wishes specialises in science, technology and engineering subjects.

The room of Churchill's birth can be viewed at Blenheim Palace. His home in Kent, Chartwell, is owned by the National Trust and preserves many of his belongings and artefacts, including a large collection of his paintings. There is a museum to his life attached to his underground wartime command centre in central London, the Churchill War Rooms, which forms part of the British Imperial War Museum. In addition, America's National Churchill Museum at Fulton, Missouri, has been created at the site of his famous 1946 'iron curtain' speech and a National Churchill Leadership Centre established at George Washington University in Washington, DC. There are Winston Churchill Memorial Trusts offering vocational scholarships in Australia, New Zealand and the United Kingdom, and an International Churchill Society in the United States, Canada and the United Kingdom, as well as a raft of other related Churchill clubs and organisations around the world. There are an incredible and diverse range of things that have been named after Winston Churchill, including plants, streets, schools, pubs, champagnes, ships, submarines and hotels. There are also many statues, some of which have recently become the focus of protests against Churchill's views on empire, class and race.

Historiography

The study of Winston Churchill has certainly been shaped by his own pen. He produced a huge number of works, many of them comprising multiple volumes, ultimately winning the Nobel Prize for Literature for his contribution to the written and spoken word (see Appendix 2 for a list of his publications). Many of these works are partially autobiographical and concern events in which he was a major actor. They were published with the intention of getting his version of the narrative before a general audience and many of them remain in print. He also assembled and preserved his personal papers as a source for his own official biography and as part of his historical legacy. These have now been digitised and published as an online resource by Bloomsbury.

The official biography of Winston Churchill runs to eight large volumes and took two decades to complete (1966–88). It was started by Churchill's son Randolph but his death in 1968 meant that the bulk of the task fell to Sir Martin Gilbert. In addition to the main volumes, there are a further twenty-three companion volumes reproducing an edited selection of key documents, the series having been completed to Sir Martin's plan after his death by Professor Larry Arnn of Hillsdale

College. This mammoth resource, which was only finished in 2019, continues to underpin study and research of Churchill's life.[7]

Other important research tools are the published edition of Churchill's (almost) complete speeches by Robert Rhodes James, the comprehensive bibliography of Churchill's writings by Ronald Cohen and the extensive work done by Richard Langworth in identifying genuine Churchill quotations and highlighting false attributions.[8]

Churchill was a prominent and controversial figure during his own lifetime. He appears in the published letters and diaries, autobiographies and memoirs of many of his contemporaries. Since his death, he has been the subject of many biographies and historical studies.

In recent years, there have been a number of more specialist works looking at Churchill as a writer, a reader of literature, an orator and a painter, and at his financial and physical health – important areas which undoubtedly influenced his political life. His family life and the lives of his wife and children have also become a focus of interest. Churchill's attitudes to empire and race form another emerging strand of the historiography, as do his legacy and role in the British national mythology.[9]

During the creation of this book, Churchill has once again become a controversial and contested figure. He tends to be characterised and often caricatured as an icon of leadership for the 'greatest generation' that fought fascism in the Second World War or as an unrepentant White supremacist. It is a debate that requires more nuance and is one that is visited in detail in Chapter 1, which examines Churchill's contested legacy.

Notes

1. A. Roberts, *Churchill: Walking with Destiny* (London: Allen Lane, 2018), p. 982.
2. G. Wheatcroft, *Churchill's Shadow: An Astonishing Life and a Dangerous Legacy* (London: The Bodley Head, 2021), p. 534.
3. Wheatcroft, *Churchill's Shadow*, p. 3; see also Roberts, *Churchill: Walking with Destiny*, pp. 965–6.
4. R. Langworth, *Churchill by Himself* (London: Ebury, 2008), p. 13.
5. Langworth, *Churchill by Himself*, p. 486.
6. W. S. Churchill, *Amid These Storms: Thoughts and Adventures* (New York: Charles Scribner's Sons, 1932), p. 213.
7. Official biography [OB]: *Winston S. Churchill* (London: Heinemann, 1966–88), R. Churchill, vol. 1, 'Winston S. Churchill: Youth 1874–1900' (1966); vol. 2, 'Winston S. Churchill: Young Statesman 1901–1914' (1967).

M. Gilbert, vol. 3, 'Winston Churchill: The Challenge of War 1914–1916' (1971); vol. 4, 'Winston Churchill: World in Torment 1916–1922' (1975); vol. 5, 'Winston Churchill: The Prophet of Truth 1922–1939' (1976), vol. 6, 'Winston Churchill: Finest Hour 1939–1941' (1983); vol. 7, 'Winston Churchill: Road to Victory 1941–1945' (1986); vol. 8, 'Winston Churchill: Never Despair 1945–1965' (1988).

Companion Volumes [CV]: R. Churchill, *Companion Volume 1* (in two parts) (London: Heinemann, 1967); *Companion Volume 2* (in three parts) (London: Heinemann, 1969). Republished as *The Churchill Documents*, volumes 1–5 (Hillsdale, MI: Hillsdale College Press, 2006).

M. Gilbert, *Companion Volume 3* (in two parts) (London: Heinemann, 1972); *Companion Volume 4* (in three parts) (London: Heinemann, 1977); *Companion Volume 5* (in three parts) (London: Heinemann, 1982). Republished as *The Churchill Documents*, vols. 6–13 (Hillsdale, MI: Hillsdale College Press, 2007–9); *The Churchill War Papers* (in three parts) (vol. 1, London: Norton & Company, 1993; vol. 2, London: Heinemann, 1994; vol. 3, London: Heinemann, 2000). Republished as *The Churchill Documents*, vols. 14–16 (Hillsdale, MI: Hillsdale College Press, 2011); *The Churchill Documents*, vol. 17 (Hillsdale, MI: Hillsdale College Press, 2014).

M. Gilbert and L. Arnn, *The Churchill Documents*, vols. 17–23 (Hillsdale, MI: Hillsdale College Press, 2015–19).

8. R. Rhodes James, *Winston S. Churchill: His Complete Speeches*, 8 vols. (New York: Chelsea Housew, 1974); R. Cohen, *Bibliography of the Writings of Sir Winston Churchill*, 3 vols. (London: Thoemmes, 2006); Langworth, *Churchill by Himself.*

9. For Churchill as a writer, see D. Reynolds, *In Command of History: Churchill Fighting and Writing the Second World War* (London: Allen Lane, 2004) and P. Clarke, *Mr Churchill's Profession: Statesman, Orator, Writer* (London: Bloomsbury, 2012). For Churchill as an orator, see R. Toye, *The Roar of the Lion: The Untold Story of Churchill's World War II Speeches* (Oxford: Oxford University Press, 2013). For Churchill as a painter, see P. Rafferty, *Winston Churchill Painting on the French Riviera* (London: Unicorn Publishing Group, 2020). For Churchill's finances, see D. Lough, *No More Champagne: Churchill and His Money* (London: Head of Zeus, 2015). For Churchill's health, see A. Vale and J. Scadding, *Winston Churchill's Illnesses 1886–1965* (Barnsley: Pen & Sword, 2020). For Churchill and empire, see W. Dockter, *Churchill and the Islamic World* (London: I. B. Tauris, 2015) and R. Toye, *Churchill's Empire: The World That Made Him and the World He Made* (London: Macmillan, 2010). For studies of Churchill's family, see M. Soames, *A Daughter's Tale* (London: Doubleday, 2011) and S. Purnell, *First Lady: The Life and Wars of Clementine Churchill* (London: Aurum Press Ltd, 2015). For a study of the women who worked for Churchill as private secretaries, see C. Stelzer, *Working with Winston* (London: Head of Zeus, 2019). For Churchill's role in the British national mythology, see S. Fielding, B. Schwarz and R. Toye, *The Churchill Myths* (Oxford: Oxford University Press, 2020) and Wheatcroft, *Churchill's Shadow.*

1

Churchill's Contested History

On 7 October 2018, Scott Kelly, the retired American astronaut and former Commander of the International Space Station, wrote a tweet commenting on contemporary American politics in which he said, 'One of the greatest leaders of modern times, Sir Winston Churchill said, "in victory, magnanimity." I guess those days are over.'[1] This led to an immediate backlash on the social media site, with several individuals questioning whether it was still appropriate to quote Churchill because of his backward views on race. Appearing on the popular television programme *Good Morning Britain*, Professor Kehinde Andrews (Birmingham City University) heavily criticised Churchill's legacy, commenting, 'Britain's impact has devastated most of the world and Churchill is a big part of that.' This led to an immediate challenge from the host, Piers Morgan, who proclaimed, 'I'm not going to be told to feel ashamed of my country just because you say we're a bunch of racists.'[2]

By January 2019, the Bomber Command Memorial in Green Park, London, along with the 'Allies' bench on New Bond Street featuring bronze figures of Winston Churchill and Franklin D. Roosevelt, had been vandalised.[3] Then, on 28 January 2019 just days after the anniversary of Churchill's death, Ross Greer, a Green Party member of the Scottish Parliament, called Churchill a 'white supremacist and mass murderer' and argued that 'Britain must be honest with its history.' The discussion quickly became politicised. John McDonnell, the UK's Labour shadow chancellor, called Churchill a 'villain' owing to his supposed role in deploying the military against striking Welsh miners at Tonypandy.[4] This in turn prompted Conservative Prime Minister Boris Johnson to accuse McDonnell of repeating 'myths of the old hard left', particularly on the subject of Churchill and Tonypandy, which Johnson said 'simply [are]n't true'.[5]

These divisions only intensified during the subsequent global pandemic, an event often referred to at the time as the greatest crisis since the Second World War. Churchill featured positively in UK coverage to mark the seventy-fifth anniversary of Victory in Europe (VE) Day on 8 May 2020, but then came the murder in the USA of George Floyd, an African American who was killed by a policeman kneeling on his neck.[6] On 7 June 2020 there were widespread demonstrations in London to support the Black Lives Matter movement, during which Churchill's statue in Parliament Square was defaced with the words 'was a racist' scrawled beneath it.[7] Twitter erupted. #Churchill, #Churchillstatue and #Churchillwasaracist trended with messages of support and condemnation for Winston Churchill.[8] The National Trust, owners of Churchill's house, Chartwell, in Kent, Churchill College and the Winston Churchill Memorial Trust all became embroiled in the ensuing debates about the extent of Churchill's racism and how to commemorate him.

More than half a century after his death, and as the events of the Second World War passed out of living memory, Churchill had become a battleground in the 'culture wars' where the politics of Brexit, postcolonial awareness and imperial nostalgia were colliding.[9] But as this chapter will show, the way in which Churchill and his legacy has been viewed has never been static.

'I Will Write the History'

Winston Churchill was only wartime prime minister for just over five years. His reputation as a successful war leader came late in life, when he was already in his sixties. Yet he had first made his mark on the national and international stage as a soldier and war correspondent in the 1890s. He had been elected to parliament in 1900, at the age of twenty-five, when Queen Victoria was still on the throne, and he had served in the British Cabinet from 1908. Both his proponents and detractors generally agree that his early political career was a rollercoaster ride that combined bravery, brilliant ability and an early meteoric rise with risk-taking, some terrible political miscalculations and a capacity to court controversy.

Figure 1.1 Cartoon from *The Sunday Graphic*, December 1929 (CAC, Churchill Press Cuttings, CHPC 10/3).

The social reformer Beatrice Webb found him 'egotistical, bumptious, shallow minded and reactionary, but with a certain personal magnetism, great pluck and some originality',[10] while the Conservative politician Rab Butler famously saw him as 'a half-breed American' and 'the greatest political adventurer of modern times'.[11] The newspaper magnate and politician Lord Beaverbrook – somewhat ironically given his own reputation – felt that Churchill on the top of a wave had in him 'the stuff of which tyrants are made'.[12] Throughout his life and career Churchill consistently generated strong, and often contradictory, opinions.

Churchill's early career, as we will see throughout this book, was complex and nuanced and left him, like most politicians, with a mixed legacy. All of this was overshadowed by success in the Second World War and by the creation, partly through wartime propaganda, of Churchill the icon. It was a part that Churchill had always felt born to play, and one that is made more interesting by the role he did then play in shaping his own reputation.

Churchill's first headmaster reported that his young charge lacked ambition.[13] That may have been true of the child; it was certainly not true of the man. He saw himself as standing in a historical tradition that stretched back to Nelson, Drake and his illustrious ancestor and military genius, the 1st Duke of Marlborough. He was part of a continuum that linked past and future, and this meant he always thought in terms of his legacy.

As a young soldier in 1897 he had written to his mother from the Indian north-western frontier, describing how: 'I rode on my grey pony all along the skirmish line where everyone else was lying down in cover. Foolish perhaps but I play for high stakes and given an audience there is no act too daring or too noble. Without the gallery things are different.'[14] A few years later, as his political star started to rise, he confided to his friend Violet Bonham Carter, 'We are all worms. But I do believe that I am a glow-worm.'[15] He knew how to play to the cameras and cultivated a very visual public image.

But he also launched and then underpinned his career with words. His early books based on his military adventures, *The Malakand Field Force*, *The River War*, *Ian Hamilton's March* and *From London to Ladysmith*, brought him to public attention and helped propel him into the British parliament. His biographies of his father and John Churchill, 1st Duke of Marlborough, helped him emphasise his own political pedigree. His multi-volume histories of the First and Second World Wars allowed him to set the tone of the historical debate, while his *History of the English-Speaking Peoples*, started in the 1930s but completed in the 1950s, was both a defence of the British Empire and a powerful articulation of his belief in the 'special relationship' and the need for the United States to play a global role alongside Great Britain.

It was the former British prime minister, Arthur Balfour, who famously described Churchill's multi-volume history of the First World War, *The World Crisis*, as 'Winston's brilliant autobiography disguised as a history of the universe.'[16] Many of Churchill's major works can be seen as autobiographical. They served not only to fund his political career and particular lifestyle but also to raise his profile and reinforce his political argument.

Similarly, Churchill's huge personal archive, housed in the Churchill Archives Centre at Churchill College, Cambridge, may have been constructed as a working resource for Churchill to support his writing, but, like his writing, it was also generated with a view to posterity. Churchill had written the biography of his father Lord Randolph Churchill and, by the time he died in 1965, he knew things had come full circle and that his son Randolph would be his chronicler. It was a task that Randolph did not live to complete, and that was taken up by the late Sir Martin Gilbert, culminating in a work of eight volumes with twenty-three companion volumes – surely the largest political biography ever written.[17] In creating the archive that underpins it, Churchill was seeking to maintain and influence his legacy and reputation from beyond the grave. And as David Reynolds has concluded, Churchill 'must surely have known as he finally slipped away, that he had won the immortality he craved'.[18]

Churchill the writer played a key role in creating Churchill the icon. But, ironically, in doing so he also raised his own profile to such a level that challenges to his reputation became almost inevitable. There were always going to be those who disagreed with what Churchill had written about them, but as more official records opened up and more memoirs came out, there were also going to be those who sought to question the veracity of different parts of his narrative and to challenge the Churchillian perspective.

This began with the published memoirs of the former head of the British army, Field Marshal Lord Alanbrooke, Churchill's doctor Lord Moran and Sir Alexander Cadogan, the Permanent Under Secretary of State at the Foreign Office. They revealed an alternative and more human picture of Churchill, depicting him as sometimes erratic, petulant, stubborn, frail and unreasonable.[19] Moran's book was viewed as a gross breach of patient confidentiality by the Churchill family and prompted members of his inner circle to publish their own book of collected memories.[20] This did not stop the psychologist Anthony Storr posthumously diagnosing Churchill with prolonged and recurrent fits of depression, which he claimed Churchill called his 'black dog'.[21] Discussion of Churchill's mental and physical health has continued since, with much speculation and amateur diagnosis, though there are now more detailed studies by Attenborough and Vale and Scadding that provide a more nuanced picture and inform our understanding of the impact of Churchill's health on his actions (see, for example, the discussion of his health during his war leadership in Chapter 13 of this volume).[22]

Challenges to the Churchill Narrative

Since Churchill's death there has been a continuous and strong strand of positive Churchill biography that can be traced from Martin Gilbert to William Manchester, Roy Jenkins and Andrew Roberts.[23] It is a tree that comes with its own interesting branches, like the direct line that can be drawn from John Lukacs' 1999 book *Five Days in London, May 1940*, which used newly opened Cabinet records to tell the story of Churchill's struggle with his Foreign Secretary Lord Halifax over whether or not to seek possible peace terms, to the 2017 movie *Darkest Hour*.[24] But there have also always been different perspectives and areas of controversy.

A deeply critical biography was written in Churchill's lifetime by Emrys Hughes, a Welsh Labour politician, journalist and author. His book *Winston Churchill in War and Peace* was first published in Britain in 1950, then in the United States in 1955 under the title *The British Bulldog: Winston Churchill – His Career in War and Peace*, and finally in Germany as *Churchill: Ein Mann in seinem Widerspruch* in 1959. While each version was slightly different, Hughes prefaced the updated American edition with the explanation that 'there has grown up a Churchill legend' and that although he had undoubtedly done great things in providing the rhetoric to help defeat the Nazis, 'when we are asked to regard him as the modern Moses ... it is time to demur'.[25]

This critique was echoed in 1969 in the edited collection *Churchill: Four Faces and the Man*, which contained essays from prominent historians including A. J. P. Taylor and J. H. Plumb, as well as the aforementioned psychological profile from Antony Storr. It was published in the USA as *Churchill Revised: A Critical Assessment* (1969), which included a publisher's preface not featured in the British version. This argued that the body of literature around Churchill was composed of three categories: biography, memoirs of those who knew him and his own works. What was missing, however, was a critical historical assessment which did not 'side step controversial issues'; the remedy, then, would be this volume, which was 'a necessary complement to the existing literature'.[26] To ease the audience into academic criticism and to echo a familiar theme, the publisher's note even assured its readers that Churchill himself had argued in his treatment of Kitchener in *The River War* that 'To do justice to a great man, discriminating criticism is necessary.'[27] The fact that these explanations were felt necessary in the American editions is itself revealing of the stature Churchill's reputation had assumed in the United States during the Cold War.

In 1970 Robert Rhodes James' *Churchill: A Study in Failure* was published and looked at the more nuanced way in which Churchill might have been remembered without the Second World War,[28] while the 1980s saw a highly critical attack on his reputation by the now discredited historian David Irving.[29] Then came a new period of reassessment in the 1990s. William Roger Louis and Robert Blake brought together thirty-seven authors to contribute to *Churchill: A Major New Assessment of His Life in Peace and War* (1993). Based on a conference at the University of Texas in Austin in 1991, the collection of essays included serious and critical examinations of Churchill's relationship with empire, India, Zionism and the Middle East, and argued that Churchill 'made certain assumptions about India, as he did about Egypt, that can only be described as racist'.[30] John Charmley's *Churchill: The End of Glory – A Political Biography* (1993), Clive Ponting's *Winston Churchill* (1994) and Norman Rose's *Churchill: An Unruly Life* (1995) all seriously critiqued Churchill.[31]

Charmley joined Alan Clark, author and Thatcherite minister, in criticising Churchill from the right. Clark revived old arguments about Churchill being a class traitor during the Edwardian era, advocating that he should have let continental Europe collapse into German domination in order to fight the real battle against communism.[32] While Charmley ended his volume with this damning verdict:

> Churchill stood for the British Empire, for British independence and for an 'anti-Socialist' vision of Britain. By July 1945 the first of these was on the skids, the second was dependent solely upon America and the third had just vanished in a Labour election victory. An appropriate moment to stop, for it was indeed the end of glory.[33]

From the left, Norman Rose and Clive Ponting illuminated Churchill's personal flaws, aristocratic views and tastes, as well as his fraught personal life with his children. According to David Marquand, himself a former Labour parliamentarian, Ponting's book painted Churchill as 'an elitist, a sexist and a racist', which clashed with 'the marmoreal slabs of Martin Gilbert's multi-volume biography', which acted as a sort of 'historiographical equivalent of a statue in Parliament Square'. Marquand, however, did not find Ponting's argument very convincing because:

> His chief message is that Churchill was not a late-20th century *bien pensant* progressive, and that this is shocking and dreadful. But how on earth could he have been? He was born in 1874, not 1974. He could no more escape the limits of time and place than Ponting can. The elitism and racism which Ponting condemns were commonplace then – and among *bien pensant* progressives as much as among reactionary aristocrats.[34]

This defence of Churchill's views as 'commonplace' and that he was 'a man of his times' has been and is still routinely used by Churchill's supporters.[35] But it is one that has also been challenged by more recent studies on Churchill and empire. Richard Toye has argued that in fact many of Churchill's views were thought of by his contemporaries and even by fellow imperialists as backward, 'old-fashioned, or even downright shocking'.[36]

Politicising Churchill

Recent Churchill historiography has moved beyond Churchill's wartime leadership to examine larger historical notions such as empire, memory and race. But it was Brexit, Britain's departure from the European Union (EU), that acted as the real catalyst for a more divisive and popular (as opposed to academic) politicising of Churchill.

Preparations for the fiftieth anniversary of Churchill's death led to a high-profile addition to popular Churchillian literature with the publication of Boris Johnson's *The Churchill Factor: How One Man Made History* (2014).[37] Though prominent historians criticised the book,[38] it generated huge sales and there can be no denying the fact that it influenced the conversation on Churchill, especially around the issues of Brexit, race and political ambition. Johnson's chapter 'Churchill the European' is instructive as it explores Churchill's views of what he called 'the United States of Europe'. The author makes clear that Churchill was one of the primary architects of an increasingly united

Europe, while also explaining why he believed Churchill backed away from British membership of the European Coal and Steel Community in the 1950s (namely because Britain could not be 'an ordinary member' and should have been 'at the table' for the negotiations, and that by 1950 'it was probably too late' because Labour had missed the boat).[39] The power of this observation lay not in its historical position but rather in the way it placed Churchill at the heart of the Leave campaign's argument for Britain exiting the EU. Not least because, not long after its publication, Johnson had joined that campaign, effectively attaching Churchill or at least Johnson's version of Churchill to the contemporary political debate.

Discussion about Churchill and Europe grew as the political divisions intensified and he was invoked by both sides. These public debates were reflected in the academic literature. (For a full discussion of Churchill's campaign, see Chapter 18 in this volume.) Felix Klos argued for Churchill as an original architect of European unity. His pamphlet *Churchill on Europe: The Untold Story of Churchill's European Project* (2016), released a year later as a full monograph titled *Churchill's Last Stand: The Struggle to Unite Europe* (2017), presented Churchill as a lifelong lover of Europe and enthusiastic supporter of European unity from the 1930s. When Boris Johnson cited Churchill in his campaign manifesto for Brexit, Klos attacked him in the British newspaper *The Telegraph*, asking, 'How can Johnson use his hero to force "Brexit" and therewith permanently damage the European project? The only way, evidently, is to paint a barbarically simplified and ill-informed picture of what Churchill stood for.'[40] To Andrew Roberts, author of *Churchill: Walking with Destiny* (2018), writing in *The Spectator*, Klos' narrative of Churchill provided 'enough evidence in this book to prove the precise opposite';[41] namely that, on Europe, Churchill was a 'friend and sponsor' but that 'is not the same as a member'.[42]

Roberts' book was a rebuttal of much of the critical writing about Churchill and a powerful restatement and modern articulation of the 'great man theory'. Indeed, *The New York Times* argued it was 'the best single-volume biography of Churchill yet written'.[43] It certainly contained new material which escaped or was not available for Gilbert's biography, such as Lawrence Burgis' verbatim reports of the War Cabinet meetings and the diary of George VI, which offered insights into Churchill's relationship with the king. It also provided a more nuanced assessment of standard Churchillian myths such as the events surrounding Tonypandy, whether Churchill's enormous appetite for alcohol made him an alcoholic and the extent of his 'black dog' of depression. The major theme of Roberts' narrative was 'greatness', beginning with Churchill's own childhood view that he would be a 'great man taking great decisions at great moments in the history of what was then the greatest empire in history'.[44] The author endows Churchill with a 'living sense of history' and makes him a symbol of the British Empire, which had 'for centuries been proactive, pugnacious and occasionally piratical'.[45] The text dwells frequently on Britain's imperial past, with references to Kipling's poems and links to Victorian figures peppered throughout the text, as well as praise for Churchill's aristocratic background, which the author acknowledges 'sits uncomfortably today with his image as the saviour of democracy'.[46]

Despite the author's admiration for his subject, Roberts is clear that he is not trying to write a hagiography. In his conclusion he develops a list with numerous examples of Churchill's failures and vices; his recklessness and his lack of sound judgement on military strategy. But these mistakes Roberts assures his readers were actually lessons in disguise. Gallipoli and the Dardanelles were simply moments Churchill could sharpen himself upon, so when it mattered later in the Second World War, he would be ready. His experience with signals intelligence at the Admiralty in the First World War would inform his support for the work of Alan Turing and the codebreakers in the Second. His youth, education and role as a solider informed his belief that the British Empire was 'the greatest force for good in the history of mankind'.[47]

Roberts argues that Churchill's problematic views should be context-ualised. He explains that Churchill's belief in the superiority of the 'British race' was commonplace when Churchill grew up, and other thinkers of the day, such as Beatrice Webb, Hugh Dalton and H. G. Wells, also subscribed to such views. However, what constitutes commonplace as opposed to exceptional on these issues continues to be strongly contested.[48] For Roberts, Churchill's faith in imperialism and colonialism was 'not just political but also spiritual'.[49] Hence, his dec-laration that the unsurpassed bravery of Indian soldiers and officers, both Muslim and Hindu, shines forever in the annals of war balances any notion of discussion that his handling of the Bengal famine of 1943 might have been callous or at least disinterested.[50] Roberts' evaluation of Churchill's racial views is that his racism, prejudice and belief in

Anglo-Saxon superiority 'ultimately served the cause of democracy well' because this would have convinced Churchill of the 'correctness of fighting on against the Germans' when others wanted peace.[51]

Churchill, Empire and Race

It is this argument on race that has not surprisingly been challenged, especially by historians working in global and less Western-centric history. Discussion of Churchill's views on empire and race and their impact on his actions forms another contested strand in the Churchill historiography. In 2002, Churchill was voted Greatest Briton of All Time in a BBC poll. The same year, John Ramsden published his largely complimentary *Man of the Century: Winston Churchill and His Legend Since 1945*. Ramsden's book explored how Churchill was still commemorated, especially in America.[52] While the author engaged with some less flattering aspects of Churchill's legacy, such as his record in Ireland and Wales, his tendency to be his own 'spin-doctor' and how his admirers have 'stifled legitimate criticism of the man',[53] he made the conscious decision not to concentrate on India, Palestine, Iraq and other colonial holdings, preferring instead to keep a tight focus on the Dominions and the 'English Speaking World'. Ramsden was clearly aware of the problems inherent in this approach but justified it on the grounds that he was following Churchill's definition of 'the English-speaking people', even if it was one that Churchill was not likely to acknowledge in public.[54] By simultaneously acknowledging and ignoring other global legacies, Ramsden adopted a methodology which avoided having to grapple with Churchill's relationship with India, race and empire.

Indian authors such as Madhusree Mukerjee, author of *Churchill's Secret War: The British Empire and the Ravaging of India during World War II* (2010), and Shashi Tharoor, who published *Inglorious Empire: What the British Did to India* (2018), have written from a very different perspective and concluded that Churchill's racial views impacted on his policy towards India and his response to the Bengal famine. These issues are discussed in the chapters by Piers Brendon (Chapter 10) and Kishan S. Rana (Chapter 11).

More recently, there have been some critical appraisals of Churchill's legacy in post-colonial and subaltern literature.[55] Remi Joseph-Salisbury argued that Churchill had become a symbol of 'White amnesia', which 'is the denial of the histories of racism and white supremacy', and by publicly challenging Churchill's appearance on the five-pound note, the author tapped into a peculiarly British '"post-racial" white supremacy'.[56] Michelle Gordon has explored Churchill's language in his book *The River War*, arguing that it contributed to 'propaganda which dehumanised the "enemy" and justified British supremacy over "inferior races" in the name of "civilization"'.[57] Farzana Shain has taken up Richard Toye's arguments around colonialism and Churchill's education, linking it to his bigoted attitudes around race later in his life when he suggested to a Conservative Party meeting the campaign slogan 'Keep England White' for the 1955 British General Election.[58] This literature had been found in academic journal articles or specialist book chapters, and – at the time of writing – it is beginning to find its way into more popular publications, such as *Churchill's Shadow* by Geoffrey Wheatcroft (2021).[59]

Conclusion

A review of the complex historiography reveals that Churchill has always been attacked and defended from both left and right. In recent years, however, the literature has become especially politicised, reflecting deep divisions in contemporary society about Britain's attitude towards its imperial past and its role in the post-Brexit world. Much of what is said and written in the public sphere is often concerned with using Churchill to justify contemporary positions and utilises his iconic status to grab headlines and assure airtime. What is lost is the complexity, nuance and fluidity of Churchill's position, which was not necessarily consistent or static (and which may not be quite as he chose to represent it). Churchill had a long political career. If there is a common strand influencing and shaping his thoughts and actions, then it surely sits at the intersection between his Western worldview, British national interests and his personal aspirations and ambitions. To a man who believed in destiny and felt himself a 'glow-worm', these three often seemed the same thing, but they were also always changing.

Historians such as Robert Gerwarth in *The Bismarck Myth: Weimar Germany and the Legacy of the Iron Chancellor* (2005) and others[60] who explore *Geschichtspolitik* or 'the politically motivated use of historical narratives in a public discourse' have long since wrestled with the historical legacies and myths in German historiography and more broadly.[61] It is perhaps revealing that English historiography around the legacy of Winston Churchill has been relatively less critical and less reflective than that for other figures such as Bismarck, Roosevelt, de Gaulle and Stalin. There are many reasons for this, though an important one is undoubtedly the enduring centrality of 1940 in Britain's popular history and culture, as evidenced by films such as *Dunkirk* and *Darkest Hour* (both 2017) and the role that Churchill played in cementing that history and creating his own legacy.

To many, and especially to British and American audiences, Churchill has remained an unblemished hero and a symbol for Western values – the embodiment of opposition to tyranny. However, viewed from a more globally inclusive perspective, Churchill's legacy can be seen as that of yet another colonial oppressor and defender of empire. In either case, he has become a symbol and a representation of something beyond himself. This chapter has summarised the state of Churchill's contested legacy at the time of writing. In doing so, it has highlighted the ever-changing nature of that debate and its relationship with the shifting public discourse. After his 1945 General Election defeat, Churchill apparently said he did not want to be 'put on a pedestal', while, as we have seen, in his own writing he argued that 'To do justice to a great man, discriminating criticism is necessary.'[62] The chapters that follow are certainly offered in that spirit and aim to provide evidence for informed debate and some starting points for further research.

Notes

1. S. Kelly, Twitter status update, 7 October 2018, viewed 18 April 2019, https://twitter.com/StationCDRKelly/status/1048967485821599744?ref—src=twsrc%5Etfw%7Ctwcamp%5Etweetembed&ref—url=https%3A%2F%2Fd-0222596446073845540.ampproject.net%2F1903141753530%2Fframe.html.
2. P. Grafton-Green, 'Piers Morgan in explosive row with academic who called Winston Churchill a "racist" and compared him to Hitler', *Evening Standard*, 9 October 2018.
3. M. Robinson, '"Why do you beat us with the things we are proud of?": Piers Morgan blasts campaigner who says WWII bombers committed a "war crime" in fiery debate about memorial vandals', *Daily Mail*, 22 January 2019.
4. J. Randerson and J. Blanchard, 'Labour's John McDonnell: Churchill was a "villain"', *Politico*, viewed 18 April 2019, www.politico.eu/article/labours-john-mcdonnell-churchill-was-a-villain.
5. B. Johnson, 'John McDonnell has lost his grip on history: Winston Churchill was the father of the worker's tea break, a true working class hero', *The Telegraph*, 14 February 2019. For more on the myth of Tonypandy, see J. Ramsden, *Man of the Century*

(London: HarperCollins, 2003), pp. 226–30 and Paul Addison, *Churchill on the Home Front* (London: Jonathan Cape, 1992), pp. 142–5.

6. 'George Floyd: Huge protests against racism held across US', *BBC News*, 7 June 2020.

7. 'Black Lives Matter protest: Why was Churchill's statue defaced?', *BBC News*, 8 June 2020.

8. Twitter metrics reveal that #Churchill had 33,437 impressions, #Churchillstatue had 28,561 impressions and #Churchillwasaracist had the most impressions at 43,123. Metadata provided by Brand24.com, 16 June 2020.

9. There were a few journalistic articles published on this in the wake of the McDonnell comments. See, for instance, D. Finklestein, 'Winston Churchill was a racist but still a great man', *The Times*, 12 February 2019; S. Edwards, 'Churchill: Hero or villain', *The Conversation*, 14 February 2019; C. Cooper, 'Why Churchill's legacy marks a fault line in British politics', *Politico*, 14 February 2019, viewed 18 April 2019, www.politico.eu/article/winston-churchill-uk-legacy-is-a-fault-line-in-british-politics.

10. M. Gilbert, *In Search of Churchill* (London: HarperCollins, 1994), p. 218, citing Beatrice Webb's diary, July 1903.

11. J. Colville, *The Fringes of Power* (London: Hodder & Stoughton, 1985), p. 122.

12. Charmley, *End of Glory*, p. 219, cited in M. Aitken, *Politicians and the War* (London: Butterworth, 1928).

13. CAC, Churchill Papers, CHAR 28/44/8, School Report for St George's School, Ascot, May–June 1884.

14. CAC, Churchill Papers, CHAR 28/2352 and 57, Letters from Churchill to Lady Randolph, 5 and 19 September 1897.

15. V. Bonham Carter, *Winston Churchill As I Knew Him* (London: Eyre & Spottiswoode, 1965), p. 16.

16. D. Reynolds, *In Command of History: Churchill Fighting and Writing the Second World War* (London: Allen Lane, 2004), p. 5.

17. See Historiography section and note 7 in the Introduction for full details.

18. Reynolds, *In Command of History*, p. 527.

19. For the first publication of the diaries of Lord Alanbrooke, see A. Bryant, *The Turn of the Tide* (London: Collins, 1957) and *Triumph in the West* (London: Collins, 1959); for Lord Moran, see Moran, *Winston Churchill: The Struggle for Survival* (London: Constable, 1966); for Cadogan, see D. Dilks, *The Diaries of Air Alexander Cadogan* (London: Cassell, 1971).

20. J. Wheeler-Bennett, *Action This Day* (London: Macmillan, 1968).

21. A. Storr, The Man. In A. Taylor et al., *Churchill: Four Faces and the Man* (London: Allen Lane, 1969), pp. 203–46.

22. W. Attenborough, *Churchill and the 'Black Dog' of Depression: Reassessing the Biographical Evidence of Psychological Disorder* (Basingstoke: Palgrave Macmillan, 2014); A. Vale and C. Scadding, *Winston Churchill's Illnesses 1886–1965* (Barnsley: Frontline, 2020).

23. For example, see M. Gilbert, *Churchill: A Life* (London: Heinemann, 1991); W. Manchester, *The Last Lion* (London: Michael Joseph, 1983); R. Jenkins, *Churchill* (London: Macmillan, 2001); and A. Roberts, *Churchill: Walking with Destiny* (London: Allen Lane, 2018).

24. J. Lukacs, *Five Days in London, May 1940* (New Haven, CT: Yale University Press, 1999).

25. E. Hughes, *The British Bulldog: Winston Churchill – His Career in War and Peace* (New York: Banner Books, 1955), pp. vi–vii. This version of the introduction exists only in the US version.

26. A. J. P. Taylor et al. (eds.), *Churchill Revised: A Critical Assessment* (New York: Dial Press, 1969), pp. 7–9.

27. Taylor et al., *Churchill Revised*, p. 7.

28. R. Rhodes James, *Churchill: A Study in Failure 1900–1939* (London: Weidenfeld & Nicolson, 1970).

29. D. Irving, *Churchill's War: The Struggle for Power* (Bullsbrook: Veritas, 1987).

30. R. Blake and W. Roger Louis (eds.), *Churchill* (New York: W. W. Norton & Company, 1993), p. 7.

31. J. Charmley, *Churchill: The End of Glory* (London: Hodder & Stoughton, 1993); C. Ponting, *Churchill* (London: Sinclair-Stevenson, 1994); N. Rose, *Churchill: An Unruly Life* (London: Simon & Schuster, 1994).

32. R. Prior and T. Wilson, Review: Reassessments of Winston Churchill. *The International History Review*, vol. 18, no. 1 (February 1996), pp. 113–26.

33. Charmley, *Churchill: The End of Glory*, p. 649.

34. D. Marquand, 'Bureaucrat bites bulldog: "Churchill" – Clive Ponting', *Independent*, 8 May 1994.

35. Roberts, *Churchill: Walking with Destiny*, p. 113; Roberts, 'Some racist', *Daily Mail*, 13 January 2005; M. Gilbert, 'Churchill and eugenics', *Finest Hour Extras*, viewed 14 August 2020, https://winstonchurchill.org/publications/finest-hour-extras /churchill-and-eugenics-1; P. Addison, The Political Beliefs of Winston Churchill. *Transactions of the Royal Historical Society*, vol. 30 (1980), pp. 39–40.

36. R. Toye, 'Yes, Churchill was a racist: It's time to break free of his "great white men" view of history', *CNN*, 10 June 2020. For examples, see Toye, *Churchill's Empire: The World That Made Him and the World He Made* (London: Macmillan, 2010), p. xv; P. Moon (ed.), *Wavell: The Viceroy's Journal* (London: Oxford University Press, 1973), pp. 4–5; and J. C. Culver and J. Hyde, *American Dreamer: A Life of Henry A. Wallace* (New York: Norton, 2000), p. 301.

37. In full disclosure, one of the authors of this chapter, Warren Dockter, was Johnson's research assistant.

38. See R. J. Evans, '"One man who made history" by another who seems just to make it up: Boris on Churchill', *The New Statesman*, 13 November 2014.

39. B. Johnson, *The Churchill Factor* (London: Hodder & Stoughton, 2014), pp. 307–8.

40. F. Klos, 'Boris Johnson's abuse of Churchill', *History Today*, 1 June 2016; B. Johnson, 'One way to get the change we want – vote to leave the EU', *The Telegraph*, 16 March 2016.

41. A. Roberts, 'Churchill's last stand: The struggle to unite Europe, by Felix Klos – Review', *The Spectator*, 17 February 2018.

42. Roberts, *The Spectator*, 17 February 2018.

43. R. Aldous, 'Is this the best one-volume biography of Churchill yet written?', *The New York Times*, 13 November 2018.

44. Roberts, *Churchill: Walking with Destiny*, p. 972.

45. Roberts, *Churchill: Walking with Destiny*, p. 973.

46. Roberts, *Churchill: Walking with Destiny*, p. 974.

47. Roberts, *Churchill: Walking with Destiny*, p. 976.

48. For example, in the Edwardian era Churchill certainly circulated memoranda from eugenics thinkers such as Alfred Tredgold in 1909, wrote his own letters linking poverty to 'feeble-mindedness', was a called a 'strong eugenicist' by his friend and contemporary Wilfrid S. Blunt, and accepted an honorary vice presidentship of the International Eugenics Congress. D. King and R. Hansen, Experts at Work: State Autonomy, Social Learning and Eugenic Sterilization in 1930s Britain. *British Journal of Political Science*, vol. 29, no. 1 (January 1999), pp. 77–107; Churchill to Asquith, December 1910, Asquith papers, MS 12, folios 224–8, Bodleian Library, Oxford; Wilfrid S. Blunt, *My Diaries: 1888–1914* (New York: Alfred A. Knopf, 1921), p. 813; Donald MacKenzie, Eugenics in Britain. *Social Studies of Science*, vol. 6, no. 3/4 (September 1976), pp. 499–532.

49. Roberts, *Churchill: Walking with Destiny*, p. 977.

50. Roberts, *Churchill: Walking with Destiny*, p. 977.

51. Roberts, *Churchill: Walking with Destiny*, p. 976.

52. Ramsden, *Man of the Century*, p. xiv.

53. Ramsden, *Man of the Century*, pp. xviii–xix.; on Ireland, pp. 259–66, on Wales, pp. 226–33; on being a spin-doctor, pp. 61–5; on admirers, see, for instance, p. 532.

54. Ramsden, *Man of the Century*, p. xviii.

55. For instance, see P. Gilroy, *Post-Colonial Melancholia* (New York: Columbia University Press, 2005). Gilroy relies on what he calls Anthony Barnett's notion of 'Churchillism', p. 82, which, according to Barnett, is a 'warp of British political culture' in which Churchill is the symbol for a wide British collation which elevated things like Anglo-Saxon democracy and the preservation of the Empire. However, Barnett is quick to point out that 'Churchillism' is quite distinct from the man himself. A. Barnett, *Iron Britannia: Time to Take the Great Out of Britain* (London: Allison & Busby, 1982), pp. 32–46. See also T. Barkawi and M. Laffey, The Postcolonial Moment in Security Studies. *Review of International Studies*, no. 32 (2006), pp. 329–52; A. Al-Hardan, Understanding the Present Through the Past: Between British and Israeli Discourses on Palestine. In R. Lentin (ed.), *Thinking Palestine* (London: Zed Books, 2008), pp. 236–53. With thanks to Amal Abu-Bakare.

56. R. Joseph-Salisbury, Does Anybody Really Care What a Racist Says? Anti-Racism in 'Post-Racial' Times. *The Sociological Review*, vol. 67, no. 1 (2019), p. 66.

57. M. Gordon, Colonial Violence and Holocaust Studies. *Holocaust Studies*, vol. 21, no. 4 (2015), pp. 272–91.

58. F. Shain, Race Matters: Confronting the Legacy of Empire and Colonialism. *British Journal of Sociology of Education*, vol. 41, no. 2 (2020), pp. 272–80. The 'Keep England White' quotation was recorded by Harold Macmillan in his diary for 20 January 1955.

59. See G. Wheatcroft, *Churchill's Shadow* (London: The Bodley Head, 2021).

60. R. Gerwarth, *The Bismarck Myth: Weimar Germany and the Legacy of the Iron Chancellor* (Oxford: Oxford University Press, 2007), p. 5. Gerwarth points to a number of German works to illustrate this point, such as E. Wolfrum, Geschichte als Politikum – Geschichtspolitik: Internationale Forschungen zum 19. und 20. Jahrhundert. *Neue Politische Literatur*, vol. 41 (1996), pp. 376–401; P. Bock and E. Wolfrum (eds.), *Umkämpfte Vergangenheit: Geschichtsbilder, Erinnerung und Vergangenheitspolitik im internationalen Vergleich* (Göttingen: Vandenhoeck & Ruprecht, 1999); and K. Schönhoven, *Geschichtspolitik: über den öffentlichen Umgang mit Geschichte und Erinnerung* (Bonn: Friedrich-Ebert-Stiftung, 2003). Other English historians of myths and memory have also explored this, such as B. Strath, Introduction: Myth,

Memory and History in the Construction of Community. In *Myth and Memory in the Construction of Community: Historical Patterns in Europe and Beyond* (Brussels: P. I. E. – Peter Lang, 2000); and P. H. Hutton, *History as an Art of Memory* (Hanover, NH: University Press of New England, 1993).

61. Gerwarth, *The Bismarck Myth*, p. 5.
62. M. Soames, *Clementine Churchill*, revised edition (London: Doubleday, 2002), p. 420; W. S. Churchill, *The River War: An Historical Account of the Reconquest of the Soudan*, vols. 1 and 2 (London: Longmans, Green and Co., 1899), vol. 2, p. 375.

Further Reading

S. Fielding, B. Schwarz and R. Toye, *The Churchill Myths* (Oxford: Oxford University Press, 2020)
J. Ramsden, *Man of the Century: Winston Churchill and His Legend since 1945* (London: HarperCollins, 2002)
A Roberts, *Churchill: Walking with Destiny* (Viking: London, 2018)
G. Wheatcroft, *Churchill's Shadow: An Astonishing Life and a Dangerous Legacy* (London: The Bodley Head, 2021)

2

The Inheritance of Winston Churchill

Winston Churchill was born in Blenheim Palace, the ancestral home of his grandfather, the 7th Duke of Marlborough, on 30 November 1874. The social elite of Victorian Britain remained largely in thrall to 'quality' of birth, which still shaped expectations of a newborn's education, career, marriage and fortune.

It is true that Charles Darwin had recently suggested that a child's upbringing might condition its character as much as its birth;[1] that the invention of the railway and steam engine had brought large quantities of grain into Britain from the prairie farms of north America, thus undermining the value of agricultural land, long the mainstay of aristocratic wealth; and that the broader voting franchise, following the First Reform Act (1832), had begun to weaken the political control of aristocratic families over the House of Commons.

Nonetheless, it is surprising that Churchill devotes less than a page of *My Early Life* (1930), written half a century later, to his birth and lineage. He acknowledges neither privileged upbringing nor assured entry into the roll of families that still dominated Britain's governing class. Ever the politician, the author paints instead a picture of a largely self-made man, whose parents were brilliant but largely absent; whose education disappointed all concerned; and who forged his own way in the world when his father died early without leaving him any money. Churchill succeeded, we infer, thanks to his wit, resilience and audacity.

This chapter explores the background to Churchill's upbringing and its bearing on his future career.

The Jeromes

The first encounter of Churchill's parents, in a British naval ship anchored off the Isle of Wight during August 1873, neatly illustrates an early shifting of the sands of Victorian society that had previously proved so solid. As the younger son of a British duke, Lord Randolph Churchill would always have been a natural guest at an afternoon ball given by the Prince of Wales; but, until a few years earlier,

Figure 2.1 Churchill's maternal grandfather, Leonard Jerome (CAC, Broadwater Collection, BRDW IV 2/1).

Miss Jeannette ('Jennie') Jerome, a nineteen-year-old visitor from the United States of America, would have been an unusual inclusion on the list.

The Jerome family had left Britain for America seven generations earlier. They settled in Connecticut before moving up the coast to the state of New York where Jennie's father, Leonard, was born one of nine children to a doctor. Leonard enjoyed a reputation for laughter and high spirits as a student, before embarking on a legal career. He married Clara Hall, a woman whose reserve contrasted sharply with his extrovert charm. It was her family money that enabled Leonard and a brother to buy a newspaper, the *Rochester Daily American*, which they sold after trebling its circulation.

Leonard moved to Brooklyn where he joined another brother trading shares on the New York stock exchange, a pursuit that suited his swashbuckling style, energy and exceptional appetite for taking risks. He put his career briefly on hold in the early 1850s while he became the American consul in Trieste, a city at the head of the Mediterranean Sea's Adriatic coast that attracted the European aristocracy each summer. Clara developed a life-long fascination for court life, although the Jeromes returned to New York shortly before Jennie was born in January 1854.

Leonard played as hard as he worked: he and his friends raced horses, sailed, partied and enjoyed music. Financial setbacks were a normal part of the early Wall Street pioneer's life: after one such event in 1858, the Jeromes repaired temporarily to Paris where the Imperial Court of Napoleon III fêted them as wealthy Americans. Back once more in New York, Leonard built an extravagant Manhattan mansion in the French style with a ballroom and theatre large enough to challenge the social pre-eminence of the city's self-styled elite of early Dutch settlers.

Leonard's fortunes peaked during the American Civil War (1861–5), when, as the leading shareholder of *The New York Times*, he supported the anti-slavery cause of the North. He took advantage of information from the battlefields, coded and passed through his own telegraph company, to deal in stocks with what contemporaries described as an almost blind risk-taking, coupled with absolute confidence in his own destiny (traits that many were to associate with his future British grandson).[2]

Clara never shared her husband's taste for adventure. Tiring of Leonard's affairs by the late 1860s, she took her teenaged daughters, with his backing, to live in Paris, where Jennie attended a *lycée*, studied piano and learned to draw, to dress and to make conversation at court. The idyll was to prove short-lived: Leonard's business affairs in New York entered a long decline, while rioters in Paris took to the streets in 1870 to protest against the excesses of the regime of Napoleon III. The emperor declared war against Prussia in an attempt to shore up his crumbling support, and Clara and her daughters had to escape to the safety of London when Bismarck's forces soon threatened the French capital.

Leonard arranged a suite of rooms in a hotel off London's Piccadilly, but the city struck them as dreary and damp after Paris. They headed in the summer for the sea air of the Isle of Wight, where Leonard, as a keen sailor, knew that the British aristocracy would assemble for the annual yachting festival at Cowes.

The Churchills

The Churchill family, by contrast, had built its fortune early in the eighteenth century, just as the Jeromes left Britain. Its chief creator, John Churchill, had grown up in the shadow of the English Civil War (1642–51), which led to the ruin of his royalist father. The restoration of the Crown under Charles II, in 1660, allowed John's sister to secure him a junior role at the court of the king's brother, James, Duke of York. It was a time when service at court provided one of the few routes to social mobility.

The young Churchill doubled his income by combining the roles of army officer and courtier, then added a third strand by marrying a fellow courtier, Sarah Jennings, an attendant to Princess Anne, the duke's younger daughter. The Churchills' fortunes flourished when the princess expanded her court on marriage and her father then became king in 1685. They safely navigated the king's downfall on account of his Catholic religion in the Glorious Revolution (1688–9), with John Churchill managing a well-timed switch of allegiance on the battlefield, earning himself promotion by the new King William and Queen Mary to the rank of Earl of Marlborough.

The full flowering of the Marlboroughs' wealth and rank had to await Queen Anne's accession in 1702. The new queen showered them both with lucrative appointments and handed the earl command of the

Figure 2.2 Churchill's paternal grandfather, the 7th Duke of Marlborough (BRDW IV 2/1).

joint armies of Britain, Holland and the German principalities in the War of the Spanish Succession (1701–14) against France. Marlborough was to score a series of successes that were sufficiently clear-cut to earn him the victor's spoils, without ever quite bringing the war to an end. First came his elevation, in his own country, to the rank of Duke of Marlborough, together with a pension for life; then, after victory at Blenheim (13 August 1704), a grant of royal land at Woodstock plus the funds from parliament with which to build a palace at public expense;

finally, Europe's princes in their turn handed over paintings, jewels, porcelain, silver and rare books to fill the palace rooms.

After a decade, the war had proved so costly that the political tide in Britain turned against the duke and duchess, who lost the queen's support. They left their palace unfinished to take refuge on the European mainland against parliament's demands in 1712 that they make substantial repayments to the public purse. There, the duke shrewdly cultivated the support of the House of Hanover, to whom the British throne was due to pass at the queen's death; two years later, he was able to return to London on the day after she died. He was too unwell to resume public office and died in 1722 in the only finished wing of his palace at Blenheim.

His widow, now the dowager duchess, decided to complete the palace out of respect for her late husband, although she considered it an expensive liability. The palace itself, its park and its treasures were protected by entail against sale by profligate Churchill heirs, but she took the additional precaution during the twenty-two years that she outlived the 1st Duke of expanding the Blenheim estate to 100,000 acres. Without ever putting the Churchills in the first rank of aristocratic landowners, her acumen allowed them to secure a firm place among the 200–300 families that dominated Britain's ownership of land and with it the exercise of political power through parliament, many of whose seats they occupied.

Yet ironically it was the dowager duchess herself whose obsessive desire to control her husband's legacy caused a split in the family fortunes that led to its decline within six generations. One of those who incurred her disapproval was her grandson Charles Spencer, who in 1733 became the 3rd Duke of Marlborough and heir-presumptive to the Blenheim estate on the death of the dowager duchess. He ignored her views on a suitable bride as well as on his gambling. When the duchess finally died in 1744, she carried out her threats to disinherit him, by leaving the half of the estate that she controlled not to the duke but to his younger brother Johnny and the Spencer line.[3]

Successive dukes struggled to run a Blenheim estate that was no longer large enough to sustain a ducal lifestyle. They veered in their personal interests between the extravagant eccentricity of artistic connoisseurs and the dutiful worthiness of political placeholders. Churchill's grandfather, the 7th Duke belonged firmly to the latter end of the spectrum: a staunch Tory, he served briefly in Prime Minister Benjamin Disraeli's Cabinet from 1867 to 1868. He had to raise money by selling off peripheral estates in Wiltshire and Shropshire as early as 1862; by the time his grandchild Winston was born in 1874, he was selling gems and land closer to home in Buckinghamshire. The Blenheim estate was reduced to one quarter of its former size.[4]

Randolph, Jennie and Winston

The Churchills and the Jeromes may have met at a time when each family was looking for a measure of financial relief; yet it was not a match made for money.[5] On that afternoon in Cowes, Jennie Jerome caught not just Lord Randolph Churchill's eye but also his ear. A recent graduate of Oxford University, Lord Randolph had enjoyed little experience of debating politics or philosophy with the daughters of British aristocrats. As in the case of his six sisters, their schooling was normally entrusted to a single governess and took place within the confines of the family home. Jennie, by contrast, had attended schools in New York as well as Paris; she was confident, widely read, bilingual and highly musical. Within seventy-two hours of their first meeting, the duke's star-struck son had proposed marriage and the Wall Street entrepreneur's impulsive daughter had accepted.

Lord Randolph had little idea of the Jeromes' background and his father's first enquiries were discouraging: 'This Mr J seems to be a sporting, and I should think, vulgar type of man', the duke told his son. 'It is evident he is of the class of speculators.'[6] Only the approval of their match by the Prince of Wales persuaded the duke to give it his provisional blessing, provided that the couple waited a year before going ahead. Then a sudden General Election at the end of 1873 gave Lord Randolph the chance to accelerate their plans. The duke had long wanted his son to enter parliament as the MP for Woodstock, the constituency next to Blenheim over which the family still held sway. Lord Randolph agreed to put his name forward on the understanding that his father would then allow the immediate start of negotiations between the Churchill and Jerome families to reach a marriage settlement (the legal instrument then used by the families of the Victorian elite to settle each family's financial contribution to a marriage and its inheritance by future generations).

The course of negotiations was to highlight the difference in cultural backgrounds between the two families. America's founding fathers had

Figure 2.3 Churchill's parents, Lord Randolph Churchill and Jennie Jerome, c.1874 (CAC, Churchill Papers, CHAR 28/41/46).

established a less patriarchic society than the one they left behind in England, deliberately omitting from their new inheritance laws any mention of primogeniture or male entail, the twin pillars of aristocratic succession in Britain. Leonard Jerome therefore expected his contribution to the settlement to produce an allowance for Jennie. 'My

Figure 2.4 Churchill with his younger brother Jack, c.1884 (BRDW IV 2/1).

daughter', he told his future son-in-law, 'is an American and ranks precisely the same as you'.[7] Lord Randolph's solicitor warned his client: 'Miss Jerome is made quite independent of you in a pecuniary sort of way, which in my experience is most unusual.'[8] The impasse was broken only a week before the wedding when Leonard conceded that half his contribution should go to Jennie and half to Lord Randolph, while warning the duke: 'Your English custom of making the wife so utterly dependent upon the husband [is] most unwise.'[9]

The newly married couple emerged from their wedding in April 1874 with Lord Randolph's debts cleared, the funds to buy a first London home and enough capital for an income of £3,000 a year (equivalent to approximately £300,000 a year in 2020).[10] Yet it soon became clear that the sum was insufficient. As an aspiring politician, Lord Randolph expected to live and entertain in the style expected of the son of a duke; absorbed by her husband's new world, the new Lady Randolph Churchill threw herself into the entertaining that it required. Both were conditioned by their different backgrounds to expect the best on offer in food, wine, clothes or furnishings; from the outset, the Churchills employed a butler, French cook, footman, valet, lady's maid and housemaid. Lord Randolph could no more give up the family penchant for gambling than Lady Randolph could discard Parisian couturiers when choosing new clothes. Like most aristocrats at the time, they lived beyond their means, surviving by paying their bills late and running up a mounting tally of debts.

All this would become a familiar feature of the landscape as the Churchills brought up their first son, Winston. He arrived only seven months after their wedding and presented his mother with a dilemma. In America, relationships between the generations were generally more relaxed than they were among the Victorian elite; parents used a lighter disciplinary touch and encouraged their children to display initiative at an earlier age. By contrast, Victorian parents imagined their children to inhabit a state of 'defective adulthood' that required them to live largely in a nursery until they had learned the rules of proper behaviour. The limited evidence available suggests that Lady Randolph veered between the American and British approaches, showing Winston more open affection than was usual for a Victorian mother, but also leaving him for long periods of time in the care of that peculiarly British invention, a nanny. Mrs Everest, the Churchills' nanny, did stay with the family for seventeen years, suggesting that she may have established a more collaborative relationship with Lady Randolph than was usual between mother and nanny.

Winston was two years old in 1877 when, as a signal of the power and reach of the British Empire, Prime Minister Benjamin Disraeli proclaimed Queen Victoria to be Empress of India. Closer to home, her son, the Prince of Wales, chose the same year to deliver a severe setback to the ambitions of the Churchills, when Lord Randolph crossed him in a dispute over a woman between the prince and Lord Randolph's brother. As a result, the heir to the throne spread the word that he would not visit any house in London that still welcomed the Churchills.

To save the family's face, the 7th Duke of Marlborough became Queen Victoria's Viceroy in Ireland, taking Lord Randolph with him as his private secretary. The family stayed in Dublin for almost three years until April 1880, during which time Lady Randolph produced a second son, John (always known as 'Jack'), while her husband witnessed poverty and famine in Ireland on a scale that gave his politics a keener edge.

On return to London in April 1880, Lord Randolph became a leading advocate of 'Tory Democracy', a new policy that encouraged his party to adopt reforms that would resonate with newly enfranchised voters rather than leave them to William Gladstone's Liberal Party. 'Our house became the rendezvous of all shades of politicians', Lady Randolph wrote of the years that followed. 'Many were the plots and plans which were hatched in my presence.'[11]

Once Winston approached the age of eight in November 1882, the Victorian social code dictated that he should leave the exciting comings and goings at home of leading politicians to join fellow sons of the elite at a 'preparatory' boarding school. It was a custom that Lady Randolph did not fight; nor is there any evidence that either Winston's mother or his father inspected their son's first school before choosing it. St George's School in Ascot was simply a fashionable establishment, known for preparing its pupils for entry into one of Britain's leading public schools at the age of thirteen. Its headmaster, however, turned out to run a brutal regime. Eighteen months later, Winston's nanny and the family doctor would combine to convince his parents to remove him for the sake of his health; on their doctor's recommendation, they chose an establishment on the south coast near Brighton. It was a gentler alternative, run by two elderly sisters, but the academic diet remained rich in classical studies.

The outside world hardly impinged on the consciousness of pupils, but at the time the guard was changing at Blenheim. Winston's grandfather, the 7th Duke, had suddenly died in 1883, leaving Lord Randolph's elder brother, George, as the 8th Duke and steward of Blenheim's dwindling estate. Before the 7th Duke died, he had persuaded his friends at Westminster to safeguard the palace's future by enacting the Blenheim Settled Estates Act of 1880, which removed the entail from certain of its treasures. Lord Randolph's father had contented himself with the sale of the library's rare books, but the new 8th Duke set about selling enough of the palace's Old Masters paintings to raise over £400,000 (at least £40 million at 2020 values).[12]

Powerless to prevent his brother, Lord Randolph consoled himself by escaping to the winter sunshine in India, leaving his ten-year-old son, increasingly a handful, in the charge of his mother and nanny. The trip to India at least paved the way to Lord Randolph's first ministerial appointment (and salary) as secretary of state for the colony when the Tory Party displaced Gladstone's Liberal government in June 1885. Although Gladstone was to recapture power six months later, the following twelve months were to prove the apogee of Lord Randolph's brief period in the political sun. Aged thirty-six, he first masterminded a decisive Tory election campaign that defeated Gladstone's policy of home rule for Ireland and drove the Liberal Party out of power for six more years; then he was rewarded by the new Tory prime minister, Lord Salisbury, with the twin posts of chancellor of the exchequer and Leader of the House of Commons. These marked him out as the government's most important figure in the House of Commons and a future leader if he played his cards with patience. His eleven-year-old son, Winston, followed reports of Lord Randolph's speeches in the newspapers at school, conscious enough of his father's fame to sell to classmates the signatures at the foot of admittedly rare letters from father to son.

The long game was not Lord Randolph's style: first he irritated Cabinet colleagues by forays into their ministerial territory (a later trademark of his son), then he wrote an impulsive letter of resignation to the prime minister in an attempt to force through cuts in his government's military spending. To Lord Randolph's surprise, Salisbury calmly accepted his departure.

No one knew so at the time, but it was the end of a political career, the meteoric trajectory of which would long dazzle contemporaries as well as his son. Writing twenty years later, Lord Rosebery, by then a former prime minister, penned a portrait of Lord Randolph as both political opponent and friend. His words could equally well have applied to Lord Randolph's son, who was by then also a young MP:

> full of charm, both in public and private life ... his unexpectedness, his impulsiveness, his tinge of violent eccentricity, his apparent

daredevilry made him a fascinating companion . . .. Whatever it might be, politics or pleasure, it possessed him entirely: he did it with gusto, with every nerve and every fibre. . . . He had few if any permanent animosities.[13]

Lord Randolph took himself off after his sudden loss of office for another long absence overseas, to lick his wounds and nurse his fragile health. Their marriage under strain, Lady Randolph found herself once again in charge of the children, who had to compete for her attention with a series of men ready to fill the gap in her life left by her husband. Winston seldom succeeded in luring her to visit him at school in Brighton; so, he reversed the tables on the occasion of Queen Victoria's Golden Jubilee in 1887, badgering his mother to let him travel to London to witness the events. A classic clash of wills with his mother, one of the first of many, ended in compromise: Winston was allowed to witness the second of two days of celebrations. The royal family had recovered from a difficult decade in the 1870s, while every schoolboy in Britain learned with pride that its empire now covered almost a quarter of the world's population and would bring them to heights of civilisation so far only reached by the Anglo-Saxons at its core. It was the start of Winston's life-long reverence for monarchy and empire.

In April 1888, the following year, Winston made the move to his 'public' school at the age of thirteen. His father had attended Eton, which had produced thirteen prime ministers, but chose for his son its rival, Harrow, which had produced five. Harrow's position on a hill was thought to be healthier than Eton's riverside for a child still prone to sickness, but Lord Randolph may already have decided that his son was no academic high-flier. Winston passed into the bottom class of his year group at Harrow, a position he barely left in the four years he spent at the school. Easily distracted, he showed little appetite for study, apart from the subject of English. There a young teacher, Robert Somervell, managed to engage Winston's interest by using pens of differently coloured inks to analyse the grammatical components of the 'noble' English sentence, as Winston, a future Nobel laureate in the subject, came to call it.[14]

Winston was still only fourteen when his father decided that his son should not be aiming at a university education (a decision that ruled out, for example, a career in the law, a frequent steppingstone into politics); instead, he should start as an officer in the army. According to Winston's account in *My Early Life*, Lord Randolph had been impressed, during a rare visit to the nursery, by his son's marshalling of a force of 1,500 miniature soldiers.[15]

As a consequence, Winston joined Harrow's army class to prepare for the army's entrance examination for would-be officer cadets into the Royal Military College at Sandhurst. The candidates spent less time studying classical languages and more time on the French language and mathematics, neither of them a favourite subject with Winston. But he and Jack enjoyed the summer holidays that they spent in the country at Banstead Manor, a property that his grandmother, the dowager duchess of Marlborough, rented for the family near Newmarket racecourse. Ostensibly it was to allow Lord Randolph to indulge his new interest in racehorses (one of his few financial successes), but the unspoken purpose was to save the young family money while they rented out their London home for the summer season.

One of the few people who knew about the extent of Lord Randolph's financial difficulties was his friend since their schooldays, Nathaniel Rothschild.[16] Towards the end of 1890, Lord Rothschild, now the head of the family bank in London, suggested Lord Randolph should lead a Rothschild-sponsored expedition to southern Africa to prospect for gold; the bank would help him to recruit a syndicate of investors, lend him money to buy his own stake and provide the necessary mining and logistical expertise.[17] Since Lord Randolph judged this one of the few ways suitable for the son of a duke to replenish the family coffers, he accepted the challenge and was able to secure additional funding from another friend, Algernon Borthwick, who commissioned regular reports on the expedition's progress for the pages of his family-owned newspaper, *The Morning Post*. (Within a decade, Winston would be reporting in the same newspaper for Borthwick's son Oliver from the military campaigns in the Sudan and southern Africa.)[18]

The eight-month expedition failed to discover any gold in commercial quantities, so its investors lost all their money; but on its way home through the Witwatersrand district, friends of the Rothschild family offered Lord Randolph the chance to become an early investor in one of the first mines in the district to be sunk deeper than was usual. Rand Mines turned out to be so successful that, once floated on the stock exchange, its shares rose to a value of more than 100 times the price that Lord Randolph had paid. The investment was to fund the Churchill family for the brief remainder of Lord Randolph's life and to form the cornerstone of his legacy.[19]

Winston was seventeen years old when his father returned from Africa. They had never been close, partly because fathers and children of the Victorian elite seldom were; partly because Lord Randolph's medical treatment (a compound of mercury administered for a diagnosis of syphilis) made him short-tempered; and partly because Lord Randolph had in any case formed a low opinion of his son's abilities. To a fatherly eye, Winston behaved erratically, spent extravagantly and seldom applied himself properly to his studies. He was, moreover, unpunctual, untidy and showed too little deference to his elders.

Lord Randolph's judgement appeared vindicated when Winston failed the army entrance examination not once, but twice. Exasperated, Lord Randolph threatened his son with the indignity of a career 'in business' before agreeing a final attempt if Winston transferred to a special London crammer that taught nothing but the army entrance exam.

On this third attempt, Winston was delighted to pass, but his placing, too low in the list to qualify for the infantry, drew only scorn from his father. 'By accomplishing the astonishing feat of getting into the Cavalry, you imposed on me an extra charge of some £200 a year', Lord Randolph complained, aware that the social life of a cavalry officer required a more costly parental subsidy.

> Make this position indelibly impressed on your mind, that if your conduct and action at Sandhurst is similar to what it has been in the other establishments in which it has [been] sought vainly to impart to you some education, then that part of my responsibility for you is over.[20]

On his arrival at Sandhurst in August 1893, officer-cadet Churchill filled a last-minute gap in the infantry list and appealed to his father for a fresh start, admitting some 'past extravagance'.[21] He seemed at first to make some headway when, on a visit to Sandhurst in November, Lord Randolph found himself impressed by the changes the army had instilled in his nineteen-year-old son. He took Winston with him to a weekend house party at Tring Park, the country home of the Rothschilds, where they met leading young politicians of the day such as Arthur Balfour and Herbert Asquith.

The thaw between father and son proved short-lived when Winston dropped his grandfather's old gold watch into a Sandhurst lake three months later. Although the watch was found and repaired, Lord Randolph decided his elder son was not to be trusted with it, handed it on to Jack and told Winston to buy a replacement with his own money. As Winston often did, he turned to his mother for help; she was usually ready to mediate or assist after briefly dressing him down out of loyalty to her husband. 'Oh! Winny, what a harum scarum fellow you are', she wrote on this occasion, while nevertheless enclosing money for a replacement.[22]

By the spring of 1894, Lord and Lady Randolph had decided to travel around the world for a year to shield Lord Randolph's children and friends from the final stages of his illness. Doctors advised a shorter trip, but agreement was reached that one of their number should accompany the Churchills and that the trip should be cut short if Lord Randolph's condition deteriorated sharply. Before his parents left England, Winston typed a letter to ask his father for an allowance of £15 a month while he was away. Lord Randolph's reply finished on a crushing note: 'If you are going to write letters to me when I am travelling, type-written & so ridiculously expressed, I would rather not receive them.'[23]

It turned out to be the last letter that Lord Randolph would send his son. By the time the Churchills reached south-east Asia in November, Lady Randolph and the doctor decided they should return straight home. At the same time, the family doctor broke the news to Winston of his father's terminal illness. It came as a complete surprise, triggering an abrupt change in the tone of his letters, which for the first time showed a concern for his mother's well being that eclipsed his own preoccupations.

Lady Randolph responded in kind after her husband's death at home in January 1895, just as Winston left Sandhurst as an army officer. From that moment onwards, according to Winston's later account in *My Early Life*, she and he 'worked together on even terms, more like brother and sister than mother and son'.[24] One of his first moves following his father's death was to secure a transfer from the infantry to the cavalry, a move that he made with the help of his mother's contacts. Lady Randolph was well placed to help him: she enjoyed warm relationships with many senior army generals as well as most of the leading figures in the Conservative and Liberal parties. Her links with the royal family were impeccable too, at a time when this still counted. Unafraid of calling in these contacts on behalf of Winston, Lady Randolph encouraged him to ask others for what he wanted, to go to the top to ask and never to accept 'no' as a final answer. They were traits which some deferential fellow members of the Victorian elite disdained as brash and American; they marked the young Churchill out from his British contemporaries and would cause him difficulties early in his career. Ultimately, they gave him an independence of mind that served him well.

Second-lieutenant Churchill emerged from his time at Harrow and the Royal Military College without, as he put it, a 'liberal education' or any guiding philosophy of life.[25] Nevertheless, he confided within months of his father's death to his mother that he planned to switch to a career in politics after four years in the army. Always disappointed by her husband's sudden fall from political grace, Lady Randolph promised to help him as best she could. Recognising that her son's weak education would prove a handicap, she suggested and supplied much of the reading material that Churchill consumed in India, where his regiment moved in the autumn of 1896. The long midday break between the end of morning training and the start of evening polo at his barracks in Bangalore gave him the opportunity for the first time to read, think and organise his mind.

Churchill sent the first statement of his political philosophy to his mother from India in a letter dated April 1897, when he was twenty-two years old. It carried conscious echoes of Tory Democracy, his father's political legacy, in its commitment to 'the present constitution – Queen – Lords – Commons', to 'Imperialism abroad' and to a 'mighty navy' but small army, as well as in its opposition to home rule for Ireland. To these traditional Tory tenets, the young Churchill added a radical domestic programme, much of which he would help implement a decade later as part of a Liberal, not a Tory, government:

> Extension of the Franchise to every male. Universal Education. Equal Establishment of all religions. Wide measures of local self-government. Eight hours. Payment of members [of parliament] (on request). A progressive Income Tax. I will vote for them all.[26]

Throughout Churchill's time in India, Lady Randolph acted as his main fixer on the home front as well as his chief correspondent. She found his first literary agent and his newspaper editors and publishers when he needed them; she spoke to top generals or politicians to ease his career path; she 'boomed' (as she put it) his early books and articles among her wide circle of friends; and she arranged his first political engagements during his periods of home leave.

The Financial Legacy

In *My Early Life* Churchill writes that his father 'died at the moment when his new fortune almost exactly equalled his debts'.[27] In reality, the Rothschilds sent Lord Randolph's executors cheques totalling £54,237 (£5.5 million), thanks to a boom in mining investments which lasted until they sold his Rand Mines shares.[28]

Lord Randolph's last will followed a traditional Victorian template by leaving his widow a modest sum of cash with which to meet immediate bills, before settling the balance into a protective trust, to be known as Lord Randolph Churchill's will trust. Lady Randolph was not entitled to use any of its capital, but she would receive all the income earned by it and by their marriage settlements. This would reach a combined sum of £5,000 a year (£500,000), handsome by any standard. Less usually, the will had left no independent allowances for Lord Randolph's sons Winston and Jack, who therefore depended financially on their mother (she had promised Winston an initial £500 (£50,000) to top up his army pay of £120 (£12,000) a year). There was one safeguard that Lord Randolph had inserted for his sons: if their mother was to remarry (and she was only forty-one when their father died), his trustees were allowed to divert half of the income from his will trust to Winston and Jack. It was an important proviso at a time when marriage prospects so often depended on financial 'expectations'; yet five years later when Lady Randolph did marry a young army officer with some financial 'prospects' but no immediate private income, nobody told Winston or Jack of the clause, which they only discovered in 1914.[29] By then they had both had to make their way in the world.

Churchill would not inherit any family money until 1921, by which time he was forty-six years old. In that year, first an Irish cousin died in a railway accident in Wales, entitling his eldest English cousin to inherit their shared great-grandmother's estate in Ireland, worth £57,000 after estate taxes (£2.5 million).[30] When Churchill's mother died in the same year, so that her remaining trust monies were shared between her two sons, he briefly enjoyed both a substantial sum of capital and additional private income. Within a decade he was to dissipate both through a mixture of extravagant spending, gambling in the south of France, trading losses on the stock exchange and the purchase of a country home at Chartwell which cost more to modernise and run than he had ever expected.

The Intangible Family Inheritance

The importance of Churchill's inheritance lies, therefore, not in terms of his finances, but in the privileged circle into which he was born and in the start that circle afforded him in each of his military, writing and political careers. The wide network of friends that his parents had cultivated exposed him from an early age to people of power in the worlds of royalty, the army, politics and newspapers. His father's political success, however brief, conferred an instant credibility on his son's name when he came to seek adoption as a parliamentary candidate by Conservative constituency associations.

Churchill took more pride in the intangible value of his family inheritance than he admits in the pages of *My Early Life*. Throughout his life he would explore (and exploit) it. He often returned to stay at Blenheim, where he chose to propose to his future wife and to be buried beside the village church. He insisted his first motor car should be painted in the precise shade of Marlborough blue, even though this delayed its delivery; he wore his father's robes when he became chancellor of the exchequer in 1924; he mined the family archives and earned handsomely by writing a biography of his father (*Lord Randolph Churchill*, 1906) and another of the 1st Duke of Marlborough (*Marlborough: His Life and Times*, 1932–8). The latter enterprise, he claimed, taught him much about the art of building alliances that proved of value while he led Britain in the Second World War.

In private, Churchill acknowledged his debt to his parents more generously than he did in the pages of *My Early Life*. On first taking up his seat in parliament at the age of twenty-five, he sent his mother, who was perennially hard-up, a cheque for £300 (£35,000), adding in a note: 'I could never have earned it had you not transmitted to me the wit and energy which are necessary'[31].

Notes

1. C. Darwin, *On the Origin of Species* (London: Murray, 1859), p. 397.
2. Box 1 CHURCHILL Collection, Longwell Papers, Columbia University, A. Hays Sulzberger, A. Memorandum, 'Meetings with CHURCHILL'.
3. C. Hibbert, *The Marlboroughs: John and Sarah Churchill, 1650–1744* (London: Viking, 2001), pp. 336, 348.
4. J. Bateman, *The Great Landowners of Britain and Ireland* (London: Harrison & Sons, 1878), pp. 472–3; A. Rowse, *The Later Churchill/s* (London: Macmillan, 1958), pp. 229–32; D. Cannadine, *The Aristocratic Adventurer* (London: Penguin, 2005), p. 6.
5. By 1907 more than 500 'dollar princesses' are said to have married titled Europeans, taking some $220 million with them to their adopted continent.
6. Letter from Duke of Marlborough to Lord Randolph Churchill, 31 August 1873, cited CV, vol. 1, pp. 12–13.
7. Letter from Leonard Jerome to Lord Randolph Churchill, 7 April 1874, Blenheim Papers, British Library.
8. Letter from F. Capon to Lord Randolph Churchill, 25 February 1875, cited CV, vol. 1, pp. 18–19.
9. Letter from Leonard Jerome to Duke of Marlborough, 9 April 1874, cited CV, vol. 1, p. 20.
10. M. Lovell, *The Churchills: A Family at the Heart of History* (London: Little, Brown, 2011), p. 41. Available at www.measuringworth.com.
11. Mrs G. Cornwallis-West, *The Reminiscences of Lady Randolph Churchill* (London: Edward Arnold, 1908), p. 126.
12. D. Lough, *No More Champagne: Churchill and His Money* (London: Head of Zeus, 2015), p. 27.
13. A. Rosebery, Earl of, *Lord Randolph Churchill* (London: Arthur L. Humphreys, 1906), pp. 34–5, 82 and 87.
14. W. S. Churchill, *My Early Life* (London: Eland, 2000), p. 17.
15. Churchill, *My Early Life*, p. 19.
16. D. Kynaston, *The City of London: Golden Years 1890–1914*, vol. 2 (London: Chatto & Windus, 1995), p. 13.
17. Transcript of letter from Lord Randolph Churchill to Lord Rothschild, 22 March 1891, Rothschild Archives London, 101/22 T 15.
18. B. Roberts, *Churchills in Africa* (London: Hamish Hamilton, 1970), p. 14.
19. Rothschild Archives London, I/8/15 a/c 198 a/c no. 4, 1893 Rothschild ledger; Lough, *No More Champagne*, pp. 28–30.
20. CAC, CHAR 1/2/66-8, Lord Randolph Churchill letter to Winston Churchill, 9 August 1893.
21. Winston Churchill to Lord Randolph Churchill, 30 August 1893, cited CV, vol. 1, pp. 402–3.
22. CAC, CHAR 1/8/59, Letter from Lady Randolph Churchill to Winston Churchill, 22 April 1894.
23. CAC, CHAR 1/2/84-5, Letter from Lord Randolph Churchill to Winston Churchill, 24 June 1894.
24. Churchill, *My Early Life*, p. 62.
25. CAC, CHAR 28/21/65, Letter from Winston Churchill to Lady Randolph Churchill, 31 August 1895.

26. CAC, CHAR 28/23/31, Letter from Winston Churchill to Lady Randolph Churchill, 6 April 1897.
27. Churchill, *My Early Life*, p. 195.
28. Rothschild Archives London, I/8/17 a/c 178, Rothschild 1895 ledger. Lord Randolph's executors were Lady Randolph Churchill, the Duke of Marlborough and a brother-in-law Lord Curzon (later Earl Howe), who was married to Georgina Churchill.
29. A full version of Lord Randolph Churchill's will is at CAC, Churchill Papers, CHAR 1/79/2-5.
30. Lough, *No More Champagne*, pp. 130–2.
31. CAC, CHAR 28/26/94, Letter from Winston Churchill to Lady Randolph Churchill, 14 February 1901.

Further Reading

D. Cannadine, *The Aristocratic Adventurer* (London: Penguin, 2005)
R. S. Churchill [OB], *Winston S. Churchill, vol. 1, Youth 1874–1900* (London: Heinemann, 1966)
W. S. Churchill, *My Early Life* (London: Thornton Butterworth, 1930)
R. Foster, *Lord Randolph Churchill* (Oxford: Clarendon Press, 1981)
D. Green, *The Churchills of Blenheim* (London: Constable, 1984)
A Leslie, *The Fabulous Leonard Jerome* (London: Hutchinson, 1954)
A. Leslie, *Jennie: The Life of Lady Randolph Churchill* (London: Hutchinson, 1969)
D. Lough, *No More Champagne: Churchill and His Money* (London: Head of Zeus, 2015)
D. Lough, *Darling Winston: Forty Years of Letters between Churchill and His Mother* (London: Head of Zeus, 2018)
A. Sebba, *Jennie Churchill, Winston's American Mother* (London: John Murray, 2007)

3

Learning Lessons
Lieutenant Churchill and Military Intelligence

When Churchill wrote his autobiographical memoir *My Early Life* (1930), he reflected on his role in the Second Boer War (1899–1902) and on the victories and failures of British military operations during that conflict. He explored the British inability to adapt to the guerrilla tactics employed by the Boers and criticised the negligently under-funded and underutilised 'intelligence branch'.[1] To illustrate how poorly intelligence was used, Churchill recounted a story in which Sir John Ardagh, who was director of military intelligence, had prepared a report[2] for General Redvers Buller, only to have Buller return the report within an hour with a message attached stating that he 'knew everything about South Africa'.[3] Churchill concluded by arguing, 'Let us learn our lessons. Never, never, never believe any war will be smooth and easy.'[4]

Winston Churchill's interest in intelligence and intrigue is well known, particularly his use of intelligence during the Second World War. He insisted on reading raw intelligence data, read the intercepts produced by the Government Code and Cypher School (the precursor to GCHQ) called Ultra and demanded frequent intelligence briefings before diplomatic meetings. But his desire for intelligence did not stop at briefings. Churchill enjoyed the romance and intrigue of espionage and intelligence operations. He told Hugh Dalton, the head of the Special Operations Executive (SOE), to 'set Europe ablaze'.[5] He was also keen on counterintelligence, misinformation and misdirection. When he approved Operation Bodyguard, he remarked that, 'In war-time, truth is so precious that she should always be attended by a bodyguard of lies.'[6] Churchill encouraged the development of the Double-Cross System[7] and other strategic deception operations such as

Operation Mincemeat[8] and Operation Fortitude.[9] But for a man who had such a long life in the service of the United Kingdom, first as a soldier and then as a statesman, his relationship with intelligence was really a matter of applying the wisdom of lessons learned as a soldier. Churchill's passion for intrigue and cloak-and-dagger stories, as well as his interest in top-secret communiques and clandestine operations, can be traced back to his youth and his own experience with intelligence collection.

It has been remarked that Winston Churchill was predisposed to the use of intelligence as a leader.[10] Indeed, the renowned historian of intelligence, Christopher Andrew, has remarked that 'no British statesmen in modern times has had a more passionate faith in the value of secret intelligence than Winston Churchill because his long involvement with intelligence went back to his early adventures at the frontiers of the late Victorian Empire'.[11] While there have been several studies on Churchill's youth and his life as a solider,[12] including Douglas Russell's excellent and comprehensive *Winston Churchill: Soldier – The Military Life of a Gentleman at War* (2005) and Richard Toye's *Churchill's Empire: The World That Made Him and the World He Made* (2010), these studies concern themselves with Churchill's military life, his role as a war correspondent or his view of empire and rarely touch on the shadowy world of intelligence. David Stafford's masterful *Churchill and Secret Service* (1997) remains a notable exception. However, the majority of Stafford's research focusses on Churchill after he entered politics and is mainly concerned with the Second World War.

Curiously, Churchill's experience in the realms of intelligence and intrigue as a soldier have been relatively underexplored.[13] This chapter will explore this relationship by examining Churchill's experiences in Cuba, on the north-west Indian frontier, during the Anglo-Sudanese War and most importantly his role in the Boer War, which had a lasting impact on Churchill's thinking around the use of intelligence and clandestine operations.

Cuba

Churchill's first expedition as a soldier (and war correspondent) was intrinsically linked to intelligence collection. After he graduated from Sandhurst and joined the Queen's Own 4th Hussars on 19 February 1895, his first foray into action was in Cuba as war correspondent for *The Daily*

Figure 3.1 An illustration from *The Daily Graphic* of Spanish troops in Cuba based on a sketch supplied by Churchill, 1895 (CAC, Churchill Papers, CHAR 8/2).

Graphic. He planned to use his army leave to join the Spanish forces led by Marshal Arsenio Martínez Campos and report from the front, but to get permission he needed to see Lord Wolseley, the Commander and Chief of the Army. He convinced a fellow subaltern, Reginald Barnes, to join him. Luckily, Wolseley was open to the idea and arranged for Churchill and Barnes to see General E. F. Chapman (director of military intelligence).[14] Churchill later reported to his mother that he had met with General Chapman, who had furnished him with 'maps and much valuable information', and that it was requested that he 'collect information and statistics on various points' and particularly on 'the effect of the new bullet[15] – its penetration and striking power'.[16] Churchill had joined the 'well established tradition of the British amateur spy sent overseas with instructions to keep his eyes and ears open'.[17]

Churchill did just that. He wrote to his mother that the 'main characteristics of the information received through Spanish sources were exaggeration and gratuitous falsehood'.[18] Churchill reported in his dispatch from the front for *The Daily Graphic* 'that while the Spanish authorities were masters of the art of supressing the truth, the Cubans were adepts at inventing falsehoods'.[19]

Despite Churchill's views of the information they gathered, a smattering of Churchill's thoughts on the weapons and bullets can be seen in his public dispatches, such as his first report when he noted that Cuban rebels would let Spanish prisoners go but keep their arms.[20] In his third dispatch, he explained that the Spanish mostly used the Mauser rifles and they were 'an excellent weapon on a similar principle to our Lee-Metford' rifles.[21] In his fourth dispatch, he wrote that 'volleys from the Mausers' typically checked the enemy's advance and noted the Cubans used Remington rifles, which had 'little puffs of smoke' that would reveal the insurgents' position.[22]

The Cuban revolt also left an impression on the young Churchill. When he arrived, he asked a Spanish officer about the location of the enemy, whose response was 'everywhere and nowhere'.[23] Churchill witnessed how the Spanish Empire's attempts to come to grips with insurrection were frustrated time and time again because the rebels might appear or disappear at any place or time, whereas the Cuban guerrillas seemed to always know how to find the Spanish troops owing to the sympathies of the Cuban public. The Spanish Empire had failed to secure the hearts and minds of their Cuban subjects and as a result the Cubans had wide-ranging intelligence on their adversaries' movements. From his first dispatch, Churchill noted: 'There is no doubt that they possess the sympathy of the entire population and hence have constant and accurate intelligence.'[24] He later compared this to Napoleon's frustrations in the Peninsula War and bluntly said the Spanish forces had been 'out-guerrilla-ed'.[25] Despite the Spanish officers 'anticipating a speedy end to the war', Churchill argued that 'as long as the insurgents choose to adhere to the tactics they have adopted ... they can neither be caught nor defeated'.[26] Such was Churchill's faith in the guerrilla tactics of the insurgents that, he concluded, 'it would take the Emperor William, with the German Army, twenty years to crush the revolt'.[27]

The North-West Frontier

Churchill's next assignment would place him as a player in the 'Great Game' or, as it was known in Russia, the 'Tournament of Shadows' between the British and Russian Empires in central Asia. Later popularised by Rudyard Kipling in his novel *Kim* (1900), the Great Game was a hotbed of intelligence collection, counterintelligence and espionage between the two Empires. Once again, he was acting as a war correspondent, this time for *The Daily Telegraph* and the Anglo-Indian paper the Allahabad *Pioneer*. But Churchill had already gleaned a serious understanding of this geo-political environment because his father, Lord Randolph Churchill, had been a player in the same game.

When Lord Randolph had been appointed secretary of state for India in June 1885, a major priority for him had been to help negotiate a settlement in the Panjdeh Crisis, when Russian forces captured an Afghani border fort and the Russian and British Empires nearly went to war.[28] He was firm in negotiations but wrote to Queen Victoria that 'there is great reason to believe that in September or October the Russians will make a further advance or aggression, just before the General Election here, causing the greatest alarm, confusion, excitement, and party feeling among the people, and consequently the greatest possible danger to the interests and security of India'.[29] His imperial stance in Asia was even noted by *The Times*, which feared his appointment was 'more likely to precipitate than to avert war'.[30] When he gave the Budget for India in August 1885, he levied an attack against the previous viceroy, Lord Ripon. Lord Randolph accused him of negligence and incompetence, saying that while Russian troops advanced in central Asia, the Indian army had been reduced, the strategic defence of the frontier neglected, and all the while 'Lord Ripon slept, lulled by the languor of the land of the lotus'. Lord Randolph painted a grim picture of Russian expansion:

> The Russian hosts absorbed the territory of Merv, and rapidly filled up the vacuum to the South which you had so incautiously and blindly left, and Lord Ripon and his counsellors were found, like the foolish virgins, with no oil in their lamps. Then followed the fruitless Frontier negotiations, and Lord Ripon came home, and Lord Dufferin went out, not one hour too soon for the safety of India, and for the tranquillity of our Indian Empire. Next we see the lonely and unsupported British Commissioner endeavouring to stop the advance of the Russian troops – troops flushed with success, and animated by the highest hopes of glory and of booty.[31]

Lord Randolph only grew increasingly hostile against Russian ambitions in central Asia. In 1888, while discussing frontier politics with the tsar on a world tour, he was insistent that Britain 'ought to take Afghanistan'.[32] The young Winston Churchill had clearly been influenced by his father's thinking. Meanwhile, at Harrow he wrote an essay on 'an imaginary future invasion of Russia by Britain – illustrating the superiority of John

Bull over the Russian bear'.[33] So when he joined the Malakand Field Force to fight the Mullah Sedullah's radical Islamic uprising, it is no surprise he saw 'Russian intrigues' in Anglo-Afghan relations and sought to thwart 'a predominance of Russian influence' which would give them 'the ability to invade India at their discretion'.[34]

Churchill's early days in Bangalore with the 4th Hussars were spent reading, preparing for the upcoming polo tournament and enjoying the life of a cavalry officer.[35] However, the encroaching spectre of Russian influence on the frontier can be seen all through his book *The Story of the Malakand Field Force*, which recorded his time on the frontier. Churchill mentioned 'Ahkund of Swat' who prophesied before his death that there would be a 'struggle between the Russians and the British' in the Swat valley, as well as a 'Russian war cloud' hanging over the region.[36] Churchill publicly argued, like his father, for a 'Forward Policy' on the north-west frontier to thwart perceived Russian ambitions in the region. He believed that the '[p]unitive expeditions had awakened an intense hostility among the tribesmen' and that the intrigues of Russia had for some time been watched with alarm by the Indian government, but 'as long as the border could remain a "No-man's land" ... all was well'. But Churchill argued 'that if any power was to be supreme, that power must neither be Russia nor Afghanistan .... The predominance of Russian influence in these territories would give them the power to invade India at their discretion', while the 'predominance of Afghan influence would make the Amir master of the situation, and enable him to blackmail the Indian Government indefinitely'.[37] Ultimately, his faith in pursuing the 'Forward Policy' on the frontier was based on a combination of 'the intense hostility of the Border tribes, the uncertain attitude of the Amir, the possibilities of further Russian aggression and the state of feeling in India'.[38]

Churchill had good reason to worry about Russian and Afghan interference. A political intelligence officer for Swat and Chitral named Major H. A. Deane befriended Churchill.[39] He had been collecting intelligence investigating how the local tribesmen came to possess their firearms. Churchill found himself once again embroiled in intelligence operations on rifles. Major Deane had received information from a local agent, Abdul Hamid Khan,[40] which indicated that Abdur Rahman Khan, the amir of Afghanistan, had begun buying weapons and dispersing them among the tribes in the Malakand (perhaps nudged on by the Russians). Deane noted in his diary that the amir paid 40,000 rupees 'to an influential Mullah in India to work up this business'.[41]

Additionally, Deane included information on Abdul Hamid Khan in a letter to Lord Salisbury, the foreign secretary, dated 31 August:

> Since the commencement of the Greco-Turkish war the Amir of Afghanistan has sent Maulvis and Talibs to excite frontier Muhammdan [sic] tribes by distributing among them books on jehad [sic]. The Amir has opened shops to sell rifles and cartridges cheap to the different tribesmen. If there were no movement from his [the amir's] side, Muhammadan [sic] tribes would never dare disturb the British Raj.

Deane's intelligence found a welcome audience in Churchill, who wrote about the arms trade which had developed in the region, noting 'all along the frontier and far down into India, rifles are stolen by expert and cunning thieves'. The most enterprising and ingenious of these, Churchill argued, was the Ut Khel tribe in the Laghman valley and that among the rifles which had been taken from them in raids, a third of them were decommissioned government martinis that 'displayed the government stamp'. But he was also quick to point out that 200 or 300 rifles were 'Russian military rifles, stolen probably from some distant posts in Central Asia'.[42]

Beyond Churchill's observations about arms, there are several passages about how intelligence might be used in operations. Here Churchill was heavily influenced by Capitan E. Henry Stanton, an intelligence officer he met while on assignment. They became fast friends.[43] Churchill wrote to Reginald Barnes that Stanton was 'a good fellow and full of knowledge of all sorts',[44] and even stayed with him later in Rawal Pindi.[45] Stanton wrote a report which argued that intelligence should be the exclusive preserve of the army's intelligence department.[46] Churchill, being a cavalry officer, married this with use of the mounted forces in modern warfare, exploring the 'formidable' use of cavalry in 'collecting intelligence', but also noting that 'reconnaissance is by no means the only opportunity for cavalry employment on the frontier'.[47] But Churchill went on to discuss how important field intelligence was on the north-west frontier and how it should be assigned and allocated. Heavily influenced by Stanton, he wrote, 'it is difficult to believe, that the collection of information as to the numbers and intentions of the enemy, would not be better and more appropriately carried out, by the Intelligence Department, and the cavalry'. But he warned about the risk of miscommunication between civil political officers with military intelligence personnel on the ground, as a civil officer would 'not be expected to understand what kind of military information a general requires'.[48] Churchill offered a solution which can be seen as a window into his thinking about intelligence in this period:

> Civil officers should discharge diplomatic duties, and military officers the conduct of war. And the collection of information is one of the most important of military duties. Our Pathan Sepoys, the Intelligence Branch, and an enterprising cavalry, should obtain all the facts that a general requires to use in his plans. At least the responsibility can thus be definitely assigned.[49]

Churchill also made a brief note on the usefulness of burgeoning signals intelligence for operational communication between field commanders. He reported: 'Signalling by heliograph, was throughout the operations of the greatest value. I had always realised the advantages of a semi-permanent line of signal stations along the communications to the telegraph, but I had doubted the practicability of using such complicated arrangements in action.' This was even more important given the geography of the region because as Churchill argued, 'In a country intersected by frequent ravines, over which a horse can move but slowly and painfully, it is the surest, the quickest, and indeed the only means of intercommunication.'[50] Churchill said he was happy to report this because he had delivered these messages himself by horse. Already Churchill was becoming fascinated with intelligence – not just the romance of intrigue or the adrenaline rush of the battle operations but the efficiency of good communication as well.

The Anglo-Sudanese War

In 1898 Churchill was able to get a position as a correspondent for *The Morning Post* and was desperate to join General Sir Herbert Kitchener's march up the Nile towards the Dervish capital of Omdurman. Though Kitchener had disapproved of Churchill's work as a war correspondent because he openly challenged his superiors' tactics, Churchill was able to use his mother's contacts with Lord Salisbury and Lord Cromer to gain admission to the 21st Lancers, another cavalry unit.[51] Churchill was

already very excited about his trip to Egypt and pondered to his friend
Ian Hamilton what he might do in the military before entering politics.
'The only thing I can think of is the IB [intelligence branch]', he wrote,
and added rather wryly, 'I have some experience.'[52] But this was no
fleeting idea. He wrote to his mother a few days later that he was
thinking of the intelligence branch because it 'might suit me or
I them'.[53] In addition to his work as a war correspondent, Churchill
was eager to engage in the usual sort of military intelligence expected of
a cavalry officer. He went on scouting and reconnaissance missions,
gathered information about the local people and regional geography
and delivered battlefield information to generals, including Kitchener
himself, much to Churchill's dismay.[54]

It was also when he got his first serious lesson in counterintelligence.
While he was out on a scouting mission south of Wadi el Abed, his
squadron came upon brush thickets so dense they had to dismount to
continue their search for signs of the Dervish. After coming upon
a deserted camp, a Dervish in a 'patch jibba and armed with several
spears emerged suddenly from the bushes'.[55] Churchill captured the
fierce warrior and returned to the camp. Churchill later wrote that he
was 'proud of my prisoner – until we reached the army'. For it turned
out that his prisoner was no ordinary Dervish. He was an agent working
for the intelligence department who, according to Churchill, had 'been
spying in Omdurman, and now returned to tell his news – news which
he might very easily have never lived to tell'.[56] Churchill was embarrassed and even pleaded with other correspondents not to telegraph the
episode to the press.[57]

Having been fooled himself, Churchill was very laudatory of the
Egyptian intelligence department in his history of the Anglo-Sudanese
War, which he titled *The River War: An Account of the Reconquest of the Sudan*
(1899). This is not surprising because, as Churchill explained, he was
indebted to the director of military intelligence, Major Reginald
Wingate, 'who gave me all the information necessary for the conduct
of the campaign, the successful result of which was greatly furthered by
the thorough knowledge acquired by the department of every detail of
the enemy's plans and positions'.[58] This included the intelligence
branch's *Handbook of the Soudan* (1898) and *Report on the Nile and Country
between Dongola, Suakin, Kassala, and Omdurman* (1898), both of which were
written by 'leading intelligence officer Lord Edward Gleichen'.[59] All of
this clearly informed Churchill's book on the war.

Churchill's tome was a history of the conflict with some added 'adventure-writing' describing his part in a larger story. This allowed him to explore the broader experience of British forces in Egypt and Sudan, as well as the evolution of the intelligence branch of the Egyptian forces. *The River War* included praise for the intelligence department, stating, 'The Intelligence Branch of the Egyptian Army rose under the direction of Colonel (now Sir Reginald) Wingate to an extraordinary efficiency' and noting that Kitchener used the Intelligence Department well and that they 'assiduously collected every scrap of information'.[60]

Churchill also demonstrated a keen interest in espionage and its importance in understanding an enemy. He noted that during the siege of Khartoum, 'Spies pervaded the town' and after the fall of Khartoum all the people of Sudan were 'the objects of a ceaseless scrutiny ... up the great river, within the great wall of Omdurman, into the arsenal, into the treasury, into the mosque, into the Kalifa's house itself, the spies and secret agents of the Government – disguised as traders, as warriors, or as women – worked their stealthy way'.[61] He appreciated the architecture of the intelligence networks and the time it took to build them. Impressed by the scope and scale of Wingate's intelligence operation, Churchill wrote that these networks 'steadily accumulated, and the diaries of the Intelligence Department grew in weight and number, until at last every import-ant Emir was watched and located, every garrison estimated, and even the endless intrigues and brawls in Omdurman were carefully recorded... . Then the reports of the spies were at length confirmed.'[62] But Churchill's admiration was also bound up with the romance and bravery of the agents and spies who served the British forces. Even as Kitchener's forces bore down on the Dervish capital, he wrote of the courage displayed by the 'Intelligence spies, who to the last – even when the forces were closing – tried' to pass on information.[63]

In January 1899, Churchill submitted his official resignation from the 4th Hussars. He planned to move into politics and had received an invitation from Robert Ascroft, the sitting Conservative MP, to be his running mate for Oldham (which then returned two MPs). In the event, Ascroft died suddenly but Churchill still contested the seat and was defeated on 7 July 1899, though he was not disheartened for the result was very close.[64]

Figure 3.2 Churchill's comments on reforming intelligence collection are lampooned in this contemporary newspaper cartoon, October 1901 (CAC, Broadwater BRDW I Press 3).

The Second Boer War

In terms of his early relationship with intelligence, Churchill's next post would be the most important. He saw an opportunity to join the war in South Africa against the Boers – not with a military appointment but as a correspondent for *The Morning Post*. He rode out from Durban on 15 November 1899 in an armoured train to Natal to cover the front. However, the train was surrounded at Estcourt by advancing Boers, forced off the track and besieged.[65] Churchill naturally helped his old comrade Alymer Haldane mount a defence, but they were overcome by Boer sharpshooters and were taken prisoner. Held as a prisoner of war, Churchill assured the authorities he was merely a 'special correspondent' and demanded release.[66] The prison received word from Boer General P. J. Joubert which heavily implied that Churchill might be a spy and that despite his press credentials, it 'appears entirely otherwise' and he 'must be guarded and watched as dangerous for our war; otherwise he can still do us a lot of harm'.[67] Churchill later wrote that he believed his Boer captors took this position because he had forfeited his non-combatant status by the part he played in the armoured train fight.[68] So he endeavoured to escape, despite knowing enough 'military law' to realise that 'a civilian in half uniform who has taken an active and prominent part in a fight, even if he has not fired a shot himself, is liable to be shot at once by drumhead court-martial'. Churchill later noted to his readers that, 'None of the armies in the Great War would have wasted ten minutes upon the business.'[69] Despite his recollection that 'spies were everywhere', he successfully returned to British-held territory, gaining a household name and a heroic status throughout the upper echelons of the British Empire, despite his still not having a formal appointment in the military.[70] He applied to the Lancashire Hussars, which came to nothing.[71] However, he was able to secure an appointment to the South African Light Horse in January 1900 from General Sir Redvers Buller owing to his new-found reputation.[72] He would even continue his career as a clandestine reconnaissance operative, riding a bicycle behind enemy lines in Johannesburg to deliver a 'heavy sheaf of telegrams full of earliest and exclusive information' between Ian Hamilton's lines and Lord Roberts' headquarters.[73] Here again Churchill noted that had he been caught, 'no court-martial that ever sat in Europe would have had much difficulty in disposing of such a case' and 'he could be tried and shot as a spy'.[74]

It was in South Africa that Churchill would develop his deepest thinking about intelligence and its applications. His deployment in the South African Light Horse taught him lessons in intelligence around three issues. The first concerned censorship and the press' relationship with intelligence; the second related to field and signals intelligence; and the final lesson centred around the use of guerrilla tactics and adapting the military to specific operations. All three of the areas would leave a major impact on how Churchill conceptualised intelligence operations for the rest of his life.

The state of British military intelligence in the early phases of the Second Boer War was not in good working order. Though the intelligence division was under the control of the thorough and intelligent Major-General John Ardagh, the branch was outrageously underfunded.[75] Despite this shortcoming, Ardagh was able to use the collected intelligence to publish the 'remarkably accurate' 'Military Notes on the Dutch Republics of South Africa', which, according to Churchill, argued that at least 200,000 British soldiers would be required to hold South Africa.[76] Ardagh sent his findings to the secretary of state for war, Lord Lansdowne, and General Redvers Buller, the commander and chief of British forces in South Africa. But his warnings were not heeded. Churchill later wrote that Buller returned the notes 'within an hour with the message that he already "knew everything about South Africa"'.[77] After the catastrophic defeats at the battles of Stormberg, Magersfontein and Colenso during the 'black week' of 10–17 December 1899, Buller was dismissed and replaced by Lord Fredrick Roberts and his second, General Kitchener, both of whom took intelligence collection very seriously. This did not keep Buller from scapegoating the intelligence division and John Ardagh on the way out. However, Ardagh was quickly vindicated and faith was restored in the intelligence division.[78]

It was into this chaotic and underfunded landscape that Churchill arrived as a war correspondent for *The Morning Post*. However, the relationship between the British press corps and military intelligence was uneasy to say the least.[79] The bloated press corps included over 88 newspapers and there were no fewer than 276 named press correspondents.[80] The rules for censoring where erratic, limited and under the purview of one officer.[81] Major Jones was responsible for press relations and administering the official licences which were granted by London, but too often correspondents would show up with no official credentials. At the War Office, Lord Lansdowne was hesitant to enforce any strict rules on censorship for fear of a public outcry over press freedoms in parliament and in high society. Moreover, this was 'compounded by the fact that no single centralised list of war correspondents existed'.[82] Yet another matter was the fact that many soldiers published their letters in local or national papers. Winston Churchill fell into just such a grey area.

Churchill had already been attacked for his public letters by fellow soldiers. After his published correspondence criticising officers' strategies in the Malakand and in Sudan, he had gained quite a reputation. An anonymous letter to the *Army and Navy Gazette* signed merely 'a general officer' complained that Churchill was 'acting as a special correspondent here, there and everywhere', that it was out of line for him to 'criticise general officers highly placed in authority and to influence public opinion' and that the feature of young subalterns as war correspondents had been 'carried in the case of Lieut Churchill to the very utmost limit of absurdity'.[83] This was followed a week later by a similar attack in the same publication by a 'field officer'.[84] Churchill fired back in a letter to the editor that these correspondents' quarrel was not with him but with 'the Army authorities'.[85] So the army authorities passed a new regulation which forbade soldiers to act as correspondents, especially in the aftermath of the Anglo-Sudanese War, where Churchill's own graphic descriptions of the battlefield had certainly contributed to the new army policy.[86] This makes Churchill's acquisition of an appointment under Redvers Buller all the more remarkable.

The chaotic nature of British press control and censorship left a mark on Churchill's thinking about intelligence. He saw the disorder created by underfunding the intelligence branch in the military and sought to rectify it. Some of his earliest speeches in parliament called for reform and reorganisation and additional funding for the intelligence division. Churchill argued in Saddleworth, Yorkshire that one does not need a 'military education to understand the importance of the [intelligence] branch'. He went on to explain that the 'intelligence service is starved for want of both money and brains' and he drew several unfavourable comparisons between the British and Boer intelligence capabilities.[87] A few months later he argued in favour of raising the funds for intelligence and was horrified to learn that the Intelligence Department only had sixteen or twenty officers. He argued that 'no department should be more fully staffed', especially since the German intelligence department had at least 200 officers. Churchill concluded that what was needed was 'an army of efficiency' and 'an army of elasticity, so that comparatively small regular units in the time of peace might be expanded into a great and powerful army in time of war. For that expansion nothing was more vital than an efficient and well-staffed Intelligence Department.'[88] When his pleas went unheard, he pushed again in April for a raise in budget for the intelligence branch.[89]

Remembering his experiences in Cuba, Churchill also spoke about the importance of censorship and in favour of the military maintaining close control over press relations. He was frustrated by the state of censorship during the war and even noted a moment when a press censor changed the wording of an intelligence telegram. This communique was meant for General John French, who was in pursuit of Boer General Louis Botha, and originally said there were '200 Boers' north of Thabanchu mountain, which the censor changed to 'small parties'. Had this small change not occurred, Churchill wrote, 'it is probable that the operations of the following day would have been attended by a greater measure of success'.[90] But Churchill did not limit his thinking to just the military application of censorship in protecting the army's secrets. His speech to the Pall Mall Club in 1900 praised another dimension of censorship: to 'protect the people from morbid and hysterical letters written for the purpose of creating a sensation and a newspaper boom'.[91] Perhaps an odd sentiment from a war correspondent and journalist. But Churchill must have been able to compartmentalise these areas in his mind. Just a few months later, he defended the role of 'well placed war correspondents who should be able to write to the public with general's supervision and the War Office's discretion'.[92]

Whatever his views about war correspondents, Churchill clung to the importance of censorship. As home secretary, he actively helped the Official Secrets Act (1911) come into being and worked with Sir Vernon Kell, the general director of MI5, to draw up a secret list of aliens who might engage in acts of espionage.[93] Perhaps inspired by the censorship used by the Spanish in Cuba, Churchill also expanded the Home Office's ability to intercept and open suspects' mail, adopting a 'general warrants authorising examination of all correspondence of particular people upon a list to which additions were continually made'.[94] Beyond the censorship of private correspondence, Churchill proposed to the general staff that there should be an informal management of the press which would be informed by an officer who could 'supply the public press with accurate information' but might be 'more readable than official dispatches'.[95] He took this idea with him to the Admiralty in 1911. In the wake of the Agadir Crisis, the Admiralty met with the War Office. The five major newspapers were in attendance as well, and at Churchill's behest they adopted a system of informal and voluntary press censorship, creating the 'D-notice' system, which stayed in place for over seventy-five years. But even then, Churchill was not totally satisfied with the level of censorship and issued a memo in 1913 to the Liberal press from the Admiralty which was met with resistance because 'Churchill seemed to be trying to influence interpretation.'[96] Having seen the shambolic nature of the British army's relationship with the press and the cavalier attitude of war correspondents first hand, Churchill used his knowledge of the practices to limit and control the press.

Another major lesson Churchill took away from the Boer War related to the importance of wartime technology, such as marrying specific weapons to tactics and the use of signals intelligence. In 1901, after his return from South Africa, Churchill was invited by Redvers Buller to address the Royal United Services Institute. Though Churchill was privately unimpressed by Buller, he remained a public ally, and Churchill used the opportunity to discuss some of his new ideas.[97] He argued for more structure in censorship and an organised use of war correspondents' material. He also argued that the cavalry's use of the sword and shock tactics were hopelessly outdated and ineffectual in the face of skilled Boer sniping and hit-and-run tactics.[98] Here he imagined that Britain could 'develop our unique and peculiar resources to meet our unique and peculiar dangers'.[99]

But his most interesting musings were on signals intelligence, where glimpses of his emerging brilliance can be seen. Churchill noticed there was no effective 'system of signalling that would effectively enable an artillery commander to direct the whole of his batteries'. Churchill argued that a liaison officer might take half an hour to relay a matter from one position to another, and then if the heliograph signals were not precise, there would be confusion, which would take precious time. Additionally, the relatively new technology of telegraph was not secure as the Boers often used the lines to gain information.[100] Churchill's solution of communicating the precise position was to fire 'a coloured shell'. When fired at a specific position, 'all the other guns ... would know that they were to concentrate their fire where this coloured shell exploded. It occurred to me that something connected with iodine might give bright purple fumes immediately visible.'[101] This would also help the artillery commander identify the location of his own troops so as to avoid them.

But not all Churchill's ideas on field intelligence were so good. Another issue he noticed was the difficulty in sending messages between divisional commanders in the field. Having significant experience of moving over difficult ground and looking for commanders who had just moved on, Churchill saw a chance to solve the issue of roving commanders whose flags were often not seen. He thought about raising a balloon so that every general had one. 'One general, one balloon. I would not suggest anything so democratic as that they should have all the same sized balloon. Each general should have a balloon in proportion to his rank in the army.' Churchill only seemed slightly concerned this might reveal the location of generals to enemy fire. He argued 'that the man at the foot of the balloon knows precisely where the general is, and the general goes no great distance from the balloon'.[102] Here he solved one problem but created a far worse one. In any case, you can see Churchill's mind working up solutions for signals intelligence on the battlefield. Moreover, these early ideas go some way towards showing why Churchill the prime minister would later adamantly support signals intelligence and cryptography in Bletchley Park, personally review raw intelligence data from the Government Code and Cypher School and look for scientific ways to solve intelligence issues.[103] Churchill had always sought technological solutions to aid in tactics and strategy.

Perhaps the most enduring lesson Churchill learned from the Boer War and indeed from his other posts was the power of a guerrilla force fighting in a known landscape with support. Churchill left South Africa in 1900 just as the war entered a guerrilla phase, which dragged on another two years in conditions that were horrific and protracted.[104] Churchill's trepidation towards guerrilla warfare was evident in *My Early Life* when he described the Boers mounting a defence of Dewetsdorp where 2,500 Boer riflemen held off 'at least ten times their number of British troops and then slipped away quietly'. Churchill added ominously that it was now 'evident that the guerrilla phase would present a problem of its own'.[105] Reflecting on the Spanish experience in Cuba, he later wrote how the Boer War had transformed 'into a guerrilla and promised to be shapeless and indefinite'.[106] Knowing his brother had been posted to South Africa as well, Churchill wrote to warn him that, 'Guerrilla warfare was just as dangerous as the other and perhaps more so.'[107] This lesson became the foundation for Churchill's own approach to asymmetric warfare in occupied France. As David Stafford has pointed out:

> Armed guerrillas with the support of the people could thwart the
> ambitions of even a great and powerful empire. The conviction had

a lifelong effect on his strategic thinking. Some forty years later, when creating the Special Operations Executive (SOE), images of heroic Boer resistance helped animate his vision. And in personally meeting its secret agents, he relived his adventure behind enemy lines in the golden days of his youth.[108]

But Churchill learned this lesson too well. Immediate effects and the cloak-and-dagger nature of guerrilla action and espionage captivated Churchill and 'exaggerated expectations of what they could achieve'.[109] As a result, Churchill was 'over-eager … to put intelligence to operational use'.[110] Perhaps the most obvious legacy of Churchill's romanticism of guerrilla warfare and espionage can be seen in his expectations for the SOE. But the SOE was not even operational until 1941 and spent more time fighting internal bureaucratic battles against the Foreign Office and Secret Intelligence Service than it initially spent in action in Europe. While Churchill's hope that it could 'set Europe ablaze' kept the SOE funded and operational, in the end it only raised a 'hopeless resistance and insurrections that produced little but bloodshed, defeat and savage reprisals'.[111]

Conclusion

An examination of Churchill's role in Victorian Britain's military intelligence provides a clear lens for viewing his future thinking on intelligence collection and operations. His brief foray into Cuba to learn about the new Mauser rifle showed him the importance of censorship and the power of a popular guerrilla insurrection. His experiences on the north-west frontier placed him in the 'Great Game', taught him the importance of reconnaissance operations and of civil and military intelligence officers working in tandem, and would leave a profound legacy for how he understood the role of Russia on the world stage. His participation in the Anglo-Sudanese War demonstrated the power and reach of Britain's spies, so much so that he was fooled himself. It also impressed upon him the power and importance of a well-organised intelligence corps. His involvement in the Boer War taught Churchill the significance of the military–press relationship and the importance of properly funding and organising the intelligence branch, and underscored the significance of censorship and guerrilla operations. In addition, it allowed him to reflect on the role of signals intelligence in action, even if some of his ideas were not practical.

Taken together, these lessons built a foundation for a leader who understood the importance of intelligence and was proactive in solving the issues relating to this wilderness of mirrors. Churchill was quick to organise a defence against the infiltration of German spies in the lead-up to the First World War and worked to create an understanding around press and government uses of military information. His genuine interest in signals intelligence and openness to using unconventional means can be seen in intelligence successes such as Operation Bodyguard, Operation Fortitude, Operation Mincemeat, the Double-Cross System and Ultra.

This foundation in intelligence work gave Churchill a footing, which meant he built 'much of his a career on a voracious appetite for and rational use of information received from a wide variety of intelligence sources' and unquestionably resulted in his being able to 'put intelligence to better use than Hitler'.[112] Historian of intelligence Michael Handel has said that, 'Although there is no ideal type of leader for the optimal use of intelligence, personality and experience are extremely important.'[113] In the case of Winston Churchill, the lessons he learned as a solider during the Victorian era helped produce a thoughtful, creative and tenacious leader who was keen to understand and use all the intelligence he could.

Notes

1. Churchill's reference to the Intelligence Branch (IB) of the War Office reveals he was using the antiquated Victorian terminology. The IB was elevated to the Intelligence Division in January 1888 and later to Intelligence Department (ID) in 1901. See C. Andrew, *Secret Service: The Making of the British Intelligence Community* (London: Heinemann, 1985), p. 49; T. Fergusson, *British Military Intelligence 1870–1914* (Columbia, MD: Arms and Armour Press, 1984), p. 85.
2. TNA, WO/33/154, Section B, Intelligence Division, War Office, *Military Notes on the Dutch Republics of South Africa*. This report was unpopular and mocked as it called for at least 200,000 soldiers to successfully defeat a Boer rebellion.
3. W. S. Churchill, *My Early Life* (London: Reprint Society, 1944), pp. 244–5.
4. Churchill, *My Early Life*, pp. 244–5.
5. H. Dalton, *The Second World War Diary of Hugh Dalton 1940–45* (London: Jonathan Cape, 1986), p. 62.
6. F. H. Hinsley, *British Intelligence in the Second World War*, vol. 4 (London: HMSO, 1990), pp. 98–102. Operation Bodyguard was a strategic deception plan developed by the Allied states before the 1944 invasion of Normandy. The plan was intended to mislead the German high command as to the time and place of the invasion. See T. Holt, *The Deceivers: Allied Military Deception in the Second World War* (New York: Scribner, 2004).

7. The Double-Cross System was a counterespionage and deception operation developed by the Security Service in 1940. See A. C. Brown, *Bodyguard of Lies* (New York: Harper, 1975); B. Macintyre, *Double Cross: The True Story of the D-Day Spies* (London: Bloomsbury, 2012).

8. Operation Mincemeat was a deception operation to disguise the 1943 Allied invasion of Sicily. See B. Macintyre, *Operation Mincemeat* (London: Bloomsbury, 2010).

9. Operation Fortitude was a set of component operations in Operation Bodyguard. It was divided into two sub-plans, North and South, with the aim of misleading the German High Command as to the location of the D-Day invasion. See J. Levine, *Operation Fortitude: The Story of the Spy Operation That Saved D-Day* (London: Collins, 2011).

10. See, for example, F. H. Hinsley, *British Intelligence in the Second World War*, 4 vols. (London: HMSO, 1979–90); D. Stafford, *Churchill and Secret Service* (London: John Murray, 1997); M. I. Handel (ed.), *Leaders and Intelligence* (London: Cass, 1988), pp. 3–39.

11. C. Andrew, Churchill and Intelligence. *Intelligence and National Security*, vol. 3 (1988), pp. 181, 183.

12. R. Churchill, OB, vol. 1 (London: Heinemann, 1968); K. Emmert, *Winston S. Churchill on Empire* (Durham, NC: Carolina Academic Press: Claremont Institute for the Study of Statesmanship and Political Philosophy, 1989); D. Jablonsky, Churchill: Victorian Man of Action. In D. Jablonsky (ed.), *Churchill and Hitler: Essays on the Political-Military Direction of Total War* (Ilford: Frank Cass, 1994); P. de Mendelssohn, *The Age of Churchill: Heritage and Adventure 1874–1911* (London: Thames and Hudson, 1961); W. Manchester, *The Last Lion: Winston Spencer Churchill: Visions of Glory 1874–1932* (Boston, MA: Little, Brown and Company, 1983); P. I. Rahe, The River War: Nature's Provision, Man's Desire to Prevail and Prospects for Peace. In James W. Muller (ed.), *Churchill as a Peace Maker* (Washington, DC: Woodrow Wilson Center Press, 1997); D. Russell, *Winston Churchill: Soldier – The Military Life of a Gentleman at War* (London: Brasseys, 2005); R. Toye, *Churchill's Empire: The World That Made Him and the World He Made* (London: Macmillan, 2010); R. Toye, 'The Riddle of the Frontier': Winston Churchill, The Malakand Field Force and the Rhetoric of Imperial Expansion. *Historical Research*, vol. 84, no. 225 (2011); F. W. Woods (ed.), *Winston S. Churchill, War Correspondent 1895–1900* (London: Brasseys, 1992).

13. There are numerous exceptions which have briefly touched on this theme but not examined it systematically. See, for instance, Andrew, Churchill and Intelligence; F. H. Hinsley, Churchill and the Use of Special Intelligence. In W. R. Louis and R. Blake (eds.), *Churchill: A Major New Assessment of His Life in Peace and War* (New York: W. W. Norton, 1993); Jablonsky, Churchill: Victorian Man of Action.

14. Winston Churchill to Lady Randolph Churchill, 19 October 1895, CV, vol. 1, p. 592.

15. The bullet in question was the 7×57 mm Mauser, which was designed by Paul Mauser for the Mauser Model 1893, which is a bolt-action rifle. This bullet was an early example of a smokeless powder rimless bottlenecked rifle cartridge. This bullet and rifle would later be used by the Boers against the British and force the British to alter their tactics. See F. Haas and W. Zwoll, *Bolt Action Rifles* (Iola, WI: Krause Publications, 2003).

16. Winston Churchill to Lady Randolph Churchill, 21 October 1895, CV, vol. 1, p. 592.

17. Stafford, *Churchill and Secret Service*, p. 14. British military intelligence during the Victorian era was often conducted by amateurs, geographers and gentlemen of

means. See S. Wade, *Spies in the Empire: Victorian Military Intelligence* (London: Anthem Press, 2007).

18. Churchill to Lady Randolph Churchill, 6 December 1895, Gran hotel Inglaterra, CV, vol. 1, p. 602.
19. Winston Churchill, 'Cienfuegos', *The Daily Graphic*, 9 November 1895, CV, vol. 1, p. 605.
20. Churchill, 'Cienfuegos', *The Daily Graphic*, 9 November 1895, Woods (ed.), *Winston S Churchill: War Correspondent 1895–1900*, p. 5.
21. Churchill, 'Cienfuegos', *The Daily Graphic*, 27 November 1895, *Winston S. Churchill: War Correspondent 1895–1900*, pp. 12–13. In this Churchill was mistaken. The Mauser rifles were superior to the Lee-Metford owing to their greater accuracy and use of black powder. See N. Murray, *The Rocky Road to the Great War: The Evolution of Trench Warfare to 1914* (Washington, DC: Potomac Books, 2013).
22. Churchill, 'Cienfuegos', *The Daily Graphic*, 15 December 1895, *Winston S. Churchill: War Correspondent 1895–1900*, pp. 16–17.
23. Churchill, *My Early Life*, p. 87.
24. Churchill, 'Cienfuegos', *The Daily Graphic*, 27 November 1895, *Winston S. Churchill: War Correspondent 1895–1900*, pp. 6–7.
25. Churchill, *My Early Life*, p. 92.
26. Churchill, 'Cienfuegos', *The Daily Graphic*, 27 November 1895, *Winston S. Churchill: War Correspondent*, p. 13.
27. Churchill, 'Tampa Bay', *The Daily Graphic*, 13 January 1896, *Winston S. Churchill: War Correspondent*, p. 19.
28. P. Hopkirk, *The Great Game: On Secret Service in High Asia* (London: Murray, 1990), pp. 425–8; E. Sergeev, *The Great Game 1856–1907: Russo-British Relations in Central and East Asia* (Washington, DC: Woodrow Wilson Centre Press, 2013), pp. 205–10.
29. Lord Randolph Churchill to Queen Victoria, 11 July 1885, Winston Churchill, *Lord Randolph Churchill* (London: Macmillan, 1906), p. 87.
30. 'The Afghan frontier question', *The Times*, 31 October 1885.
31. Lord Randolph Churchill, 'India Budget', *Hansard*, House of Commons Debates, vol. 300, cols. 1286–1385, 6 August 1885.
32. Churchill, *Lord Randolph Churchill*, vol. 2, p. 362.
33. Toye, *Churchill's Empire*, p. 18; J. Golland, *Not Winston, Just William? Winston Churchill at Harrow School* (Harrow: Harrow Publications, 1988), p. 13.
34. W. S. Churchill, *Malakand Field Force* (London: Macmillan, 1897), pp. 344–5.
35. Churchill developed a significant love of polo while he was in India, where he also underwent his 'self-education': Churchill, *My Early Life*, pp. 110–31. On the importance of polo in the development and nuancing of colonial attitudes, see M. Marsden, All-Male Sonic Gatherings, Islamic Reform, and Masculinity in Northern Pakistan. *American Ethnologist*, vol. 34, no. 3 (2007), pp. 473–90.
36. Churchill, *Malakand Field Force*, pp. 28, 72.
37. Churchill, *Malakand Field Force*, p. 247.
38. Churchill, *Malakand Field Force*, p. 250.
39. Churchill mentioned Deane nineteen times in the *Malakand Field Force*, noting on multiple occasions that he had given 'valuable assistance in collecting intelligence and supplies'. See Churchill, *Malakand Field Force*, pp. 262, 266, 271.
40. Abdul Hamid Khan was a local agent who worked with Major Deane as well as Churchill's other intelligence officer friend, H. E. Stanton, who said he was 'of good

Afghan refugee family which for three generations has been conspicuous in its loyalty in Government Service'. See TNA, WO 106/290. David Stafford further points out that Abdul Hamid Khan spoke four languages and was intelligent and discreet. See Stafford, *Churchill and Secret Service*, p. 16.

41. British Library, India Office, L/PS/7/98/1293/No. 81, Major H. A. Deane, Diary, 29 July 1897; K. Surridge, The Ambiguous Amir: Britain, Afghanistan and the 1897 North-West Frontier. *The Journal of Imperial and Commonwealth History*, vol. 36, no. 3 (2008), p. 422.

42. Churchill, *Malakand Field Force*, pp. 131–2.

43. According to Stafford, Captain Henry Stanton was an 'important figures in Churchill's introduction to intelligence work'. Stafford, *Churchill and Secret Service*, p. 15.

44. Churchill to Reginald Barnes, Nawagai, CV, vol. 1, p. 787.

45. Churchill to Lady Randolph Churchill, Bombay, CV, vol. 1, p. 910. Churchill told his mother he was 'a clever fellow in the Intelligence Department'.

46. See H. E. Stanton, 'Extracts from reports on the working of the Intelligence Branch with the Chitral Relief Force, Tochi Field Force, Malakand and Buner Field Forces', TNA, WO 106/290.

47. Churchill, *Malakand Field Force*, p. 208.

48. Churchill, *Malakand Field Force*, pp. 224–5.

49. Churchill, *Malakand Field Force*, pp. 224–5.

50. Churchill, *Malakand Field Force*, p. 237.

51. OB, vol. 1, pp. 392–5. On the importance of the 21st Lancers in Britain's Victorian expansion, see R. Dutton, *Forgotten Heroes: The Charge of the 21st Lancers at Omdurman* (Prenton: Infodial, 2012).

52. Churchill to Ian Hamilton, Bangalore, 18 April 1898, CV, vol. 2, p. 914.

53. Churchill to Lady Randolph, Bangalore, 25 April 1998, CV, vol. 2, p. 922.

54. Churchill, *My Early Life*, pp. 186–7.

55. Churchill, *The River War*, vol. 2 (1899), p. 69.

56. Churchill, *The River War*, vol. 2 (1899), p. 73.

57. David Stafford noted that it was unsurprising that Churchill left out this episode of his running afoul of the Intelligence Department in *My Early Life*: Stafford, *Churchill and Secret Service*, p. 17. But Stafford is correct that this must have seriously bruised Churchill's ego because the episode was also cut out of the second edition of *The River War*, which condensed the two earlier volumes and was published a year later.

58. Churchill, *The River War*, vol. 2, p. 430. Churchill also thanked him in the first volume for supplying expensive maps and plans which he could use to write his history. Churchill, *The River War*, vol. 1, p. ix.

59. Stafford, *Churchill and Secret Service*, p. 16.

60. Churchill, *The River War*, vol. 2, pp. 166, 359.

61. Churchill, *The River War*, vol. 1, pp. 88, 166.

62. Churchill, *The River War*, vol. 1, p. 167.

63. Churchill, *The River War*, vol. 2, p. 67.

64. Churchill was within 1,200 votes of his competition in the Radical Party, *Manchester Courier*, 7 July 1899, Randolph Churchill (ed.), CV, vol. 2, p. 1036.

65. For a full of account of the incident with the armoured train, see Russell, *Winston Churchill: Solider*, pp. 258–62.

66. Churchill to Louis de Souza, 18 November 1899, Pretoria, CV, vol. 2, p. 1074.

67. P. J. Joubert to F. W. Reitz, 19 November 1899, Ladysmith, CV, vol. 2, p. 1075.
68. Churchill, *My Early Life*, p. 282.
69. Churchill, *My Early Life*, p. 271.
70. Churchill, *My Early Life*, p. 297; R. Toye, *Winston Churchill: A Life in the News* (Oxford: Oxford University Press, 2012), pp. 40–3.
71. Russell, *Winston Churchill: Solider*, p. 263.
72. Toye, *Churchill: A Life in the News*, p. 43.
73. Churchill, *My Early Life*, p. 365.
74. Churchill, *My Early Life*, p. 363; Stafford, *Churchill and Secret Service*, p. 19.
75. The intelligence department only received £11,000 annually; by comparison, the Transvaal intelligence department received £92,000 annually and the German general staff received £270,000 annually. See Fergusson, *British Military Intelligence 1870–1914*, p. 112.
76. Fergusson, *British Military Intelligence*, p. 113; Churchill, *My Early Life*, p. 244.
77. Churchill, *My Early Life*, pp. 144–5.
78. D. P. McCracken, John Ardagh (1840–1907): The Irish Intelligence Scapegoat for Britain's Anglo-Boer War Debacles. *Études irlandaises*, vol. 38, no. 1 (2013), pp. 60–3.
79. D. P. McCrachen, The Relationship between British War Correspondents in the Field and British Military Intelligence during the Anglo-Boer War. *Scientia Militaria, South African Journal of Military Studies*, vol. 43, no. 1 (2015), pp. 99–126.
80. McCrachen, War Correspondents, p. 100.
81. Identified as Major Jones by the chief press censor at Cape Town, assistant adjutant-general Lord Edward Stanley's report on Press Censorship; TNA, WO 108/262.
82. McCrachen, War Correspondents, p. 104.
83. Anonymous letter to the editor of the *Army and Navy Gazette*, 17 December 1898; CV, vol. 2, p. 999.
84. Anonymous letter to the editor of the *Army and Navy Gazette*, 24 December 1898; CV, vol. 2, p. 1000.
85. Churchill to the editor of the *Army and Navy Gazette*, 8 January 1899; CV, vol. 2, p. 1001.
86. De Mendelssohn, *The Age of Churchill*, pp. 122–34; M. Gordon, Viewing Violence in the British Empire: Images of Atrocity from the Battle of Omdurman, 1898. *Journal of Perpetrator Research*, vol. 2, no. 2 (2019), pp. 65–100.
87. Churchill, 'The War in South Africa', 4 October 1901, Rhodes James, *Complete Speeches*, vol. 1, p. 101.
88. Churchill, 'Army Estimates', 21 March 1902, Rhodes James, *Complete Speeches*, vol. 1, p. 157.
89. Churchill, 'The Budget', 14 April 1902, Rhodes James, *Complete Speeches*, vol. 1, p. 178.
90. Churchill, *Ian Hamilton's March*, p. 97.
91. Churchill, 'The War in South Africa', 25 October 1900, Rhodes James, *Complete Speeches*, vol. 1, p. 60.
92. Churchill, 'The War in South Africa', 27 April 1900, Rhodes James, *Complete Speeches*, vol. 1, p. 75.
93. Andrew, Churchill and Intelligence, p. 186, on Churchill helping pass the Official Secret Acts (1911) and on Vernon Kell's list, which by July 1913 contained 29,000 names. Stafford, *Churchill and Secret Service*, pp. 35–9.
94. Andrew, *The Secret Service*, p. 65.
95. Stafford, *Churchill and Secret Service*, p. 38.

96. Toye, *Winston Churchill: A Life in the News*, p. 88.
97. See Toye, *Winston Churchill: A Life in the* News, p. 43.
98. Churchill, Some Impressions of the War in South Africa. *The RUSI Journal*, vol. 45, no. 281 (1901), pp. 102–13, 107–10.
99. Churchill, Some Impressions of the War in South Africa, p. 111.
100. McCrachen, War Correspondents, p. 110.
101. Churchill, Some Impressions of the War in South Africa, p. 106.
102. Churchill, Some Impressions of the War in South Africa, p. 107.
103. Andrew, Churchill and Intelligence, p. 189.
104. For more on the horrific conditions of the last phase of the Boer War, see E. van Heyningen, The Concentration Camps of the South African (Anglo-Boer) War, 1900–1902. *History Compass, vol. 7*, no. 1 (2009), pp. 22–43; J. de Reuck, Social Suffering and the Politics of Pain: Observations on the Concentration Camps in the Anglo-Boer War 1899–1902. *English in Africa*, vol. 26, no. 2 (October 1999), pp. 69–88; S. V. Kessler, The Black Concentration Camps of the Anglo-Boer War 1899–1902: Shifting the Paradigm from Sole Martyrdom to Mutual Suffering. *Historia*, vol. 44, no. 1 (1 May 1999), pp. 110–47.
105. Churchill, *My Early Life*, p. 356.
106. Churchill, *My Early Life*, p. 367.
107. Churchill to Jack Churchill, 31 July 1990, CV, vol. 2, p. 1188.
108. Stafford, *Churchill and Secret Service*, p. 19.
109. Andrew, Churchill and Intelligence, p. 183.
110. Andrew, Churchill and Intelligence, p. 182.
111. Stafford, *Churchill and Secret Service*, pp. 186–8.
112. Handel, *Leaders and Intelligence*, p. 6.
113. Handel, *Leaders and Intelligence*, p. 6.

Further Reading

C. Andrew, *Secret Service: The Making of the British Intelligence Community* (London: Heinemann, 1985)
R. Churchill [OB], *Winston S. Churchill: Youth, 1874–1900* (London: Heinemann, 1968)
W. S. Churchill, *The Story of the Malakand Field Force: An Episode of Frontier War* (London: Longmans, 1898)
W. S. Churchill, *The River War: An Historical Account of the Reconquest of the Soudan*, vols. 1 and 2 (London: Longmans, Green and Co., 1899)
W. S. Churchill, *London to Ladysmith via Pretoria* (London: Longmans, Green and Co., 1900)
W. S. Churchill, *Ian Hamilton's March* (London: Longmans, Green and Co., 1900)
W. S. Churchill, *My Early Life: A Roving Commission* (London: The Reprint Society, 1944)
F. H. Hinsley, Churchill and the Use of Special Intelligence. In W. R. Louis and R. Blake (eds.), *Churchill: A Major New Assessment of His Life in Peace and War* (New York: W. W. Norton, 1993)
D. Russell, *Winston Churchill: Soldier – The Military Life of a Gentleman at War* (London: Brasseys, 2005)
D. Stafford, *Churchill and Secret Service* (London: John Murray, 1997)
R. Toye, *Churchill's Empire: The World That Made Him and the World He Made* (London: Macmillan, 2010)

4
_____

Churchill As a Writer and Orator

Churchill's lifespan coincided with the golden age of print. When he was growing up in the late nineteenth century, the cheap newspaper press and the electric telegraph were busy transforming communications, while international copyright protection and the adoption of payment of royalties were making the authorship of books more profitable. By the end of his active life, though television was by then getting into its stride in dominating popular culture, the era of today's electronic media had yet to dawn. Churchill's career was thus bounded by the primacy of the printed word, both in his activities as a politician and in his professional dependence on writing for the bulk of his income.

As a politician, Churchill was not alone in spending a great deal of preparation time on speeches that would not only sound well when delivered to a particular audience but would also read well in print, whether in newspapers or in subsequently published volumes. He often spoke at public meetings at a time when the platform still attracted large audiences, especially in his twenty-one election campaigns. His favourite venue, however, was the House of Commons, which he entered at the age of twenty-five and learned to master through assiduous preparation. At first he tried memorising his speeches – a fallible method, as he found out. His later procedure was to dictate a full text which would by typed up by secretaries, cadence by cadence, in what became known as 'psalm format'.

Churchill was already in his sixties when he tackled the new problem of communicating effectively through radio. Even then, his wartime broadcasts on the BBC were not as universally well received as the later myth would suggest. His legendary 'finest hour' speech in 1940 was judged 'magnificent' in the House of Commons by one strongly supportive MP (Harold Nicolson), who nonetheless thought 'it sounded ghastly on the wireless'.[1] Here, too, Churchill improved with practice. But his best speeches were always those that read well in print, a medium that helps their words transcend the particular occasions of their delivery. They remain quotable partly because they were always intended to be so.

Churchill's mastery of literary craftsmanship (on which Rudyard Kipling was one writer who complimented him) was no accident. Like Benjamin Disraeli, another author who became prime minister, Churchill lacked a university education, though the boy's talents in his schooldays were not as deficient as the later legend had it. Instead, it was in the army in India that the young Churchill had purposely educated himself, with an impressive breadth of reading of authors who, even at that time, seemed rather old-fashioned. Among his favourites were Edward Gibbon, Samuel Johnson, Edmund Burke and – above all – Thomas Babington Macaulay, with whose *History of England* Churchill had a lifelong fascination. His own literary and oratorical style was influenced accordingly: what Evelyn Waugh, in his novel *Men at Arms*, later derided as 'sham Augustan'.

True, Churchill often consciously harked back to the formal grand manner of an earlier era, though he knew how to leaven this, both in his speeches and in print, with a sudden swoop into the vernacular catch-phrases of his own day. He was thus fully in control of the diverse stylistic devices by which he conveyed his message, with a professionalism of which he was justly proud. When he was saluted by both Houses of Parliament on his eightieth birthday in 1954, with inevitable emphasis on his role and oratory in the Second World War, he said in response: 'if I found the right words you must remember that I have always earned my living by my pen and by my tongue'.[2]

Apprenticeship

Winston Churchill's early career was as a soldier. Although his father, Lord Randolph, had been an undergraduate at Oxford, no such path was indicated for young Winston, partly through financial constraints, since his parents were conspicuous spendthrifts at a time when the Churchill family fortunes were at a low ebb. Hence Winston's direction into the army class at Harrow School and his subsequent commission in the 4th

Figure 4.1 Churchill at his desk, c.1901 (CAC, Broadwater Collection, BRDW IV 2/1).

Hussars. At the time of Lord Randolph's early death in 1895, so Winston later suggested, his father's debts virtually cancelled the value of his estate; and while this seems not to be accurate, it is certainly true that Winston himself could expect little benefit, given his mother's appropriation of any proceeds to meet her own extravagant spending habits.[3] The net result was to throw this young aristocrat upon his own resources, albeit aided by his family connections. He had to rely on his talents, not in a military career but through his ability as a writer. And what the young soldier could write about, naturally enough, was warfare. If keeping up Lady Randolph's lifestyle and social position was part of the problem, exploiting it also became part of the solution. An attractive widow of forty, she adroitly used her connections to promote Winston's career as a war correspondent.

Hence Churchill's first book, *The Story of the Malakand Field Force* (1898), was compiled from the dispatches he had sent to *The Daily Telegraph* reporting on a British expedition to India's north-west frontier. Churchill had got himself loosely attached to the force, engaged in the perennial quest of subduing Afghanistan, with some of his mordant reflections on this intractable task subordinated to an overall message supporting its necessity.[4] His efforts were well received in high places; he was summoned to a personal interview with the prime minister, the great Lord Salisbury. Moreover, Churchill received from reviewers the sort of praise that his own father had never given him, which excited his ambition to write further books.

This fuelled his determination to seize another suitable opportunity in a forthcoming British military assault on the Sudan under General Sir Herbert Kitchener, despite his commander's reluctance to accept a young man who seemed simply a well-connected opportunist. The two volumes of *The River War* (1899), published after Churchill had left the army, in a sense vindicated both men: these showed off Churchill's talents, if not as a career soldier, then as a promising writer. Moreover, he spent much of the first volume unpicking the history of British involvement in the country, thus now delving into printed sources for the first time. Much of the second volume was devoted to a graphic first-hand depiction of the military action, notably in the one-sided battle at Omdurman, where the Islamic warriors were mown down by modern British technology. A further pointer to where Churchill's talents really lay – or plainly did not lie – was seen with the publication of a romantic adventure novel that he had meanwhile dashed off, *Savrola* (1899), on which his own later comment may well stand: 'I have consistently urged my friends to abstain from reading it.'[5]

What remains notable is that, before his twenty-sixth birthday in November 1900, Churchill had published no fewer than five books. This tally was made up by two further volumes on early British campaigns in the Second Boer War (1899–1902) in South Africa, during which this now famous war correspondent escaped from capture by the Boers, in an incident that, of course, became a publicist's dream. *London to Ladysmith* (1900) was published five days before the relief of Mafeking and sold 14,000 copies. It was followed by *Ian Hamilton's March* (1900), which sold 8,000, published in October of the same year. By this point Churchill, safely back at home, was standing as a Conservative candidate in the so-called Khaki Election of 1900 and was elected for the cotton town of Oldham. Obviously, the circumstances of the time account for the contemporary success of these books, which comprise graphic and efficient reporting rather than great literature. But they were milestones in the making of Churchill's career, not only as a budding politician but also as an apprentice author who could finance himself through his literary earnings. His lecture tour of North America, undertaken as soon as the General Election was over, was another spin-off; and his own total earnings from his pen and his tongue, as he proudly told his mother, now amounted to £10,000 – about £1 million in today's money.

Here was his own war chest for a political career, at a time when there was no salary for MPs. Winston was now financially independent and able to renounce his allowance from his mother; but he was also able to cash in on the political legacy of his father's reputation. A biography of Lord Randolph Churchill, with his dazzling and scandal-ridden career still a vivid memory, was obviously attractive to publishers; and Winston now had the keys to the family archive, not least through his good relationship with his cousin 'Sunny', the current duke of Marlborough. The authorised biographer thus began work in 1902 and was initially appalled at the scale of the task when he explored the papers held at Blenheim. He exploited family connections to seek access to the other side of correspondence with his father's old friends, notably the former Liberal Prime Minister Lord Rosebery and the current Conservative Prime Minister Arthur Balfour (who had now succeeded his uncle, Lord Salisbury). Both were charmingly uncooperative; but a third political giant of that era, Joseph Chamberlain, formerly a Liberal and now a key figure in the Unionist government, offered sustained support to young Winston, who later wrote: 'I must have had a great many more real talks with him than I ever had with my own father.'[6] The fact that Chamberlain had changed sides in politics in the 1880s, just as Winston was about to do so himself, gave this connection a further twist.

Churchill thus had many advantages, with personal connections that simultaneously aided his rapid rise to political prominence and endowed his authorship of *Lord Randolph Churchill* (1906) with unusual interest. Its two volumes were deliberately published during the General Election campaign in January 1906, resulting in a landslide victory for the Liberal Party, to which Winston himself had recently become a star recruit. How, then, would this dashing young Liberal convert deal with the political legacy of his father, famous for his slogan of 'Tory Democracy'?

The current political situation had made it possible for the author to extract particularly favourable financial terms. He had already been made an offer of an advance of £4,000 from Longmans, previously his publisher in London; but his father's old friend from the demi-monde, Frank Harris, took on a last-minute challenge to do better. He hawked the biography around the leading London houses – Heinemann,

Methuen, Cassell, Hutchinson, John Murray – before securing an offer totalling £8,000 from Macmillans in October 1905. After paying Harris a well-deserved £400, Churchill himself thus pocketed £7,600 (around £750,000 today). This compares with an annual salary of £2,000 in Churchill's first Cabinet post in 1908.

The biography of Lord Randolph had a great critical success, partly because it steered such a well-judged course between the ingrained prejudices of both the main political parties. The noble project of Tory Democracy that Lord Randolph was depicted as upholding was the aspect that Conservatives could readily applaud. Conversely, the alleged betrayal of this cause by others in Lord Randolph's own party allowed Liberals to suppose that they might inherit his legacy. At different times in his career, Winston Churchill himself read the moral of this story either way. In giving his account at the time, he had certainly exercised considerable latitude in the way he cited the evidence. Some of this was simply a matter of not washing the family linen in public; the shaky state of Lord Randolph's marriage was spared inquiry, as were the circumstances of his death (on which Frank Harris was later to break the silence by attributing it to syphilis). All this was understandable from a loyal son; his readers at the time would have had no complaint.

Moreover, they would have had no means of checking on the use of original sources to which the author had been given privileged access. This was just as well since the correspondence that Churchill cited was exploited in ways that plainly lack the sort of scholarly rigour that subsequent historians naturally expect. It is apparent to us now just how much the impact of the work depended not only on omission and elision but also on Churchill's cavalier alteration of quotations whenever it suited him, not only for reasons of personal tact but also in order to sustain his own interpretation against the grain of the evidence.[7] Two big issues were thus dealt with in an adroit but question-begging way. First, the project of Tory Democracy was endowed with a long-term consistency that allowed young Winston to reproach the Conservative Party of his own day for abandoning it. Lord Randolph was thus shown as a man of principle. Secondly, however, when his crucial decision in 1886 to back Ulster Unionist opposition against Irish Home Rule was discussed, Lord Randolph was quoted as saying lightly that 'the Orange card would be the one to play'.[8] Here, it seemed, the move was merely tactical, so although Winston was now both a Liberal and a Home Ruler, he was implying no real breach of his father's true principles. To his own satisfaction at least, the author had squared the circle for the politician.

Winston's War: 1

Churchill published further books after taking office in the Liberal government. He wrote about a long official visit he made to Africa as a junior minister at the Colonial Office in *My African Journey* (1908), which is distinctive in sometimes departing from official views of the benefits of empire for Indigenous peoples.[9] Here we see the irrepressible marginalia of a politician famous for stretching the rules. He also published *Liberalism and the Social Problem* (1909), which reflects his engagement with major policy issues in this field; but this is a compilation of the speeches he had given as a minister, unusual in quality rather than in kind from what might be expected of any working politician. There were also later editions of *Savrola* that similarly would not have been published but for the fame generated by Churchill's political career.

This quite naturally consumed the time and energy of a man who was by now married and in due course the father of four surviving children. His immediate financial need for income, which had driven him into authorship in the first place, was handsomely abated by a regular salary of £5,000 a year from 1910. In today's money this was worth no less than £500,000, but by the time of Churchill's post-war periods in office, inflation was to cut the value of such a salary by about 50 per cent. This was in itself a significant reduction, but the effect was even more striking because of subsequently heavier levels of taxation. His total liability for taxes before 1914 would have been less than 10 per cent of his total income; by 1919 it was around 40 per cent. Crucially, since any literary earnings could be spread over three years, and assessment for taxation was retrospective, actual payment of tax on a lump sum advanced against royalties could be deferred for several years into the future. Here was a system with a potentially devastating impact on a feckless author – as Churchill was duly to discover in the post-war period.

The opening of his career in government marked a watershed in Churchill's career as a writer by permanently altering his way of working. He now had a civil service staff with professional expertise in translating their minister's expressed intentions into tightly drafted documents; and this was also the era in which the modern typewriter mechanised this process. Churchill's official private secretary, Edward Marsh, was to become a lifelong friend: a man whom many regarded as a pedant but someone who cared deeply about literary style, and who provided versatile assistance for Churchill in many subsequent publications. Whereas Churchill had literally penned all his previous books in longhand, in his official role he now naturally took to dictating memoranda and other documents to members of staff, usually women, who took down his words in shorthand and then typed up the drafts. This way of transacting government business and composing speeches, notably through dictation, henceforth became the model for all Churchill's own professional literary production, whether of newspaper and magazine articles or the many volumes that he was later to publish. Hence the phrase he coined to describe the process: 'I lived in fact from mouth to hand.'[10]

The first of his books to be produced in this way was *The World Crisis*, ultimately running to five volumes (or six if we count an appended account of the war on the Eastern Front). Though the title suggests a work of very wide scope, the early volumes also have a specific personal agenda: to defend Churchill's record as first lord of the admiralty, especially the perceived failure of the Gallipoli offensive against Turkey. The very full contemporary documentation printed in *The World Crisis* is a function not only of Churchill's privileged access to the official archives but also of the fact that, while still in office, he had already prepared a detailed defence of his conduct in testimony for the committee of inquiry on the episode.

So when Churchill signed a contract to produce his book at the end of 1920 while still a Cabinet minister in the post-war Lloyd George coalition government, he had a vast amount of the relevant evidence already marshalled in support of his case. He continued working on such drafts while serving in the Cabinet until October 1922. All this helps to explain how the first two fat volumes of *The World Crisis* could then be published within twelve months of his losing office. Churchill's prior reputation as an author undoubtedly enhanced the terms of the contract that he secured for the book in 1920: £27,000 in all (worth up to £1 million today).

Churchill's account begins with his appointment as first lord of the admiralty in 1911 and there is a lengthy discussion of the strategic role of the navy in an era when technological advances put its traditional supremacy under pressure. The evolution of Churchill's position, from that of a leading pre-war critic of increased naval estimates to that of their foremost champion, is explicated, with much corroborative detail but not without irony. One central claim, of course, is that when war came in 1914, the fleet was ready. But, as an author, Churchill well appreciated that the circumstances of his dismissal from the Admiralty in 1915 constituted a problem that he would need to explain at length, not simply by challenging details.

The World Crisis accordingly set the choices open to the Allies in 1915 in terms of grand strategy, often memorably phrased, arguing that Britain as 'the Great Amphibian' could have exploited its naval mastery in the eastern Mediterranean to avert and avoid the military horrors of the Western Front.[11] One telling quotation was his own plea to Asquith at the time: 'Are there not other alternatives than sending our armies to chew barbed wire in Flanders?'[12] As it was, the gallant effort to take the Gallipoli peninsula, notably by the ANZAC troops involved, was insufficiently supported, leaving this 'great army hanging on by its eyelids to a rocky beach'.[13] It was the tragically premature decision to end the Dardanelles campaign that had led to this tragedy, argued an author whose eloquence responded to the sombre mood of his post-war readers in 1923. It is true that, as with his composition of Lord Randolph, the author falls below the level of modern scholarship in the suppressions and deletions he made in some of his quotations.[14] But if his account failed to stifle the derision that Churchill knew he faced in Australia in particular, he at least showed that Gallipoli was an open question at a moment when public opinion was retrospectively turning sceptical about the rival grand strategy, as seen in the mass carnage of the Western Front.

The later volumes of The World Crisis do not sustain the earlier level of compelling personal interest, often dealing with issues in which Churchill had had little direct participation. Here he was more reliant on the efforts of the team of advisers he had assembled, led by Major-General Sir James Edmonds, the editor of the British official war history. The fact that the third and fourth volumes were published in 1927 while Churchill was again in Cabinet office speaks for itself; it was a remarkable feat, but one achieved under inevitable constraint. We now know that his reason for pressing ahead was pecuniary. After taking office as chancellor of the exchequer, Churchill had formally retired from his profession as an author in 1925; so long as he did no further writing, receipts from his publishers would be treated as capital sums, which in those days went untaxed in Britain. But within a year, despite his official salary, he still needed to get his hands on further advances. So, in 1926 he had obtained official approval for reversing his 'retired' status, without prejudice to the fiscal holiday he had meanwhile enjoyed.[15]

A fifth volume, *The Aftermath*, also published while Churchill was in office in 1929, shows an interesting engagement with the controversies over the Versailles Peace Treaty, for example a commendation of the case made against its economic impact by John Maynard Keynes. But the subsequent decision to append a further volume to *The World Crisis* dealing with the Eastern Front, taken by Churchill on financial grounds during his own financial crisis in 1931 and knowing that he could devolve much of the work onto his assistants, did not bolster the author's reputation.

Professional Writer

Churchill was out of office in the period 1929–39, and it was then that his home at Chartwell became his 'word factory', thus helping him to pay the bills for its expensive upkeep by taking on multiple contracts. He not only had shorthand typists to take his dictation but, increasingly, commissioned advisers to undertake research on his historical works. While still in office he had begun a further book of memoirs, *My Early Life* (1930), as usual in desperate need of the advance. He had largely completed it while nominally on holiday at Chartwell in the late summer of 1928, assuring the prime minister (Baldwin): 'I have had a delightful month – building a cottage & dictating a book: 200 bricks & 2000 words per day.'[16] Only to his wife Clementine did Winston reveal the real toll of such labour. Yet the resulting book remains a joy to the reader, with its sensitive evocation of the aristocratic society in which the young Winston grew up and its vivid revisitation of the fields of his military adventures on the frontiers of the British Empire.

Churchill had not expected the Conservatives to lose the General Election at the end of May 1929; so when he had signed a further contract earlier that month to write a major biography of his ancestor the 1st Duke of Marlborough, he had envisaged performing this feat while still in Cabinet office. The five volumes of *The World Crisis* had been published by Thornton Butterworth in London and in New York by Scribners, a much larger firm, who now put in their own offer for *Marlborough* of $25,000 for the American rights. This was worth £5,000 in sterling, a sum matched by *The Daily Telegraph* for the serial rights, and was topped up by £10,000 from the London publishers Harraps, making a total of £20,000 in all (about £1 million today). Envisaged as a supplement to a government salary of £5,000 a year, this sum would have seen Churchill well provided for the next five years while he completed the work.

This scenario failed to materialise in almost every respect. Instead, Churchill found himself out of office and out of pocket; his own reckless investments in New York collapsed in the Great Crash; his deferred tax bills from more prosperous years continued to fall due. The cumulative effect was to make Churchill acutely dependent on his earnings as an author, with a subsequent trade-off between quality and quantity. Commissions for newspapers and magazines were now sometimes ghost-written by others; for example, he enlisted the loyal Edward Marsh to write a series of six 'Great Stories of the World Retold' for the salacious *News of the World*, for which Churchill received £2,000, of which he paid Marsh £150. Such projects, including scenarios for films, were simply too lucrative to resist.

Marlborough was different. On this Churchill had recognised from the first that he needed scholarly assistance. He was lucky to find Maurice Ashley, a recent graduate with First Class Honours in History at Oxford and later a distinguished independent scholar specialising in the seventeenth century. Ashley was happy to accept £300 a year to work half-time on the family archive at Blenheim, which the current duke meanwhile closed to other scholars, notably Professor G. M. Trevelyan, who was engaged in a major study of the period.

Despite his own lack of progress on *Marlborough*, by the summer of 1931 Churchill was proposing yet another big contract for yet another big book. It was the entrepreneurial Brendan Bracken, now active in Churchill's entourage, who picked up on an airy notion that Churchill had earlier suggested to his American publisher Charles Scribner during a visit to New York: 'a history of the English-speaking race' in two volumes. Yet Scribner himself was already waiting for other promised volumes – on the Eastern Front and, above all, *Marlborough* – for which he had paid large advances, so it is not surprising that he dropped out of the bidding. Nor, for much the same reasons, were Harraps interested. Uniquely, it was the proprietor of Cassells, Newman Flower, who eventually took the risk.

The contract for a projected *History of the English-Speaking Peoples*, signed in February 1933, was notable in that Cassells, rather than paying royalties, would buy the work's copyright for a lump sum of £20,000, payable on delivery of a completed manuscript within five years. With no capital gains tax in that era, Churchill would thus not have to pay income tax (though he could draw some advance payments for his expenses). Flower had been assured that the first volume of *Marlborough* would be published by Harraps within a year, with the highly optimistic promise that its concluding volume would follow within six months. In fact, the interlocking commitments for these two big contracts were to hang over Churchill for the next seven years.

Chartwell was the scene of operations, with the long table in Churchill's study laden with papers and books, and shorthand typists in attendance to take down dictation as he paced up and down. The first volume of *Marlborough* was indeed ready to be published in October 1933, thanks largely to Ashley, who had now put in four years on the project. He wrote later of how the text had been dictated by Churchill, usually late at night: 'As his research assistant, I sat by in case he needed any facts supplied or verified, but he had such a marvellous memory that he rarely got them wrong.'[17] Churchill, at nearly sixty, lacked neither energy nor acumen; but he did lack first-hand contact with the archival sources, where he relied upon Ashley to select, assess and synthesise the relevant documents.

Trevelyan, engaged on his own three-volume work, *England under Queen Anne*, was not only an academic historian but also Macaulay's great-nephew; and in his first volume, published in 1930, he had supported a notorious charge of treacherous double-dealing against Marlborough, famously made by his great-uncle. Churchill disputed this in his own first volume of *Marlborough* in 1933, at disproportionate length and with passion to match – 'Such evidence would not hang a dog.'[18] He was thus in a sense continuing a longstanding family quarrel within the British elite; but it can also be said that he won the point against the best-known historian of his day and in terms that are still acknowledged with respect by academic scholars today. Churchill's first volume was generally well received at the time.

Further volumes of *Marlborough*, at ever greater length, proved less happy, competing for Churchill's attention with many other claims. He even stole time in order to complete his volume of biographical essays, *Great Contemporaries* (1937), which is indeed a literary gem, full of insight, especially when dealing with other politicians who were also men of letters. Churchill did it because he needed the money, but his *Marlborough* paid the price through a growing lack of discipline that fostered unnecessary prolixity. In London, two volumes became three, three volumes became four; only a virtual mutiny by Harraps ultimately prevented the fourth volume from being split so as to produce a fifth. In New York, Scribners had already published the first volume in two parts and were to end up with a six-volume edition, which sold poorly.

Meanwhile, the publishers of Churchill's other promised volumes on the *History of the English-Speaking Peoples* had to wait, fobbed off with excuses that wore increasingly thin with repetition. The Oxford don Keith Feiling, who had originally recommended his former pupil Ashley as historical adviser, was himself engaged in October 1934 on a part-time basis at £500 a year. Although nominally charged with planning the *History*, Feiling was also trying to finish off *Marlborough*, with Churchill repeatedly complaining to him that he was 'much burdened by politics', with little time to spare for his literary commitments.[19]

For two years Feiling sought to square the circle here with a plan for the *History* as a work in three volumes: one up to the American Declaration of Independence in 1776, a second on the Industrial Revolution and the first half of the nineteenth century, and a third culminating in 'The Relation of the English Speaking Races before the Great War'. A comparison with the four volumes finally published in 1956–8, which reach the War of Independence only halfway through the third volume and barely stretch to the end of the nineteenth century, shows the extent to which the focus slipped. The explanation is twofold: not only that, like *Marlborough*, the work grew haphazardly in the making, but also that the *History* was never finished by its ostensible author.

With *Marlborough* finally off to the publishers, Churchill turned belatedly to the long-promised, long-overdue *History* and set out to write a thousand words a day from August 1938. He was confident that in sixteen months he could produce his promised 400,000 words for his publisher, Newman Flower – who now threatened to cancel the contract if the extended deadline of December 1939 was not met. The problem was not that Churchill lacked appetite for the task; in fact, his thirst for learning about the early period meant that he produced far more than planned, fundamentally shifting the balance of the work and denying himself the opportunity of giving crucial developments in the modern period the attention that had been promised. Churchill's dictated narrative, night by night, expanded with undisciplined amateur enthusiasm. At his elbow in this task, in succession to Ashley and Feiling, it was now the turn of William Deakin, a young historian of the modern era who found his versatility challenged by confronting the problems of the medieval period. An older historian, G. M. Young, was also brought in, alongside the faithful Marsh, in giving the resulting text a degree of scrutiny that it certainly needed.

Some of what Churchill included simply shows his own delight in good stories, especially ones he had heard since his boyhood, such as King Alfred burning the cakes. And Churchill found himself fascinated by the Dark Ages, taking the expression rather literally in what he dictated: 'They fought among themselves. But they left no records of their conflicts.' Young's marginal comment on the proofs – 'Then how do you know?' – scotched this particular Churchillian comment (though some others were reinstated in the 1950s).[20] It was not that Churchill was simply distracted by trivia, but he sensed too late that there was a big story here of which he had not been fully conscious. As he told Ashley in April 1939, 'the theme is emerging of the growth of freedom and law, of the rights of the individual, of the subordination of the State to the fundamental and moral conceptions of an ever-comprehending community. Of these ideas the English-speaking peoples were the authors, then the trustees, and must now become the armed champions.'[21] The newspaper columns he reprinted in June 1939 – including one with the title 'The Gathering Storm' – are evidence of how his political agenda now fed, rather late in the day, into his work on the History.[22]

Much of what Churchill dictated in his 1938–9 draft speaks to this theme, not didactically but with many hints about the 'gleaming' or 'glowing' way in which later developments seemed foreshadowed. This was no narrow nationalistic account – Joan of Arc and George Washington are both heroic figures. So, of course, is the 1st Duke of Marlborough; indeed, Churchill thriftily solved the problem of writing again about his ancestor by getting permission from Harraps to incorporate no fewer than 50,000 words of his published biography into the History that he was to send to Cassells.

Churchill brazenly claimed that he had 530,000 words of text ready for his publishers at the outbreak of war in September 1939. The fact is that he had only finished about 320,000. On joining Chamberlain's Cabinet as first lord of the admiralty, Churchill actually continued working on his *History*, in a clandestine way, with whatever assistance Deakin could spare from the start of his own military service. Not until mid-December was the text duly submitted, ending abruptly with the American Civil War. The work was rejected by Cassells because it clearly did not fulfil the contract. Only the intervention of Bracken, ruthlessly playing the patriotic card with Cassells, saved the situation. He cut a deal that was to give Churchill the full sum contracted, with only £1,000 held back – and all of it tax-free. At the time it looked as though Cassells had the worst of this bargain, forced to pay up and left with a virtually unpublishable manuscript on their hands; their only consolation was that they had managed to sell the North American rights to Dodd, Mead and Company in New York and to McClelland and Stewart in Toronto.

Winston's War: 2

On taking government office in September 1939, Churchill again retired as an author; or so his tax lawyers were subsequently successful in arguing. He was thereby disbarred from any further literary work, except for revising the *History*. The first volume of his wartime speeches was formally edited by Randolph Churchill, so that he could share the

Figure 4.2 Churchill at his desk, c.1939 (CAC, Broadwater Collection, BRDW V 3/3).

royalties with his father, thus reducing income tax liability; but the copyright of later volumes, edited by the journalist Charles Eade, was sold outright, thus becoming tax-free. In these speeches it is not surprising that Churchill now drew upon so many of the images, themes and rhetoric of the *History*, still fresh in his own mind even though its publication had been indefinitely deferred. The idea that the English-speaking peoples had a common heritage and a common destiny was deployed by Churchill to rally support for the beleaguered British Empire from the United States, both before and after it entered a world war with the Japanese attack on Pearl Harbor.

That Churchill would eventually write his own war memoirs was taken for granted from an early point, in a scenario where he never acknowledged any outcome except ultimate victory. Moreover, even amid his new tasks, he was fully conscious of the huge rise in his personal stock as an author. This was exemplified in the sale of the film rights of *Marlborough* in 1943 and of the *History* in 1944, each for £50,000 (together worth up to £4 million today) and in each case tax-free as windfalls for a retired author. To sell the film rights on the *History*, however, Churchill had needed the consent of Cassells, which was obtained by giving them an option on any war memoirs that he might write. The awkward fact that he had already granted next-book options to both Harraps and Macmillans was brushed aside by invoking Churchill's standing as saviour of his country.

As it turned out, these wartime deals were to bring Cassells enormous profits through the post-war publication of the six volumes of *The Second World War* (1948–54), followed by the four-volume edition of the *History* (1956–8). And for the author, the ultimate return was to be measured in many millions, protected by ingenious fiscal devices. The most crucial of these was the creation of a family trust as proprietors of all his relevant papers, with the ability to commission Churchill to 'edit' them for publication, on a relatively modest salary, thus emerging from his tax shelter of notional retirement as an author. The point was that the big money from publishers, not least from serialisation in the USA, would now pass as a capital transaction, tax-free.[23]

As with *The World Crisis*, the first volume of *The Second World War* is the most distinguished in literary terms, and for much the same simple reason: that it is most fully the work of Churchill himself. Its own title, *The Gathering Storm*, hints at the fact that half the book is devoted to the pre-war years in which Churchill had sought to warn of the danger from

Nazi Germany. He had a good story to tell here and made the most of it, with an account that rendered the word 'appeasement' a pejorative term for a generation or more. The enthusiastic reception of this volume set the tone for the rest; in particular, in 1948 a long review-essay by Isaiah Berlin helped to enshrine the image of Churchill not simply as a warrior, and certainly not just as a politician, but in displaying 'an historical imagination so strong, so comprehensive, as to encase the whole of the present and the whole of the future in a framework of a rich and multi-coloured past'.[24] This was recognition of Churchill as author as much as man of action.

His claims to authorship, as well as to leadership in waging war, have received definitive treatment in a fine scholarly study which explores in detail the way in which Churchill's account was constructed.[25] The extent to which it was the result of teamwork by a group of trusted assistants (including the veteran Marsh) should come as no surprise. Deakin, who had done so much on the *History*, was brought back as the key figure in the 'Syndicate' that was assembled to provide Churchill with all the necessary support, not just in exploiting his unique access to official papers but also in providing drafts from which Churchill would refine the final text. He was still, of course, a major figure in politics in these years, though his parliamentary duties as Leader of the Opposition were often delegated to others. Still, it is a remarkable tribute to his own drive, energy and grasp in his mid-seventies that he was able to super-intend the work so closely. The successive bulky volumes included long appendices of documents, partly to protect the work's favourable fiscal status as an edition.

A sixth and final volume was not published until November 1953 in the United States (and a few months later in Britain), by which time Churchill was again serving as prime minister. The official story was that it had already been finished before he took office; in fact, others discreetly completed the work in a routine already well established. The first five volumes had had spectacular sales of 1.75 million copies in Britain, 1.76 million in the United States and 77,000 in Canada, so the financial rewards were already secure. Moreover, in October 1953 Churchill received the news that he was to be awarded the Nobel Prize for Literature. There is good reason to believe that, on an earlier shortlist of twenty-five, there had been six other anglophone names, including such distinguished writers as E. M. Forster, Robert Frost, Graham Greene, Ernest Hemingway, Walter de la Mare and Carl Sandburg.

Hemingway subsequently made no secret of his opinion that Churchill's mastery was of the *spoken* word; and it is true that the Nobel commendation mentioned the wartime speeches but not the volumes of *The Second World War*.

The belated publication of the *History* followed in 1956–8. It was now one of the hottest literary properties in the world and was to be marketed accordingly, with a print run of 130,000 for Cassells' first volume in April 1956, and the American edition (the property of Dodd, Mead) selling 50,000 plus a further 224,000 for the Book of the Month Club, while McClelland and Stewart sold 15,000 in Canada. The three later volumes were equally successful, boosted by generally uncritical plaudits. 'Yes, pages of unending flattery', commented Churchill.[26] The *History* thus set the final seal upon his fame as an author. But what was published was not the text that had been submitted in 1940 to Cassells. In the interim, Churchill had paid for expert advice in 1945 from the historian Denis Brogan, who made cogent suggestions for revision, which were subsequently ignored or forgotten. It was during Churchill's convalescence after his stroke in 1953, with the last volume of his war memoirs now in the press, that the proofs of the *History* were again retrieved at Chartwell.

Here was Churchill's planned project for when he finally quit government. But the task was actually put in the hands of Alan Hodge, editor of the magazine *History Today* (founded by Bracken). Under Hodge, a programme of reconstruction of the text of the *History* was improvised as successive pre-war drafts were exhumed for further scrutiny. Cassells were induced to lubricate the process by agreeing to regard their outright purchase of the copyright (under the 1933 contract) as simply an advance on future royalties. These would now additionally accrue to Churchill, but to avoid income tax he needed (for the third time) to retire as an author in 1957.

Hodge not only assembled his own team of experts for the work; he also covered the traces of what they actually contributed by purposely destroying much of the archival evidence, with the intention of protecting Churchill's reputation as author. The fact remains that, of the four volumes of the *History* as published in 1956–8, only the first two are substantially as Churchill left them in 1939. The third volume (with much material reprinted from *Marlborough*) is his up to 1714, and the remainder mainly by others, some of them historians whom Churchill never even met. Hardly any of the fourth volume is by Churchill, except for the section on the American Civil War. The fact that he had jumped ahead to this episode, out of sequence, was testimony to his own visceral enthusiasm for military history – a lifelong passion that had, of course, animated his career as an author in the first place.

Notes

1. R. Toye, *The Roar of the Lion: The Untold Story of Churchill's World War II Speeches* (Oxford: Oxford University Press, 2013), p. 58.
2. OB, vol. 8, p. 1075.
3. D. Lough, *No More Champagne: Churchill and His Money* (London: Head of Zeus, 2015), pp. 35–6.
4. R. Toye, *Churchill's Empire: The World That Made Him and the World He Made* (London: Macmillan, 2010), pp. 42–5.
5. W. S. Churchill, *My Early Life* (London: Fontana, 1965), p. 161.
6. W. S. Churchill, *Great Contemporaries* (London: Fontana, 1962), p. 63.
7. R. Foster, *Lord Randolph Churchill: A Political Life* (Oxford: Oxford University Press, 1981), pp. 392–9.
8. W. S. Churchill, *Lord Randolph Churchill* (London: Macmillan, 1906), vol. 2, p. 59.
9. J. Rose, *The Literary Churchill: Author, Reader, Actor* (New Haven, CT: Yale University Press, 2014), p. 623.
10. W. S. Churchill, *The Second World War*, 6 vols. (London: Cassell & Co Ltd, 1948–54), vol. 1, p. 62.
11. W. S. Churchill, *The World Crisis, 1911–1918*, 2 vols. (London: Odhams, 1938), vol. 1, p. 456.
12. Churchill, *The World Crisis*, vol. 1, p. 484.
13. Churchill, *The World Crisis*, vol. 2, p. 779.
14. R. Prior, *Churchill's 'World Crisis' as History* (London: Croom Helm, 1983), p. 281.
15. Lough, *No More Champagne*, pp. 165–9.
16. R. Jenkins, *Churchill* (London: Macmillan, 2001), p. 421.
17. R. I. Cohen, *Bibliography of the Writings of Sir Winston Churchill*, 3 vols. (London: Thoemmes, 2006), p. 408.
18. W. S. Churchill, *Marlborough: His Life and Times*, 2 vols. (London: Harrap, 1947), vol. 1, p. 380.
19. P. Clarke, *Mr Churchill's Profession: Statesman, Orator, Writer* (London: Bloomsbury, 2012), p. 182.
20. P. Clarke, *Mr Churchill's Profession*, p. 212.
21. P. Clarke, *Mr Churchill's Profession*, p. 224.
22. W. S. Churchill, *Step by Step* (London: Odhams, 1947), p. 62.
23. D. Lough, *No More Champagne*, chapters 21–3.
24. I. Berlin, *Mr Churchill in 1940* (London: Murray, 1964), p. 12.
25. D. Reynolds, *In Command of History: Churchill Fighting and Writing the Second World War* (London: Allen Lane, 2004).
26. Lord Moran, *Winston Churchill: The Struggle for Survival, 1945–60* (London: Robinson, 2006), p. 407.

Further Reading

(For a full list of works by Winston Churchill, see Appendix 2.)

M. Ashley, *Churchill as Historian* (London: Secker & Warburg, 1968)

I. Berlin, *Mr Churchill in 1940* (London: Murray, 1964)

P. Clarke, *Mr Churchill's Profession: Statesman, Orator, Writer* (London: Bloomsbury, 2012)

R. I. Cohen, *Bibliography of the Writings of Sir Winston Churchill*, 3 vols. (London: Thoemmes, 2006)

R. Foster, *Lord Randolph Churchill: A Political Life* (Oxford: Oxford University Press, 1981)

R. Jenkins, *Churchill* (London: Macmillan, 2001)

C. Levillain, An Art of Translation: Churchill's Uses of Eighteenth-Century British History, XVII–XVIII. *Revue de la Société d'études anglo-américaines des XVIIe et XVIIIe siècles*, vol. 76 (2019), pp. 1–15.

D. Lough, *No More Champagne: Churchill and His Money* (London: Head of Zeus, 2015)

J. H. Plumb, The Historian. In *Churchill: Four Faces and the Man* (London: Allen Lane, 1969)

R. Prior, *Churchill's 'World Crisis' as History* (London: Croom Helm, 1983)

D. Reynolds, *In Command of History: Churchill Fighting and Writing the Second World War* (London: Allen Lane, 2004)

J. Rose, *The Literary Churchill: Author, Reader, Actor* (New Haven, CT: Yale University Press, 2014)

R. Toye, *The Roar of the Lion: The Untold Story of Churchill's World War II Speeches* (Oxford: Oxford University Press, 2013)

M. Weidhorn, *Sword and Pen: A Survey of the Writings of Sir Winston Churchill* (Albuquerque: University of New Mexico Press, 1974)

5

Churchill and Social Policy

Winston Churchill's public reputation today rests almost entirely on his management of warfare, not welfare. Unlike his predecessor as prime minister, Neville Chamberlain, Churchill had no experience of local government and a limited understanding of the day-to-day delivery of public services. Yet social policy featured prominently in Churchill's career from the moment he entered the Cabinet in 1908 until he left 10 Downing Street for the final time in 1955. His life coincided with the development of the modern British 'welfare state' and the emergence of social policy as a major field of competition between the political parties. Churchill's contribution to this process also became an important part of his personal myth, allowing him to soften his sometimes abrasive image by pointing to his record as a social reformer. During the 1951 election campaign, for instance, Churchill boasted of 'the great measure of social reform – Unemployment Insurance, Labour Exchanges, safety in the coalmines, bringing old age pensions down from seventy to sixty-five years of age, the widows' and orphans' pensions – for which I have been responsible both as a Liberal and a Conservative Minister'.[1] This chapter explores how far Churchill's claims were justified, and what imprint he ultimately left on the social responsibilities of the British state.

In some ways, Churchill was an unlikely social policy-maker. His temperament was hardly suited to the minutiae of social administration, and when Herbert Asquith offered him the presidency of the Local Government Board in 1908, he reportedly reacted with horror, telling his private secretary that he refused to be 'shut up in a soup kitchen with Mrs. Sidney Webb'.[2] What Churchill brought to the field instead was a quintessentially Edwardian interest in social *politics* – that is, in the ways in which political leaders could use tax, benefits and public services to mobilise support and manage class tensions. He frequently echoed the classical liberal fear that mass democracy would lead to over-spending and over-taxation, and repeatedly warned against lavish electoral promises, as Richard Toye has recently shown.[3] In truth, however, Churchill was not above using public policy to bid for votes. For instance, the income tax reforms which he announced in his 1925 budget were carefully calibrated to consolidate Conservative support by easing the tax burden on the lower middle and skilled working classes.

Churchill's engagement with social policy was perhaps inevitably coloured by the perspective from which he approached it. This can be seen in at least four respects. Firstly, he was primarily an executive politician rather than a constituency MP or a social campaigner. He reached the Cabinet at the age of thirty-three and spent more than fifty of his sixty-two years in parliament on the government benches; as a result, he viewed social questions largely from the perspective of the state. Secondly, his ministerial career mainly brought him into contact with the economic dimension of social policy, most obviously at the Board of Trade (1908–10), the Ministry of Munitions (1917–19) and the Treasury (1924–9). Churchill thus knew much more about employment and labour relations than services such as health, education, poor relief or housing, which – especially in the early part of his career – were mostly delivered by local authorities. Thirdly, Churchill wore his party identity lightly, defecting from the Conservatives to the Liberals over free trade in 1904 and back again in the 1920s. Though he could be fiercely partisan at times, his policy ideas were rarely a straightforward expression of party shibboleths. Finally, he approached social policy from the perspective of a privileged (if not always financially secure) White man. As the son of a Cabinet minister and the grandson of the 7th Duke of Marlborough, Churchill was never likely to be dependent on state education or social insurance himself. The Labour politician Herbert Morrison noted wryly during the Second World War that this had double-edged implications: 'He's the old benevolent Tory squire who does all he can for the people – provided always that they are good obedient people and loyally recognise his position, and theirs.'[4]

Throughout his front-line career, Churchill spoke the language of the 'national minimum', suggesting that the state had a responsibility to prevent poverty and deprivation among its citizens. Yet Churchill's paternalistic sympathy for the plight of 'the left-out millions' was always balanced by a strong sense of the sturdiness and respectability of most British workers. Churchill was convinced that Britons of all classes were deeply attached to 'small-c' conservative values of personal freedom, dignity and independence, expressed in conventionally gendered ways through paid work and family care-giving. This coloured his approach to social policy in a variety of spheres: his interest in 'cheap food' and working-class consumption, his attachment to the contributory principle and his fraught but grudgingly respectful relationship with organised labour. It is perhaps no coincidence that two of the hallmarks of Churchill's 1951–5 administration were the abolition of rationing and the pursuit of a modus vivendi with the unions.

Churchill and the Edwardian Welfare Reforms, 1905–1915

Churchill's first serious engagement with social policy came as a minister in the Liberal governments of 1905–15, which presided over a piecemeal but cumulatively significant expansion of state welfare provision. The list of reforms introduced in this period is justly famous: school meals, old-age pensions, unemployment and health insurance, labour exchanges, a major shift towards progressive taxation, and the introduction of trade boards to set minimum wages in 'sweated industries'. As Chris Renwick has shown in his recent book *Bread for All* (2017), these policies were driven by a range of factors, including new forms of social research (such as Seebohm Rowntree's study of poverty in York, which Churchill read), concern about 'national efficiency' and pragmatic electoral calculations.[5]

   Churchill's personal contribution to these welfare reforms was twofold. Firstly, alongside David Lloyd George, he was one of the earliest and most prominent exponents of the 'new Liberal' agenda, drawing on the ideas of 'advanced' Liberal writers such as J. A. Hobson and L. T. Hobhouse to articulate a distinctive rationale for expanding the role of the state in a modern industrial society. Beginning with a speech in Glasgow in October 1906, when the government's social policy agenda was at best part-formed, Churchill argued that the modern Liberal had to be 'both an individualist and a collectivist' – combining the economic dynamism of market competition with 'the universal establishment of minimum standards of life and labour, and their

Figure 5.1 Churchill with David Lloyd George, c.1918 (CAC, Broadwater Collection, BRDW II 8).

progressive elevation as the increasing energies of production may permit', if necessary through methods which might be considered 'Socialistic'.[6] Six months later, he argued in *The Nation* that the Liberal Party had 'not abandoned in any respect its historic championship of Liberty', but had 'become conscious of the fact that political freedom is utterly incomplete without a measure at least of social and economic independence', which required a new openness to state activity.[7] As the government's legislative programme took shape, Hobson hailed a volume of Churchill's speeches – published under the title *Liberalism and the Social Problem* (1909) – as 'the clearest, the most eloquent, and the most convincing exposition' of the new Liberal position.[8]

Churchill was well aware of the difficulty of turning this rhetoric into action. When he discussed the presidency of the Local Government Board with Asquith in March 1908, he outlined 'a policy which I call the National Minimum Standard' but expressed doubts about his 'power to give it concrete expression', particularly in the face of scepticism from Gladstonian Liberals such as John Morley.[9] Churchill eventually agreed to take the post, but Asquith then changed his plans at the last minute and made him president of the Board of Trade instead.[10] As a result, Churchill found himself responsible for developing the 'national minimum' in the labour market – in some ways the most complex of all social policy areas. Periodic trade depressions had thrust unemployment on to the political agenda during the 1880s and 1890s, and trade unions and some local authorities pressed for central government to finance relief works.[11] At the same time, the unemployment issue intersected with the debate over Poor Law reform (championed by Sidney and Beatrice Webb, and studied at length by a Royal Commission from 1905 to 1909) and raised difficult questions about the impact state intervention might have on work incentives and wage bargaining. Churchill's two years at the Board of Trade coincided with a new cyclical downturn and strong demands for the Liberal government to take action, particularly from unions representing skilled workers in depressed industrial areas such as north-east England.

Churchill's second main contribution to the Liberal government's welfare reforms, then, was to develop and carry through an unemployment policy. He was not averse to the use of public works as a temporary measure, and persuaded the Cabinet to relax the conditions for local relief works under the previous Unionist government's 1905 Unemployed Workmen Act.[12] Under the influence of the Webbs and the *Morning Post* journalist William Beveridge, however, Churchill focussed most of his energies on developing a more 'scientific' policy designed to 'decasualise' the labour market, in the hope that this would reduce the need for ad hoc support. Churchill recruited Beveridge to the Board of Trade as an unestablished civil servant and commissioned Beveridge and the permanent secretary Hubert Llewellyn Smith to develop plans for a national system of labour exchanges, together with contributory unemployment insurance for workers in the most volatile industrial trades (particularly construction, engineering and shipbuilding). Like Lloyd George, Churchill was much impressed by 'the successful experiences of Germany in social organisation' and saw his unemployment policy as part of a larger attempt to 'thrust a big slice of Bismarckianism over the whole underside of our industrial system'.[13] At the same time, he resisted proposals to make the use of labour exchanges compulsory, and only grudgingly accepted that workers should be disqualified from benefit if they lost their jobs through dishonesty or drunkenness. Where the Webbs' conception of a national minimum included penal labour colonies for those who refused to work, Churchill's approach was more libertarian.[14] In his eyes, one of the great advantages of social insurance was that it allowed working men to claim benefit as of right, instead of 'mixing up moralities and mathematics' by imposing new restrictions on their behaviour.[15]

As José Harris and Tomoari Matsunaga have pointed out, much of the detailed work on unemployment policy was undertaken by officials and drew on ideas which had been circulating within the Board of Trade before Churchill became its president.[16] Moreover, even though Churchill announced his plans for labour exchanges and unemployment insurance together in May 1909, only the first part had passed into law by the time he moved to the Home Office in 1910. Unemployment insurance was held back while Lloyd George and the Treasury worked out the details of a health insurance scheme, to which it was harnessed (somewhat uneasily) in the 1911 National Insurance Act.[17] Nevertheless, Churchill played a crucial role in championing unemployment insurance within government, assuaging the concerns of unions and employers and – with Lloyd George – promoting the idea to the public at large. As Paul Addison has noted:

> It was Churchill who decided to act in advance of the report of the
> Royal Commission on the Poor Law; Churchill who gave instructions
> for proposals to be drawn up, discussed, and submitted to the
> Cabinet; and Churchill who bore the responsibility for persuading the
> Cabinet and the House of Commons to accept them.[18]

Given the diversity of opinion within the Liberal Party and the wide range of options canvassed in Edwardian public debates, the importance of this ministerial leadership should not be underestimated.

The same philosophy of creating a national minimum through piecemeal policy interventions was also visible in the 1909 Trade Boards Act, which formed Churchill's other main achievement at the Board of Trade. This created a new system of trade boards with power to set minimum wages in four 'sweated trades' (chain-making, machine lace-making, ready-made tailoring and the manufacture of paper boxes) where wages were 'exceptionally low' and working conditions were 'prejudicial to physical and social welfare'.[19] Unemployment insurance was designed to help male manual workers deal with the effects of the trade cycle, whereas the trade boards were intended to protect mainly female workers from exploitation, but both were narrowly targeted at particular groups and dealt with some of the most egregious faults of the capitalist system. They were also relatively uncontentious (in sharp contrast to Lloyd George's health insurance scheme, which provoked a firestorm of criticism). Indeed, the Trade Boards Act passed through its second and third readings without a division.

The Home Office which Churchill managed for twenty months in 1910–11 was responsible for the regulation of working conditions and the oversight of children in care, as well as for prisons, policing and the criminal law; in a sense, then, it was also a social welfare department. Churchill's main preoccupation here was penal reform, where he hoped to reduce the number of young offenders and debtors sent to prison; this 'ambitious programme' was only partly complete when he moved to the Admiralty in October 1911, but Addison has nevertheless described it as 'the pinnacle of his achievement in social policy'.[20] Churchill also piloted the 1911 Coal Mines Act on to the statute book, consolidating and tightening mine safety regulations. However, any sense of gratitude the miners might have felt was outweighed by bitterness over Churchill's decision to deploy troops to the Rhondda to help the Glamorgan Constabulary deal with rioting during a strike. For years afterwards, he would be plagued by references to 'Tonypandy'.[21]

Churchill's role in the development of the Asquith government's reforming agenda was thus marked by a paradox. In his rhetoric, Churchill positioned himself at the radical edge of the 'new Liberalism', championing new forms of state intervention in the name of 'constructive social reform'; in the heated debate over the 1909 'People's Budget', for instance, he baited the House of Lords and mocked Tory complaints that the aristocracy would be ruined by land taxes.[22] Partly by accident and partly by design, however, the policies he found himself carrying through as a minister were much less controversial. This pattern of pragmatic policy-making, cloaked in partisan invective, would re-emerge after the First World War when Churchill found himself back on the Conservative benches.

From Radical Liberal to Tory Reformer, 1915–1940

Churchill's move to the Admiralty in 1911 marked a turn away from social policy which prefigured the Liberal government's mutation into a war ministry. Between 1914 and 1918, the dynamics of economic and social policy were transformed by the experience of mobilisation for total war, while the landscape of party politics was transformed by the feud between Asquith and Lloyd George and the growing disintegration of the Liberal Party. In this context, signs of conservatism which had already been visible in Churchill's politics before the First World War became increasingly pronounced, particularly in the face of the 1917 Bolshevik revolution in Russia and growing trade union militancy. As secretary of state for war (1919–21) in Lloyd George's peacetime coalition, he attempted to throw British support behind the 'white' forces in the Russian civil war, seriously damaging his relationship with Labour and the unions. After losing his seat at Dundee in 1922 and resurfacing in a Conservative Cabinet as Stanley Baldwin's chancellor of the exchequer in 1924, Churchill became the face of the Treasury's deflationary policy of taking sterling back on to the gold standard at its pre-war parity. His bellicose approach to the 1926 General Strike confirmed his reputation as a figure of the right who had left Edwardian radicalism far behind him.

Yet Churchill's approach to social questions was always more complex than a left–right dichotomy would allow. During the First World War, he took a notably activist approach to the war economy, pressing for public control of shipping and railways to prevent profiteering alongside the conscription of labour. After he resigned from government over the Dardanelles fiasco, he called for the introduction of food rationing on the grounds that restricting consumption 'merely through the agency of price' was 'cruel' and 'unfair': 'In time of war particularly you should have regard for the broad claims of social justice.'[23] As minister of munitions at the end of the war, he found himself dealing with significant industrial unrest, and sought to conciliate skilled workers with wage increases which turned out to have damagingly inflationary effects.[24] During the 1918 General Election he urged Lloyd George to levy a steep tax on war profits, and declared himself in favour of rail nationalisation.[25] All in all, this added up to a highly statist form of centrist liberalism which sought to defuse social unrest – and marginalise the growing Labour Party – by subordinating private interests to the needs of the nation.[26]

At the end of the war, Churchill hoped that Lloyd George's coalition could turn this centrist liberalism into the basis for a new political settlement, forging an alliance between Tories, moderate Liberals and patriotic workers. During the early 1920s, however, this vision disintegrated as the post-war boom collapsed, Lloyd George sacrificed education and housing to the 'Geddes Axe', and socialist and 'anti-waste' campaigners stoked class tensions. By the time Churchill became chancellor in 1924, the focus of economic policy had shifted decisively to an orthodox pursuit of price stability and industrial competitiveness. In many ways, Churchill was never really a 'Treasury man': he was privately uneasy about the return to gold, pressed the Bank of England to keep interest rates down and became notorious for raiding the sinking fund and the Road Fund in order to balance his budgets. In classic liberal vein, however, Churchill used social policy to 'flank' deflationary economics and so give tangible support to Baldwin's rhetoric of social harmony.

As Martin Daunton has shown in *Just Taxes* (2002) and in his contribution to this volume (see Chapter 9), Churchill's 1925 budget formed the centrepiece of this integrative strategy.[27] Churchill took 6d off the standard rate of income tax, cut 'super-tax' and raised earned income relief from one tenth to one sixth, in order to reduce the tax burden on 'black coated working men' and improve incentives for 'professional men, small merchants and businessmen' – what Churchill called 'superior brain workers of every kind'.[28] At the same time, Churchill sought to 'balance' these characteristically Tory tax cuts in two ways: firstly, by raising death duties by £10 million in order to pay for the super-tax cut, and secondly, by announcing plans for a new scheme of widows' and old-age pensions. His goal (as he put it in the peroration of his budget speech) was not only to balance the budget 'in pounds, shillings and pence' but also 'to balance it fairly in the scales of social justice between one class and another in our varying community'.[29]

The 1925 Widows', Orphans', and Old Age Contributory Pensions Act was largely Neville Chamberlain's work, but Churchill provided crucial Treasury support – not least because it allowed him to burnish his credentials as a champion of social insurance. The Asquith government's 1908 Act had provided for means-tested pensions for the over seventies; the 1925 Act reduced the pension age to sixty-five and removed the means test for the 15 million workers paying National Insurance contributions, and so began the process of shifting the state pension on to a contributory basis. The wives and widows of insured workers, and all widowed mothers with children up to the age of fourteen, would also be entitled to a pension. Churchill presented the scheme as an extension of Lloyd George's 1911 reforms, but as John

Macnicol has shown, its structure also reflected Tory preoccupations. The contributory principle was designed to encourage self-help, and most of the cost would fall on workers and employers (through contributions) rather than on general taxation. The scheme also reinforced the male-breadwinner orientation of the 1911 Act by linking pension rights to claimants' history of labour-market participation.[30]

As minister of health, Chamberlain followed up contributory pensions with the wide-ranging 1929 Local Government Act, which abolished the Poor Law Guardians and introduced a new system of block grants to local authorities. Churchill was again closely involved, and spearheaded plans for relieving agriculture and industry of local rates in order to stimulate production. As the depression loomed, however, Churchill's approach to social policy became increasingly difficult to distinguish from that of other Conservatives. For instance, he criticised Ramsay MacDonald's 1929–31 Labour government for raising unemployment benefit rates and abolishing the 'genuinely seeking work' clause, and claimed that these decisions had 'stripped our incomparable insurance system of every vestige of dignity or equity and … converted it into a vast dole-spreading agency'.[31] When the National Government took office in August 1931 he supported its austerity measures, and was more concerned about the impact on public investment than about the controversial benefit cuts.[32] Churchill's increasingly right-wing image was reinforced by his conversion to tariff protection and by the hard line he took on Indian self-government. Even when the lines of political controversy were redrawn by the debate over appeasement, it was Chamberlain, not Churchill, who remained the standard-bearer for Tory social reform.

War and Reconstruction, 1940–1945

Churchill's ascent to the premiership in May 1940, however, drew him back into a reluctant engagement with social policy questions. To an even greater extent than in 1914–18, the needs of total war prompted a rapid expansion of the role of the state (for instance, through evacuation, rationing, rent controls and food subsidies), followed by extensive planning for post-war reconstruction. As prime minister, Churchill was reluctant to enter into major policy commitments during the war or to allow discussions of reconstruction to distract attention from the war effort, and historians such as Kevin Jeffreys have largely dispelled the notion of a wartime 'consensus'.[33] Nevertheless, the Churchill coalition set the parameters for post-war developments in many fields of economic and social policy.[34]

During the early part of the war, social policy was closely tied up with the issue of mobilisation for the war effort, which risked being hampered by the hostility that had emerged between Conservative ministers and the trade unions during the 1920s and 1930s. Where Chamberlain kept the unions at arm's length, Churchill thought it was 'vitally important that organised labour in industry should be directly represented' in his Cabinet, and so invited Ernest Bevin to become minister of labour.[35] Bevin accepted on the condition that the ministry could shape 'the actual organisation of production' and would not be expected to maintain 'the status quo in the matter of the social services for which it was responsible'.[36] Bevin quickly took over the Factory Inspectorate from the Home Office and used Orders in Council to require large firms to expand their medical provision and provide canteens for workers; he also secured the abolition of the household means test.[37] Likewise, it was largely trade union pressure for reform of the workmen's compensation scheme which kept social security on the agenda, and so prompted the appointment of the Beveridge Committee on Social Insurance and Allied Services in June 1941. While Bevin focussed on the production side, Churchill took a closer interest in matters of consumption. He was highly sensitive to the political importance of food – a legacy, perhaps, of his political formation in the tariff reform debates of the 1900s. In contrast to his position in the First World War, however, he found it difficult to see how rationing and 'fair shares' would improve morale, and offered only grudging support for Lord Woolton's efforts to curtail the consumption of luxury foods. As a frustrated Woolton noted in his diary, Churchill was 'benevolently hostile to everything that involved people not being fed like fighting cocks'.[38]

Yet it was in matters of post-war reconstruction, rather than wartime policy, that Churchill found himself cut adrift from the leftward trajectory of public opinion. This became most visible in his response to the Beveridge report, which set out plans for unifying pensions with unemployment and sickness benefits in a single scheme of contributory social security. In many ways Beveridge's scheme represented a logical culmination of the social insurance plans Churchill had developed with

Lloyd George in 1908–9 and expanded with Neville Chamberlain in 1925, extending the insurance principle to the whole working population. Coming in the wake of the Allied victory at El Alamein at the end of 1942, the report was also enormously popular: 635,000 copies were sold, and a poll by the British Institute of Public Opinion found that 86 per cent of respondents were in favour. Yet Churchill was instinctively reluctant to legislate on social security while the war was still on, and faced pressure from the Treasury and Tory MPs to water down the proposals. As he argued in a memorandum to the War Cabinet,

> We do not know what conditions will be at the end of the war or how the expenditure on social insurance will fit with other social expenditure desired or how this scope of betterment expenditure can be reconciled to the needs of maintaining strong naval and air forces.[39]

Churchill told his parliamentary private secretary, George Harvie-Watt, that Beveridge was an 'awful windbag and a dreamer', and insisted that the British public would not be impressed by 'false hopes and airy visions of Utopia and Eldorado'.[40]

This lukewarm attitude left the government badly exposed when the House of Commons debated the Beveridge report in February 1943. More than a hundred Labour, Liberal and independent MPs (including the ageing Lloyd George) supported an amendment calling for 'early implementation' of the scheme – a huge rebellion which risked turning social security into a party question. Churchill was forced to shore up his position in a BBC radio broadcast which set out a 'Four Years' Plan' for the post-war period. Though he complained about 'attempts to over-persuade or even to coerce His Majesty's Government' to commit itself to 'great new expenditures', he promised that the coalition would prepare 'five or six large measures' of social reform so that a new government could implement them quickly after a post-war election.[41]

Churchill assured his listeners that social security would 'have a leading place in our four-year plan' and reminded them that he had been 'prominently connected with all these schemes of national com-pulsory organised thrift from the time when I brought my friend Sir William Beveridge into the public service thirty-five years ago'. Despite this rhetorical invocation of his past, however, Churchill's approach to post-war reconstruction differed from his previous practice in two sig-nificant ways. Firstly, instead of playing up the importance of social insurance, he sought to shift public attention away from it by emphasising the need to attend to 'other large matters', such as agriculture, education, public health and 'the replanning and rebuilding of our towns and cities'. Public spending in these fields seemed to be more productive and less open-ended than Beveridge's plans for cash benefits, and most of the departments involved were run by loyal Conservatives. Secondly, Churchill embarked on a conscious attempt to depoliticise social policy. Instead of tailoring tax and benefits to his party's electoral needs, as he had done before and after the First World War, he now emphasised the practical nature of the issues involved and warned against a premature revival of the 'party fights of peacetime'.

This desire to neutralise the political impact of Beveridge contributed to Churchill's support for the Education Bill, which R. A. Butler drew up during 1943 and carried through parliament in the following year. Churchill worried that educational reform would re-open the rivalries between Anglicans, Catholics and Nonconformists which had flared up in 1903, but once Butler brokered a compromise on the religious issue, he allowed him to go forward with his plans for a tripartite system of free secondary education up to the age of fifteen.[42] (The chancellor of the exchequer, Sir Kingsley Wood, told Butler he would 'far rather give money for education than throw it down the sink with Sir William Beveridge'.)[43] Negotiations over health care proceeded more slowly, not least because general practitioners and the voluntary hospitals resisted efforts to place them under the control of local authorities. Although the 1944 White Paper on *A National Health Service* committed the government to providing a comprehensive service, free at the point of use, the structure and finance of the system continued to be fiercely debated.[44] In both cases, Churchill's direct involvement seems to have been limited, and the locus of policy-making largely departmental. In health, as in many other areas of policy, crucial issues remained unresolved when the coalition broke up in 1945.

The Conservatives and the Welfare State, 1945–1955

Churchill's attempt to depoliticise social policy while attacking 'socialism' – for instance, in his notorious 'Gestapo' speech – fell flat in the 1945 General Election.[45] Not only was Churchill's tone widely seen as partisan and strident, but many voters seem to have thought Labour was more likely to deliver the plans for social security and housing the coalition had developed. Labour MPs' greater enthusiasm for the Beveridge report may have been one reason for this judgement; the party's argument that welfare provision and full employment required economic planning was probably another.[46] Stung by defeat, Churchill played little role in domestic policy debates during the late 1940s (though, like other Conservative MPs, he voted against Aneurin Bevan's 1946 National Health Service Act).[47] As the years drew on, however, the distinction Churchill drew between the government's social reforms and its 'socialist' economic policies became increasingly resonant. Churchill rallied disaffected Liberals and middle-class voters to the Tory banner by arguing that he could 'set the people free' from rationing and controls without reversing social advances.

In defining the Conservatives' position on the welfare state, Churchill returned to the Edwardian concept of the national minimum. Where Labour sought social equality and uniformity of provision for their own sake, he argued, the Tories believed in establishing a floor, with 'competition upwards – not downwards' from those 'minimum standards'.[48] In a well-received radio broadcast in the 1951 election, he added the concept of a 'ladder'. The Conservatives were committed to encouraging personal responsibility and individual betterment, but if anyone slipped off, 'We shall have a good net and the finest social ambulance service in the world.'[49]

What this rhetoric meant in policy terms was never very clear. In some ways, it hinted at the agenda Iain Macleod and Enoch Powell would set out in *The Social Services: Needs and Means* (1952), based on a move away from tax-funded universal provision towards greater use of means testing, contributions and charges, but Churchill was well aware of the political risks of moving in this direction. He resisted pressure to draw up a detailed programme in opposition, partly as a matter of principle and partly because he recognised that Labour was only too keen to portray the Tories as 'the enemies of social welfare and improvement'.[50] The 1951 Conservative manifesto contained one main positive proposal – to build 300,000 houses a year, a target the leadership had been bounced into at the 1950 party conference – together with vague commitments in other areas: for instance, the Party would 'provide better services' in health and education by using existing budgets more effectively and 'review the position of pensioners ... and see that the hardest needs are met first'.[51] The Tories were widely thought to be most vulnerable over their plans to cut Labour's £400 million food subsidy programme, but Lord Woolton sought to reassure voters that any changes would not take place immediately and that the rise in food prices would be offset by tax cuts and increased benefits.

Churchill's electoral caution meant that the social policy of his 1951–5 government had (in Timothy Raison's words) 'a curiously uncomplicated flavour', focussed on laying to rest the ghosts of the 1930s.[52] Churchill put Harold Macmillan in charge of the housing drive and helped him secure the resources required (not only in money but also materials and labour), while R. A. Butler at the Treasury raised benefits, cut income tax and scaled back the food subsidies, but in other areas action was limited. As Anthony Seldon has concluded in his study of the government, there was 'little attempt to think out a coherent and balanced social policy' and Churchill took 'little detailed interest in the work of the social policy Ministries'.[53] Some Treasury officials hoped that independent enquiries into pensions (chaired by Sir Thomas Phillips) and the National Health Service (chaired by the Cambridge economist Claude Guillebaud) would prepare the ground for a major shift away from universal state provision, but neither ultimately did so.

This cautious approach suited the Conservatives' political needs well, and Churchill was not shy of boasting about it. Far from 'wielding a Tory axe to cut the Social Services', he told a conference of Conservative women in May 1954, 'we have improved all the Social Services and we are spending more this year on them than any Govt. at any time'.[54] In fact, the share of GDP spent on health, education and social security was broadly flat during the early 1950s, and capital investment in hospitals and schools remained very low, prompting complaints about poor facilities and overcrowding. This partly stemmed from parsimony (and a desire to reduce the tax burden), but it was also a by-product of the priority the Tories gave to housing.

Conclusion

Perhaps because of Churchill's drift to the right over the course of his career, historians of the British welfare state have tended to be sceptical of his claims to be a pioneer of social reform. Though he helped create unemployment insurance in 1908–9, his attitude to social security became increasingly cautious thereafter, as seen in his response to the Beveridge report. By the time he became prime minister and later Conservative Party leader, the concept of a national minimum had long ceased to be a radical cry and had become a way of limiting the expansion of state provision. None of the major social innovations which emerged from the Second World War – such as the 1944 Education Act or the National Health Service – owed much to Churchill's patronage or influence.

All this is true. Yet Churchill left a deeper mark on the welfare state than is often realised. Once Churchill and Lloyd George had set the development of social insurance in motion, it took on a life of its own – a classic case of ideological and institutional 'path dependency'. In similar vein, the idea that the state's role was to set minimum standards (which tapped into elements of the Poor Law tradition) became deeply embedded in British political discourse.[55] If Churchill was keen to keep the welfare state within limits, control its cost and maintain traditional work and gender norms, so too were many other politicians and voters. As David Edgerton has pointed out, even the 1945 Labour government saw social services as 'secondary to production' and the export drive required to reduce the dollar deficit.[56] Partly as a result, the pattern of social provision in 1950s Britain arguably fitted more closely with Churchill's instincts and values than with the aspirations of welfare enthusiasts such as T. H. Marshall or Richard Titmuss. For better or worse, the mid-century British welfare state was a product of its time and place, and Churchill's longevity and political resilience meant that he did more than most politicians to shape it.

Notes

1. Speech at Huddersfield, 15 October 1951, reported in *Manchester Guardian*, 16 October 1951, p. 10.
2. Quoted in B. B. Gilbert, Winston Churchill versus the Webbs: The Origins of British Unemployment Insurance. *American Historical Review*, vol. 71 (1966), pp. 846–62, at 852.
3. R. Toye, The Electoral Promises of Winston Churchill. In D. Thackeray and R. Toye (eds.), *Electoral Pledges in Britain since 1918: The Politics of Promises* (London: Palgrave Macmillan, 2020), pp. 165–84.
4. Quoted in P. Addison, *Churchill on the Home Front, 1900–1955* (London: Jonathan Cape, 1992), p. 341.

5. C. Renwick, *Bread for All: The Origins of the Welfare State* (London: Allen Lane, 2017), pp. 58–125.
6. Speech at Glasgow, 11 October 1906, in W. S. Churchill (ed.), *Never Give In: The Best of Winston Churchill's Speeches* (London: Pimlico, 2003), pp. 23–5, at p. 24.
7. W. S. Churchill, 'The untrodden field in politics', *The Nation*, 7 March 1907.
8. Quoted in Addison, *Churchill on the Home Front*, p. 89.
9. Quoted in Addison, *Churchill on the Home Front*, p. 61.
10. CAC, Churchill Papers, CHAR 2/39/119–21, Winston Churchill to John Morley, 23 December 1909.
11. The definitive study, on which this paragraph draws, is J. Harris, *Unemployment and Politics: A Study in English Social Policy, 1886–1914* (Oxford: Oxford University Press, 1972).
12. Harris, *Unemployment and Politics*, p. 275.
13. CAC, Churchill Papers, CHAR 2/36/50–1, Winston Churchill to Herbert Asquith, 29 December 1908.
14. Gilbert, Winston Churchill versus the Webbs.
15. Winston Churchill to H. Llewellyn Smith, 'Notes on malingering', 6 June 1909, quoted in Gilbert, Winston Churchill versus the Webbs, p. 856.
16. Harris, *Unemployment and Politics*, pp. 273–347; T. Matsunaga, The Origins of Unemployment Insurance in Edwardian Britain. *Journal of Policy History*, vol. 29 (2017), pp. 614–39.
17. J. Harris, *William Beveridge: A Biography*, 2nd ed. (Oxford: Oxford University Press, 1997), pp. 180, 187–90.
18. Addison, *Churchill on the Home Front*, pp. 72–3.
19. CAC, Churchill Papers, CHAR 11/16/200–1, Winston Churchill memorandum to Cabinet on Trade Boards Bill, 12 March 1909, at p. 200.
20. Addison, *Churchill on the Home Front*, p. 110.
21. For a succinct overview of this episode, see R. Jenkins, *Churchill* (London: Macmillan, 2001), pp. 197–200.
22. See, for instance, speech at Leicester, 4 September 1909, in *Never Give In*, pp. 34–5.
23. *Hansard*, House of Commons Debates, vol. 85, cols. 2505–29, at col. 2514, 22 August 1916.
24. Addison, *Churchill on the Home Front*, pp. 188–91.
25. Addison, *Churchill on the Home Front*, pp. 197–8.
26. For the concept of 'centrist liberalism', see M. Freeden, *Liberalism Divided: A Study in British Political Thought, 1914–1939* (Oxford: Oxford University Press, 1986).
27. M. Daunton, *Just Taxes: The Politics of Taxation in Britain, 1914–1979* (Cambridge: Cambridge University Press, 2002), pp. 122–41.
28. CAC, Churchill Papers, CHAR 18/3/41–9, Winston Churchill to Sir Richard Hopkins, 28 November 1924, at p. 42.
29. *Hansard*, House of Commons Debates, vol. 183, cols. 34–89, at col. 89, 28 April 1915.
30. J. Macnicol, *The Politics of Retirement in Britain, 1878–1948* (Cambridge: Cambridge University Press, 1998), pp. 200–24.
31. *Hansard*, House of Commons Debates, vol. 237, cols. 848–60, at col. 860, 28 March 1930.
32. *Hansard*, House of Commons Debates, vol. 256, cols. 700–12, 15 September 1931.
33. K. Jefferys, *The Churchill Coalition and Wartime Politics, 1940–1945* (Manchester: Manchester University Press, 1991).

34. R. Lowe, The Second World War, Consensus, and the Foundation of the Welfare State. *Twentieth Century British History*, vol. 1 (1990), pp. 152–82.

35. P. Weiler, *Ernest Bevin* (Manchester: Manchester University Press, 1993), p. 102.

36. CAC, Churchill Papers, CHAR 20/11/59–60, Ernest Bevin to Winston Churchill, 13 May 1940, at pp. 59, 60.

37. Weiler, *Ernest Bevin*, pp. 128–30.

38. Quoted in Addison, *Churchill on the Home Front*, p. 340.

39. CAC, Churchill Papers, CHAR 23/11/11, 'War Cabinet. Beveridge Report. Note by the Prime Minister', 15 February 1943.

40. Quoted in Jefferys, *Churchill Coalition*, p. 119.

41. W. S. Churchill, 'Four Years' Plan' broadcast, 21 March 1943.

42. P. H. J. H. Gosden, *Education in the Second World War: A Study in Policy and Administration* (London: Methuen, 1976).

43. Quoted in Renwick, *Bread for All*, p. 246.

44. C. Webster, *The National Health Service: A Political History* (Oxford: Oxford University Press, 1998), pp. 8–12.

45. In Churchill's election broadcast of 4 June 1945 he claimed a socialist government would 'have to fall back on some form of Gestapo'.

46. P. Sloman, Rethinking a Progressive Moment: The Liberal and Labour Parties in the 1945 General Election. *Historical Research*, vol. 84 (2011), pp. 722–44.

47. *Hansard*, House of Commons Debates, vol. 422, cols. 407–17, 2 May 1946.

48. Speech to Conservative Central Council, 14 March 1947, quoted in Addison, *Churchill on the Home Front*, p. 393.

49. Radio broadcast, 8 October 1951, quoted in Jenkins, *Churchill*, pp. 841, 842.

50. *Hansard*, House of Commons Debates, vol. 468, cols. 1615–26, at col. 1622, 27 October 1949.

51. Conservative Party, *The Manifesto of the Conservative and Unionist Party: General Election 1951* (London: Conservative Party, 1951); H. Jones, 'This Is Magnificent!' 300,000 Houses a Year and the Tory Revival after 1945. *Contemporary British History*, vol. 14, no. 1 (2000), pp. 99–121.

52. T. Raison, *Tories and the Welfare State: A History of Conservative Social Policy Since the Second World War* (Basingstoke: Macmillan, 1990), p. 32.

53. A. Seldon, *Churchill's Indian Summer: The Conservative Government 1951–1955* (London: Hodder & Stoughton, 1981), pp. 246, 247.

54. CAC, Churchill Papers, CHUR 5/54A/28–57, 'Speech to a Mass Meeting of Conservative Women, Albert Hall, 27 May 1954', at p. 46.

55. J. Harris, From Poor Law to Welfare State? A European Perspective. In D. Winch and P. K. O'Brien (eds.), *The Political Economy of British Historical Experience, 1688–1914* (Oxford: Oxford University Press, 2002), pp. 409–37.

56. D. Edgerton, *The Rise and Fall of the British Nation: A Twentieth Century History* (London: Allen Lane, 2018), p. 218.

Further Reading

P. Addison, *Churchill on the Home Front, 1900-1955* (London: Jonathan Cape, 1992)

P. Bridgen and R. Lowe, *Welfare Policy under the Conservatives, 1951–1964: A Guide to Documents in the Public Record Office* (London: Public Record Office, 1998)

M. Daunton, *Just Taxes: The Politics of Taxation in Britain, 1914–1979* (Cambridge: Cambridge University Press, 2002)

J. Harris, *Unemployment and Politics: A Study in English Social Policy, 1886–1914* (Oxford: Oxford University Press, 1972)

K. Jefferys, *The Churchill Coalition and Wartime Politics, 1940–1945* (Manchester: Manchester University Press, 1991)

A. Seldon, *Churchill's Indian Summer: The Conservative Government 1951–1955* (London: Hodder & Stoughton, 1981)

6

Churchill, the 'Irish Question' and the Irish

If you search the Internet for the most hated figures in Irish history, Winston Churchill is often ranked in the top ten.[1] He is accused of creating the Black and Tans, the armed auxiliary unit sent to support the police force in Ireland in 1920 which was under attack from Irish republicans who had rebelled against the Crown. The patchy guerrilla-style conflict from 1919 to 1921 that foreshadowed Irish independence – and commonly remembered today as the War of Independence – occupies a treasured place in Ireland's national memory. On its centenary, a proposal to commemorate the members of the police force that had been targeted by republicans – and by extension, the Black and Tans who had been killed – caused political outcry not unlike the outrage unleashed among sections of the British public in 2020 when the less savoury aspects of Churchill's character were brought to light in the Black Lives Matter protests. The year 1940 is as important to Britain's national identity as 1919–21 is to many people in the Republic. The love–hate relationship that Churchill's memory inspires across the two islands is not so different to his personal perception of Irish affairs over his long tenure in office, or how he was himself viewed by various groups of Irish people during his career. But he was one of the most influential politicians in shaping relations both within and between Britain and Ireland, and his legacy endures today.

The Irish Question and Home Rule

Churchill played a formative role in the so-called Irish Question, the Irish nationalist demand for self-government within the United Kingdom, which gathered pace after 1880 under the leadership of

Figure 6.1 Churchill's scheme for devolved parliaments, as seen by *The Liverpool Daily Courier*, September 1912 (CAC, Churchill Papers, CHAR 2/58/8).

Charles Stewart Parnell and the Irish Parliamentary Party (IPP). Home Rule, the term under which the demand for self-government was made, intended to reform the 1801 Act of Union. The Act had abolished the old

Irish parliament in place of governance from Westminster, inspiring both constitutional and revolutionary Irish nationalist movements to 'repeal' the Union across the long nineteenth century (Irish republicans still seek to 'undo' the last vestiges of the Union in their campaigns to re-unify Ireland). Home Rule would have granted Ireland a measure of self-government within the United Kingdom and British Empire, establishing a parliament in Dublin with limited control over domestic affairs, but in the late nineteenth century the Irish Question was not simply a deliberation over whether to reform the constitution. It inspired heated debates about major political issues, such as the Empire, religion, citizenship, nationality, democracy, governance and minorities. It was thus one of the most intractable questions of the late Victorian era.

In the 1880s the long-serving statesman and Liberal Prime Minister William Ewart Gladstone took up the cause of self-government and proposed two Home Rule Bills for Ireland in 1886 and 1893. While Gladstone had many supporters, the notion of limited devolution for Dublin sparked considerable opposition. The first Bill split the Liberal Party and was defeated in both the Commons and Lords. Conservatives were deeply opposed and refashioned themselves as the 'Conservative and Unionist Party' – a designation deemed politically useful for many Conservatives ever since. They allied with Unionists across the island of Ireland who formed the Irish Unionist Alliance in 1891. When the second Home Rule Bill passed the Commons and was thrown out by the Lords in 1893, unionism in Ireland began to shift northwards, and by 1905 had become better organised and significantly more powerful in Ulster. Irish emigrants and their descendants across the British Empire and in the USA also took sides and fed the debate with their views, funds and activism. The question of Irish self-government energised British politics in its widest sense.

At the beginning of his career, Churchill was a Unionist. Several generations of Churchills had connections with Ireland. Winston's earliest years were spent in Dublin, as his father Randolph became aide to Winston's grandfather, the 7th Duke of Marlborough, who served as the Queen's representative in Ireland from 1876 to 1880 (the official role was Lord Lieutenant of Ireland). Following Gladstone's conversion to Home Rule, Randolph helped to foster Unionist Ulster's opposition. In February 1886, in preparation for a speech in Belfast's Ulster Hall, he wrote to a friend: 'I decided some time ago that if the GOM [Grand Old

Man, i.e. Gladstone] went for home rule, the Orange card would be the one to play. Please God it may turn out the ace of trumps not the two.'[2] As Peter Clarke has astutely observed, 'There is seldom a smoking gun in politics.'[3] Randolph's speech was an exception. His views were summarised in a public letter published shortly after the event and set the defensive tone of Ulster Unionist resistance for the rest of the nineteenth century – and for much of the twentieth as well: 'Ulster will fight, and Ulster will be right.'

Winston inherited his father's sympathy for Ulster and initially had good relations with leading unionists such as his cousins, the Londonderrys.[4] His imperially minded ideals were fostered when he spent time as an officer in the 4th Hussars and then as a journalist during the second South African War. Even when Churchill entered the House of Commons and crossed the floor to the Liberal Party in 1904, he did not support Irish self-government. In April he told the president of the North-West Manchester Liberal Association, 'I remain of the opinion that the creation of a separate Parliament for Ireland would be dangerous and impracticable.'[5] However, over the coming months and years his tone softened. He became colder towards Conservatives and Unionists who opposed any changes to the United Kingdom's polity and claimed that these groups were loyal only to their own interests.[6]

Whether Churchill had a Damascene conversion to Home Rule or saw it as a political necessity now he was in the Liberal Party remains unclear. By 1906 he had come around to the Gladstonian notion that self-government could only benefit the Empire, a view which was strengthened during his time as undersecretary of state for the Colonial Office (1905–8). As home secretary in March 1911, he revived the notion of federalism, an imaginative proposal first aired by Liberal Unionist MP Joseph Chamberlain in 1886. 'Home Rule All Round' was designed to simultaneously strengthen the United Kingdom and take the heat out of the Irish nationalist demand by reforming the United Kingdom polity and its relationship to the Empire. Scotland, Wales and Ireland would each receive their own parliament; England would be divided into a series of legislative authorities; all would be subservient to the imperial parliament at Westminster.[7] While the proposal didn't gather enough steam to gain parliamentary traction during the 1910s, major aspects of it substantively came to pass at the end of the twentieth century in the form of devolution under New Labour. In the years leading up to the First World War, it is frequently forgotten that there were several roadmaps as to how the Irish Question might be solved that placed the problem within wider UK and imperial contexts. Churchill contributed to the imaginative thinking that proved too radical for the 1910s – but a necessity for the 1990s.

The Edwardian era was ripe with political opportunities and challenges. During his time in the governments of 1906–10, social reform was on the Liberal ticket and Churchill identified himself with the radical wing, at least initially.[8] Alongside Welsh radical, David Lloyd George, he sought to increase expenditure on social policy at the cost of making economies elsewhere, and one major reform which the duo supported was the adoption of the Old Age Pensions Act in 1908, which entitled most men and women aged seventy years and above to a weekly pension. Two years after its introduction, 22.2 per cent of those drawing the pension across the United Kingdom lived in Ireland, even though Ireland's share of the total number of pensioners was only one in seven persons. The Act had a transformative impact on the Irish, especially elderly working women who typically had low earnings throughout their lifetimes. Claimants whose income was less than £21 p.a. were entitled to a full five shillings a week; between one third and two fifths of a pensioner's annual income. Contemporary reports reveal its immediate impact in impoverished rural Ireland. In Roscommon, 'neighbours ferried cartloads of aged female pensioners to the post office'. 'In Galway two very elderly pensioners wondered out loud why they could not claim back time', while in Ennis, Co. Clare, the post office required a police presence to keep order. How to finance the pension was one of the most difficult questions for the new Irish state from 1922 and an issue upon which elections were won and lost in independent Ireland. Churchill's legacy continued to be felt even when the Liberal influence appeared to be history.[9]

One of the great political questions of the Edwardian era – though many politicians felt it was marginal, even an annoyance – was the question of women's suffrage. Churchill's position on women's enfranchisement seems to have been positive. On a private members' Bill in 1904, he voted with most Liberal members to propose a limited measure of enfranchisement.[10] Nor did he oppose the 1918 Representation of the People Bill, which, when it became an Act, enfranchised all men over the age of twenty-one and women over the age of thirty, with qualifications. But he had zero tolerance for the violence of the suffragettes or any disruption to the gender order and was not afraid of using police repression when protesters were considered to have stepped out of line. When Sylvia Pankhurst interrupted a meeting at which Churchill was speaking on 5 January 1906 and asked would he use his influence to secure votes for women, he replied he had voted in favour of it on an occasion before, but 'in view of the destruction of great meetings by the advocates of women's suffrage, nothing would induce him to vote for giving women the franchise'.[11] His views softened once Pankhurst was ejected from the meeting, but he insisted that he would not be 'hen-pecked' into declaring his support. Churchill could countenance women's suffrage but was hostile towards campaigners who went against the gendered notion of a quiescent, pacifistic woman, especially when they challenged the 'masculine' space of formal politics and adopted 'masculine' forms of behaviour, such as interrupting meetings, heckling and throwing objects.

The question of suffrage also preoccupied Irish activists, though divisions had appeared between suffragists who agitated for enfran-chisement through Westminster on existing terms, those who believed that suffrage should be attained before independence and those who argued that Ireland should secure independence first – and that inde-pendence should be based on sex equality.[12] When Churchill as first lord of the admiralty (1911–15) visited Belfast in 1912 to deliver a speech in support of Home Rule, suffragettes such as Hanna Sheehy Skeffington, the co-founder of the Irish Women's Franchise League, which paralleled the militancy of the Pankhursts' Women's Social and Political Union, heckled 'the first lord'.[13] Churchill had refused to meet a deputation and during his speech was frequently interrupted by members with remarks such as, 'Will you give self-government to the women of Ireland?'[14]

In pre-war Ireland, suffrage, labour and the national question were causes that frequently intersected with the politics of radical nationalist women.[15] When Churchill was appointed president of the Board of Trade in 1908, it was common practice for newly appointed Cabinet ministers to resign as MP for their constituency and stand for re-election. Churchill expected to be re-elected without controversy in Manchester North-West, which he had easily won in 1906. However, the Irish played a role in his surprising defeat, not least the radical sisters, Constance Markievicz and Eva Gore-Booth, who campaigned against him because of his support for the controversial Licensing Bill, which proposed to restrict barmaids' right to work. Proponents of the

Bill argued it would protect women from the attentions of inebriated male customers, but simultaneously blamed female servers for men's drunkenness because their sexual allure was allegedly driving men to excess. In light of his orthodox views on gender, it isn't surprising that Churchill emerged as a prominent supporter of the Bill and was one of several MPs who considered further restrictions on women's employment by making it illegal for women to work beyond 8 p.m.[16] In response, Gore-Booth established the Barmaids' Political Defence League and both sisters led a vocal and demonstrative campaign to support Churchill's rival candidate, the Conservative William Joynson-Hicks, who was against the Licensing Bill and even opposed Irish Home Rule. For radical nationalist women, some causes were just as important as self-government, and Churchill was defeated by 529 votes.[17] Though the defeat was of little professional consequence – he was re-elected in Dundee the following month, where he was also dependent on Irish nationalist votes – the episode was formative in other ways. It was Markievicz's first experience of radical political protest and Sonja Tiernan has argued that it propelled her towards activism. That year, she joined the nationalist women's organisation, Inghinidhe na hÉireann (Daughters of Ireland), and the republican party, Sinn Féin. She later acted as a combatant in the 1916 Easter Rising and was the first female MP elected in the 1918 UK General Election, though didn't take her seat as she stood for Sinn Féin, which abstained – and continue to abstain – from Westminster.

The growth of labour and the unionisation of workers was another challenge for Churchill as home secretary (1910–11). Between 1910 and 1914, trade unionism flourished in Britain and Ireland; in the former, union membership increased from 2,477,000 to 4,315,000.[18] In urban Ireland, strikes were often led by the Irish Transport and General Workers' Union whose leader, James Larkin, played a prominent role in the Liverpool dockers' strikes and other unrest during 1905–6.[19] The coercive streak in Churchill came to the fore when managing strikes in Britain. He had few qualms about deploying the police and army against miners, railwaymen, dockers and carters during the strikes of 1909–11: occupations which had significant Irish representation.[20] His hatred of syndicalism was shared by prominent Dublin employers, several of whom saw Churchillian tactics as a solution to the industrial unrest following the 1911 Irish railway strike and during the major industrial dispute known as the Dublin Lockout during 1913–14, when over 20,000 workers struck against 300 employers.[21]

Political developments in the Edwardian era were far from dull and in the 1910s, the question of Home Rule became more acute. Churchill's support for an Irish parliament had been strengthened when writing his father's biography, as he came to read Parnellite works of history to further understand the longue durée of the Irish Question. In 1890, Parnell had been ousted from his party by an alliance of the Catholic Church, its loyal supporters and several IPP members following the revelation that he had been having an affair. He suddenly died in 1891. His fall from grace had all the hallmarks of a Greek tragedy, as did the rapid transformation of his memory in the years that followed (Parnell is still colloquially known as 'the Uncrowned King of Ireland' because of his efforts to put Home Rule at the top of the British parliamentary agenda). Churchill admired Parnell, ranking him one of his 'great contemporaries' in his later book of that name.[22]

In 1912, Churchill became more outspoken about Irish Home Rule. He wrote the introduction to a pamphlet published by the nationalist MP Jeremiah MacVeigh and made the case for the restoration of the Dublin parliament to 'thus express once more what has been the persistent and consistent desire of the great majority of the Irish people ever since the Act of Union more than a hundred years ago'.[23] In his visit to Belfast in February 1912 when first lord of the admiralty, he spoke alongside Parnell's successor to the IPP leadership, John Redmond. Churchill's speech to the estimated crowd of 7,000 persons, mostly nationalists, was important, as it was his first made in Ireland and presaged the heated developments of that year. He spoke of the Irish of all backgrounds as a global people, reflecting his awareness that the 'Irish Question' extended beyond the island (indeed, more Irish-born persons lived outside Ireland than within it in 1911). He argued that the diasporic Irish had demonstrated their aptitude for government. How could it be denied to nationalists in Ireland when 'in every other part of the English-speaking world [the Irish] have won their way out of all proportion to their numbers to positions of trust, affluence, and ability (hear, hear) – particularly political authority'? He recognised their strategic power, not least of all in America: 'They have on more than one occasion unfavourably deflected the policy of the United States. They are now the most serious obstacle to Anglo-American friendship.'[24] Churchill's concern with the transatlantic alliance was a long-term preoccupation, and the potential negative influence of Irish Americans on that alliance troubled him at various points throughout his career.

However, most of the speech was presented through an imperial lens. Churchill declared that the Irish were fundamentally a monarchical people, evidenced by the triumphant visit of King George to Dublin in 1911 (the visit had been a success, opposed only by a minority of advanced nationalists, though to describe attendees as 'monarchical' would no doubt have raised eyebrows). He declared that any measure of Irish Home Rule would have to be in harmony with imperial federation, demonstrating his foremost concern, but self-government would ultimately be a 'boon' to the Empire. He asked Unionists why 'this constitutional sentiment of Irish loyalty should be repulsed'.[25] His vision was not out of sync with that of moderate nationalists; indeed, mainstream Irish nationalism in 1912 was qualitatively more moderate than the republicanism which emerged as a political force in 1918. Redmond was an Irish Catholic loyalist.[26] He wrote in the introduction to *The Open Secret*, a pro-Home Rule book written by nationalist MP Tom Kettle: 'the grant of full self-government to Ireland will reveal to England the open secret of making Ireland her friend and helpmate, the brightest jewel in her crown of Empire'.[27] Nor was his a minority view, as Redmond could draw on several examples of Irish participation in – and 'service' to – the Empire, not least in the army and Indian civil service, though participation within that superstructure and loyalty to the Crown were not two sides of the same coin.[28] The Irish also had a rebellious history and it was this history that was commonly recalled by many British politicians, especially Conservatives. Churchill was not immune and linked Irish rebellion to the cause of Home Rule: 'Irishmen overseas have done us much harm in the past. They have been an adverse force in our Colonies . . . . If we had their aid instead of their enmity, their help instead of their opposition, how much smoother our path, how much quicker our progress – (cheers) – what new possibilities would be opened, what old dangers would vanish away.'[29] It is difficult not to agree with him, and as politicians dithered over what to do about Ireland, opposition to Dublin rule intensified in Ulster.

If Churchill had not realised that professions of nationalist 'loyalty' held little traction with Unionists, he was clearer on that front by the end of his visit. Belfast Unionists were incensed by his proposal to speak in the Ulster Hall, where Winston's father delivered his celebrated 'smoking gun' speech in 1886. Consequently Winston's venue was changed to the nationalist Celtic Park. Upon arrival, Churchill and his wife Clementine were confronted by angry Unionist crowds who carried placards which read 'Down with Churchill' and 'No Home Rule'. Union flags were common, as were military parades and renditions of 'God Save the King'.[30] The *Irish Times* recorded: 'Indeed, from the very moment that they emerged on the footpath until they got away, they appeared to be in danger, and had it not been for the prompt and vigorous action of the police, serious consequences might have followed.'[31] The Unionist press remarked that 'Mr. Churchill probably never delivered a duller speech.'[32] These reactions contrasted starkly to the nationalist reception, where the Churchills were greeted by a cheering crowd and his speech was reported as 'momentous' and 'important', but there too Churchill would have sensed the visceral emotions the Home Rule debate had stirred. The Irish, Papal and American flags were much in evidence. Two effigies of Sir Edward Carson, the Irish unionist leader, and Churchill's cousin, Lord Londonderry, were hung from a line and labelled, 'Carson and Londonderry, turncoats'.[33]

Over the next two years, Unionist Ulster put Randolph's threat into practice. On 28 September 1912, Unionists marked the day 'Ulster Day' and signed the Ulster Solemn League and Covenant, a pledge suffused with religious and imperial arguments, as well as concerns over citizenship, to demonstrate their opposition to Home Rule. The pledge also contained a declaration to reject the authority of an Irish parliament if self-government came to pass. In all, 237,368 men signed the document while 234,046 women signed an accompanying Women's Declaration to preserve the orthodox gendered distinction between men and women. Major constitutional developments had catalysed Unionist opposition. The Parliament Act of 1911 had removed the power of the House of Lords to veto bills from the Commons, conferring instead the right to delay legislation for a maximum of two years. Thus the single greatest obstacle to the second Home Rule Bill of 1893 was now removed. The third Home Rule Bill, presented to the Commons for its second reading by Liberal prime minister, Herbert H. Asquith, in April 1912, looked likely to pass if it was accepted by the House, which duly happened in May. The third and final reading passed in January 1913. Unionists were incensed. That month, the Ulster Volunteer Force (UVF) militia was formed to resist any enforcement of Home Rule on Ulster. The organisation comprised as many as 110,000 members at its zenith in mid-1914.[34]

In September, the Ulster Unionist Council endorsed the creation of a provisional government for Ulster, which would sit illegally if one were established in Dublin.[35]

Churchill found himself intimately involved in these events. In early March 1914, Asquith appointed a special committee including Churchill to deal with the 'Ulster Question'. Its members issued confusing instructions to General Arthur Paget, who commanded the military in Ireland, giving the impression that unionists in Ulster were about to be coerced. Senior cavalry officers, many of whom were from the same class, educational and social backgrounds as the upper middle classes who led the northern Unionist opposition to Home Rule, refused to deploy the army against Ulster if they were required to do so.[36] The episode had the unmistakeable whiff of a developing mutiny. Then in April 1914, unionists successfully – and illegally – imported 25,000 rifles and 3 million rounds of ammunition to Larne, Co. Antrim, and its surrounding environs.[37] Churchill was willing to deploy force against the UVF and Bew has argued that the period between March and July marked a low point in leading Unionists' relationships with him. At the same time, however, Churchill remained convinced that some form of separate treatment was needed for Ulster, though he believed that any concessions should be within the framework of an Irish settlement.[38] And most of all, within a settlement favourable to the Empire.

To add fuel to the fire, nationalists took inspiration from the unionist example and formed their own militia in November 1913, the Irish Volunteers, to defend Home Rule when it became law. At its height, the organisation comprised at least 170,000 men.[39] They even attempted their own gun-running exercise in Howth, Dublin on 26 July 1914, but were thwarted by the police. Later that day, an altercation between civilians and a detachment of the British army resulted in four civilian deaths and at least thirty injuries when troops fired into the crowd. In the months leading up to the outbreak of the First World War, Ireland looked on course for civil war, though it was unclear who would be fighting whom, and Irish affairs dominated parliamentary debates in the last days of July 1914. In the first of his epic volumes on *The Great War*, Churchill captured what is almost difficult to believe retrospectively – that Irish affairs were *the* dominant topic in parliament while war was brewing on the continent. Under the heading 'The Crisis, July 24–30', the first entry lists 'Fermanagh and Tyrone': the two majority nationalist Ulster counties in contention for being excluded from the Home

Rule settlement if an exclusionary measure were introduced for Ulster. Only the second read 'The Austrian Ultimatum to Serbia', the important document initiating the sequence of events that resulted in the outbreak of the Great War.[40]

War and Rebellion

As July became August, the Ulster Question was rapidly overshadowed by escalating hostilities on the continent. On 4 August, the United Kingdom (including Ireland) declared war on Germany. Immediately the atmosphere in Ireland changed as both unionists and nationalists threw their weight behind the British war effort. Churchill accurately recalled the change in his *World Crisis* series: 'The quarrels of North and South faded in the glare of the struggle, and throughout the green island Catholics and Protestants alike hastened to the recruiting offices.'[41] In September 1914, Redmond declared that Irishmen should go 'wherever the firing line extends', precipitating a split in the ranks of the Irish Volunteers between the bulk of members who agreed with him and a minority who did not think that Irishmen should go to the front to fight in the British army. This split would become important in 1916 but in the interim, the Irish public of all backgrounds was full throttle behind the war effort, notably so in urban centres. By the end of September 1914, three new divisions had been raised in Ireland for active service with Lord Kitchener's New Armies: the 10th, 16th and 36th divisions. The 16th contained many nationalists; the 36th contained many Unionists; and the 10th contained a mixture of both. The latter would be the first to see active service and Churchill played a decisive role in its fate.

In November, Churchill, first lord of the admiralty since 1911, was appointed by Asquith to a new War Council charged with overall direction of military operations. In January 1915, the Council – now renamed the Dardanelles committee – authorised a naval attack on the Dardanelles Strait, a sixty-mile stretch of water that separated Europe from Asia and a historically important trading route. Churchill remained on the committee following the May 1915 government reshuffle.[42] Addison has argued that Churchill suffered under the delusion that he possessed military genius. He believed that Germany's position would be considerably weakened if the Ottoman Empire were knocked out of the war, a plan that had theoretical merit but in practice underestimated the Ottoman forces. Churchill helped to plan the British Empire's assault. Regular units of the British army found themselves engaged in the first wave of landings in February 1915. By mid-May, numerous casualties were reported in the Irish press and units such as the Royal Irish Rifles, the Royal Irish Regiment and the Royal Dublin Fusiliers suffered heavily (see Chapter 7 for more on the Dardanelles operation and resulting Gallipoli campaign).[43]

In August, the 10th was initiated at Gallipoli. Unlike the earlier engagement, the Division's losses had a different impact on public opinion because this was the first time that Irish volunteers, most of whom were from the professional middle classes, saw action. Within days, an estimated 2,017 men were killed and over two months the 10th sustained 9,000 casualties: more than half its fighting strength and a figure comparable to the losses suffered by the Australian and New Zealand Army Corps.[44] While Churchill later acknowledged the Irish actions in the campaign,[45] he did not single them out for commendation, which typified reactions in Westminster. Frustration at the lack of recognition from the government stirred discontent among nationalists and southern Unionists alike.[46]

It is well known that Gallipoli was the sword upon which Churchill temporarily fell. His removal from the committee resulted in his resignation in November, and from then until July 1917, Churchill was not involved in prosecuting the war or in managing events in Ireland. Since September 1914, the splinter-group of Irish Volunteers had reorganised. Backed by the Irish Republican Brotherhood, a forerunner to the Irish Republican Army (IRA), a group of advanced nationalists led by writers, poets and playwrights embarked on a rebellion on Easter Monday 1916 to establish an Irish Republic while the government was preoccupied with continental affairs. The rebellion, indelibly stamped on popular memory as the Easter Rising, centred on Dublin. Approximately 1,200 rebels occupied key locations across the capital, one of which was the General Post Office on Sackville Street (now O'Connell Street) where the ringleader, Patrick Pearse, read the Proclamation of the Irish Republic (Poblacht na hÉireann) to bemused passers-by. The British military responded under the command of General Reginald Dyer and for six days rebels fought the British army. In total, 450 people were killed, most of whom were civilians; more than 2,600 were injured; and the inner city was considerably damaged. From 3 to 12 May, fifteen rebel leaders were executed without trial under the Defence of the Realm Act.[47] One further rebel was hanged in August.

The Rising was initially unpopular with the nationalist public, but the long-drawn-out series of executions and their extra-judicial nature stirred old memories of coercive policies dealt out by past British governments and of republican martyrdom. It was with regard to these executions that Churchill wrote in *The World Crisis*, 'The grass soon grows over a battlefield but never over a scaffold.'[48] Over subsequent months, the government introduced further repressive policies including internment and martial law, and hundreds of predominantly innocent men and some women – including Markievicz – were jailed. The IPP protested in the Commons but its inability to alter post-Rising policy affected its trust with the nationalist public, and as the months crept by, it began to suffer by-election challenges and defeats from the better-organised and pro-women's suffrage Sinn Féin. Lloyd George, now minister of munitions, revived the question of Home Rule, and when he offered Redmond immediate self-government with the temporary exclusion of Ulster, Redmond initially agreed; however, he withdrew his approval when he realised that Carson had been offered the same deal but with Ulster's permanent exclusion. Redmond had been tricked and Sinn Féin made political capital out of his error. A solution involving partition – rather than imperial federation or other alternatives – was now moving up the list of possible solvents to the Irish Question, though this outcome was still not guaranteed. From June 1917 to April 1918, a representative convention of Irishmen was tasked with solving the question of Irish self-government. Sinn Féin did not participate in the Irish Convention, a strategy which came to serve them well as 1918 progressed. It was in this context that Churchill returned to office in July 1917 to take up Lloyd George's position as minister of munitions.

Since late 1916, the political environment in Westminster had changed. Carson had led a backbench revolt, putting the wheels in motion that resulted in the resignation of Asquith and appointment of Lloyd George as prime minister on 6 December 1916.[49] Prosecution of the war was effectively in the hands of a small War Cabinet weighted to the right and this new environment suited Churchill, who was emerging as a politician who could easily wear different political stripes, as could Lloyd George. Since January 1916, compulsory military service had been enacted in Britain – a policy Churchill had favoured – though

Ireland avoided the measure because the British administration in Dublin warned the Cabinet that it would be a wrong-headed policy to conscript nationalists. In October 1916, the Lord Lieutenant, Lord Wimborne, told Lloyd George: 'The fact is that it does not appear to be feasible to demand national service from any community without a general measure of consent, and of such general consent there is at present no evidence.'[50]

Circumstances changed in March 1918 when, following the collapse of the Eastern Front, Germany sent the might of its arsenal and forces to the West, where the British Third and Fifth Armies held the line. The seriousness of the German Spring Offensive was such that it convinced the Cabinet to conscript Ireland alongside expanding the age range of men called up across Britain – a measure which Adrian Gregory has noted was designed to pacify British public opinion even though the government knew it would cause uproar in Ireland.[51] The British administration in Dublin protested to no avail. General Byrne, head of the Royal Irish Constabulary (RIC), was against it, and the chief secretary for Ireland, Henry Duke, quipped, 'We might almost as well recruit Germans.'[52] To make matters worse, when the Bill was introduced in April 1918, Lloyd George indirectly tied it to the results of the Irish Convention, effectively offering self-government for Ireland if the Irish agreed to conscription. He later amended this when he dismissed the Convention's report entirely, but the damage was done. The demand for Irish Home Rule had now moved from offering self-government to all Ireland in 1914 (albeit while kicking the Ulster 'problem' into the long grass) to a partitioned form of Dublin government in exchange for conscription. Echoes of colonial rule were soon heard in Ireland and Churchill later commented that 'the question of Irish conscription was handled in such a fashion during 1918 that we had the worst of both worlds, all the resentment against compulsion and in the end no law and no men'.[53] The horror at the prime minister's confused message and hatred of the conscription proposal provoked one of the largest popular reactions among nationalists that had been seen since the crisis of 1912–14. Hundreds of thousands of nationalists backed by the Catholic Church demonstrated their hostility through protests, petitions to Irish, British and American representatives who had social and political influence, and a massive £250,000 anti-conscription fund, which the Catholic hierarchy inaugurated and which people at home and abroad amassed over a four-month period.[54] At the heart of the protest was the principle that Westminster should not legislate for Ireland, which was itself a distinct nation; one which had freely contributed to the war effort and which was now about to be further coerced. The policy was enacted but not one man was compelled. As Churchill wrote, it 'spread disaffection through the whole Irish people'.[55] It is difficult to disagree with him. Though nationalists celebrated the armistice of 1918 in much the same way as Unionists – roughly between a quarter and a third of all available young men in Ireland served in the conflict; 57 per cent of recruits were Catholics – 'moderate nationalism' had been overtaken.[56] The General Election of December saw Sinn Féin win a landslide majority. Churchill wrote: 'The Nationalist Party, which had represented the Irish democracy for sixty years, vanished overnight …. Here was the spirit of the Easter rebellion embodied in eighty Members of the House of Commons.'[57] Churchill was concerned about the influence Sinn Féin might have on the Empire when its members took their seats and was relieved when the Party declared it would abstain from Westminster.[58] In January 1919, Sinn Féin established an Irish parliament, the Dáil, and passed a Declaration of Independence. Coincidentally, on the same day, the newly formed IRA began to shoot policemen, now deemed enemies of the state, marking the beginning of Ireland's War of Independence.

The next two years permanently impacted the island and reconfigured the United Kingdom. Churchill played a key role in these transformations, though it took until 1920 for the government to pay much attention to the insurgency at its back door. Churchill's mood was not compromising: 'Personally I wished to see the Irish confronted on the one hand with the realisation of all that they had asked for, and of all that Gladstone had striven for, and upon the other with the most unlimited exercise of rough-handed force.'[59] He hated the IRA. In his new role as secretary of state for war and air, he advocated hanging IRA members and floated the wild proposal of 'arming 20,000 Orangemen to relieve the troops from the North', leading Field Marshal Sir Henry Wilson, Chief of the Imperial General Staff in 1918 and from February 1922, an Ulster Unionist MP, to describe him as a 'perfect idiot as a statesman'. Churchill also encouraged the creation of an emergency gendarmerie to reinforce the police, which happened in 1920 when Crown forces were sent to assist the RIC. The notorious Black and Tans and Auxiliaries engaged in reprisals, tacitly and explicitly sanctioned by the British state, including Churchill.[60] It was this act that would cast a long shadow over Churchill's legacy in Ireland.

But he simultaneously pursued a strategy of negotiation. He chaired a Cabinet committee regarding Ireland in summer 1920, despite having a multitude of distractions to manage in other unstable parts of the Empire. In May 1921 he was part of a minority of five in the Cabinet to advocate a truce with republicans, partly because the war was damaging Britain's reputation abroad and Churchill was once again concerned about Irish America – especially as the UK was so heavily indebted to the USA following the war – but also because Churchill strongly desired an Irish settlement.[61] Space opened up for negotiation with republicans when the Government of Ireland Act, which had been hurriedly concocted and rushed through parliament at the end of December 1920, came into operation following the May 1921 Irish elections. The Act partitioned Ireland, creating two parliaments on the island and a shared council of Ireland, and while much of it was soon redundant, the creation of a new Northern Irish parliament for six counties of Ulster unexpectedly came to stay. For the majority of Unionist MPs from Ulster, the Act preserved most of Ulster's place in the Union, but not everyone was content. Around eighty Ulster unionists, predominantly from the three southern Ulster counties but also including Carson himself, voted against it. For northern nationalists, partition was viewed as nothing short of a disaster. Most refused to recognise the legitimacy of the devolved administration, leaving the door open for one-party rule by the Unionists, who deemed the region their own. In the short term, the Act triggered a refugee crisis and sectarian violence in Belfast, largely against Catholics.

In late 1921, Bew notes that it was the carrot of reclaiming territory from Northern Ireland which the Act had granted that brought republicans to the negotiating table. So did their own fatigue with conflict, concern with nationalist public opinion and the fact that Britain had initiated the offer to negotiate – an attractive proposition which implicitly raised their status from a 'murder gang', as described by Lloyd George in October 1920, to the new leaders of Irish nationalism. Relationships were important to the success of the negotiations. Churchill had little time for Éamon de Valera, the new president of the Dáil, who refused to attend the talks in London and sent plenipotentiaries, whom Churchill was more impressed with. Arthur Griffith, the Sinn Féin founder, was 'a man of great firmness of character and of high integrity' and Collins 'had elemental qualities and mother wit which were in many ways remarkable'.[62] In the early hours of

6 December 1921, following months of negotiations underpinned by the threat of 'immediate and terrible war' from Lloyd George,[63] the Anglo-Irish Treaty was signed. This was a feat for both sides and Churchill felt the way was now open to Irish reunification. Nine days later he said in parliament: 'We do not at all conceal the fact that we hope that some day – surely we are permitted to do so – Ulster will join herself with Southern Ireland, and that the national unity of Ireland within the British Empire will be attained.'[64] However, problems rapidly arose. A substantial minority in the Dáil led by de Valera opposed the Treaty. When a vote was taken and the Treaty carried by seven votes (sixty-four versus fifty-seven), de Valera resigned and anti-Treaty supporters, now referred to as the republicans, walked out. The new Irish political divisions were between pro- and anti-Treatyites, and many British politicians (including unionists) were divided on whether there was a distinction between them.

Churchill had to manage these new realities and did so to Britain's advantage. Shortly after the Treaty had been signed, he was appointed chairman of a Cabinet committee for Irish affairs and his energies were directed towards 'bedding down' the two new Irish administrations while keeping republicans at bay. His role in accelerating the rapid transfer of power between Britain and a new Irish provisional government, in keeping lines of communication open between North and South, and in defending the Treaty settlement in parliament when other forces threatened to tear it apart made him the single most important person in ensuring that the two-state solution for Ireland would endure. This looked far from certain in early 1922. Collins wrote to him in anger about unionist repression in Belfast, especially the killings of Catholics by the new northern security service, the Ulster Special Constabulary, which Churchill had helped to finance (republicans mistakenly thought that Sir Henry Wilson was behind the creation of the Constabulary and the notorious 'B-Specials', remembered because of their viciousness against Catholics in the name of 'security', and duly assassinated him at his London home in June 1922). Conversely, James Craig, the first prime minister of Northern Ireland, wrote to Churchill blaming IRA provocation in which Collins was allegedly involved, and senior figures in London were perturbed at reported attacks on Protestants in the South, chiefly in Cork. Churchill played an important mediatory role. He invited both Craig and Collins to London in January and March to engineer pacts to improve North–South relations, though in the end both pacts failed. In February 1922, Churchill introduced the Irish Free State Bill in parliament and his memoirs recall his private misgivings. He was not certain whether Collins and Griffith would betray him by succumbing to pressures from anti-Treaty diehards and there was considerable parliamentary opposition to the Bill from Conservatives and all the Ulster unionist members. Yet his formidable speech concealed those suspicions and the majority in favour was over-whelming: 302 ayes to 60 noes.[65]

While it is difficult to know how much influence Churchill exercised over Collins, his memoirs record cordial, even warm relations between them during the crucial months between February and April 1922. Churchill pressed Collins to hold an election so that the Irish people could determine whether they supported the Treaty – a strategy that could have backfired, but Churchill, as we have seen, was inclined to view Irish nationalism more favourably than his unionist colleagues and was willing to bet on a positive outcome. However, his anxiety increased when Collins and de Valera signed a compact on 20 May arranging for a rigged election.[66] Anti-Treaty factions would be given considerable representation in the Dáil, which, as Bew has noted, 'meant the Treaty was *ipso facto* broken'.[67] Another interpretation might hold that it was a clever strategy to prevent growing internal dissent. For Churchill, however, the Treaty relied on sidelining dissident republican elements because they sought to undo what had been agreed in Westminster. In his view, co-opting republicans into a rigged election meant that the deal signed in London was off. But the compact between Irish factions did not hold and divisions between pro- and anti-Treaty sides had their own momentum. In April, republicans seized the Four Courts in Dublin. In June 1922, an election was held and pro-Treaty candidates won 75 per cent of the vote. It is difficult to know what might have happened in subsequent months had it not been for the decisive role of Churchill. After the assassination of Wilson, Churchill's tolerance for dissenting republicans dissipated and he demanded that Collins respond to the takeover of the Four Courts, putting an end to Collins' prevarication. Collins wrote to Churchill for military supplies and not only did Churchill grant Collins this wish, he also told his colleagues that he intended to support the Free State Army by sending 'up to 30,000 rifles'. His vigour in pursuing a military response to squashing dissenting republicans contributed to the development of the Irish civil war, leaving a bitter legacy in Ireland in the decades that followed. At the same time, he defended his actions in parliament against those who saw the Irish – whether Free Staters or republicans – as part of the same network of dissidents that had assassinated Crown forces in 1920.[68] By August 1922, both Griffith and Collins were dead: Griffith of a cerebral haemorrhage and Collins was assassinated in his home county, Cork. Churchill's support for the settlement was now the only viable option for the coalition government and the Treaty was ratified in December 1922, creating the Irish Free State, a twenty-six-county Dominion within the British Empire. The civil war came to a close in May 1923 when the anti-Treaty republicans surrendered.

Throughout these years and beyond, one issue bubbled beneath the surface. The Treaty contained a provision for a Boundary Commission to review the frontier between North and South. The sheer vagueness of its remit was its ultimate brilliance in the eyes of those who supported the creation of Northern Ireland and the ultimate tragedy for those who lamented partition. Collins and his supporters had vested considerable hopes that the Commission would lead to significant transfers of territory and people to the Free State, while Craig and his supporters wanted no changes to the makeup of Northern Ireland, refusing to acknowledge the Treaty if there were any alterations to the border.[69] The civil war delayed the Commission's implementation and it started work in 1924. The original intention was for Britain, the Free State and Northern Ireland to send representatives, but unionist Ulster was so against the Commission that none was sent (Westminster appointed a deputy on its behalf). Over several months, the Commission spoke to respondents – primarily middle class and male – who lived along the border to assess their views regarding the partition, and on 7 November 1925 the findings were leaked to *The Morning Post*. By this date, both Irish administrations had had time to 'bed down'. The carrot of revising the border had been sufficiently delayed, making it difficult to undo what had been passed for Unionist Ulster in December 1920 and agreed with Free State representatives in December 1921.

Nonetheless, the Commission proposed some significant changes that would transfer about 130,000 acres and 24,000 citizens to the Free State. The problem was that it would also transfer land and people in the other direction and, overall, the changes were minor in the eyes of nationalists, who had dreamed of vast restorations of people and territory to the Free State. The largely nationalist counties of Fermanagh and

Tyrone, which had exercised parliamentary debate in 1914 and which Churchill recalled in his *World Crisis* series, would remain within Northern Ireland. The Commission fell like a lead balloon on nationalist ears and the new Free State government, now under William Cosgrave, moved to suppress the report in the aftermath of civil war. Craig was equally pleased to do so, having boycotted the Commission from the start, and Churchill played the decisive role. Since July 1924, Churchill had crossed the floor to the Conservatives and was now chancellor of the exchequer under Prime Minister Stanley Baldwin. He proposed to waive most of the debt the Free State owed Britain under Article 5 of the Anglo-Irish Treaty: an attractive option in the economically challenging environment of the early 1920s. On 3 December 1925, the governments of the United Kingdom, the Free State and Northern Ireland revoked the Boundary Commission's powers and formalised acceptance of partition. Eighty per cent of the Free State's debt was waived: 'the largest debt relief episode in the twentieth century'.[70] Churchill played the trump card in this phase of the Irish Question, seemingly closing the problem for the British. But where one question ends another typically starts, and Churchill helped to leave an even more serious question in his wake, that of partition: a question which fifty years later during the Northern Ireland 'Troubles', and now again in the aftermath of Brexit, continues to exercise politics not only in the island of Ireland but also in Britain, Europe and even the USA.

The resolution of 1925 marked an end point of sorts in this phase of the Irish Question and Churchill had been a decisive actor over the decades. On the one hand, he showed a belligerent readiness to use force against people he saw to be enemies of the state, whether they were strikers, suffragettes, the UVF, IRA or anti-Treaty republicans; yet, on the other, he was far from the Colonel Blimp-type character that is commonly remembered. His inconsistency when dealing with Ireland was thus largely consistent when compared with how he handled other vexed 'questions' within the United Kingdom. Whether or not he deserves the reputation as one of the ten most hated figures in Irish history largely depends on which aspect of his character is best recalled, but his popular association with war across these islands – and coercion in Ireland – has meant that his Colonel Blimp side is better remembered. Such a memory has obscured the multifaceted ways he dealt with and thought about the Irish. Unlike several of his contemporaries, he took Ireland seriously. 'Whence does this mysterious power of Ireland come?' he quipped in December 1921. 'How is it she has forced generation after generation to stop the whole traffic of the British Empire, in order to debate her domestic affairs?'[71]

Sage words that have no doubt been uttered by many a prime minister, but few have been so intimately involved as Churchill, which is probably why he makes the Irish Web's alternative top ten.

Notes

1. I have borrowed this observation from Paul Bew in his preface to *Churchill and Ireland* (Oxford: Oxford University Press, 2016).
2. Randolph was referring to the ideologies and practices of the Orange Order, a Protestant fraternal association created in the late eighteenth century which, in this period, was fundamentally sectarian and anti-Catholic.
3. P. F. Clarke, *Mr Churchill's Profession: Statesman, Orator, Writer* (London: Bloomsbury, 2012), p. 63. See also Chapter 4 in this volume.
4. P. Bew, *Churchill and Ireland* (Oxford: Oxford University Press, 2016), pp. 4–5.
5. *Irish Times*, 19 April 1904.
6. *Hansard*, House of Commons Debates, vol. 141, col. 713, 20 February 1905.
7. CAC, Churchill Papers, CHAR 21/22, image 38–9, March 1911.
8. P. Addison, *Churchill on the Home Front*, 3rd ed. (London: Faber & Faber, 2013), p. 108.
9. The pension might have added £13 to an annual pensioner's income of £39. C. Ó. Gráda, 'The Greatest Blessing of All': The Old Age Pension in Ireland. *Past & Present*, vol. 175, no. 1 (2002), pp. 124–61.
10. He was on record alongside Edward Grey, Richard Haldane and Lloyd George as a supporter in contrast to Herbert Asquith, Herbert Samuel and Reginald McKenna. Addison, *Churchill on the Home Front*, p. 129.
11. *Manchester Evening News*, 6 January 1906.
12. For further information, see L. Ryan and M. Ward, *Irish Women and the Vote: Becoming Citizens* (Dublin: Irish Academic Press, 2007).
13. National Library of Ireland, Sheehy Skeffington Papers, MS 33,620 (10), handwritten account of heckling Winston Churchill in Belfast, February 1912.
14. *Irish Independent*, 8 February 1912; *The Freeman's Journal*, 9 February 1912.
15. For further information, see S. Pašeta, *Irish Nationalist Women* (Cambridge: Cambridge University Press, 2013).
16. See this debate, for instance: *Hansard*, House of Commons Debates, vol. 195, cols. 796–907, 2 November 1908.
17. S. Tiernan, *Eva Gore-Booth: An Image of Such Politics* (Manchester: Manchester University Press, 2012), pp. 123–30.
18. Addison, *Churchill on the Home Front*, p. 141.
19. J. Sexton, *Sir James Sexton, Agitator: The Life of the Dockers' M. P.* (London: Faber & Faber, 1936).
20. Addison, *Churchill on the Home Front*, pp. 110–51.
21. D. Keogh, William Martin Murphy and the Origins of the 1913 Lock-Out. *Saothar*, vol. 4 (1978), p. 18.

22. Bew, *Churchill and Ireland*, pp. 36–7; W. S. Churchill, *Great Contemporaries* (London: Thornton Butterworth Limited, 1937).
23. J. MacVeigh, *Home Rule in a Nutshell*, 3rd ed. (London: The Daily Chronicle, 1911), p. iii.
24. *Belfast Telegraph*, 9 February 1912.
25. *Irish Independent*, 9 February 1912.
26. J. McConnel, John Redmond and Irish Catholic Loyalism. *The English Historical Review*, vol. 125, no. 512 (2010), pp. 83–111.
27. T. Kettle, *The Open Secret of Ireland* (London: W.J. Ham-Smith, 1912), p. x.
28. In 1830, for instance, the Irish represented 42.2 per cent of the British army. E. M. Spiers, Army Organisation and Society in the Nineteenth Century. In T. Bartlett and K. Jeffery (eds.), *A Military History of Ireland* (Cambridge: Cambridge University Press, 2008), p. 337.
29. *Irish Independent*, 9 February 1912.
30. *Irish Independent*, 8 and 9 February 1912.
31. *Weekly Irish Times*, 17 February 1912.
32. *Irish Times, Belfast Newsletter*, 9 February 1912.
33. *Irish Independent*, 9 February 1912.
34. T. Bowman, *Carson's Army: The Ulster Volunteer Force, 1910–22* (Manchester: Manchester University Press, 2007), p. 1.
35. The Ulster Unionist Council was formed in 1905 to demonstrate Ulster's opposition to Home Rule. It is generally seen as an important marker in the shifting of Irish unionism towards the northern province.
36. Bew, *Churchill and Ireland*, pp. 68–79.
37. A. Jackson, *Ireland 1798–1998: War, Peace and Beyond*, 2nd ed. (Chichester: Wiley-Blackwell, 2010), p. 234.
38. Bew, *Churchill and Ireland*, pp. 68–79.
39. Jackson, *Ireland 1798–1998*, p. 167.
40. W. S. Churchill, *The Great War* (London: George Newnes, 1933), p. i.
41. W. S. Churchill, *The World Crisis, Volume IV: 1918–1928 – The Aftermath* (London: Bloomsbury Academic, 2015), p. 189.
42. Addison, *Churchill on the Home Front*, p. 216.
43. Approximately 96 per cent of the 1st Battalion Royal Dublin Fusiliers officers and 63 per cent other ranks were killed, wounded or reported missing after their attempted landing at 'V' beach on 25 April 1915. N. Gallagher, *Ireland and the Great War: A Social and Political History* (London: Bloomsbury, 2020), pp. 134–8.
44. Gallagher, *Ireland and the Great War*, p. 137.
45. W. S. Churchill, *The World Crisis, Part II: 1915* (New York: Rosetta Books, 2013), pp. 248–52, 337–52.
46. Gallagher, *Ireland and the Great War*, pp. 134–40.
47. F. S. L. Lyons, The New Nationalism, 1916–18. In W. E. Vaughan (ed.), *A New History of Ireland, Volume VI: Ireland Under the Union, II: 1870–1921* (Oxford: Clarendon Press, 1996; repr. 2010), pp. 224–39.
48. W. S. Churchill, *The World Crisis, Volume IV*, p. 289.
49. E. Mulhall, 'A very British coup – Carson, the press and the fall of Asquith', RTE Century Ireland, www.rte.ie/centuryireland/index.php/articles/a-very-british-coup-carson-the-press-and-the-fall-of-asquith.

50. Wimborne to Lloyd George, Beaverbrook Library, London, LG MSS, E3/9/1, 2 October 1916, cited by Alan J. Ward, Lloyd George and the 1918 Irish Conscription Crisis, *The Historical Journal*, vol. 17, no. 1 (March 1974), p. 108.

51. A. Gregory, 'You Might As Well Recruit Germans': British Public Opinion and the Decision to Conscript the Irish in 1918. In A. Gregory and S. Pašeta (eds.), *Ireland and the Great War: 'A War to Unite Us All?'* (Manchester: Manchester University Press, 2002), pp. 113–32.

52. Gregory, 'You Might As Well Recruit Germans', p. 110.

53. Churchill, *The World Crisis, Volume IV*, p. 190.

54. Gallagher, *Ireland and the Great War*, pp. 150–1.

55. Churchill, *The World Crisis, Volume IV*, p. 190.

56. D. Fitzpatrick, The Logic of Collective Sacrifice: Ireland and the British Army, 1914–1918. *The Historical Journal*, vol. 38, no. 4 (1995), p. 1025; P. Bew, Moderate Nationalism and the Irish Revolution, 1916–1923. *The Historical Journal*, vol. 42, no. 3 (1999), pp. 729–49.

57. The Party won seventy-three seats, not eighty as Churchill mistakenly declared. Churchill, *The World Crisis, Volume IV*, p. 190.

58. Churchill, *The World Crisis, Volume IV*, p. 191.

59. Churchill, *The World Crisis, Volume IV*, p. 196.

60. Bew, *Churchill and Ireland*, p. 94; Churchill, *The World Crisis, Volume IV*, pp. 193–4.

61. Bew, *Churchill and Ireland*, pp. 104–11.

62. He had less to say about the other Irish representatives – Eamon Duggan, George Gavan Duffy and Robert Barton – who he claimed were 'overshadowed by the two leaders'. Churchill, *The World Crisis, Volume IV*, pp. 205, 259.

63. D. G. Boyce, How to Settle the Irish Question. In A. J. P. Taylor (ed.), *Lloyd George: Twelve Essays* (London: Hamish Hamilton, 1971), p. 162.

64. *Hansard*, House of Commons Debates, vol. 149, col. 175, 15 December 1921.

65. Churchill, *The World Crisis, Volume IV*, pp. 242–4, 248.

66. Churchill, *The World Crisis, Volume IV*, p. 255.

67. Bew, *Churchill and Ireland*, p. 125.

68. *Hansard*, House of Commons Debates, vol. 150, col. 1193, 16 February 1922.

69. Churchill, *The World Crisis, Volume IV*, pp. 256–7.

70. J. Fitzgerald and S. Kenny, 'Till Debt Do Us Part': Financial Implications of the Divorce of the Irish Free State from the United Kingdom, 1922–1926. *European Review of Economic History*, vol. 24, no. 4 (2020), pp. 818–42.

71. *Hansard*, House of Commons Debates, vol. 149, col. 182, 15 December 1921.

Further Reading

P. Addison, The Search for Peace in Ireland. In James W. Muller (ed.), *Churchill as Peacemaker* (Cambridge: Cambridge University Press, 1997), pp. 186–209.

P. Addison, *Churchill on the Home Front*, 3rd ed. (London: Faber & Faber, 2013)

P. Bew, *Churchill and Ireland* (Oxford: Oxford University Press, 2016)

R. Fanning, *Fatal Path: British Government and Irish Revolution, 1910–1922* (London: Faber and Faber, 2013)

N. Gallagher, *Ireland and the Great War: A Social and Political History* (London: Bloomsbury Academic, 2019)

A. Jackson, *Home Rule: An Irish History, 1800–2000* (London: Weidenfeld & Nicolson, 2003)

A. Jackson, *Ireland 1798–1998: War, Peace and Beyond*, 2nd ed. (Chichester: Wiley-Blackwell, 2010)

S. Pašeta, *Irish Nationalist Women* (Cambridge: Cambridge University Press, 2013)

A. T. Q. Stewart, *The Ulster Crisis* (London: Faber, 1967)

M. Walsh, *Bitter Freedom: Ireland in a Revolutionary World, 1918–1923* (London: Faber and Faber, 2015)

7
_____

Churchill's First World War

Perhaps the most telling moment of Churchill's First World War
experience was marked, according to Asquith's account of it to his
confidante, Venetia Stanley, with an outburst of uncontrollable laughter
around the Cabinet table.[1] In October 1914 Churchill telegraphed from
Antwerp, where he was directing an improvised defence of the town
against the invading Germans, with the suggestion that he should stand
down as first lord of the admiralty, the Cabinet post he had held since
1911, and be appointed instead to a senior military position in the field.
The assembled ministers thought the idea so startling and ridiculous
that, after a moment of numbed surprise, they broke into 'incredulous
laughter'.[2] Perhaps not surprisingly, Churchill does not mention this
detail in his own account of the matter, but he does mention that his
proposal enjoyed the support of the one Cabinet minister who did have
an understanding of military matters, the secretary of state for war, Lord
Kitchener.[3]

Churchill had gone to Antwerp at the beginning of October to assess
the situation and give heart to the Belgians, who seemed on the point
of abandoning the town; however, his flamboyant arrival and breezy
personal style had not only encouraged the Belgians to keep fighting
but had also persuaded him that he should stay on and lead them.
Churchill's predilection for military adventure was hardly a secret and
had long attracted both political and press criticism; however, since his
actual military experience amounted to no more than a bit of colonial
campaigning in his youth, much of it as a war correspondent, and his
one serious battle experience was the celebrated but futile charge of
the 21st Lancers at Omdurman, his Cabinet colleagues' incredulity is
perhaps understandable. The press, too, was scathing: the *Morning Post*

even accused him of wanting to establish himself as a dictator.[4] Recent historians, however, have largely agreed with Kitchener's more favourable view: Addison goes so far as to call Churchill's defence of Antwerp, which delayed the German advance for the better part of a week, 'superb'.[5]

However, the importance of the Antwerp episode lies less in its military significance, which was creditable rather than decisive, than in its political implications. Was Churchill essentially a military figure who happened to have gone in for politics, or was he a civilian politician who happened to have a military background? The issue is of more importance than simply reaching a judgement on a larger-than-life maverick. The First World War saw a struggle for power between military and civilian authority in nearly all the major combatant powers. In Germany, the military and the politicians were in constant dispute over war aims and strategy, with ultimately disastrous results; in France, the deadly struggle at Verdun provoked a political coup which reasserted clear civilian control of the war and replaced the previous supreme military commander, General Joffre, with separate commanders for different fronts. However, it was in Britain that the war's tendency to blur the distinction between civilian and military authority was most marked and where it carried the most radical constitutional implications.

The obvious example of this blurring of the lines was the figure of Kitchener, the first soldier to sit in the Cabinet since Wellington (and he had done so as a civilian). His position, including his habit of wearing his field marshal's uniform, challenged the strict constitutional exclusion of the military from politics that had been jealously maintained since Cromwell's day. His 'New Army', which consisted of the thousands of young men, often referred to as 'Kitcheners', who had responded to his pointing finger in the famous recruiting poster, was essentially a civilian force in uniform and subject to military discipline; cartoonists at the time had great fun showing drill sergeants' exasperation at the unmilitary ways of these educated, somewhat precious new recruits from the urban and suburban middle classes.[6] Even more significantly, the issue of conscription, which was being seriously debated by 1915, threatened virtually to erase the traditional distinction between civilian and military, subjecting citizens going about their business to military interference and control to a degree not seen since the Press Gang. In this context, Churchill's very public hopping between civilian and military command might appear, if it were not kept in check, as a worrying sign of the gradual militarisation of British public life.

First Lord of the Admiralty

Churchill's role in the early stages of the war did indeed seem to indicate that he was combining military, naval and political leadership in his own person. The navy, for which Churchill assumed responsibility in 1911, was still in the throes of the revolution set in motion by Admiral Sir John 'Jackie' Fisher, the First Sea Lord who had championed the new *Dreadnought* class of battleship and swept away cherished older vessels and traditions with equal abandon. Although Fisher had retired in 1910, Churchill, equally contemptuous of naval traditions and prejudices, maintained the same momentum of change, improving pay and promotion prospects for the men, instituting a Royal Naval Air Service and clearing out dead-wood senior admirals, much as Fisher had cleared out obsolete ships. It was thanks to Churchill that the Grand Fleet, as the home-waters fleet was now dubbed, was not only in far better shape for the war than the army but was actually in the right place: he had mobilised it and ordered it to its new base at Scapa Flow even before war had been declared. His decision in 1914 to appoint the cautious, prudent Sir John Jellicoe as its commander proved inspired, not least because Jellicoe was very different from the sort of dashing, pugnacious commander Churchill usually preferred, like his debonair naval secretary, Rear-Admiral Sir David Beatty. In a much-quoted phrase from *The World Crisis*, Churchill described Jellicoe as 'the only man on either side who could lose the war in an afternoon'.[7] The navy could not hope to win the war for the allies on its own, but were Jellicoe to lose control of the North Sea and the Channel, allowing German warships and submarines to operate unchecked in British waters, not only would Britain's vital imports of food and munitions be jeopardised but it would be impossible to maintain the British army in France. If Britain were then to pull out, France would be unlikely to carry on and the war would indeed be lost. For this reason, it was Jellicoe's primary task not to win battles and certainly not to risk his battleships, but to maintain an iron grip on the North Sea.[8]

In many ways both Churchill's strengths and his weaknesses as a wartime first lord of the admiralty lay in his background as a journalist: he knew very well how to raise public expectation and how to exploit good news to best advantage, but he also knew that a slow, cautious policy, however wise, makes very poor copy. England expected a Nelsonian victory and looked to Jellicoe to provide it. Churchill himself added to this heightened air of expectation with an unfortunate phrase in a public speech in Liverpool, where he compared the task of drawing the German fleet out of harbour to enticing rats out from a hole.[9] The reality, as Churchill was in a very good position to know, was that the navy's strategy could only be a long-term one: in the immediate term the naval news was always likely to be much more mixed. Daring German surface raiders attacked British merchant shipping with virtual impunity – the most famous of them, the *Emden*, even bombarding the port of Madras before eventually being cornered and sunk. The first proper naval battle of the war, fought off the Chilean coast at Coronel, far from being a new Trafalgar, saw the complete defeat of a British squadron by the German Admiral von Spee, including the sinking of the British Admiral Cradock's flagship; Churchill naturally made the most of the avenging of Coronel a month later by the defeat of von Spee's own force off the Falkland Islands, calling it a 'sizzling coup', but there was no denying the naval war had got off to a very unsatisfactory start.[10]

Normally the first lord's responsibility for the detail of naval operations would be limited, but Churchill's 'hands-on' style meant he was bound to be in the firing line in the case of any failure. His weakness for daring plans led him to back a proposal for a raid on the German fleet in its home waters in the Heligoland Bight; however, the plan was not properly communicated to Jellicoe, which not only led to British submarines mistakenly launching torpedoes at British ships but at one point the raid's commander signalled for help against the very ship he was signalling to.[11] The Heligoland action was, nevertheless, successful and was much celebrated in Britain, but it had come perilously close to grief and for this Churchill and the First Sea Lord, Prince Louis of Battenberg, must bear much of the responsibility: it was a pursuit of headlines without proper planning and preparation. Perhaps less blame can be attached to Churchill for the sinking on 22 September 1914 off the Dutch coast of three warships, *Aboukir*, *Hogue* and *Cressy*, by a single German submarine. The ships were elderly and Churchill had in fact given orders that they be withdrawn, but his instructions had been circumvented, which led to an unedifying blame game within the Admiralty. If Churchill cannot be directly blamed for the ships' loss, he can be held ultimately responsible for the inner workings of his department that had put the ships in danger in the first place.

More serious than the loss of three antiquated battleships were Churchill's failures with regard to the Mediterranean. At the very start of the war he took the difficult but wise decision to impound two battleships being built on the Tyne for the Turkish government, then still neutral. Although it made good sense (and headlines), his decision provoked fury in Turkey, where the ships were regarded as symbols of national pride and identity. At the same time, Churchill's instructions to Admiral Milne, the British commander in the Mediterranean, where two German warships, the *Goeben* and the *Breslau*, were at large, were grand in style but too open to interpretation: Milne was to safeguard French transportation of troops from North Africa, if possible bringing to action any German ships, like the *Goeben*, which might appear on the scene, but not to engage with 'superior forces', however that phrase might be defined, except in combination with the French.[12] The result was that Milne shadowed but did not engage the German ships, which therefore reached Constantinople safely, where they were promptly bought by the Turkish government before sailing off to bombard southern Russia, thereby bringing Turkey into the war on the German side. Clearly Churchill's own responsibility for the escape is outweighed by Milne's, but the episode does show Churchill's weakness for grand language rather than precise, if less colourful, instructions.

If Churchill had confined himself to the naval war, he might well have got credit for overseeing it through its inevitably difficult opening months and shared some of the credit for Jellicoe's eventual success; however, he blurred the distinction between land and sea command just as much as he did between the political and operational aspects of his office. He infuriated Kitchener by entering into regular correspondence with Sir John French about strategy on the Western Front in a manner that Kitchener thought, not without reason, threatened to undermine his authority. Keen for as many men under his command as possible to get to grips with the enemy, Churchill threw together a Royal Naval Brigade from 'surplus' marines and seamen, essentially creating a regiment of the army, and sent the Royal Naval Volunteer Reserve off to the trenches with them. He then turned himself, as we have seen, from a visiting politician into a military commander in the defence of Antwerp. This fusion of roles might have made some sense when he was prime minister in the Second World War; in 1915 it merely led him into the decision which was to mark his whole wartime reputation and which he was to carry for the rest of his life: the assault on the Dardanelles.

Fisher and the Dardanelles

It is almost impossible to discuss the Dardanelles campaign calmly and objectively, so strong are the emotions it still engenders. The arguments about whether it was a brilliant plan let down by the commanders on the spot or a mad scheme which could not be rescued by the hapless men on the ground go back and forth.[13] Although the government's Committee of Inquiry exonerated Churchill from blame for the disaster, and even the most hostile historians recognise that his personal responsibility largely ceased once the troops had gone ashore, nevertheless public blame for the failure and the heavy losses of the Dardanelles campaign stuck firmly to him, as he himself recognised. He devoted the whole second volume of *The World Crisis* to a detailed exculpation of his role, but, while this largely satisfied his readers at the time, it has by no means quietened the controversy since. Even the most cursory look at a map reveals the difficulties of the terrain, with its steep cliffs and narrow strait: how could Churchill possibly have thought the offensive would work?

In fact, politically, an assault on the Dardanelles made perfect sense. The British and Russians had long contemplated dividing Turkey between them; Churchill's plan for an Anglo-French assault would allow the French to have their share too. A successful landing in the Dardanelles would leave Constantinople itself wide open to be taken, with Russian help if need be.[14] This would not only remove Turkey from the war at a stroke but would also allow material aid to get through to Russia and even a possible Allied attack through the Balkans against the Austrians; deprived of both their allies, the Germans might even be forced to sue for peace. Militarily, too, there was every reason for optimism: the Turks' recent military record was lamentable and Enver Pasha, minister of war in the 'Young Turks' government, had just displayed his military incompetence in a humiliating defeat at the hands of the Russians at Sarikamish.[15]

The problem with the campaign was the confusion over whether it was to be a purely naval operation or a joint military-naval one, and the blame for this confusion must lie at least in part with Churchill's decision in 1914 to bring Lord Fisher out of retirement to replace the ineffective Battenberg as First Sea Lord. Churchill and Fisher each found himself faced, for once, with an ego as big as his own, and although they developed a close, almost intimate relationship, it could also be tempestuous.[16] Both were men in a hurry – Fisher's energetic writing style, with its free use of underlinings and exclamation marks, is a good indication of his frenetic state of mind – when a complex invasion plan against a defended coastline required careful, methodical preparation. The initial naval attack began well but ran into a minefield that sank three ships and severely damaged three more; small wonder Admiral de Robeck decided to cut his losses and withdraw. Churchill was later to insist that the attack could have been maintained, now the position of the minefields was known, and that the Turks would not have been able to resist if it had been; it is impossible to know this for certain.[17] As it was, the naval bombardment merely served to alert the Turks to the likelihood of a military landing, so that, when it came a month later, they were ready for it: Allied troops ran into determined resistance and suffered heavy casualties, especially the Australian and New Zealand troops, whose boats drifted to the wrong place and who were pinned down literally on the beaches. The overall result was a campaign that could not advance far inland and which was for whole stretches confined to the beachheads. When the decision was finally taken to withdraw, the campaign had achieved nothing in military terms but delivered a major blow to British prestige in political ones.

The Dardanelles disaster brought Churchill's apparently unstoppable progress as a naval-military-political leader to a shuddering halt. Fisher resigned in May 1915, saying he could not possibly work with Churchill; when Asquith formed a coalition government in the spring, Churchill, whom the Conservatives had never forgiven for deserting them for the Liberals back in 1904, was himself sacrificed: he lost the Admiralty and was made chancellor of the Duchy of Lancaster, a sort of political consolation prize. He clung doggedly to his belief in the Dardanelles campaign but he was rapidly finding himself the only one who did: 'What about the Dardanelles?' became a regular taunt by angry hecklers at public meetings.[18] Interestingly, it was also at this point that Churchill discovered he had a talent for painting. Painting requires careful, even minute, observation on the part of the painter and helps develop a keen sense of perspective; it is possible to discern both in Churchill after his Dardanelles debacle.

Figure 7.1 Churchill in French steel helmet, c.1916 (CAC, Churchill Press Photographs, CHPH 1B).

Trenches and Munitions

Churchill's fall after the Dardanelles was a sharp reminder to him of the ultimate authority in the British political system, even in wartime, of the prime minister. It also prompted him to take the unexpected step of resuming his military commission and heading to the Western Front. There was clearly an element of personal expiation in his decision, but it also gave him an opportunity to do more for the war than he could achieve on the outskirts of the Cabinet: an indication of a change of perspective in his outlook. After a time acclimatising himself to trench warfare with the Grenadier Guards, he joined the Royal Scots Fusiliers as Lieutenant Colonel of their 6th battalion. Understandably, he was at first viewed askance by the men of his new command, but he soon won them over with a combination of competent efficiency, obvious care for the wellbeing of his men and indulgent hospitality with food and drink sent from England.[19] Churchill's frontline soldiering was no act: he took it seriously and was taken seriously in return; he was lucky, however, that he was not in the line during any major engagement. Was this a return to his true vocation? It is difficult not to conclude that he was trying to find this out, though he was clearly not intending to be a typical officer: instead of the Fusiliers' regimental glengarry, for example, he sported a French helmet, claiming it fitted his head better; this may have been true, but it also gave him a distinctive 'look', which enabled him to stand out in photographs (Figure 7.1).[20] In any case, his time in the trenches seems to have helped him finally decide that his true field of battle was the political one. In March 1916 he seized the opportunity of a spell of leave to give a speech in the House of Commons which went a long way to restoring his reputation, until he spoiled the effect right at the end by calling for Fisher to be recalled.[21] Nevertheless, it reminded him of where his heart lay; a couple of months later he took advantage of a reorganisation of his regiment to leave the front and return to Westminster, where the tussling for power of civilian and military was about to enter a new phase.

In December 1916 David Lloyd George executed what amounted to a political coup against the prime minister, Asquith: he formed a joint Liberal-Conservative committee to run the war, but without the prime minister. Faced with a fait accompli, Asquith resigned and Lloyd George took power. He and Churchill were old colleagues, but, for all his admiration for him, Lloyd George knew Churchill well enough to realise he needed to be kept under tighter control than Asquith had managed; he felt much the same, and for similar reasons, about Sir Douglas Haig, the commander of the British Expeditionary Force, whom he blamed for the appallingly heavy casualties of that year's offensive on the Somme.[22] Relations between Haig and Lloyd George grew steadily worse; Haig resented any political interference in his control of the war; Lloyd George saw Haig as wasting his men's lives on pointless offensives and insisted that Haig accept his subordination to civilian (or, better, French) authority. Churchill was no supporter of the sort of costly offensives Haig launched, but Lloyd George, determined to establish his authority over the war, was in no hurry to appoint the warrior-minister to a position where he could repeat the military posturing that had marked his time at the Admiralty, especially as Bonar Law's Conservatives were so opposed to working with him. When he finally appointed Churchill to ministerial office in July 1917, it was as minister of munitions.

Lloyd George had himself galvanised the munitions industry as minister and Churchill had the right dynamic temperament to carry on where he had left off; on the other hand, munitions, essential though it was, did not carry War Cabinet rank: Churchill would be called to Cabinet as and when the Cabinet wished to hear from him. As it was, Churchill took full advantage of his new post to opine and advise – some might say interfere – in all branches of the government's war work. He also visited the front regularly to observe operations and was even given the use of a small château behind the lines as his headquarters, for all the world like a general. It is not difficult to imagine that, had he actually been in Lloyd George's War Cabinet, he would have found the temptation to try to take over the running of the war difficult to resist. It is no coincidence that Lloyd George waited until January 1919, barely two months after the end of the war, to make him secretary of state for war.[23]

Legacy

If it was the Second World War that established Churchill's international reputation, it was the First World War that marked and shaped him. He experienced it from a quite astonishing range of perspectives: as a strategist in charge of the naval war and also shaping part of the land campaign; as a technical innovator, introducing both a naval air service and sponsoring the development of the tank; as a makeshift general in charge of the defence of Antwerp; as a battalion commander at the front; as a minor Cabinet minister; as a backbench MP out of office; and finally as a minister in charge of industrial production. When one adds to this his service immediately after the war, overseeing military operations against the Bolsheviks in Russia; directing a counter-insurgency campaign against the Irish Republicans; negotiating the Anglo-Irish Treaty; and manoeuvring for maximum British advantage in the post-war settlement of the Middle East, it is difficult to conceive of how Churchill could have had a better military, political and diplomatic apprenticeship for his role in the Second World War. The First World War gave him a holistic understanding of how modern war works, with first-hand experience of strategy and tactics at every level from Grand Strategy to the front line, as well as experience of the direction of a wartime economy. He saw first hand the advantage of coalition government in running a war, while Lloyd George's dynamic style and his improvised 'garden suburb' of administrative offices

Figure 7.2 A post-First World War cartoon which captures the enduring impact of the Dardanelles on Churchill's political career, November 1923 (CAC, Broadwater Collection, BRDW I Press 23).

sprawling across the nearby parks was an obvious precursor of Churchill's famous 'Action This Day' memos and his hastily assembled underground Cabinet War Rooms. The war showed the importance of unity of command: Lloyd George maintained a tight inner War Cabinet, while Foch's position as Supreme Allied Commander was crucial to the successful Allied counter-offensives in 1918: there are obvious echoes of Eisenhower. To those with the eyes to see it, and Churchill was certainly one of those, the war also revealed the potential of the United States to turn the tide of war, both in military and economic terms; it is no coincidence that American involvement was to be so central to his strategic thinking in the Second World War.

However, the war also revealed those aspects that were to leave Churchill so politically isolated for so much of the time that lay ahead. Throughout the war he operated essentially as a lone figure: even with his regiment he chose his distinctive style of dress so as to set himself apart. His one period of working closely in partnership was with Fisher and it produced disaster; never again would he work so closely with another figure. The war destroyed much of the world he had grown up in: the glittering European empires of his youth came crashing down and the sort of skulking anarchists and revolutionaries he had once seen cornered at Sidney Street were now elevated to the government of Russia. The Irish Republicans forced Britain out of most of Ireland and in India the nationalists were clearly hoping to do the same. It is hardly unusual for people to become more conservative as they get older; in Churchill's case, his rightward drift was exacerbated by the sense that he seemed to be virtually alone in regretting the passing of the world he had known. So, the loneliness of his backbench voice in the 1930s, and even of his wartime premiership, had its origins in the First World War: no wonder he was able to make standing alone in 1940 sound so appealing. Above all, the war resolved once and for all the conundrum that had surrounded Churchill: he was indeed essentially a civilian politician who happened also to have a strong military side to him. It was a lesson in civilian authority that the generals of the next war, whom he happily appointed or sacked as he pleased, would learn the hard way.

Notes

1. M. Gilbert, CV, vol. 3, part 1, pp. 165–6.
2. R. Rhodes James, *Churchill: A Study in Failure, 1900–1939* (London: Weidenfeld and Nicolson, 1970), p. 62.
3. W. S. Churchill, *The World Crisis, 1911–1918* (London: Penguin, 2007), p. 200.
4. P. Addison, *Churchill: The Unexpected Hero* (Oxford: Oxford University Press, 2006), p. 72, quoting *The Morning Post*, 23 October 1914.
5. P. Addison, *Winston Churchill* (Oxford: Oxford University Press, 2007), p. 32.

6. See, for example, E. Wallace, *Kitchener's Army and the Territorial Forces: The Full Story of a Great Achievement* (London: George Newnes, 1915).

7. Churchill, *The World Crisis*, p. 602.

8. Churchill, *The World Crisis*, p. 601.

9. He was speaking at the Tournament Hall, Liverpool, on 21 September 1914: 'So far as the Navy is concerned, we cannot fight while the enemy remains in port. We hope a decision at sea will be a feature of this war. Our men, who are spending a tireless vigil, hope they will have a chance to settle the question with the German Fleet, and if they do not come out and fight they will be dug out like rats in a hole. [Cheers.]', https://en.wikisource.org/wiki/Great—Speeches—of—the—War/ Churchill—(2). Churchill later regretted the phrase and acknowledged it had been foolish; *Hansard*, House of Commons Debates, series 5, vol. 80, col. 1425, 7 March 1916.

10. Churchill to Fisher, 10 December 1914, in Gilbert, CV, vol. 3, part 1, p. 302.

11. R. K. Massie, *Castles of Steel: Britain, Germany and the Winning of the Great War at Sea* (London: Jonathan Cape, 2004), p. 106.

12. Massie, *Castles of Steel*, p. 31.

13. For a forthright critical account, see P. Hart, *Gallipoli* (London: Profile, 2013), which castigates Churchill's 'strategic incompetence'. For a more measured analysis, see S. McMeekin, *The Ottoman Endgame: War, Revolution and the Making of the Modern Middle East, 1908–1923* (London: Penguin, 2015), which points out that, in geographical and political terms, the plan made sense, but that neither Churchill nor Fisher were aware of how strongly the Dardanelles had been fortified by the Germans since the start of the war.

14. S. McMeekin, *The Russian Origins of the First World War* (Cambridge, MA: Belknap Press, 2013), p. 128.

15. P. Hopkirk, *On Secret Service East of Constantinople: The Plot to Bring Down the British Empire* (New York: Oxford University Press, 2001), pp. 73–7.

16. P. Brendon, *Churchill: A Brief Life* (London: Pimlico, 2001), pp. 72–3; J. Morris, *Fisher's Face* (London: Viking, 1995), pp. 211–14.

17. As Churchill himself put it, 'And yet if the Navy had tried again they would have found that the door was open.' Churchill, *World Crisis*, p. 412.

18. Rhodes James, *Churchill*, p. 86.

19. G. Best, *Churchill and War* (London: Hambledon Continuum, 2006), p. 69.

20. R. Jenkins, *Churchill* (London: Pan, 2007), p. 297.

21. *Hansard*, House of Commons Debates, vol. 80, cols. 1421–30, 7 March 1916.

22. D. Lloyd George, *War Memoirs* (London: Odhams, 1938), pp. 635–8 on Churchill; p. 322–6 on Haig and the Somme.

23. 'What is the use of being War Secretary if there is no war?' wondered Churchill, when offered the post. 'If we thought there was going to be a war we wouldn't appoint you War Secretary' was Bonar Law's rejoinder. Brendon, *Churchill: A Brief Life*, p. 91.

Further Reading

W. S. Churchill, *The World Crisis, 1911–1918*, 5 vols. (London: Thornton Butterworth, 1923–9)

A. D. Gibb, *With Winston Churchill at the Front / by Captain X* (London: Gowans and Gray, 1924)

M. Gilbert, [OB] *Winston S. Churchill*, vol. 3, *The Challenge of War 1914–1916* (London: William Heinemann Ltd, 1971)

M. Gilbert, [CV] *Winston S. Churchill*, vol. 3: Companion, part I, Documents, July 1914–April 1915 (London: Heinemann, 1972)

P. Hart, *Gallipoli* (London: Profile, 2013)

D. Lloyd George, *War Memoirs* (London: Odhams, 1938)

S. McMeekin, *The Ottoman Endgame: War, Revolution and the Making of the Modern Middle East, 1908–1923* (London: Penguin, 2015)

8
_____

Churchill, Art and Politics

On the evening of 28 April 1949 Sir Alfred Munnings, then president of the Royal Academy (PRA), London, addressed an audience of the
great and the good at Burlington House. During his now infamous
presidential speech, which was broadcast live on the BBC, Munnings
delivered an uninhibited denouncement of 'the follies and excesses of
modern art'.[1] Raising his voice against the rain thundering on the roof,
the PRA lambasted modern artists:

> I find myself a President of a body of men who are what I call
> shilly-shallying. They feel that there is something in this so-called
> modern art ... this affected juggling, this following of what shall
> we call it – the School of Paris.[2]

He raged against those who were 'helped by foolish men ... encouraging
all this damned nonsense'.[3] Henri Matisse, Pierre-Auguste Renoir and
Pablo Picasso were singled out as the proponents of 'this nonsense'. On
the last named, Churchill, who was sitting next to Munnings during his
tirade, was drawn into the fray by Munnings' suggestion that the two
shared the same view on the most famous artist in the world.

> Winston Churchill. He, too, is with me because . . .. And I know he is
> behind me because he once said to me, 'Alfred, if you met Picasso
> coming down the street, would you join with me in kicking his
> something, something, something . . .' (*Laughter*). I said, 'Yes sir,
> I would!' (*More laughter*).[4]

Churchill is said to have later rebuked Munnings for revealing and
misrepresenting a private conversation.[5] However, this unfortunate
episode raises questions about Churchill's views on modern art, as

a spectator, a writer and a practitioner. The following essay will explore, chronologically, various themes within Churchill's relationship with art: his encounter with painting, his mentors and influences, painting, politics and the tension between tradition and modernism in the art of his age, the reception of his works, and the question of the amateur versus the professional artist.

As a practitioner of painting, Churchill's own works have largely been studied only to a limited degree, mainly by Churchill enthusiasts and family members, therefore this aspect of Churchill's life has remained marginal to the study of his legacy in the twentieth century. This is due, in part, to Churchill's own commentary on his painting as a 'pastime'; historians have engaged with Churchill's art along the lines the artist himself laid out. As David Coombs has written, the fact that Churchill 'painted because he wanted to, and not because it was a way of making a living, leads some people to dismiss him as an amateur, with the corollary that his work cannot be taken seriously'.[6]

This limited approach also overlooks his painterly interests in the broader context of the history of art in the twentieth century. Moreover, the narrative of Churchill as a recreational painter ignores the fact that he was in correspondence with some of the most highly regarded painters of his time, among them Sir John Lavery RA, Richard Walter Sickert and Sir William Nicholson. Furthermore, an interpretation of Churchill as a 'hobbyist' painter would also seem at odds with his work being very successfully presented in public and private galleries, as well as his being made an Honorary Academician Extraordinary at the Royal Academy, London, and reviewed by critics and art historians, including Thomas Bodkin, Ernst Gombrich and John Rothenstein. In short, then, as David Cannadine has recently suggested, 'Churchill's involvement with oils, brushes, easels and canvases was more complex and revealing than his own writings on these subjects suggest.'[7]

Motivations

It has been argued that perspective and colour, light and shade gave Churchill respite from dark worries, heavy burdens and the clatter of political strife – that painting was the perfect antidote to his 'black dog' of depression. It is clear that painting initially came as a source of respite from the stresses of Churchill's military career. His encounter with painting began after he had thrown himself into military strategy during the First World War. As first lord of the admiralty, Churchill was prematurely held personally responsible for the Dardanelles campaign, 1915–16. His initial attempt to secure the Dardanelles Strait by ships alone proved unsuccessful and led to the costly and equally ill-fated Allied landings on the Gallipoli peninsula. As a result, he was sacked from the Admiralty and subsequently resigned from government. His career seemed in tatters and his public reputation was only partly rehabilitated by the Dardanelles commission, which concluded that he was not personally responsible for the failure of the operation. During this period Churchill was preparing to defend himself against charges of incompetent and reckless leadership:

> I had long hours of utterly unwonted leisure in which to contemplate the frightful unfolding of the War. At a moment when every fibre of my being was inflamed to action, I was forced to remain a spectator of the tragedy, placed cruelly in a front seat. And then it was the Muse of Painting came to my rescue.[8]

It was by way of his sister-in-law's watercolours while staying at Hoe Farm, Surrey that painting first drew his attention – Churchill having previously claimed that he had demonstrated no appreciation of art at any time during the first forty years of his life. His London neighbour, Hazel Lavery, encouraged him to be bold and take up the more robust medium of oil paints: 'Painting! What are you hesitating about? …. Splash into the turpentine, wallop into the blue and white, frantic flourish on the palette – clean no longer.' He responded, 'Anyone could see that [the canvas] could not hit back. No evil fate avenged the jaunty violence. The canvas grinned in helplessness before me. The spell was broken.'[9] The episode evidently had an emotionally cathartic effect on Churchill: 'Everyone knows the feelings with which one stands shivering on the spring-board, the shock when a friendly foe steals up behind and hurls you into the flood, and the ardent glow which thrills you as you emerge breathless from the plunge.'[10]

Churchill would go on to draw an analogy between painting and military leadership when he wrote:

> In all battles two things are usually required of the Commander-in-Chief [firstly,] to make a good plan for his army and, secondly, to keep a strong reserve. Both these are also obligatory upon the painter. To make a plan, thorough reconnaissance of the country where the battle

is to be fought is needed . . .. But in order to make this plan, the General must not only reconnoitre the battle-ground, he must study the achievements of the great Captains of the past. He must bring the observations he has collected in the field into comparison with the treatment of similar incidents by famous chiefs . . .. But it is in the use and withholding of their reserve that the great commanders have generally excelled. After all, when once the last reserve has been thrown in, the commander's part is played. If that does not win the battle, he has nothing else to give. The event must be left to luck and to the fighting troops. But these last, in the absence of high direction, are apt to get into sad confusion, all mixed together in a nasty mess, without order or plan – and consequently without effect. Mere mass count no more. The largest brush, the brightest colours, cannot even make an impression. The pictorial battlefield becomes a sea of mud mercifully veiled by the fog of war.[11]

Churchill's engagement with painting would become inseparable from his military and political ambitions in a number of ways; through the visual politics of his art, through his use of art as a means of cultural diplomacy and via his political engagement with the art and the institutions to which he was affiliated. Churchill would eventually produce over 500 canvases, while crediting the practice with helping him to hone his visual acuity, powers of observation and memory. The 'pastime' would flourish, and perhaps even, as some commentators have suggested, assist him as he furthered his career as a writer, orator and politician.

Churchill was further encouraged to develop his new-found passion for painting by the Laverys under the supervision of Sir John, a technically highly skilled painter who had risen to prominence as an artist of the aristocratic life. Lavery had studied in London and Paris, enjoying great success as a fashionable portrait painter in Paris and Berlin in the early 1900s. He was commissioned to produce a portrait of Churchill in May 1915. As a consequence, Churchill became a regular visitor to his neighbour's studio on Cromwell Place, London. This contact deepened Churchill's artistic impulse. While attending the studio, he painted a number of canvases, including a portrait of Lavery at his easel in a 'singular sitter's eye view' of the artist – which Churchill gifted to his friend. The painting was later loaned to the Royal Society of Portrait Painters for their annual exhibition at the Grafton Galleries, London in 1919. This was the first recorded public showing of a painting by Churchill.

Lavery would later write of the reciprocity of their friendship, 'we have often stood up to the same motif, and in spite of my trained eye and knowledge of possible difficulties, he, with characteristic fearlessness and freedom from convention, has time and again shown me how I should do things. Had he chosen painting instead of statesmanship, I believe he would have been a great master with the brush, and as P. R. A. would have given stimulus to the art world.'[12]

Art, Politics, Diplomacy and War

It was at Lavery's suggestion that Churchill gave a short speech at the opening of an exhibition at the New Burlington Galleries in London on 27 July 1937. The show was devoted to 'Sea Power in Art' and included paintings of Royal Navy ships and the British merchant marine. A few days prior, on 19 July 1937, an exhibition entitled *Entartete Kunst* had opened at the Institute of Archaeology in the Hofgarten, Munich, Germany. The day before the exhibition opened, Hitler delivered

Figure 8.1 *Tower of the Koutoubia Mosque* by Churchill, January 1943 (CAC, Churchill Heritage Collection, CHHE C381). Reproduced courtesy of Churchill Heritage Ltd.

a speech declaring 'merciless war' on cultural disintegration by attacking the 'chatterboxes, dilettantes and art swindlers'. The so-called Degenerate Art was defined as artworks that 'insult German feeling or destroy or confuse natural form or simply reveal an absence of adequate manual and artistic skill'. Hitler had denounced all such work as 'Jewish' or 'Bolshevik'. Nazi authorities had confiscated some 17,000 works of modernist art from German museums over the same summer, works by German and non-German artists including Klee, Mondrian and Picasso.

In his speech at the opening of the 'Sea Power' exhibition, Churchill invoked 'a master of propaganda' who has 'favoured us with his views on art'. These views, he continued, contained 'very drastic and formidable pronouncements'. He stopped short of defending modern art but added that 'I would feel it a very hazardous employment in some countries to be an amateur artist. If you had only the alternatives of being hung if your picture were accepted or hanged if it were rejected.'[13] Despite the fact that he did not appreciate modern art and abstract painting, Churchill understood that freedom of artistic expression was essential to any society that valued liberty.

In the following year, Churchill spoke at the Royal Academy, London, where he offered a carefully balanced view on the relationship between tradition and novelty in art. He remarked on the 'disaster' that would abound if a 'particular school of artistic thought' were to take control of the machinery of the cultural institution. 'In this hard material age of brutal force we ought indeed to cherish the arts.' Churchill spoke of the Academy's responsibility to 'hold a middle course between tradition and innovation'. He argued that 'Without tradition, art is a flock of sheep without a shepherd.' Conversely, 'Without innovation, it is a corpse.' But innovation, Churchill went on, had its limits: 'it is not the function of the Royal Academy to run wildly after novelty'. Now, more than ever, he believed, it was the purpose of the Academy to give 'strong, precious and enduring aid which can be given to British painting and sculpture'.[14] As David Cannadine has observed, Churchill's sympathies were with conservatives, rather than the modernists, 'but he took care to be tactful'.[15]

From late 1939 to mid-1945, during the intervening war years, Churchill put his own painting practice on hold. The exception was a single canvas produced in January 1943, entitled *Tower of the Koutoubia*

Mosque, a view of Marrakesh rising towards the peaks of the Atlas Mountains (Figure 8.1).

Churchill and his US counterpart, Franklin Roosevelt, had attended the Casablanca Conference, an Allied strategy conference, where Churchill was able to convince the American president to take a five-hour drive to a place he termed the 'Paris of the Sahara', having fallen for it during a wilderness years painting trip in the winter of 1935–6. He even managed to have the wheelchair-bound Roosevelt conveyed to the top of the tower in the place where they stayed – an oasis called Villa Taylor in what is now the Gueliz district – as he wanted him to witness the sunset over the Atlas Mountains. He would later gift the painting to the US president as a memento of their time together. This was both an act of friendship and political diplomacy at the outset of the 'special relationship'.[16]

Tower of the Koutoubia Mosque captures a view over the Marrakesh incorporating its most famous landmarks, with the tower of the Koutoubia Mosque in front of the snow-capped Atlas Mountains. The tiny figures in the foreground give the scene a sense of scale, set against the rising peaks in the far distance. The scene is drenched in golden afternoon light falling on the ochre-coloured buildings. The city is suffused with pink and purple shadows raking across the façade of the city walls, which recede into the greenery of palms, directing the viewer's gaze upwards to the high peaks of the mountains beyond. The purple mountains are dusted with snow, which is contrasted with the rich blue of the gradient sky. The painting adopts a palette of sandy pinks, azure greens and the deep blues of the desert sky. The brushwork is rapid and broken into separate dabs in order to render the fleeting daylight.

Influences

The painting offers insight into Churchill's most important artistic influences, both modern and traditional. Having discovered Morocco in late 1935, Churchill enjoyed the warmth, the sunlight and the views of the dramatic North African landscape. He considered the paintings produced there 'a cut above anything I have ever done so far'.[17] Sir John Lavery had established a winter studio in Morocco in 1903, in Tangier. The pioneering French artist Henri Matisse had also visited the country in 1912, where the culture had had a similarly profound impact on his work. Each of the painters was inspired by the luminous North African light and completed many important works during that time.

The work of Matisse, and the Impressionists before him, had a profound effect on the work of Churchill. Indeed, the impact of the modern movement cannot be overemphasised, as Churchill himself wrote:

> Have not Manet and Monet, Cézanne and Matisse, rendered to painting something of the same service which Keats and Shelley gave to poetry after the solemn and ceremonious literary perfections of the eighteenth century? They have brought back to the pictorial art a new draught of *joie de vivre*; and the beauty of their work is instinct with gaiety, and floats in sparkling air. I do not expect these masters would particularly appreciate my defence, but I must avow an increasing attraction to their work.[18]

The fascination with the techniques of Monet, and those painters who followed Impressionism, is clearly evident in Churchill's own paintings, and remained an enduring legacy throughout his practice. This is made clear in his own account of those who inspired his paintings:

> Chance led me one autumn to a secluded nook on the Cote d'Azur, between Marseilles and Toulon, and there I fell in with one or two painters who revelled in the methods of the Modern French School. These were disciples of Cézanne. They view Nature as a mass of shimmering light in which forms and surfaces are comparatively unimportant, indeed hardly visible, but which glean and glows with beautiful harmonies and contrasts of colour . . .. Now I must try to represent it by innumerable small separate lozenge-shaped patches of colour – often pure colour – so that it looked more like a tessellated pavement than a marine painting. It sounds curious. All the same, do not be in a hurry to reject the method. Go back a few yards and survey the results. Each of the little points of colour is now playing his part in the general effect.[19]

Although originating in France, Impressionism had great influence overseas, and included artists working in Britain, among them Richard Walter Sickert; he had developed a personal version of Impressionism, which favoured a muted colour palette, for his portrayals of the London music halls.

During the late 1920s Churchill had taken detailed advice and instruction from Sickert. Churchill's wife, Clementine, introduced him to the German/Danish artist who had been a friend of her family in her youth. The two men got along so well that Churchill wrote to his wife that, 'I am really thrilled by the field he is opening to me. I see my way to paint far better pictures than I ever thought possible before. He is really giving me a new lease of life as a painter.'[20]

It was Sickert who had passed on his enthusiasm for French painters such as Degas, Corot and others. Thereafter, Churchill spent years scrutinising the works of other painters, such as Camille Pissarro (whom Clementine had met in Paris). Collectively, what all of these painters have in common is the subject of the most famous remark by Cézanne that, 'Painting from Nature is not copying the object; it is realising one's sensation.' And, as a poem is made of words arranged on a page, then painting too should be seen as ordered patches on a flat, blank surface. Here, painting's task was not to describe but to express. By this means, colour could claim the sensibility of emotion itself.

It was Sickert who taught Churchill to work directly from photographs, which served as both preliminary material for paintings and as an aide-memoire for later use, for example when completing a landscape later in this studio. The artist also instructed him on how to use a 'magic lantern' to project a negative or slide directly on to the canvas, thereby negating the need for draftsmanship. For the most part, Churchill was drawn to scenes of interiors, in the landscape or of the sea, as well as still-life compositions, for his paintings. Yet, under Sickert's mentoring, Churchill painted a number of portraits based on photographs, rendering a particularly striking image of Clementine in 1955.

Sickert, and later Sir William Nicholson, gave Churchill extensive technical advice. Both artists would write down instructions on methods and for the handling of oil paints. As with the Impressionists, Churchill would often paint directly onto a white canvas with no ground colour, sketching out the composition with thin lines in blue paint, after which he laid down colours with larger brushes. His brushstrokes were loose, open and direct, as he tried to capture moments in time with the fleeting effects of lights and shadow – which excited him most. Thus, his paintings had to be executed swiftly; after a few hours the atmospheric effects on the given scene would change dramatically.

Nicholson

Sir William Nicholson was initially commissioned by friends of the Churchills to paint a conversational piece of Sir Winston and his wife Clementine for their silver wedding anniversary. The artist started visiting Chartwell around 1933 and 'stayed for many months ... [leaving] innumerable funny little drawings around the house'.[21] The pair instantly struck up a friendship.

During his stay, Nicholson and Churchill would sometimes paint together, side by side, which enabled Winston to consult the artist on the many challenges he faced in painting. Nicholson had a profound effect on Churchill's output. Significantly, Nicholson differed from many other artists of his time in his adamant refusal to fit into any of the 'schools' or artistic 'narratives' of the period – though his son Ben would go on to define Modernism in Britain. Nicholson's effect on Churchill is rendered through his use of a subtler, quieter palette of colours, which were atypical of Churchill's output prior to this period.

Hitherto, a characteristic of Churchill's paintings was his bold use of vibrant colours, sometimes straight from the tube. His enthusiasm for a vivid palette is noted in *Painting as a Pastime* where he wrote, 'I cannot pretend to be impartial about colours. I rejoice with the brilliant ones and am genuinely sorry for the poor browns.'[22] Walter Sickert had urged Churchill to subdue his palette in the belief that it would improve his work, which had limited success. Churchill noted his independence from Sickert's influence, telling Sir John Rothenstein, then director of the Tate Gallery, that although Sickert 'had imparted to me all his considered wisdom about painting ... I wasn't an apt pupil, for I rejoiced in the highest lights and brightest colours'.[23] It was only under Nicholson's mentorship that Churchill adopted a much more restrained and sensitive palette for his work. This shift was encouraged by Clementine who, when writing to Churchill while he was in France, asked, 'Are you keeping [your paintings] cool and pale *à la* Nicholson?'[24] Significantly, Churchill would later suggest, 'I think the person who taught me most about painting was William Nicholson.'[25]

It has been suggested that, arguably, Churchill reached his peak as a painter in the 1930s, which was his most prodigious period and the time when the influence of Nicholson was at its greatest.[26]

Exhibitions

In the post-war years, Churchill's relationship with the Royal Academy became much closer, largely thanks to initiatives of its president, Sir Alfred Munnings. Munnings was regarded as one of the finest equine painters of his generation. He was spontaneous, naturally gifted and highly prolific, working from both life and photography. Munnings had been made PRA in 1944 and revived the Royal Academy Summer Exhibition following a pause during the war years. He was a great supporter of Churchill's art, relentlessly encouraging him to show at the Academy. Hitherto, Churchill's only outing had been an exhibition in Paris in 1921, when he'd used the pseudonym of Charles Morin. Consequently, the show sold four of the five landscapes for thirty pounds each.

In response to Munnings, the modest artist in Churchill would only hand in works with the rest of the 'outsiders' (common entries) under a pseudonym: 'Unless you treat me as an outsider and put my work in with the rest to go before the selecting committee, I do not wish to send', Churchill wrote to Munnings. Using the pseudonym 'David Winter', Churchill submitted paintings for the Royal Academy Summer Exhibition in 1947 and 1948, having works selected each year. While Munnings was its president, the Royal Academy voted unanimously to honour Churchill as a Royal Academician Extraordinary, in consideration of his 'services to ... achievements in the Art of Painting'. From then on Churchill had a right as a member to have a painting in the annual exhibition.

It was also at this time that Churchill chose to republish *Painting as a Pastime*. The text had first appeared as a two-part essay published in *Strand Magazine* in December 1921 and January 1922 and had included reproductions of seventeen of his paintings. The essay was written in a light-hearted, self-deprecating tone. The book was published by Odhams Press and well received by critics and the general public. It also sold well in the USA, where it was published in 1950 and sold over 25,000 copies.

Painting became an essential part of Churchill's Anglo-American fame. As further evidence of the 'special relationship' between the UK and the USA, an exhibition was conceived by Joyce C. Hall of Hallmark cards in conversation with President Eisenhower. Churchill received a letter from the latter who wrote, 'a travelling exhibition of your paintings in the United States would not only attract a good deal of attention among all people here interested in painting, but I am certain it would serve in a very definite way to strengthen the friendship between our two countries …. The tour would create a wave of good will across our country that would be both exciting and valuable.'[27]

Until this time, Churchill had been reluctant to exhibit his paintings. This was the first solo show of his canvases, and it proved an enormous success. The exhibition opened at the Nelson Gallery of Art, Kansas City, in 1958. It displayed thirty-five of Churchill's paintings and the president wrote the foreword to the exhibition catalogue. Among the visitors was Eisenhower's predecessor, President Truman, who pronounced the pictures, 'Damn good. At least you can tell what they are and that is more than you can say for a lot of these modern painters.'[28] In any case, it was a record-breaking success.

In Kansas the show was extended for two days. The *Kansas City Times* reported that it was 'the first time [the gallery] opened on a Monday in its history'.[29] The paintings were seen by 25,500 visitors, with 6,019 in a single day. It then went on to tour extensively in both the USA and Canada. The Detroit Institute of Arts, Metropolitan Museum of Art, Smithsonian Institution, Dallas Museum of Fine Arts and the Museum of Art of the Rhode Island School of Design all took part in exhibiting the works. However, some galleries were dismissive; the assistant director of the Carnegie Institute in Pittsburgh said, 'I understand that Churchill is a terrific bricklayer too, but nobody is exhibiting bricks this season'; the director of the Art Institute of Chicago, Daniel Catton Rich, stated that 'We have certain professional standards …. We do not show the work of amateurs unless they have been passed by professional juries, and we do not feel that Mr. Churchill's work rates as professional.'[30] Boston also rejected the idea. In Canada the exhibition toured through Toronto, Montreal, Fredericton and Vancouver.

A request came from Australian Prime Minister Robert Menzies to take the show to Australia, mentioning that New Zealand were also interested. As with the US president, Menzies wrote the foreword to the catalogue and added one of his own paintings by Churchill to the exhibition, which toured through Canberra and Sydney, as well as The Queensland National Art Gallery, Brisbane; The National Gallery of Victoria, Melbourne; The Tasmanian Museum and Art Gallery, Hobart; The National Gallery of South Australia, Adelaide; and The

Art Gallery of Western Australia, Perth. In New Zealand the paintings were displayed in Dunedin, Christchurch, Wellington and Auckland.

The exhibition came to London the following year, in March 1959, in response to an earlier approach from the president of the Royal Academy. Churchill had hitherto resisted the idea of a solo show in his lifetime but, emboldened by the success of the shows in North America, Australia and New Zealand, he relented. The expanded show contained sixty-two of Churchill's paintings, including the thirty-five that had been on world tour. As in other parts of the world, the exhibition proved a major success with the public, attracting 141,000 visitors in the five months the paintings were on show. Moreover, the exhibition was rehung across three rooms, rather than the original two, to accommodate the number of visitors. The president of the Royal Academy suggested that the exhibition tour the UK, offering Manchester, Cardiff, Glasgow, Edinburgh and Belfast as possible venues. Churchill declined, as he did not wish to 'prolong their absence'.

Amateur or Professional?

The reviews of the show were on the whole complimentary. David Carritt in the *Evening Standard* wrote 'There is nothing intellectual in Sir Winston's painting, but there is nothing stupid either.' He continued by offering a summary of Churchill's influences:

> He belongs to a generation that idolised Sargent and Lavery;
> dangerous models whose chief virtue was a sparkling illusionism . . . .
> But he soon became aware of their limitations. He began to look at Sir
> William Nicholson and Augustus John. From them he learned to
> paint with subtle simplicity in clear bold outlines and areas of
> unbroken sonorous colours. Monet seems to have become one of his
> heroes, his *Rocks Near Cannes* (1948) is a brilliant tribute to the artist.
> He even seems to have looked long and hard at the landscapes of
> Andre Derain and Pierre Bonnard, at a time when other English
> Academicians considered the post-Impressionists a bunch of
> bungling imposters.[31]

Others were less forgiving of Churchill's 'lack of the professionally trained painter's ability', while the British *Daily Mail* newspaper focussed on the commercial value of such works, in monetary terms, rather than their artistic worth: 'The P.R.A. tells me that the pictures are insured for an agreed middle value of £1200 each, or £63,000 in all ... truly a remarkable sum for an amateur.'[32]

Ultimately, though, as the critic Ernst Gombrich suggested, art criticism can never be truly objective:

> No critic is free of prejudices in the original sense of the word, as prejudgements. When it comes to the work of an amateur who is also one of the most famous and controversial figures of his age, objectivity becomes doubly impossible. His fame enlists our interest but makes us suspicious; his amateur status spikes the critic's guns. To judge these paintings by professional standards would be unfair; to make allowances would be patronising. No wonder that crowds flocked, but critics frowned, when a group of Churchill's landscapes and still lifes toured the United States.[33]

Gombrich goes on to suggest that Churchill's paintings have their value as personal documents, but raises the question of whether they are art. Many other commentators have been forthright by stating that Churchill was not a great painter. In the end, it remains questionable whether it matters if his paintings may be considered 'great' or not; what matters is the astonishing fact that Churchill chose to paint at all. It meant that painting became inseparable from his thinking as a politician, strategist and statesman.

As for Churchill's position on modern artists, the former director of the Tate, John Rothenstein, wrote in 1970: 'Always retentive of matters that annoyed him, he referred, without mentioning Munnings by name, to his association of himself with abuse of Picasso and Matisse, and as though by way of an additional repudiation he described how on a recent visit to France he had been studying books on Cézanne, Van Gogh and certain of their contemporaries.'[34] As if by reciprocation, it has been claimed that Picasso said: 'If Churchill were a painter by profession, he'd have no trouble making a living.'[35]

Notes

1. Sir Alfred Munnings, Presidential Speech, 28 April 1949. In T. Wilcox, *Munnings vs the Moderns* (Manchester: Manchester City Art Gallery, 1986), p. 11.
2. Munnings, Presidential Speech, p. 11.
3. Munnings, Presidential Speech, p. 11.
4. Munnings, Presidential Speech, p. 12.

5. 'I … heard with surprise your statement that we were walking up the street together when I spoke to you about kicking Picasso if we met him. I do not think we have ever walked up a street together, and anyhow this is not the sort of statement that should be attributed to me. I know you speak on the impulse of the moment, but I protest none-the-less against these utterances.' Churchill to Sir Alfred Munnings, 8 May 1949. In M. Soames, *Winston Churchill: His Life as a Painter* (Boston, MA: Houghton Mifflin, 1990), p. 157.

6. D. Coombs, *Churchill: His Paintings* (London: Hamish Hamilton, 1967), p. 12.

7. D. Cannadine, *Churchill: The Statesman as Artist* (London: Bloomsbury Continuum, 2018), p. 2.

8. W. S. Churchill, *Painting as a Pastime* (London: Odhams Press, 1948), p. 16.

9. Churchill, *Painting as a Pastime*, p. 17.

10. Churchill, *Painting as a Pastime*, p. 18.

11. Churchill, *Painting as a Pastime*, p. 20.

12. J. Lavery, *The Life of a Painter* (London: Cassell & Company Ltd., 1940), p. 18.

13. W. S. Churchill, 'Sea Power in Art', in Cannadine, *Churchill: Statesman as Artist*, p. 90.

14. W. S. Churchill, 'We Ought Indeed Cherish the Arts', in Cannadine, *Churchill: Statesman as Artist*, p. 94.

15. Cannadine, *Churchill: Statesman as Artist*, p. 26.

16. Churchill sometimes gave paintings as gifts to people he admired. Presidents Roosevelt, Truman and Eisenhower, Viscount Montgomery and General George C. Marshall were among those who received such gifts.

17. M. Soames, *Speaking for Themselves: The Personal Letters of Winston and Clementine Churchill* (London: Doubleday, 1998), p. 411.

18. Churchill, *Painting as a Pastime*, p. 27.

19. Churchill, *Painting as a Pastime*, p. 25.

20. Soames, *Speaking for Themselves*, p. 309.

21. D. Coombs with M. Churchill, *Sir Winston Churchill's Life Through Painting* (London: Chaucer, 2003), p. 146.

22. Churchill, *Painting as a Pastime*, p. 24.

23. Soames, *Winston Churchill: His Life as a Painter*, p. 175.

24. Soames, *Winston Churchill*, p. 86.

25. Soames, *Winston Churchill*, p. 84.

26. S. Schwartz, *William Nicholson* (New Haven, CT: Yale University Press, 2004), p. 137.

27. Coombs with Churchill, *Sir Winston Churchill: His Life Through His Paintings*, p. 199.

28. Coombs with Churchill, *Sir Winston Churchill*, p. 202.

29. *Kansas City Times*, 1 February 1958.

30. *The Ottawa Citizen*, 22 April 1958.

31. D. Carritt, *Evening Standard*, 11 March 1959, p. 5.

32. P. Jeannerat, *The Daily Mail*, 11 March 1959.

33. E. Gombrich, Winston Churchill as Painter and Critic. *The Atlantic*, vol. 215 (1965), pp. 90–3.

34. J. Rothenstein, A Great Presiding Presence. In Cannadine, *Churchill: Statesman as Artist*, p. 168.

35. Q. Reynolds, *All About Winston Churchill* (London: W. H. Allen, 1964), p. 128.

Further Reading

D. Cannadine, *Churchill: The Statesman as Artist* (London: Bloomsbury Continuum, 2018)

W. S. Churchill, *Painting as a Pastime* (London: Odhams Press, 1948)

D. Coombs, *Churchill: His Paintings* (London: Hamish Hamilton, 1967)

D. Coombs with M. Churchill, *Sir Winston Churchill's Life Through His Paintings* (London: Chaucer, 2003)

9

Churchill's Economics

When Stanley Baldwin invited Winston Churchill to be chancellor of the exchequer in 1924, he feigned astonishment. 'I should have liked to have answered, "Will the bloody duck swim?" – but as it was a formal and important conversation I replied, "This fulfils my ambition."' In reality, Churchill was gratified to follow his father to the Treasury and his appointment was not surprising.[1] Peter Clarke remarks that Churchill came to the role 'better prepared than predecessors like Lloyd George, Baldwin, or even Neville Chamberlain', and that 'if one is looking for consistency in his political career in the period up to 1930, it is to be found more clearly in his economic ideas than almost anywhere else'.[2]

Liberalism, Free Trade and Individual Responsibility

Above all, Churchill's economic ideas rested on free trade – the issue on which he joined the Liberals in 1904, and a major reason for Baldwin's invitation. Support for a general tariff contributed to the Conservatives' defeat in 1923, and Churchill returned to the Party when it abandoned the policy. Baldwin needed to show that the Party was genuinely committed to free trade – and Churchill made his position clear during the election in 1924. 'I am still a free trader and opposed to the protective taxation of food and to a general tariff.'[3]

Before the war, Churchill accepted that duties imposed for revenue did not breach free trade principles. Otherwise, duties must be 'based on the commercial principle of the equal treatment of all nations, and the most-favoured nation treatment from those nations in return'.[4] Free trade made Britain 'the richest nation in the world'. Low costs for raw materials gave a competitive edge and led to expanding trade based on comparative advantage in a multilateral system. 'There can be no exportation without a corresponding importation .... The goods which are bought and sold between great Powers are not paid for in money. They are exchanged one with the other.' The system was self-regulating, for imbalances were corrected through the gold standard. If Britain bought too much from overseas, the deficit was covered by shipments of bullion and an increase in the bank rate which 'immediately corrects and arrests the very trade which has given rise to the disparity'. He accepted the self-correcting specie-flow mechanism of classical economics.[5]

Free trade guaranteed dynamic, competitive firms, whereas tariff reform – a duty on imports with a preference granted to goods from the Empire – meant the 'small manufacturer ... will find himself bought out – absorbed, like in America and Germany, in some vast syndicate – no longer his own master and an independent man, but the salaried servant of a great combine'.[6] His line followed the economic analysis of Alfred Marshall who stressed a combination of free trade with cooperative competition between independent, small manufacturers in industrial districts as superior to the high managerial costs of large, unresponsive, firms.[7] Churchill followed liberal political economy from J. S. Mill onwards in fearing that private monopolies in gas or railways might replicate the monopolies of chartered companies and impose a tax on the consumer.[8] He argued for municipal enterprise:

> I am on the side of those who think that a greater collective element should be introduced into the State and municipalities. I should like to see the State undertaking new functions, stepping forward into new spheres of activity, particularly in services which are in the nature of monopolies. There is a wide field for State enterprise. But when we are told to exalt and admire a philosophy which destroys individualism and seeks to replace it absolutely by collectivism, I say that is a monstrous and imbecile conception.

As Churchill remarked, 'Socialism attacks property, Liberalism attacks monopoly.'[9]

An open economy based on competition led to cheapness and efficiency that benefited workers as consumers. Churchill rejected the counter-argument that foreign competition threatened workers as producers. Rather, tariffs 'warped and restricted the growth of the industries of the nations who have adopted them' and prevented dynamic adjustments of industry. Free trade created market incentives for 'readjustment of labour and redistribution of capital are more easy, where enterprise is more varied and elastic'. In Churchill's view, old countries lacked new resources and therefore needed to look beyond basic industries that faced competition from countries with abundant resources, and 'gradually to move on to the more complicated and secondary processes of manufacture, and in the higher grades of manufacture to obtain the expansion of their trade which they need'. Competitive adaptation meant that 'our industries move forward into those higher grades where labour is more skilled, more varied, more generously rewarded, and by proficiency in which an old country can alone maintain that "leadership" in respect to quality vital to her industrial strength'.[10]

To Churchill, free trade 'enshrines certain central truths, economic truths, and, I think, moral truths'.[11] Monopoly and tariffs corrupted the state by 'predatory interests' that turned politics into 'a cash transaction throughout, with large profits and quick delivery. Every little would-be monopolist in the country is going to have his own association to run his own particular trade.' The result would be 'a deadly injury to the purity of English public life'. Tariffs would also corrupt the Empire by turning it into a matter of economic calculation, for 'the British Empire is held together by moral not by material forces'. Far from strengthening imperial ties, 'a policy of Preferential tariffs will lead to much friction between the Colonies and the mother country, and if it is based upon the taxation of food, will estrange the masses of our countrymen from the Imperial idea'. Any benefits from tariff reform would be 'very small compared with the enormous boon of keeping the field of Colonial politics separate from the social and economic issues on which Parties in this country are so fiercely divided'.[12]

What the Empire needed was social rather than tariff reform:

> I see little glory in an Empire which can rule the waves and is unable to flush its sewers. The difficulty has been so far that the people who have looked abroad have paid no attention to domestic matters, and those who are centred on domestic matters regard the Empire merely as an encumbrance. What is wanted is a well-balanced policy ... something that will coordinate development and expansion with the progress of social comfort and health.[13]

Social reform is considered in Peter Sloman's Chapter 5 in this volume. Here, we shall note that it was designed, like free trade and the attack on monopoly, to sustain the 'mainspring' of society – 'competitive selection' which 'is all we have got between us and barbarism'.

> I do not want to see impaired the vigour of competition, but we can do much to mitigate the consequences of failure. We want to draw a line below which we will not allow persons to live and labour, yet above which they may compete with all the strength of their manhood. We want to have free competition upwards; we decline to allow free competition to run downwards. We do not want to pull down the structure of science and civilisation but to spread a net over the abyss.[14]

Social reform would encourage self-reliance rather than replace prudence, just as free trade was intended to encourage industrial adaptation. Economic fluctuations beyond the control of working families would overwhelm their own efforts, but the state could stimulate self-reliance 'by giving them for the first time a practical assurance that those efforts will be crowned with success'.[15]

This approach was complemented by policies to remove imperfections in markets. Monopolists with the power to exploit consumers needed to be restrained, as did employers of 'sweated' labour. Churchill supported trade boards that set minimum wages and cited Marshall in support: the gross returns received by an employer should take account of the wear and tear on the life of the worker and on the next generation, so that – in Marshall's words – 'the replacement of inefficient and stunted human lives would be a gain of a higher order than any temporary material loss that might have been occasioned on the way'. Some employers were parasitic, for they did not pay the full costs of labour which were passed to workers and society. The laws of supply and demand alone would not secure adequate minimum standards in sweated trades, for there was no parity of bargaining. Workers were not unionised and were drawn from widows or the wives of the poorest casual labourers who lacked mobility. Neither were industrialists organised, so that any employer who paid a decent wage was undercut. Churchill cited Mill's argument that the wages of sweated labour bore no relation to the ultimate price of goods which might be an expensive luxury. The market was distorted and these trades were 'diseased', so that intervention was needed to raise 'the degenerate and parasitical portion of these trades up to the level of the most efficient branches of the trade'.[16]

Churchill also supported the use of public employment – both ordinary contracts and extraordinary relief works – to smooth trade cycles:

> There is nothing economically unsound in increasing temporarily and artificially the demand for labour during a period of temporary and artificial contraction. There is a plain need of some averaging machinery to regulate and even-up the general course of the labour market, in the same way as the Bank of England, by its bank rate, regulates and corrects the flow of business enterprise.

Further, labour exchanges could remove imperfect knowledge that put workers at a disadvantage. Modern industry had become national; labour had not and was still hired through antiquated and demoralising personal application.[17]

Churchill's political economy rested on a belief that the wide diffusion of property to 'vast numbers of persons who are holders of interest-bearing, profit-bearing, rent-earning property' provided 'the essential stability of modern States', so that any attempt to overthrow society would 'encounter an overwhelming resistance ... from the selfish power of the haves'.[18] But it was not only the widespread ownership of property that mattered. It was vital that 'property is associated in the minds of the great mass of the people with ideas of justice and of reason'.

> When and where property is associated with the idea of reward for services rendered, with the idea of recompense for high gifts and special aptitudes displayed or for faithful labour done, then property will be honoured. When it is associated with processes which are beneficial, or which at the worst are not actually injurious to the commonwealth, then property will be unmolested; but when it is associated with ideas of wrong and of unfairness, with processes of restriction and monopoly, and other forms of injury to the community, then I think you will find that property will be assailed and will be endangered.[19]

Churchill's defence of property as the source of social stability was therefore complemented by an attack on the monopoly power of land. It 'is by far the greatest of monopolies; it is a perpetual monopoly; and it is the mother of all other forms of monopoly'. It led to unearned wealth that imposed costs on enterprising members of society – like parasitic sweated trades – and personal benefit was not aligned with social costs.

Churchill denied that the same argument applied to other processes such as an increase in the value of stocks or railways, or the sale of a painting, for the unearned increment in land 'arises from a wholly sterile process, from the mere withholding of a commodity which is needed by the community'. Landowners were operating 'in restraint of trade and in conflict with the general interest', unlike higher share values or railway profits that were 'part of a natural and healthy process, by which the economic plant of the world is nourished'. By contrast, landowners gained from public investments in trams, roads, water and gas to which they did not contribute, and their high price hit the profits of industrialists and the wages of workers. This burden was a more serious threat than foreign tariffs, for 'every form of enterprise, every step in material progress, is only undertaken after the land monopolist has skimmed the cream off for himself'. Churchill looked to a new political economy in which the blessings of free trade would no longer be undermined by

> the evils of an unreformed and vicious land system. In no great country in the new world or the old have the working people yet secured the double advantage of free trade and free land together, by which I mean a commercial system and a land system from which, so far as possible, all forms of monopoly have been rigorously excluded . . .. We are met in an hour of tremendous opportunity. 'You who shall liberate the land', said Mr Cobden, 'will do more for your country than we have done in the liberation of its commerce.'[20]

Although Churchill did not attack unearned increments beyond land, he did support differentiation of the income tax between earned and unearned income:

> No one wants to penalise or to stigmatise income derived from dividends, rent, or interest; for accumulated capital, apart from monopoly, represents the exercise of thrift and prudence, qualities which are only less valuable to the community than actual service and labour. But the great difference between the two classes of income remains.[21]

Unearned income from capital continued regardless of health and active engagement in the economy; income from employment would be lost in the event of ill-health or an economic recession, and required savings or insurance to provide a safety net. It was equitable to impose a lower rate of tax to reflect this difference – and also to tax inheritances that led to passive rather than active wealth. The result, as Churchill saw, was a new attitude of the state to wealth:

> Formerly the only question of the tax-gatherer was, 'How much have you got?' …. But now a new question has arisen. We do not only ask to-day, 'How much have you got?' we also ask, 'How did you get it? Did you earn it by yourself, or has it just been left you by others? Was it gained by processes which are in themselves beneficial to the community in general, or was it gained by processes which have done no good to anyone, but only harm? Was it gained by the enterprise and capacity necessary to found a business, or merely by squeezing and bleeding the owner and founder of the business? Was it gained by supplying the capital which industry needs, or by denying, except at an extortionate price, the land which industry requires?'[22]

Churchill's political economy before 1914 rested on interventions to remove monopoly power and market imperfections that would allow 'competitive selection' by free enterprise and encourage individual responsibility. The state or collective action would sustain individualism.[23] Free trade and the gold standard were part of a self-regulating system with no role for the Treasury in managing the economy. After the war, strains appeared in this coherent set of assumptions.

Conservatism, Creative Accounting and the Return to Gold

A major concern after the war was how to handle the war debt that was attacked by Labour as a drain by parasitical rentiers on workers and active capital. Labour's solution was a capital levy – a one-off charge on all property. In 1920, Churchill supported Austen Chamberlain's tentative proposal for a levy on wartime increases in wealth as a way of establishing a 'democratic platform' and responding to complaints that the coalition government was 'too tender to trusts, plutocrats and profiteers':

> Look at the position of Capital if you fail to carry with you the working classes …. It will be said that we are in the grip of the plutocracy and it will be said with a certain truth. It will be very hard anyway to hold this immense electorate by reason and not by force and still hold the capitalist system. … The present taxation is crushing, and my principal aim is to rectify our finances and give

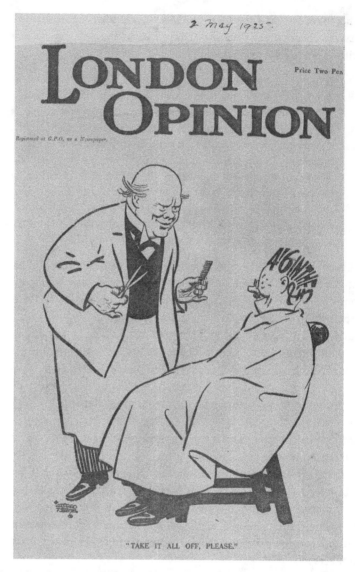

Figure 9.1 The new chancellor depicted in tax-cutting mode, May 1925 (CAC, Broadwater Collection, BRDW 1 Press 26).

remission to the income tax payers . . .. If we lose this chance, we become a plutocratic and not a national Government – the chance of getting the honest comradeship of the men who saved the country.

His plea to the Cabinet was ignored and he continued to worry about the political dangers of excessive debt service paid from high taxation.[24] In 1922, he supported the fiscally unorthodox approach of the chancellor, Robert Horne, who wished to reduce taxation to help business and maintain social reform. The only way to square the circle was to budget for a deficit and raid the sinking fund that paid off the national debt. In the event, orthodoxy was preserved when revenues recovered and produced an unexpected surplus.[25] Churchill reverted to similar ideas during his time as chancellor.

In 1921, Churchill accepted safeguarding of industry from goods dumped by foreign competitors and the protection of key industries. Otherwise, he remained loyal to free trade.[26] But his Edwardian combination of free trade and a commitment to minimum wages was starting to fracture, as he discovered in his constituency – Dundee – where competition from India led to increased demands for protection of the jute industry. Churchill rejected protection and argued that 'It was not foreign imports or foreign competition that was injuring this country as a whole . . .. It was the failure of our export trade owing to the collapse of foreign markets.' He failed to satisfy the protectionists yet offended supporters of untrammelled free trade by support for safeguarding. Divisions also opened over trade boards. In 1919, a trade board was established for jute and a minimum wage was set at the peak of the post-war boom. By 1921, employers were calling for wage cuts and abolition of the board. Churchill supported the employers and aimed to 'promote the unity of anti-socialist forces'. He wrote to Lloyd George that 'I was originally the author of this legislation, but over and again to Parliament I declared that it was to be confined to parasitic trades, and that no trade that was capable of forming an effective trade union should be subjected to this special and invidious control.' Minimum wages were inappropriate as a response to competitors paying low taxes and wages, and he had no solution other than wage cuts in Dundee and opposition to fiscal autonomy in India that would allow it to impose tariffs on British goods. Churchill had little to offer to resolve Dundee's economic problems, and could only observe that 'where competition was between peoples living under wholly different modes of life, Government would have to formulate principles of equity and economy for regulating such competition; these principles were not at present apparent to him'. His hope that a free trade economy could respond to competition by adjustment to industrial structure was falsified, and he lost Dundee in the General Election of 1922.[27] The internal contradictions of his position were less apparent in his constituency of Epping.

Churchill's tenure at the Treasury alarmed the permanent secretary, Warren Fisher, who characterised him as an irresponsible child rejecting caution in favour of spectacular schemes that would get the national finances in a mess.[28] Churchill claimed to be a reformed man, and assured Lord Salisbury that his 'maturer views of life' meant he abandoned the frontal attack on accumulated wealth. The attack on land was dropped in the coalition government and Churchill adopted a gradual policy of adjusting the tax system to create incentives for personal ambition. He continued to believe that the capitalist system and private property provided the foundation of civilisation and material well-being, and that 'an attempt to hunt down "the idle rich", whoever they are, wherever they may be found, might be attended with so much friction and injury to the general system of capital and to the freedom arising under a capitalist system that it would be more trouble than it is worth'. He believed that 'the existing system of death duties is a certain corrective against the development of a race of idle rich. If they are idle they will cease in a few generations to be rich. Further than that it is not desirable for the legislature to go.'[29] As before the war, Churchill's ambition remained 'the appeasement of class bitterness, the promotion of a spirit of cooperation, the stabilisation of our national life'.[30] This strategy could be pursued by reducing taxation of active wealth at the expense of inherited wealth and cutting the tax burden on moderately well-to-do middle-class families who were crucial to the Conservative base.

Churchill feared that the Treasury's policies of maintaining taxes and a budgetary surplus to redeem debt could lead to accusations that the government was exalting the 'Money Trust' in preference to other 'social, moral or manufacturing' interests. He argued that 'there is more in the life of a nation than the development of an immense class quartered in perpetuity upon the struggling producer of new wealth', and he was concerned that large charges of servicing the debt 'will not be allowed to continue indefinitely in a country based on an adult suffrage'. At the end of 1924 he asked the Treasury to consider conversion of the debt to a lower rate of interest or a reduction in the sinking fund, and in 1927 he proposed a forced loan at a low rate of interest.[31]

At the Treasury, Otto Niemeyer accepted that 'compared with other persons the Rentier is getting too much' and that some taxation might be appropriate. What he could not accept was a reduction in the sinking fund. To the Treasury, the sinking fund was sacrosanct and any surplus left at the end of the financial year should also be used to reduce the national debt. The Treasury argued that redemption was beneficial to industry by releasing funds from government loans and making them available for investment and economic recovery. Its position was to maintain a high level of taxation and debt redemption through cuts in expenditure.[32]

Churchill was sceptical. During his time as chancellor, the rate of redemption of the national debt was slower, and he used a number of creative accounting devices in order to give the appearance that the budget was balanced when he was, in reality, running a deficit. In 1925, he gave the net rather than gross expenditure of the government, which allowed him to appear to reduce the scale of government spending. Churchill also adopted devices to boost the government's income. He 'raided' the sinking fund, took money set aside for debt redemption and drew on the reserve of the Road Fund. By such means, Churchill was able to create sufficient freedom to modify the income tax in pursuit of economic recovery and political stability. Senior officials at the Treasury were scandalised by Churchill's creative accounting, and Montagu Norman characterised Churchill as the 'Blondin of finance'. Churchill did not dissent, remarking that his budget of 1927 was 'as good a get-out as we could get'. Even the prime minister had the honesty to inform the king that Churchill's budget was 'a mischievous piece of manipulation ... a masterpiece of ingenuity'. As Peter Clarke remarked, Churchill talked like Gladstone and behaved like Mr Micawber.[33]

Churchill realised that the Treasury's approach, for all its financial probity, might alienate taxpayers aggrieved by the high rate of extraction, and the poor and unemployed who would suffer from lower welfare spending. The Treasury's concern was predominantly with debt redemption and financial stability; Churchill had concerns for the legitimacy of the state and the need to build an electoral coalition. Discussions over adjustments to the tax regime in the budget of 1925 started with death duties, and whether they should be reduced from the high rate imposed in 1919. The Treasury thought that duties paid at death were 'psychologically a much less onerous charge' than an annual income tax, with less effect on enterprise. Churchill agreed. The rate on small and medium estates between £12,500 and £1 million was raised and the revenue devoted to cuts in income tax. The threshold for super-tax on large incomes had not been increased despite inflation, so that more members of the middle class came into liability. Churchill left the upper levels of super-tax unchanged so that very rich individuals remained 'stranded on the peaks of taxation to which they have been carried by the flood'. Cuts in taxation were concentrated on 'the lower and medium classes of Super Tax payers, giving the greatest measure of relief to the lowest class comprising professional men, small merchants and businessmen – superior brain workers of every kind'. These changes in the super-tax and death duties meant that

> The doctor, engineer and lawyer earning 3 or 4 thousand a year and with no capital will get the greatest relief; the possessor of unearned income derived from a capital estate of 2 or 3 hundred thousands, the smallest relief; while the millionaire will remain substantially liable to the existing scales of high taxation.

Meanwhile, 'the great mass of the Income Tax payers subside into the refreshing waters of the sea' through a reduction in the standard rate of income tax on the earned income of active creators compared with passive recipients of income from investments. This change would benefit the 'very large class of deserving people who have to maintain a certain status of living, who are sometimes called "the black coated working men"'. The strategy had continuities with the pre-war policy of removing 'a grave discouragement to enterprise and thrift' that would 'relieve the pressure upon the highly-creative faculties of the community'. The result would be

> an encouragement to people to bestir themselves and make more money while they are alive and bring up their heirs to do the same. The process of the creation of new wealth is beneficial to the whole community. The process of squatting on old wealth though valuable is a far less lively agent . . .. We shall never shake ourselves clear from the debts of war and break into a definitely larger period except by the energetic creation of new wealth. A premium on effort is my aim and a penalty on inertia may well be its companion.[34]

Churchill was aware that concessions to earned income and enterprise demanded a 'necessary counterpoise' so that they did not appear to benefit only the middle class. He turned to contributory widows', orphans' and old-age pensions (see Peter Sloman's Chapter 5 in this volume) as a 'means of striking the balance fairly between class and class' and giving 'millions of people a stake in the country which they will have created largely by their own contributory efforts . . .. Everyone will realise that violent disorder, confusion, revolutionary disturbance, repudiation of liabilities, injury to public credit, confiscatory finance, etc., will endanger the insurance arrangements from which the vast majority expect to derive benefits.' His aim in the budget of 1925 was to bring classes together in a society based on enterprise, self-reliance and social stability which would deal with the 'twin supreme objects of public policy . . .. Security of the home of the wage-earner against exceptional misfortune and encouragement of enterprise through a relief of the burdens resting upon industry.'[35] Churchill continued the pre-war strategy of uniting property in support of capitalism and enterprise, now purged of radical attacks on the unearned increment of land.

The budget of 1925 is remembered mainly for the return to the gold standard – an event that provoked Keynes to ponder, 'Why did he do such a silly thing?' Keynes answered his question:

> Partly perhaps, because he has no instinctive judgement to prevent him from making mistakes; partly because, lacking this instinctive judgement, he was deafened by the clamorous voices of conventional finance; and, most of all, because he was gravely misled by his experts.[36]

Churchill came to think it the 'biggest blunder' and that he was led into error by Niemeyer and Montagu Norman at the Bank, whom he came to think by 1931 deserved to be hanged.[37] The reality was more complicated.[38] Churchill was aware of the arguments against a return to gold of Keynes and Reginald McKenna, the former chancellor who was now chairman of the Midland Bank. They saw that a high bank rate to defend the exchange rate would lead to unemployment, and that deflation to bring British prices in line with the United States would lead to industrial unrest. In January 1925, Churchill and Niemeyer discussed the risks with Max Beaverbrook, who responded with an attack in the *Daily Express* on the Treasury's preference for the City over industry. It was a view with which Churchill had sympathy, as we saw over the costs of servicing the national debt. The next day, he sent 'Mr Churchill's exercise' to the Treasury and Bank. It drew on the arguments of the opponents of return and he requested 'good and effective answers to the case which I have, largely as an exercise, indicated in this note' so that he could 'answer any criticisms which may be subsequently made upon our policy'. Why, he wondered, could the existing managed currency not be continued? And the decision could not be considered only in terms of finance, for manufacturers, workers and consumers might have different concerns. A higher bank rate to defend the pound would be a 'very serious check' on trade, industry and employment, and could lead to accusations of favouring 'the special interests of finance at the expense of the special interest of production . . . . It would be difficult to rebut such a charge, the burden of which would fall upon the Chancellor of the Exchequer. Only very plain and solid advantages would justify the running of such a risk.' He sought to be instructed: 'I am ready and anxious to be convinced as far as my limited comprehension of these extremely technical matters will permit' – a statement with an element of irony.[39] It was not that Churchill was hostile to gold as part of a self-regulating system that complemented free trade. Rather, he wanted convincing arguments against the opponents of the decision to return.

Norman's response lacked substance. Gold, he asserted, was 'the best "Governor" that can be devised for a world that is still human, rather than divine'. It was 'the guarantee of good faith' and the basis for international banking and finance. He confirmed Beaverbrook's complaint in castigating opponents as ignorant, gamblers and 'antiquated industrialists' compared with the 'instructed' supporters of gold. He accepted that a higher bank rate would be needed, but he dismissed the demand for 'cheap money' as 'the Industrialists' big stick' which should be dismissed. And managed currency only worked as a prelude to a 'golden 1925'.[40] Niemeyer was more reasoned. A failure to return would lead to a loss of confidence and withdrawal of balances, a drop in the exchange rate and hence an increase in the bank rate. As a result, 'We might very easily thus reap all the disadvantages which some fear from a return to gold without any of the advantages.' He pointed out that only a few theoretical advocates of managed currency – above all Keynes – opposed return. Other critics admitted immediate difficulties but still supported a return. Niemeyer agreed: 'is it not better to get over any discomforts at once and then proceed on an even keel rather than have the dislocation (if dislocation there be) still before us?' Bankers, he asserted, were not opposed to manufacturers and did not pursue their own interests: the real difference was that they took a longer view based on what was good for trade and industry. Indeed, returning to gold was a policy for increased employment by restoring trade. In his view, 'no very heroic step' was needed to maintain the pre-war parity. A balanced budget and sound credit based on gold were mutually supportive, for unsound money would lead to inflation, which increased the money revenue of the government and permitted it to behave in an extravagant manner until the bubble burst and the budget was left in ruins.[41]

Churchill continued to press the officials, and called for further papers, including on the return to gold after the Napoleonic wars. He read Keynes' recent article that pointed to the 'paradox of unemployment amidst dearth' and accused officials of not facing its 'profound significance'. He asked Niemeyer whether there was a link between 'the unique British phenomenon of chronic unemployment and the long, resolute consistency of a particular financial policy'. He realised that the interests of finance and industry did not coincide and complained that 'The Governor shows himself perfectly happy in the spectacle of Britain possessing the finest credit in the world simultaneously with a million and quarter unemployed.' Churchill admitted that he could not see how financial policy could bridge the gap between a dearth of goods and a surplus of labour: 'Still, if I could see a way, I would far rather follow it than any other. I would rather see Finance less proud and Industry more content.' Despite these doubts, Churchill remarked to Niemeyer that 'You and the Governor have managed this affair. Taken together I expect you know more about it than anyone else in the world …. But the fact that this island with its enormous resources is unable to maintain its population is surely a cause for the deepest heartsearching.' To settle the matter, Churchill held a dinner party on 17 March attended by Keynes, McKenna and Niemeyer. McKenna accepted that the return would be 'hell' but that there was no alternative. Keynes was isolated. In the end, Churchill could not go against the advice of Treasury officials and the Bank, or his own 'deeply internalized convictions' that coincided with their assumptions.[42]

Later in 1925, Churchill defended his decision against Keynes' proposal that a 'manipulated currency' could be a 'shock absorber'. The idea was, Churchill argued, 'altogether out of harmony with the sound and rugged principles on which British financial policy has been built up'. The gold standard meant that, 'Whatever our troubles may be, it is much better that all classes should face them with open eyes, that they should know the truth about what is taking place.' By contrast, a 'manipulated currency could be used by a capitalist government to undermine wages, by a socialist government to threaten property, and by an incompetent government to drift. And in all cases, a weaker currency would subsidise exports at the expense of consumers – just like tariffs.[43]

Churchill soon realised that the economy had not recovered as promised. The gold standard could not operate as it had before the war, for more attention needed to be paid to the domestic consequences of mass unemployment and excess capacity in staple industries. Churchill was in dispute with Norman over increases in the bank rate to defend sterling which harmed industry and made government debt more expensive.[44] In 1927, he complained to Niemeyer that an economic policy based on 'deflation, debt repayment, high taxation, large sinking funds and Gold Standard' might improve credit and strengthen the exchange rate at the expense of 'bad trade, hard times, an immense increase in unemployment'. By contrast, taxation in Germany was lower and debt had been reduced through 'a vast act of national repudiation extinguishing the *rentier* class'. It was, he thought,

> a strange contrast to be produced by military victory and financial orthodoxy on the one hand, and by decisive defeat and dishonourable repudiation on the other. That will be a contrast from which most misleading deductions might easily be drawn by a democratic electorate.

The situation in Britain worried him, for the cost of debt service would bring 'the forces creating new wealth into serious competition with the interests of the old wealth as represented by the bondholders'. He feared that 'gigantic taxation and an enormous *rentier* class' would 'lie like a vast wet blanket across the whole process of creating new wealth by new enterprise':

> I shall certainly have to meet the criticism that the policy of the Treasury and the Bank favours the Capitalists' interests and in particular the *rentier* class to such an extent that the nation will never be free from the debt in any period which can be foreseen .... The fact that such a policy obtains keep approval among the banking classes and in the City of London is no answer. Indeed, it might be considered quite natural that they should welcome a policy which undoubtedly tends to foster to its highest point the interests of creditors and inert citizens of all kinds at the expense of all those forces which by fresh efforts are perennially replacing what is consumed.[45]

As he explained to James Grigg, his private secretary, in 1928, 'the complacency of the Treasury and the Bank and their indifference to all other aspects of our national problem make it a duty to put the opposite case sometimes. They have caused an immense amount of misery and impoverishment by their rough and pedantic handling of the problem.'[46]

In 1928, as in 1925, challenging the Treasury did not mean rejection of its core tenets. Churchill was a defender of sound finance, and Grigg thought that 'his financial administration as a whole displays a great hankering to be considered orthodox'.[47] His breach of the balanced budget was a surreptitious response to immediate political difficulties rather than an explicit statement of the benefits of deficit finance. He did not develop his pre-war thinking on the stabilising effect of government employment as did Keynes and Lloyd George prior to the election of 1929. In his final months at the Treasury, Churchill was actively involved in developing the 'Treasury view' against their case for public works. Keynes thought that Churchill was sympathetic and needed to be rescued from 'the timidities and mental confusions of the so-called "sound finance" which established as an end to be worshipped what should only be pursued so long as it is successful as a means to the creation of wealth and the useful employment of men and things'.[48] Keynes misjudged Churchill, who defended orthodox finance in the Cabinet and remarked in private that 'We should not try to compete with [Lloyd George] but take our stand on sound finance.' He played an active role with Treasury officials in drafting 'the orthodox argument against a policy of large Government loan expenditure to give increased employment'.[49] In his final budget, he argued that the impact on employment of spending on public works was

> so meagre as to lend considerable colour to the orthodox Treasury doctrine which has steadfastly held that, whatever might be the political or social advantages, very little additional employment and no permanent additional employment can in fact and as a general rule be created by State borrowing and State expenditure.[50]

The Treasury, with Churchill's support, took its last stand in defence of sound finance that had dominated its thinking since the days of Gladstone.

The tensions in Churchill's economics were becoming apparent. His search for a positive policy to deal with unemployment and depressed regions led to the removal of three quarters of the local rates on industry. Churchill thought it 'economically unsound to tax instruments of production' and claimed that this concession would make industry profitable and so increase employment. It was a trivial response to the problems. Above all, it reflected his strategy of creating balance. Merchants and bankers gained from the return to gold; producers paid for debt service; and a reduction in local rates offered compensation to producers that would, unlike tariffs, not harm consumers. It was not an adequate response to the economic problems of the country, and the tide was turning towards tariffs.[51]

Looking back a year after he ceased to be chancellor, Churchill explained the 'classical doctrines of economics' followed by the Treasury and the Bank of England for the previous century:

> In their pristine vigour these doctrines comprise among others the following tenets: Free imports, irrespective of what other countries may do and heedless of the consequences to any particular native industry or interest. Ruthless direct taxation for the repayment of debt without regard to the effects of such taxation upon individuals or their enterprise or initiative. Rigorous economy in all forms of expenditure whether social or military. Stern assertion of the rights of the creditor, national or private, and full and effectual discharge of all liabilities. Profound distrust of State-stimulated industry in all its forms, or of State borrowing for the purpose of creating employment. Absolute reliance upon private enterprise, unfettered and unfavoured by the State.

These propositions were, he pointed out, part of 'one general economic conception, amplified and expounded in all the Victorian textbooks' – and he commented in 1930 that 'we can clearly see that they do not correspond to what is going on now'.[52] During his time as chancellor, Churchill remained committed to free trade, with any departure justified as a revenue duty that did not affect necessities. He departed from the Treasury and Bank who prioritised repayment of debt, which reflected his long-standing suspicion that passive rentiers harmed active enterprise, though now he turned from an attack on land that set types of property against each other in favour of an alliance of property against socialism. He wished, both before the war and as chancellor, to use the tax system and social welfare to sustain enterprise and self-reliance. Despite his creative accounting for pragmatic political reasons, he remained a devotee of sound finance and balanced budgets, and he did not accept that the state could create employment.

After Churchill left the Treasury in 1929, he took little systematic interest in economics. He reflected in the Romanes lecture of 1930 that 'The compass has been damaged. The charts are out of date', and he did not make any serious attempt to construct a new way of navigating the treacherous economic waters of the Great Depression and post-war reconstruction. Churchill's coherent political economy of free trade and the gold standard collapsed and he had nothing in its place. In Peter Clarke's words, he was 'a disillusioned agnostic in his economic ideas, dealing with issues of economic policy in a purely pragmatic way'.[53]

In 1932, Churchill welcomed the Ottawa agreement on imperial preference in public; in private, he was sceptical. As prime minister in the war, he presided over a Cabinet split over trade policy between supporters of imperial preferences and advocates of a restored multilateral system of trade. Churchill's concerns were immediate: to secure assistance through Lend Lease without succumbing to American pressure for an end to imperial preference as a price for support. Churchill delayed discussion of trade policy that threatened to split the Cabinet and officials lacked clear direction. Neither did he engage with the details of the plans for a post-war monetary order that culminated in the Bretton Woods agreement of 1944. He claimed to be too busy to read the papers, and adopted a defensive and cautious line, in part from a fear of repeating the difficulties of the rigid exchange rates of 1925. He was sceptical about ambitious statements on the post-war world, commenting that the would-be peace planners 'should not overlook Mrs Glass's Cookery Book recipe for Jugged Hare: "First catch your hare"'. Although he was not in the vanguard of multilateralism, he was willing to let the Atlanticists take the lead. Indeed, in April 1944 he assured members of the Conservative Party that 'It's all about dear food; we beat you on that before and will beat you again' – seeming to forget that he was no longer a Liberal in 1906.[54] When the Bretton Woods agreement and post-war loan came to the Commons in December 1945, Churchill instructed Conservative MPs to abstain – a decision castigated by the American ambassador as weak, though probably a sensible response to internal divisions in the Party.[55] He was reluctant to fight the elections of 1950 and 1951 on a detailed programme, an approach he justified by the chancellor's autonomy in taxation. After his return to office, he was initially attracted by the proposal of the chancellor in 1952 to restore convertibility of the pound by allowing the exchange rate to be set by the market, which would have destroyed the Bretton Woods regime. He soon backed down, and certainly did not develop any reasoned case about monetary policy as in 1925. What he did continue to accept, as he did in the Liberal government before 1914, was that planning was not the best approach to the economy – a sentiment that led to copies of Hayek's *Road to Serfdom* being supplied to Conservative candidates in the election of 1945.

Notes

1. M. Gilbert, *OB*, vol. 5 (London: Minerva, 1990), pp. 56, 57.
2. P. Clarke, Churchill's Economic Ideas. In Robert Blake and William Roger Louis, eds., *Churchill* (Oxford: Clarendon, 1996), pp. 79, 82.
3. F. Trentmann, *Free Trade Nation: Commerce, Consumption, and Civil Society in Modern Britain* (Oxford: Oxford University Press, 2008), p. 236; G. C. Peden, *The Treasury and British Public Policy, 1906–1959* (Oxford: Oxford University Press, 2000), pp. 193–5; Clarke, Churchill's Economic Ideas, p. 82.
4. Churchill to *Oldham Chronicle*, 28 October 1902 in R. Churchill, *CV*, vol. 2, part 1, p. 169.
5. Churchill to J. Mitford, 9 July 1903, in R. Churchill, *OB*, vol. 2, p. 64 and *CV*, vol. 2, p. 208; R. Rhodes James, *Complete Speeches*, 8 vols. (New York: Chelsea House, 1974), vol. 1, p. 945.
6. Trentmann, *Free Trade Nation*, p. 75, quoting W. S. Churchill, *For Free Trade* (London: A. L. Humphreys, 1906), p. 61.
7. A. Marshall, *Principles of Economics* (London: Macmillan, 1890) and *Industry and Trade* (London: Macmillan, 1919).
8. J. S. Mill, *Principles of Political Economy* (London, 1848), book 4, chapter 11.
9. W. S. Churchill, *Liberalism and the Social Problem* (London: Hodder & Stoughton, 1909), pp. 155, 156.
10. W. S. Churchill, *The People's Rights* (London: Hodder & Stoughton, 1909), p. 96; Rhodes James, *Complete Speeches*, vol. 1, pp. 212, 238, 315.
11. Rhodes James, *Complete Speeches*, vol. 1, p. 872.
12. Trentmann, *Free Trade Nation*, p. 166, quoting Churchill, *For Free Trade*, pp. 72–3; letter from Churchill to Mitford, pp. 207–8; Churchill to J. Moore-Bayley, 20 May 1903, in CV, vol. 2, part 1, p. 57; Churchill, *Liberalism*, pp. 121, 233–4.
13. Churchill to J. Moore-Bailey, 23 December 1901, in CV, vol. 2, part 1, pp. 104–5.
14. Churchill, *Liberalism*, pp. 82–3.
15. Churchill, *Liberalism*, p. 376.
16. Churchill, *Liberalism*, pp. 182–3, 242–3, 251.
17. Churchill, *Liberalism*, pp. 199–200, 257.
18. Churchill, *Liberalism*, pp. 77, 144–5, 395.
19. Churchill, *Liberalism*, pp. 318–19.
20. Churchill, *Liberalism*, pp. 278–1, 319–27, 335–6.
21. Churchill, *Liberalism*, p. 336.

22. Churchill, *Liberalism*, pp. 377–8.

23. Churchill, *Liberalism*, pp. 80–1.

24. University of Birmingham Library, Austen Chamberlain Papers, AC25/4/24 and 25, Cabinet discussions on 2 and 4 June 1920.

25. M. Daunton, How to Pay for The War: State, Society and Taxation in Britain, 1917–24. *English Historical Review*, vol. 101 (1996), p. 909.

26. Trentmann, *Free Trade Nation*, p. 303.

27. J. Tomlinson, Churchill's Defeat in Dundee, 1922, and the Decline of Liberal Political Economy. *Historical Journal*, vol. 21 (2010), pp. 995, 1003, 1005–6.

28. University of Birmingham Library, Chamberlain Papers, NC 2/21, 1 November 1925.

29. Churchill to Salisbury, 9 December 1924 in Gilbert, CV, vol. 5, part 1, p. 297.

30. M. Gilbert, *Churchill's Political Philosophy* (Oxford: Oxford University Press, 1981), p. 53.

31. TNA, T176/28, Churchill to Hopkins, 26 January 1927; T176/39, Churchill to Niemeyer, 26 January 1927.

32. M. Daunton, *Just Taxes: The Politics of Taxation in Britain, 1914–1979* (Cambridge: Cambridge University Press, 2002), pp. 126–7.

33. K. Middlemass, ed., *Thomas Jones: Whitehall Diary vol. 2: 1916–30* (Oxford: Oxford University Press, 1969), p. 98; Baldwin to George V in Gilbert, CV, vol. 5, part 1, p. 986; Clarke, Churchill's Economic Ideas, p. 80; Daunton, *Just Taxes*, pp. 128–32; Peden, *Treasury*, pp. 205–9.

34. *Hansard*, House of Commons Debates, series 5, vol. 183, cols. 64–5, 85–6, 28 April 1925; Gilbert, CV, vol. 5, part 1, p. 466, Churchill to George V, 23 April 1925; TNA, T171/239, Churchill to Hopkins, 28 November and 14 December 1924.

35. Gilbert, CV, vol. 5, part 1, p. 271, Churchill to Baldwin, 28 November 1924; Churchill to George V, 23 April 1925; TNA T171/239, Churchill to Hopkins, 28 November 1924; *Hansard*, House of Commons Debates, series 5, vol. 183, cols. 64, 71–2, 28 April 1925.

36. J. M. Keynes, The Economic Consequences of Mr Churchill. In *Collected Writings of John Maynard Keynes vol. 9: Essays in Persuasion* (London: Macmillan, 1972), p. 212.

37. Lord Moran, *Winston Churchill: The Struggle for Survival, 1940–65* (London: Constable, 1966), p. 330; Gilbert, *Prophet of Truth*, p. 411.

38. Details in D. E. Moggridge, *British Monetary Policy 1924–1931* (Cambridge: Cambridge University Press, 1972), chapter 9 and Peden, *Treasury*, pp. 197–202.

39. Printed in Moggridge, *British Monetary Policy*, pp. 260–2.

40. Moggridge, *British Monetary Policy*, pp. 270–2.

41. Moggridge, *British Monetary Policy*, pp. 262–9.

42. Peden, *Treasury*, pp. 200–1; Moggridge, *British Monetary Policy*, pp. 75–6.

43. *Hansard*, House of Commons Debates, series 5, vol. 187, cols. 1462–9, 5 August 1925.

44. Peden, *Treasury*, pp. 203–4; Moggridge, *British Monetary Policy*, pp. 161–3.

45. Gilbert, CV, vol. 5, part 1, Churchill to Niemeyer, 26 January 1927, pp. 924–5 and Churchill to Niemeyer, 20 May 1927, pp. 997–9.

46. Moggridge, *British Monetary Policy*, note 4, pp. 75–6.

47. P. J. Grigg, *Prejudice and Judgement* (London: Jonathan Cape, 1948), p. 195.

48. D. E. Moggridge, ed., *The Collected Writings of John Maynard Keynes, vol. 19, Activities 1922–1929: The Return to Gold and Industrial Policy* (London: Macmillan, 1981), p. 766.

49. Middlemass, ed., *Whitehall Diary*, II, pp. 175–6; P. Clarke, *The Keynesian Revolution in the Making, 1924–36* (Oxford: Clarendon, 1988), pp. 62–5.

50. *Hansard*, House of Commons Debates, series 5, vol. 227, col. 54, 15 April 1929.

51. Peden, *Treasury*, pp. 210–11; Daunton, *Just Taxes*, pp. 343–7; TNA, CAB27/365, CP (8) memo by the chancellor of the exchequer, 20 January 1928.
52. Quoted in Clarke, Churchill's Economic Ideas, p. 80.
53. Clarke, Churchill's Economic Ideas, p. 95.
54. R. Toye, Churchill and Britain's 'Financial Dunkirk'. *Twentieth Century British History*, vol. 15 (2004), pp. 331–3; Robert Skidelsky, *John Maynard Keynes: Fighting for Britain, 1937–1946* (Basingstoke: Macmillan, 2000), pp. 326–7, 329; David Reynolds, *The Creation of the Anglo-American Alliance, 1937–1941: A Study in Competitive Cooperation* (Chapel Hill: University of North Carolina Press, 1982), p. 363, quoting Churchill to Anthony Eden, 18 October 1942.
55. Toye, Churchill and Britain's 'Financial Dunkirk', pp. 337–45.

Further Reading

W. S. Churchill, *Liberalism and the Social Problem* (London: Hodder & Stoughton, 1909)
P. Clarke, Churchill's Economic Ideas, 1900–1930. In Robert Blake and William Roger Louis, eds., *Churchill* (Oxford: Clarendon, 1996), pp. 79–95
M. Daunton, How to Pay for the War: State, Society and Taxation in Britain, 1917–24. *English Historical Review*, vol. 101 (1996)
M. Daunton, *Just Taxes: The Politics of Taxation in Britain, 1914–1979* (Cambridge: Cambridge University Press, 2002)
M. Gilbert, *Churchill's Political Philosophy* (Oxford: Oxford University Press, 1981)
J. M. Keynes, The Economic Consequences of Mr Churchill. In *Collected Writings of John Maynard Keynes, vol. 9: Essays in Persuasion* (London: Macmillan, 1972)
G. C. Peden, *The Treasury and British Public Policy, 1906–1959* (Oxford: Oxford University Press, 2000)
F. Trentmann, *Free Trade Nation: Commerce, Consumption, and Civil Society in Modern Britain* (Oxford: Oxford University Press, 2008)

10

Churchill, the Roosevelts and Empire

The British Empire provided the context in which both Winston Churchill and Franklin Roosevelt (FDR) came to maturity and to a remarkable extent it defined and aggravated their differences as national leaders. An apt starting point therefore is 1897, the date of Queen Victoria's Diamond Jubilee and the year often taken to mark the apogee of the British Empire. As the celebrations were acclaiming the providential supremacy of the Anglo-Saxon race, Churchill, aged twenty-two, was a supremely confident and energetic officer bent on defending the far reaches of the Empire and ambitious soon to beat his sword into an iron despatch box. By contrast, the fifteen-year-old Roosevelt was at Groton, an insecure mother's boy who hero-worshipped his thrusting cousin Theodore (TR) but would ask pertinently, when debating America's acquisition of Hawaii, 'Why should we soil our hands with colonies . . .? Why take away the nationality of a free people?'[1]

Perhaps because this was the noon-day of aggressive imperialism, there were also forebodings, on both sides of the Atlantic, about the sunset of empire. Addressing the Naval War College, Teddy Roosevelt said that if America were to lose 'the virile, manly qualities, and sink into a nation of mere hucksters, putting gain above national honour, and subordinating everything to mere ease of life; then we shall indeed reach a condition worse than that of the ancient civilisations in the years of their decay'.[2] Returning from military service in India in 1897, Churchill indulged in Gibbonian musings amid the ruins of the Capitol in Rome about whether the British Empire would suffer a similar decline and fall. The prospect of imperial doom, which FDR welcomed and eventually tried to precipitate, cast a shadow over Churchill's entire life.

Winston and Teddy

Yet, in his first political speech, made in May 1897, Churchill denounced the croakers who prophesied that the British Empire would go the way of Babylon, Carthage and Rome. He set out the standard case, adumbrated by Disraeli and elaborated by his father Lord Randolph Churchill and others, for 'the greatness and the empire of England'.[3] Its expansion stemmed from Anglo-Saxon vitality. And its colonial possessions would be maintained by naval might, by loyalty to the throne and by a determination 'to pursue that course marked out for us by an all-wise hand and carry out our mission of bearing peace, civilisation and good government to the uttermost ends of the earth'.[4] This was a theme Churchill developed for its own sake and because it gave scope for grandiloquent oratory. But his view of the British Empire was by no means summed up, then or subsequently, in a set of Victorian platitudes. As his doubts about the future suggest, it was more complex and more mutable, reflecting the play of different and often conflicting influences on his powerful and volatile mind.

Much of Churchill's imperial drum-beating might have been echoed at the time by Theodore Roosevelt, who resembled him in a variety of ways. The Australian prime minister Billy Hughes was especially struck by how similar the American Bull Moose was to the British Bulldog: 'of all the leaders of men I have known he stands out in my memory as cast in the same mould as Churchill'.[5] Both men admired Kipling and believed in bearing the White man's burden. They both emphasised the connection between imperialism and social reform. Yet both justified ruthless measures in wars between 'civilisation' and 'savages', these being the most righteous of all wars in TR's estimation, although 'apt to be the most terrible and inhuman'. Roosevelt scorned the notion that whole continents should be the preserve of scattered tribes, 'whose life was but a few degrees less meaningless, squalid, and ferocious than that of the wild beasts with whom they held joint ownership'.[6] Churchill denied that 'a great wrong has been done to the Red Indians of America, or the black people of Australia ... by the fact that a stronger race, a higher grade race ... has come in to take their place'.[7]

Roosevelt and Churchill also shared a passion for adventure in wild places. They courted danger and fame. Roosevelt's charge with the Rough Riders at San Juan Hill anticipated by only two months Churchill's charge with the 21st Lancers at Omdurman – a feat soon followed by his most celebrated exploit, escaping from Boer captivity during the South African War. President by 1901, Teddy felt for the Boers but backed the British. En route to Cuba he had read Edmond Demolins' *Anglo-Saxon Superiority* (1898) and it confirmed his faith in the race's extraordinary aptitude to civilise. He believed that it was to the advantage of humankind to have English spoken south of the Zambesi. Teddy considered the Boers to be as medieval as the Spaniards, against whom John Bull had given Uncle Sam much-appreciated moral support, and he even covertly provided Pinkerton detectives to sniff out Irish-Boer collaboration. In 1909 Roosevelt wrote about India in terms that might have been dictated by Churchill: its successful administration had been 'one of the most notable achievements of the white race during the past two centuries' and if British control were withdrawn, 'the whole peninsula would become a chaos of bloodshed and violence'.[8]

Franklin Chooses His Own Path

Young Franklin notoriously identified with his cousin, fantasised about becoming a Rough Rider and was so excited by the Spanish-American War that he planned to escape from Groton in a pie-man's cart in order to enlist – instead he caught scarlet fever. It is true that he ranged himself against Theodore by his staunch opposition to the British Empire during the South African War, belying his Harvard nickname 'the feather-duster'. 'Hurrah for the Boers!' he wrote in 1899, during his first political disagreement with his overbearing mother: 'I entirely sympathise with them.'[9] As his ambitions ripened, however, Franklin modelled his own career path on that of TR: assistant secretary of the navy, governor of the empire state, president. FDR was eager to profit politically from the relationship and he readily subscribed to TR's imperialistic views (which softened over time). FDR backed American intervention in Haiti and even claimed (falsely) to have written the Haitian constitution. He favoured acquiring bases and territories elsewhere in America's sphere of influence, if necessary by force. In 1922 he urged both Democrats and Republicans to accept that the independence of the Philippines, Puerto Rico, Haiti and San Domingo could not be contemplated for many years. FDR aspired to imitate something of his cousin's robust style, saying that he too wanted to be a *'preaching President'*.[10] But he lacked TR's bark and his bite, what one journalist called 'the castanet-like ecstasy of his snapping teeth'.[11]

Moreover, his admiration for TR was tempered by a need to distance himself and to be his own man. Often this meant being all things to all men, embodying optimism rather than dogma, appealing to the widest possible constituency, becoming the chameleon on plaid. His desire to appear progressive became acute in an era indelibly marked by the liberal doctrines of Woodrow Wilson, when Victorian imperialists such as TR and Churchill seemed to represent an obsolescent order. So during the decade after his cousin's death, FDR executed a gradual volte face on the subject of imperialism. In 1928 he paid tribute to Wilson's 'restoration of high moral purpose to our foreign affairs' and said that the United States should adopt 'new principles of a higher law, a new and better standard in international relations'.[12] On becoming president he pushed for the Philippine Independence Act (1934), declaring that 'Our Nation covets no territory; it desires to hold no people against their will over whom it has gained sovereignty through war.'[13]

Roosevelt claimed that his antipathy to the expansion of British power overseas, for commercial as well as political reasons, was a family tradition dating back to the American Revolution. Whatever the truth of this, FDR's hostility to the British Empire was plainly inspired by genuine idealism as well as calculating pragmatism. He detested the exploitation of subjugated races and felt a sincere concern for the welfare of global underdogs, a concern evidently deepened by his own crippled state. But the British Empire was guilty in other respects. It did not pay its war debts. It engaged in global power politics which threatened to lead the United States into entangling alliances. It behaved as if North America below the 49th parallel were an 'errant Dominion'.[14] Finally, like many Americans, Roosevelt tended to believe both that the British Empire was over-stretched and moribund and that it was a colossus threatening global domination. As a leader who (like Churchill) thought primarily in terms of power, FDR wished to diminish that threat.

Churchill's Imperial Destiny

Roosevelt would have found much to justify his aversion to the British Empire in the early conduct of Winston Churchill. As a soldier, Churchill defended the imperial frontiers, engaging in a vicious form of warfare that included burning Pathan villages and killing all who resisted. As a young politician he espoused harsh methods against the Empire's enemies. Yet Churchill often expressed strikingly liberal sentiments about the Empire. He preferred conciliation to coercion and in 1898 described reliance on terror as 'the debauched Imperialism of Ancient Rome'.[15] He condemned the slaughter of wounded Dervishes at Omdurman and 'the disgusting butchery of natives'[16] in Natal, which he dubbed 'The hooligan of the Empire'.[17] He deplored injuries inflicted on Indigenous people, whether by colonial officials, White settlers, speculators or missionaries. On occasion he even expressed doubts about the worth of the Empire, except insofar 'as it is undertaken in an altruistic spirit for the good of the subject races'.[18] Churchill's own spirit of imperial altruism reached its zenith in July 1920 when he denounced General Dyer's massacre of Indian civilians at Amritsar.

However, the pugnacious imperialist came to the fore after the Great War. This was chiefly because the British Empire, which had survived the conflict as the Russian, German, Austro-Hungarian and Ottoman Empires had not, was now assailed from many quarters. Among its foes were Bolshevik revolutionaries, Churchill's bêtes noires, whose ambitions were neatly summed up in a Russian pamphlet sent to him entitled, 'The destruction of the British Empire as planned by the Communist International.'[19] In India and Egypt nationalists attempted to cast off the British yoke. Violence periodically erupted in Palestine and Mesopotamia. After a bloody struggle, the Irish Free State was born. At the War Office (1919–21) and subsequently at the Colonial Office (where Churchill proposed that his title should be changed to secretary of state for imperial affairs), he strove to preserve the strength and restore the prosperity of the Empire. This meant defending distant possessions on the cheap and, as he put it, buckling them together with the economical new instrument of aviation. 'The first duty of the Royal Air Force', he declared, 'is to garrison the British Empire.' Still more vital was sea power and Churchill supported the creation of an 'impregnable'[20] naval base at Singapore and the ratification of the Washington Naval Treaty, which limited battleship construction. At the same time he endorsed the termination of the Anglo-Japanese naval alliance, looking forward instead to 'an ever closer association between the United States and the British Empire'. Churchill gleefully quoted from the rash Guildhall speech of the American Admiral William Sims, Anglophile protégé of both Roosevelts: 'I am sure that if the time should ever come when the British Empire is seriously menaced by an external enemy, its people can count on every man, every dollar, every ship, and every drop of blood of their kindred across the ocean.'

Churchill's citing this pronouncement would have fed Franklin Roosevelt's suspicion that he wished to tap the power of the United States in order to shore up the crumbling fabric of the British Empire. FDR was not far wrong about this. Churchill recognised that, after the Washington Treaty, Britannia no longer ruled the waves and America was a rival, even a potential foe. Yet no one better appreciated the value of transatlantic amity. Thus he extolled the common racial and cultural identity of the English-speaking peoples. All too aware of the danger of over-extension, he talked up 'the consolidation of the British Empire'.[21] Indeed, as if to quell his own fears about its 'passing',[22] Churchill allowed his imperial imagination to soar. As Lord Curzon sardonically remarked, he was 'spreading his wings over the universe'.[23] Churchill forecast that the Empire was entering its most resplendent period. Its intimate – and equal – relationship with the United States offered 'the brightest hopes for the progress of mankind'.[24]

After 1929, when Churchill lost office for what would be a decade, he became much more pessimistic about the future of the British Empire. This was mainly because a cross-party consensus was emerging that India should soon receive dominion status. Until 1935, when it obtained provincial self-government, Churchill led a campaign against this policy. Home rule for India, he said, would herald 'the decline and fall of the British Empire' and bring about a catastrophe 'more horrible than anything we have experienced even in the awful times through which we have lived'.[25] Despite such apocalyptic language, Churchill vehemently denied repeated accusations that he was a reactionary. Indeed, he claimed to be a progressive, like the British Empire itself. As he wrote in the preface to a never-published 'Biographical Dictionary of the British Empire' (1937), it would survive because it adapted to modern conditions, combining authority with liberty and reconciling the duties of government with the rights of individuals. Old but not senile, diversified but coherent, it would survive 'not so much through force as through understanding, not so much through strength of arms and genius of statesmanship as through the wide dispersal of its burdens and honours'. The protagonist in the imperial drama, he concluded, did not 'apprehend the approach of a final curtain'.[26] All this sounded like whistling in the dark. Yet Churchill truly saw himself as the standard-bearer of British civilisation, whereas he viewed Gandhi, with his spin-ning-wheel and his dhoti, as the embodiment of Indian backwardness.

When war broke out in 1939 Churchill returned to the Admiralty (where his first act was to order a bottle of whisky) and expressed the intention to draw on 'the vast latent power' of the British Empire, including India. He supported the Viceroy's declaration of war on India's behalf and maintained in his first ministerial broadcast that its 'heart and moral conviction'[27] were on Britain's side. There was scant evidence for this, as indicated by Churchill's simultaneous insistence that no constitutional change should take place during the war and that the Congress Party should be side-lined. He particularly rejoiced in its renewed quarrel with the Muslim League and hoped that it 'would remain bitter and bloody'.[28] And he was dismissive of socialists such as Sir Stafford Cripps who declared that Britain could not fight for freedom and democracy while denying both to India.

When Churchill became prime minister he dramatised Albion's chiv-alric past in a way that made it supremely relevant to the present. Minting phrases that were treasured up as oracles at the time and have since become proverbial, he sought to revive the ancient spirit of valour dissipated by the appeasers of Hitler and Gandhi. Mobilising the English language, all the more sonorous for encompassing the fate of Greater Britain overseas, he summoned the nation and the Empire to battle . . . and to victory. He looked to kith and kin in the self-governing dominions to help 'rescue not only Europe but mankind' from Nazi tyranny. In a paean of defiance following the fall of France, he declared that Britain would never surrender. But if, as he did not believe, it were 'subjugated and starving, then our Empire beyond the seas, armed and guarded by the British Fleet, would carry on the struggle, until, in God's good time, the New World, with all its power and might steps forth to the rescue and the liberation of the old'.[29]

As this pronouncement shows, Churchill appreciated from the outset that American participation in the war was the key to victory. His first message to Roosevelt after becoming prime minister, written on 15 May 1940, made the point bluntly: if the voice and force of America were withheld for too long, the result might be the swift establishment of 'a completely subjugated, Nazified Europe'. Churchill asked for moral and material aid, notably the loan of some fifty old destroyers, and with Australia and Britain's eastern Empire in mind, he looked to Roosevelt 'to keep that Japanese dog quiet in the Pacific, using

Singapore in any way convenient'.[30] Alert to the strength of isolationist opinion in an election year, FDR temporised. Ever more desperate, Churchill told Roosevelt that he would go down fighting but that his successors might bargain away the British fleet, which could be turned on America. Privately he referred to 'those bloody Yankees'.[31]

Yet even while anguished about national survival, Churchill remained committed to imperial solidarity. He would only offer token concessions to India and said that rather than accepting its separation from the British Crown, he would 'go out into the wilderness and fight'.[32] He was incensed when in August 1940 the prime minister of Canada, Mackenzie King, concluded a joint defence agreement with the United States. He also resented Roosevelt's extracting bases in the British West Indies as the price for the old (and defective) destroyers, doubtless recognising that the president was, as Secretary of State Cordell Hull noted, using 'American aid as a knife to open up that oyster shell, the empire'.[33] Nevertheless, Churchill had no option but to attempt to mix up together, as he delicately phrased it, the affairs of the 'two great organisations "of the English-speaking democracies, the British Empire and the United States'. For notwithstanding the meagreness of Roosevelt's assistance, he was, Churchill told King, 'our best friend'.[34]

The New World Against the Status Quo

Despite stresses and strains, of which their dispute over the British Empire was the most fundamental, there is no doubt that the friendship between Churchill and Roosevelt, a friendship first of pen and then of sword, was fundamentally sound. True, it was essentially political, based on reasons of state, and it never amounted to the holy alliance Churchill conjured up in his romantic and partisan war memoirs. But nor was it the cat-and-dog relationship portrayed by Elliott Roosevelt in his post-war volume, As He Saw It. The two leaders had much in common. They were both former naval persons, of course, and keen students of Alfred Thayer Mahan's thesis that sea power was the essential constituent of national greatness. They shared a patrician concern for the forgotten men of society. Despite his suspicions about the New Deal, Churchill said that it had nothing to do with communism, let alone Nazism – 'To compare Roosevelt's effort with that of Hitler is to insult, not Roosevelt, but civilisation.'[35] Churchill and Roosevelt both

Figure 10.1 Churchill and Roosevelt meet with Chiang Kai-shek of China, 1943 (BRDW I Photo 8).

reflected, though in varying fashions, the racial prejudices of the day. But both leaders had a real loathing of persecution and tyranny, as well as a commitment to Western culture and values. Both professed liberal principles and often, though not always, practised them. Both had expressed admiration for Mussolini, had sympathised with Franco and had wobbled over appeasement. Both had a fascination with secret intelligence and toyed with what their military advisers called, respectively, cigar-butt and cigarette-holder strategy.

However, there were individual differences as well as political and strategic disagreements. Roosevelt was adulterous and respectable; Churchill was faithful and disreputable. Roosevelt was a virtuoso of dissimulation; Churchill found it hard not to speak his mind. Roosevelt enjoyed persiflage and raillery; Churchill preferred wit and irony. Roosevelt was irritated by the ceaseless pertinacity of Churchill's late-night harangues. Churchill was bored by Roosevelt's stamp collection. Roosevelt was irrepressibly buoyant and delegated cheerfully. Churchill was hyper-active and would really have preferred both to direct the war and to fight it, like his hero Napoleon. Roosevelt gave orders informally.

Churchill was literally a dictator, conducting a war of words via busy secretaries and, as he put it, living from mouth to hand. Roosevelt talked to the American people in 'fireside chats', using the modern medium of radio like a master of dramatic art and delivering the clear, natural and intimate addresses which did much to make him a trusted father figure. Churchill gave the lion's roar as though bestriding a music hall stage.

The British Empire became a source of disagreement between the two leaders from the moment of their first wartime meeting, at Placentia Bay, Newfoundland, in August 1941. According to Elliott Roosevelt, his father aimed to establish from the start that America would not be used as a good-time Charlie to get the British Empire, which rode roughshod over its subject peoples, out of a tight spot. Churchill looked apoplectic, Elliott continued, when FDR said to him, with reference to India: 'I can't believe that we can fight a war against fascist slavery, and at the same time not work to free people all over the world from a backward colonial policy.' No records were kept of their private discussions and maybe the president did not speak with such uncharacteristic forthrightness. But Elliott provides copious evidence that his father went on reproaching Churchill and his entourage about the Empire, 'sticking his strong fingers into sore consciences, prodding, needling'.[36]

Churchill had arrived at Placentia Bay with high hopes that Roosevelt would take a decisive step towards belligerency, but when these were dashed he had to concoct a propaganda victory. He took immense pains to present their meeting as a display of comradeship, an exhibition of moral unity. He also had to dress up the Atlantic Charter, a joint declaration of high-sounding principles for the post-war betterment of the world, as an implicit Anglo-American alliance. In its formulation the British Empire was a major bone of contention. Churchill successfully resisted American pressure to change the system of preferential tariffs on imperial goods. But he accepted Article 3, which affirmed the right of all peoples to choose their own form of government, later even claiming credit, quite unjustifiably, for drafting such forward-looking sentiments. Actually, in his anxiety to woo and win Roosevelt, he had given a hostage to fortune. The Atlantic Charter was greeted throughout the colonial world with enthusiasm similar to that generated by President Wilson's Fourteen Points. Nationalists were correspondingly enraged, especially in India and Burma, when

Churchill announced in parliament that the Charter's promise of self-determination only applied to countries in Nazi-occupied Europe. He was unmoved by their protests. In fact, as Roger Louis has pointed out, Churchill turned the principle of self-determination into a two-edged sword, a weapon for defending the Empire. He argued, for example, that Arabs might claim by majority that 'they could expel the Jews from Palestine'.[37]

After the attack on Pearl Harbor, which was carried out, Roosevelt stressed, by the *Empire* of Japan, Churchill was less inhibited about rejecting interference in imperial affairs. When the president canvassed the matter of Indian self-government during Churchill's visit to the United States in December 1941, the prime minister, as he later recorded, 'reacted so strongly and at such length that he never raised it verbally again'.[38] Yet Roosevelt persisted, though more circumspectly. Embedded in his denunciation of Nazi and Fascist attempts to goose-step to world power over the bodies of other races, for example, was the assertion that no people on earth were 'fit to serve as masters over their fellow men'[39] or had a right to deny them nationhood, which was a tacit condemnation of the British Empire. But its collapse in south-east Asia under the Japanese assault shocked him almost as much as it did Churchill.

Advancing far more swiftly than Churchill had anticipated, the Japanese seized Hong Kong, occupied Malaya, forced the surrender of Singapore and invaded Burma. As India came under threat, Roosevelt despatched a series of missives urging Churchill to invigorate the sub-continent by granting some form of dominion status. The prime minister thought this would be 'an act of madness'. In the severest criticism of the president contained in his history of the war, Churchill ascribed Roosevelt's meddling to historical error and misplaced idealism. Turning the tables on FDR, who equated the Congress Party with American revolutionaries fighting George III, the prime minister accused him of living in the past. As for his high-minded attitude towards Indian independence, it was adopted at British expense and 'without regard to the consequences of ruin and slaughter'.[40]

The Asian disasters not only blasted the fabric of the British Empire but also irretrievably damaged its prestige. Churchill was obliged to make a conciliatory gesture towards India, not least to satisfy America. So he sent Cripps, a new member of the War Cabinet, to negotiate with the nationalists. Simultaneously Roosevelt despatched a personal representative to Delhi, Louis Johnson, in the hope that he would facilitate a deal. Johnson pressed Cripps to offer major concessions to Congress, among them handing over the defence portfolio to an Indian. But Churchill prevented Cripps from making more than overtures. Johnson told Roosevelt that 'London wanted a Congress refusal'.[41] Wishing to steer clear of the Indian imbroglio, the president gave no definite lead to Johnson, whom the prime minister tried to undermine. Nevertheless, Roosevelt did tell Churchill that Americans believed the deadlock to have been 'caused by the unwillingness of the British Government to concede to the Indians the right of self-government'.[42] Churchill turned the night air blue with curses. More soberly, he warned that an independent India could well seek an armistice with Japan and that he himself might resign over the issue, though this was probably a bluff. In any case, since Cripps was unable to offer Congress enough, his mission proved abortive. Churchill rejoiced, dancing round the Cabinet room and intoning, 'No tea with treason, no truck with American or British Labour sentimentality, but back to the solemn – and exciting – business of war.'[43]

Gandhi substantiated Churchill's prognostications by announcing that India had no quarrel with Japan and by mounting a campaign of civil disobedience under the banner of 'Quit India'. The Viceroy, Lord Linlithgow, responded with repression. Gandhi and other Congress leaders were imprisoned, along with 65,000 of their followers. Roosevelt's initial instinct was to keep quiet, reckoning that anything which impaired Britain's ability to withstand the Japanese would itself jeopardise the cause of Indian independence. But when Wendell Willkie, his Republican opponent in the election, denounced colonialism in the autumn of 1942, the president virtually endorsed his view. He also stated openly that the Atlantic Charter applied to all humanity. Churchill was irate, reminding Willkie of 'a Newfoundland dog in a small parlour which had wiped its paws on a young lady's blouse and swept off the tea cups with his tail'.[44] The prime minister punctuated his private discourse with frantic tirades about Britain's sacrifice of blood and treasure in defence of India and the humiliating prospect of being kicked out by 'the beastliest people in the world next to the Germans'.[45] In public, buoyed up by the victory at El Alamein, he famously declared on 10 November 1942: 'We mean to hold our own. I have not become the King's First Minister in order to preside over the liquidation of the British Empire.'[46]

This upset public opinion in the United States, where many hoped that a new global order would emerge from the conflict. 'America', wrote *Fortune* magazine, 'owes the world a substitute for the *Pax Britannica*, which is dead.'[47] Churchill remained belligerent about the Empire, threatening to defend it by force of arms if necessary, but he did see the post-war settlement in terms of a *Pax Americana*. Indeed, he drafted a parliamentary speech proposing that the United States should adopt a major peace-keeping role in post-war Europe, comparable to Britain's mediating presence in India. Europe resembled India, he argued, in being a continent riven by diversity. When Europe obtained 'independence' after the fall of the Roman Empire, it used that

> independence to have, with a few lucid intervals, an unending succession of bloody and devastating wars, of which we are passing through the latest. However there is hope that after this war is over we may build up some sort of central presiding power, which will bring to an end or at least to a prolonged pause the merciless struggle which has brought infinite miseries in its train.

The Raj had given India peace, stability, prosperity and progress in 'one of the noblest works that any European nation or white race has ever accomplished'. In fact, British rule had rendered to India, Churchill asserted, 'exactly that function of central control, including an external element, which is what we seek to create … [by bringing the] vast steadying power of the United States into the new Council of Europe'. Here was an ingenious justification for Britain's imperial stewardship, which might come to an end, Churchill concluded, 'but to India it may well be the age of the Antonines'.[48]

However, he did not deliver the speech. Probably this was because it seemed bound to offend Americans, imbued as it was with resentment against India and hatred of Gandhi. Churchill regarded the hunger strike he began in February 1943 as an odious form of moral blackmail. He disdained Roosevelt's new representative in India, David Phillips, who got the president's authorisation to express American concern over the Mahatma's fast. Churchill was jubilant when it ended, proposing to express on the radio his conviction that Gandhi never had any intention of

> starving himself to death or running any risk of squandering the world's record nuisance value. I was quite sure that as soon as he realised that none of this bluff and fraud and sob-stuff made the

slightest impression upon the Viceroy or upon His Majesty's Government he would take all the necessary steps to restore himself to health, and this is exactly what happened.[49]

This Blimpish broadcast, hardly calculated to conciliate Americans, was also undelivered. Instead Amery transmitted an audacious piece of sophistry over the air waves designed, as he told the prime minister, 'to clear up the absurd charge, continually reiterated, that you deliberately excluded India from the Atlantic Charter'.[50] Churchill remained intransigent. At Roosevelt's behest he met Phillips but he furiously rejected his plea to transfer more power to Indians. As the focus of the war moved away from India by mid-1943, the president was ever more inclined to wash his hands of the whole subject and he was, indeed, likened to Pontius Pilate.

Even when it became impossible to ignore the Bengal famine, which killed some 3 million people in 1943–4, Roosevelt did nothing that might impede the war effort or embarrass Churchill. The prime minister himself, with the agreement of the War Cabinet, denied and diminished shipments of food to India. This has led to accusations that he was guilty of genocide. They are unwarranted. As Churchill told Lord Wavell, Linlithgow's successor as Viceroy, 'the wellbeing of the masses' in India constituted 'for us a sacred duty'.[51] In fact, there was an acute shortage of shipping, compounded by heavy losses in the Bay of Bengal, and Churchill felt bound to heed the paramount claims of the global struggle and to direct resources to the crucial theatres of war. Roosevelt concurred despite considerable pressure from the press, which lambasted the British Raj for its failures. When Churchill belatedly asked for American help in transporting Australian grain to India in April 1944, the president replied that despite humanitarian considerations, the chiefs of staff were 'unable on military grounds to consent to the diversion of shipping'.[52]

However, Churchill set out his priorities in brutal fashion: 'the starvation of anyhow under-fed Bengalis is less serious [than that of] sturdy Greeks'.[53] He may have thought that the Congress Party would take aid as a sign of weakness and he was perhaps, as Madhusree Mukerjee claims, moved by a 'will to punish' the recalcitrant subcontinent.[54] Certainly his outbursts against Indians, as recorded by Amery, Jock Colville and R. A. Butler, were outrageous even by the standards of the day. Andrew Roberts has recently attempted to depict them as instances of Churchill's 'provocative humour'.[55] Doubtless his wish that Bomber Harris could send surplus aircraft to destroy the 'foul race'[56] of Hindus was a joke – in execrable taste. But most of Churchill's statements on the subject were clear expressions of atavistic prejudice. In April 1944, for example, he told the state department adviser Isaiah Bowman that Indians

> marry young, they are immature mentally, they breed far in excess of reason, seeming to think that to stretch their limbs out in the sun and let the light of Heaven shine on them is the chief aim of their existence. How can you expect government from such people?[57]

It is hard to avoid the conclusion that Churchill's reluctance to alleviate the Bengal famine stemmed, at least in part, from a racist animus.

By contrast, Roosevelt went out of his way to express sympathy towards the deprived inhabitants of colonial hell-holes. In February 1944, for example, he regaled members of the Negro Newspaper Publishers Association with an account of his stopover in the British colony of Gambia. Painting a vivid picture of the country's neglected and exploited state, FDR said that it was 'the most horrible thing I have ever seen in my life'. In the interest of preparing Gambia's people for eventual self-rule, he apparently warned Churchill, 'If you Britishers don't come up to scratch – toe the mark – then we will let the world know.'[58] Roosevelt may have exaggerated all this but time and again he did insist that America would not be wheedled into abetting Britain's imperial ambitions. 'A new period is opening up in the world's history,' he told Churchill at the Tehran Conference, 'and you will have to adjust to it.'[59]

The tension did not abate at Yalta, where they met for the last time. The president wanted to facilitate decolonisation by awarding the trusteeship of various dependent territories to the United Nations. Churchill was outraged: 'While there is life in my body, no transfer of British sovereignty will be permitted.'[60] He would never consent to 'forty or fifty nations thrusting interfering fingers into the life's existence of the British Empire ... never, never, never'.[61] Reassured on that point, he inadvertently agreed that the UN's role should include territories such as Germany's former colonies held by Britain under League of Nations mandates. This would open the door to the international vilification of the Empire, which contributed to its fall. If Churchill was inattentive, Roosevelt was visibly failing at Yalta and he did not implement his rhetoric about bestowing independence on colonised peoples. But he became more outspoken about Churchill's incorrigible

Victorianism and his inability to appreciate the plight of huddled masses yearning to breathe free. The president confessed to being tired, having 'spent the last five years pushing Winston uphill in a wheelbarrow!'[62]

At every stage the British Empire came between them. It bedevilled the issue of strategy, Churchill always having an eye on British interests in the Mediterranean, Roosevelt wanting to cross the Channel straight for the German jugular. It caused friction over the Far East, Roosevelt propping up Chiang Kai-shek's nationalist China and favouring the Burma campaign, Churchill anxious to use sea power to preserve every 'inch of the territory that was under the British flag'.[63] The British Empire helped to alienate Roosevelt from de Gaulle. 'Interests coincide', Roosevelt told his son. 'The English meant to maintain their hold on their colonies. They mean to help the French maintain *their* hold on *their* colonies. Winnie is a great man for the status quo. He even *looks* like the status quo, doesn't he?'[64] The British Empire complicated relations with the Soviet Union: Roosevelt suspected that Churchill had sinister imperialistic motives for his initiatives in eastern Europe and the Balkans, which might undermine cooperation with Stalin. According to Robert Nisbet, it was Roosevelt's 'ineradicable hatred of ... British imperialism'[65] that prompted him to curry favour with Stalin at the expense of Churchill, though the president was perhaps more concerned about the balance of power in post-war Europe.

Certainly Churchill's dispute with Roosevelt on the subject of the British Empire went to the heart of the relationship between a Democrat president who wanted to create a new world order imbued with American values and a Conservative prime minister who aimed to maintain the old world in all its glory. This disjunction threatened the stability of the wartime alliance. As Oliver Harvey, Anthony Eden's private secretary, wrote in October 1942: 'With Roosevelt straining to put the British Empire into liquidation and Winston pulling in the opposite direction to put it back to pre-Boer War, we are in danger of losing both the Old and the New World.'[66] Each leader was prepared to take the risk. With hindsight it is obvious that the Empire was doomed, as Churchill had long feared. Franklin Roosevelt, having decisively emerged from his cousin Theodore's shadow, rode the wave of the future. Churchill was unable to hold back the tide of history. But during the struggle against the Axis powers nothing better illustrated Churchill's resolve than his stubborn rearguard action in defence of the British Empire.

Notes

1. E. Roosevelt (ed.), *The Roosevelt Letters: Early Years* (London: Harrap, 1949), p. 152.
2. W. H. Harbaugh, *The Life and Times of Theodore Roosevelt I* (New York: Collier, 1963), p. 101.
3. R. Blake, *Disraeli* (London: Methuen, 1974), p. 523.
4. W. S. Churchill (ed.), *Never Give In!* (London: Pimlico, 2003), p. 4.
5. W. M. Hughes, *Policies and Potentates* (Sydney: Angus and Robertson, 1950), p. 230.
6. T. Roosevelt, *The Winning of the West*, 4 vols. (New York: Putnam, 1894), vol. 3, pp. 44–5.
7. W. Dockter, *Churchill and the Islamic World* (London: Tauris, 2015), p. 178.
8. E. S. Rubin, America, Britain, and *Swaraj*: Anglo-American Relations and Indian Independence, 1939–1945. *India Review*, vol. 10 (2011), p. 45.
9. Roosevelt (ed.), *Roosevelt Letters*, p. 311.
10. A. M. Schlesinger Jr., *The Age of Roosevelt: The Coming of the New Deal* (Boston, MA: Houghton Mifflin, 1960), p. 539.
11. P. Collier and D. Horowitz, *The Roosevelts: An American Saga* (London: Deutsch, 1995), p. 59.
12. F. D. Roosevelt, Our Foreign Policy: A Democratic View. *Foreign Affairs*, vol. 6 (July 1928), pp. 575 and 584.
13. S. I. Rosenman (ed.), *The Public Papers and Addresses of Franklin D. Roosevelt*, 13 vols. (Harper: New York, 1938), vol. 3, p. 118.
14. D. Reynolds, *The Creation of the Anglo-American Alliance 1937–41* (London: Europa, 1981), p. 15.
15. Rhodes James, *Complete Speeches*, vol. 1, p. 30.
16. R. Toye, *Churchill's Empire: The World That Made Him and the World He Made* (London: Macmillan, 2010), p. 102.
17. P. Brendon, Churchill and Empire. In B. P. Farrell (ed.), *Churchill and the Lion City: Shaping Modern Singapore* (Singapore: NUS Press, 2011), p. 14.
18. W. S. Blunt, *My Diaries*, 2 vols. (New York: Knopf, 1921), vol. 2, p. 284.
19. CAC, CHAR 2/139/2, pamphlet: 'The destruction of the British Empire as planned by the Communist International.' Published by the Russian National Students' Association, 1924.
20. D. Stafford, *Oblivion or Glory: 1921 and the Making of Winston Churchill* (New Haven, CT: Yale University Press, 2019), pp. 186 and 178.
21. Rhodes James, *Complete Speeches*, vol. 3, pp. 3065 and 3144.
22. R. Hyam, Churchill and the British Empire. In R. Blake and W. R. Louis (eds.), *Churchill* (Oxford: Oxford University Press, 1994), p. 169.
23. J. Darwin, *Britain, Egypt and the Middle East* (London: Palgrave Macmillan, 1981), p. 114.
24. Rhodes James, *Complete Speeches*, vol. 3, p. 3140.
25. CAC, CHAR 9/98, 'India', pp. 79 and 83.
26. CAC, CHAR 8/556, pp. 9 and 15.
27. Rhodes James, *Complete Speeches*, vol. 6, p. 6613.
28. J. Colville, *The Fringes of Power* (London: Hodder and Stoughton, 1985), p. 103.
29. Churchill (ed.), *Never Give In!*, pp. 209 and 218.
30. W. F. Kimball (ed.), *Churchill and Roosevelt: The Complete Correspondence*, 3 vols. (London: Collins, 1984), vol. 1, pp. 37–8.
31. Colville, *Fringes of Power*, p. 136.

32. J. Barnes and D. Nicholson (eds.), *The Empire at Bay: The Leo Amery Diaries 1929–1945* (London: Hutchinson, 1988), p. 637.

33. J. Charmley, Churchill and the American Alliance. In D. Cannadine and R. Quinault (eds.), *Winston Churchill in the Twenty-First Century* (Cambridge: Cambridge University Press, 2004), p. 151.

34. M. Gilbert, *OB*, vol. 6 (London: Heinemann, 1983), pp. 743 and 473.

35. Schlesinger, *Coming of the New Deal*, p. 474.

36. E. Roosevelt, *As He Saw It* (New York: Duell, Sloan and Pearce, 1946), pp. 37–8.

37. W. R. Louis, *Ends of British Imperialism: The Scramble for Empire, Suez and Decolonization* (London: Tauris, 2006), pp. 593–4.

38. W. S. Churchill, *The Second World War*, 6 vols. (London: Cassell, 1951), vol. 4, p. 185.

39. Rosenman (ed.), *Public Papers of Roosevelt*, vol. 10, p. 69.

40. Churchill, *Second World War*, vol. 3, p. 194.

41. K. J. Clymer, Franklin D. Roosevelt, Louis Johnson, India and Anticolonialism: Another Look. *Pacific Historical Review*, vol. 57 (1988), p. 272.

42. Kimball (ed.), *Churchill and Roosevelt*, vol. 1, p. 446.

43. W. F. Kimball, *Forged in War: Churchill, Roosevelt and the Second World War* (London: HarperCollins, 1997), p. 140.

44. K. J. Clymer, *Quest for Freedom: The United States and India's Independence* (New York: Columbia University Press, 1995), p. 105.

45. Barnes and Nicholson (eds.), *Empire at Bay*, p. 842.

46. *Churchill by His Contemporaries: An Observer Appreciation* (London: Hodder and Stoughton, 1965), p. 97.

47. Quoted by S. Wolton, *The Loss of White Prestige: Lord Hailey, the Colonial Office and the Politics of Race and Empire in the Second World War* (Basingstoke: Palgrave Macmillan, 2000), p. 101.

48. CAC, CHAR 9/191A/3–12, 30 March 1943.

49. CAC, CHAR 9/191 A-B/35.

50. CAC, CHAR 9/191 A-B/53.

51. CAC, CHAR 20/165/43, Churchill to Wavell, 27 May 1944.

52. Kimball (ed.), *Churchill and Roosevelt*, vol. 3, p. 155.

53. Barnes and Nicholson (eds.), *Empire at Bay*, p. 943.

54. M. Mukerjee, *Churchill's Secret War: The British Empire and the Ravaging of India During World War II* (New York: Basic Books, 2010), p. 273.

55. A. Roberts, *Churchill: Walking with Destiny* (London: Allen Lane, 2018), p. 787.

56. Colville, *Fringes of Power*, p. 563.

57. Rubin, 'America, Britain, and *Swaraj*', p. 48.

58. Rosenman (ed.), *Public Papers of Roosevelt*, vol. 13, pp. 68–70.

59. Rubin, 'America, Britain, and *Swaraj*', p. 49.

60. W. D. Leahy, *I Was There* (New York: Whittlesey, 1950), p. 313.

61. J. J. Sebrega, The Anti-Colonial Policies of Franklin D. Roosevelt: A Reappraisal. *Political Science Quarterly*, vol. 101 (1986), p. 76.

62. K. Sainsbury, *Churchill and Roosevelt at War: The War They Fought and the Peace They Hoped to Make* (New York: New York University Press, 1994), p. 15.

63. W. R. Louis, *Imperialism at Bay: The United States and the Decolonization of the British Empire 1941–1945* (Oxford: Oxford University Press, 1977), p. 548.

64. Roosevelt, *As He Saw It*, p. 71.

65. R. Nisbet, *Roosevelt and Stalin: The Failed Courtship* (Washington, DC: Gateway, 1989), p. 102.

66. Quoted by W. Kimball, Churchill, Roosevelt and Post-War Europe. In R. A. C. Parker (ed.), *Winston Churchill: Studies in Statesmanship* (London: Brassey, 1995), p. 141.

Further Reading

P. Brendon, Churchill and Empire. In B. P. Farrell (ed.), *Churchill and the Lion City: Shaping Modern Singapore* (Singapore: NUS Press, 2011), pp. 10–35

W. S. Churchill, *The Second World War*, 6 vols. (London: Cassell & Co. Ltd, 1948–54)

W. Dockter, *Churchill and the Islamic World* (London: Tauris, 2015)

R. Hyam, Churchill and the British Empire. In R. Blake and W. R. Louis (eds.), *Churchill* (Oxford: Oxford University Press, 1994), pp. 167–85

W. F. Kimball, *Forged in War: Churchill, Roosevelt and the Second World War* (London: HarperCollins, 1997)

D. Reynolds, *The Creation of the Anglo-American Alliance 1937–41* (London: Europa, 1981)

T. Roosevelt, *The Winning of the West*, 4 vols. (New York: Putnam, 1894)

11

Churchill, India and Race

Churchill, Empire, Race and India

Winston Churchill remains a highly controversial and contested figure in India (see Chapter 1 in this volume by Allen Packwood and Warren Dockter on Churchill's contested legacy). It is easy to see why. In 2019, leading historian Ramachandra Guha published a short essay in an Indian newspaper called 'The Two Faces of Winston Churchill'.[1] Guha cited Churchill's 1932 note to a parliamentary committee on Indian constitutional reforms, which argued that India could not become self-governing 'in any period which men can foresee'. Churchill went on to compare India with Europe, claiming it was not a political entity but a 'geographic abstraction' and could never be an independent nation. This chapter seeks to analyse why Churchill felt so strongly about the subcontinent and to explore the impact of these views on his policies and actions.

Churchill's India Sojourn

As a young officer Churchill spent twenty-two months 'in-country' living in India (including his two spells at the Afghan frontier). This represented his longest concentrated stay anywhere outside of Britain.

His arrival in India marked the start of his military career as a newly created subaltern, following his initiation into his regiment and his enjoyment of that exhilarating short attachment to Spanish troops in Cuba in 1895 (see Chapter 3 in this volume by Warren Dockter). His cavalry regiment, the 4th Hussars, was being rotated into India for a typical six- to twelve-year spell. As a young officer, Churchill lived a carefree life of conspicuous comfort, even luxury. Sequestered among British companions of his own class, he also enjoyed high-society contacts among the elites of British India, a product of his upper-class social connections, reinforced by a discreet push from his mother, Lady Randolph, who used her extensive political and military contacts to advance his career. Churchill disdained the Anglo-Indians he encountered, a term which in those days referred to the Britons who had spent long years in India, in the Indian Civil Service, the Indian Army and elsewhere.[2] His prejudice had the effect of precluding dialogue with those Britons who knew India intimately, enhancing his intellectual isolation. And he complained bitterly about this isolation in his frequent letters to his mother. The only Indians with whom he fully engaged were the princely polo-playing elites of the Indian states who lionised Churchill for his prowess at the sport and for his aristocratic lineage – his father, Lord Randolph, was well remembered for his four-month visit to India in 1884–5 (directly before his appointment as the secretary of state for India). The early and still recent demise of Lord Randolph, in January 1895, would also have evoked their sympathy. Churchill's only quotidian Indian contacts, beyond the ordinary Muslim troopers that he came to know during a brief attachment with a Punjab Muslim regiment in 1897, were with sundry personal attendants, plus the service providers, not forgetting the moneylenders at the cantonment fringes, who also figure in his informative personal letters.

Churchill idolised his father. Lord Randolph's Victorian vision of imperial rule became his personal compass, as he repeatedly attested throughout his political life. This severely damaged India when he was prime minister between 1940 and 1945. Churchill's political persona, in its conception, was forged in these military years, partly through his reading of England's two greatest historians, Gibbon and Macaulay. He found ample time for self-education amid the set routines his regiment. He also engaged in deep personal reflection on what he sought from life. His 1897 essay, *The Scaffolding of Rhetoric*, reveals his aspirations, developed in that period of intense seclusion, to become an orator and politician. In parallel, he embarked on another quest, a calculated, risky pursuit of military distinction, explicitly designed to launch his political career. In this manner, the Empire and its permanence became the bedrock of deep-seated conviction. Protecting them also became Churchill's life goal. Through happenstance, those career-building actions coincided with India's nationalist upsurge for self-rule and independence. That created a deeply personal challenge for Churchill, which was played out during his public life with a particular intensity.

1919–1929: Interwar Political Career

The Jallianwala Bagh massacre of 13 April 1919 was one of the most brutal actions in Britain's Indian colonial record. It involved the killing of hundreds of men, women and children, all part of a peaceful crowd that had gathered at an enclosed garden near Amritsar's Golden Temple, the premier shrine of the Sikh community. Their misfortune was that as a consequence of wider political agitation across India, and some attacks in Amritsar against Britons, there was tension in the city. Brigadier General Reginald Dyer responded with overwhelming force, mobilising armoured cars with machine guns and then ordering Indian troops (and Gurkhas) armed with rifles to open fire.[3] Thereafter, Dyer was recalled to London where an army board decided to remove him from the Army List, in effect sending him into retirement at half-pay.

By this time, Churchill was back in the Cabinet as secretary of state for war and air, a position he would hold until 1921. He confirmed the decision to remove Dyer and it then fell on him, and the secretary of state for India Edwin Montagu, to defend the government's action in parliament, in the face of a growing upsurge of British opinion that favoured Dyer. On 8 July 1920, Montagu opened that debate, but failed adequately to defend the government's position. Churchill's speech, which followed immediately, was a model of restrained, forensic and persuasive argument. Confronting angry heckling over the government's removal of Dyer, in which some members of his own side joined the opposition critics, Churchill analysed the issue, asserting that the repression against peaceful political demonstrators, which culminated in the Jallianwala massacre, was:

> not the British way of doing business . . . . The slaughter of nearly 400 persons and the wounding of perhaps three or four times as many . . . [is] an episode which appears to me to be without precedent or parallel in the modern history of the British Empire . . . . It is an extraordinary event, a monstrous event, an event which stands in singular and sinister isolation.[4]

That speech transformed the mood of the House; some have held it as Churchill's most effective parliamentary performance. It was certainly a singular public expression of empathy for the Indian people – perhaps a final unequivocal utterance of that nature.

The limits of Churchill's liberalism towards India would quickly become apparent. In 1921, when Edwin Montagu developed the Liberal government's ideas for Indian political evolution, formulated in the 1919 India Act, Churchill warned him that he was getting into 'deep waters' and that 'reaction was gathering' against this.[5] In the wake of the Indian national movement's first *Satyagraha*, nation-wide demonstrations which coincided with the five-month 1921–2 India tour by the Prince of Wales (future King Edward VIII), Churchill even urged that Gandhi be arrested and deported.[6] This was just the beginning. Many of Churchill's friends, from the 1920s onwards, came to believe that he had developed an India obsession.

Appointed secretary of state for the colonies (1921–2), Churchill made a bid to enlarge the ambit of that office by suggesting for himself the nomenclature 'secretary of state for imperial affairs'. Lord Curzon, foreign secretary at the time, unsurprisingly shot it down.[7] In 1924 Stanley Baldwin took office as prime minister and, Churchill having abandoned the Liberal Party for the Conservatives, seriously considered appointing Churchill secretary of state for India, only to be talked out of the idea by those he consulted.[8] Instead, Churchill won the bigger prize, becoming chancellor of the exchequer, after Neville Chamberlain had turned down that post. His period in that office has come to be viewed as a failure, with his abandonment of the gold standard seen as folly (see Chapter 9 in this volume on Churchill's economics by Martin Daunton).[9] A greater failure may have been his reduction in funds for the navy to build capital ships, leaving it short of the strength it would need when the Second World War broke out ten years later and contributing to Britain's inability to defend the Empire in the east. It is an episode that does not say much for the prophetic powers of the historian, in spite of Churchill's frequent claim that looking back sharpened one's understanding of the future.

Between 1908 and 1945, Churchill held positions of Cabinet rank for long stretches. The exceptions were: 1915–17, when he resigned after the failed Dardanelles attack, and served in the First World War trenches commanding an infantry battalion; 1922–4, when he lost three elections (the 1922 General Election and two by-elections in 1923 and 1924); and finally, from 1929 to 1939, when he was in the political wilderness, quitting Baldwin's shadow Cabinet in 1931 but remaining a backbench

Conservative MP. Those final ten years of exile from high office were self-inflicted, caused in large part by his diehard opposition to the evolution of self-rule in India which helped to convince Baldwin, Chamberlain and others that he was temperamentally unsuited for a return to the Cabinet. It was a subject that obsessed him. Perhaps no British political figure of the time spoke as much, and as often, on Indian affairs and the Empire as did Churchill.

British India's Constitutional Evolution

Churchill's six-year campaign against the India Act of 1935 was conducted at enormous political cost to himself, as it followed his Party's clear decision in October 1929 to support the ruling Labour Party in its moves towards gradual constitutional changes in British India. In the eyes of the leadership of his Conservative Party, plus an overwhelming majority of its parliamentary members, this was an extreme act of indiscipline and led to his resignation from the shadow Cabinet.

Churchill was supported in this by a handful of his own party MPs, and lost round after round of voting when he tried to block the legislation presented to parliament in its tortuous passage towards acceptance. From 1930, to buttress his campaign against self-rule, he used the Indian Empire Society. It drew its membership from those who opposed the government's moves towards constitutional reform, including many arch-conservatives and imperial diehards who would previously have regarded Churchill as a traitor for his 1904 defection to the Liberal Party.

Repeatedly, Churchill explained his actions in terms of defending the Empire; he attacked the very notion of self-governance for India. That made sense only if one also bought into Churchill's notion that the people of India were intrinsically unfit to run their own affairs. And that harked back to the colonial thinking of the nineteenth century, which saw the colonised natives as unschooled, politically immature and incapable of running their own affairs, their survival in safety and peace resting upon supervised governance by the benign harbingers of Western civilisation.

Churchill saw India as composed of four segments: the Hindus as exemplified and led by the Congress Party; these he viewed as intrinsically untrustworthy (and many different racist epithets were added in

elaboration). The other three were presented as Britain's allies: the
Muslims, a bastion of solid support; the princely states, also Britain's
constant supporters; and the Untouchables (i.e. the 'oppressed' classes),
who suffered at the hands of Hindus and were thus useful for Britain.
Churchill did not care if this analysis ran against facts on the ground and
did not take account of the width and depth of the country's surging
national movement for independence, which grew continually in
strength during this period.

In 1931 Churchill published a pamphlet consisting of ten of his
speeches on the India Act and the Empire.[10] There were three running
themes. First, Churchill stressed, in his famous denunciation, the incon-
gruity of Gandhi, a 'half-naked fakir' and 'seditious' Middle Temple
lawyer striding up the steps of the Viceregal Palace to treat on equal
terms with the king-emperor's representative. Secondly, he pointed to
the danger of 'Brahmin domination' under Congress rule. The charge
might have fitted Nehru's caste affiliation but not his political stance,
which was far from casteist. His accusation that Indian nationalists
communicated with one another using the English language was
equally misplaced: he was seemingly unaware that Hindustani was the
idiom for most Indian political speeches. Thirdly, Churchill held that
Muslims faced extinction at the hands of Hindus. He alleged that under
Hindu rule over 70 million Muslims would be 'bled and exploited'.[11]
This showed no understanding of the complex relationships among all
of India's religious communities.

Churchill advanced two further arguments, both economic, which
merit closer study. One was that although Britain had done little for
India's economic advancement, it could do much more.[12] British failures
in this respect are entirely borne out by the figures of India's long-term
economic growth in the colonial era.[13] But Churchill did not suggest
how the situation might be rectified, beyond some generalities. Nor did
he pursue this thinking, much less act on it, during the five years of his
prime ministership. The other major point Churchill advanced was in
indirect contradiction to British concern for India, namely the assertion
of Britain's 'essential rights' in the subcontinent.[14] He argued that the
coming struggle in Europe required that Britain assert its interests in
the Empire. That was a key point in his BBC broadcast of 30 January 1935
(see later in this chapter).[15] The problem with this approach is that it
undercut his argument that Britain should do more for India's

advancement. Britain's economic gains were the result of exploitation of this 'crown jewel'.

What was the net outcome? Few of Churchill's supporters, even those he counted as his friends, understood his logic or shifted their positions to back him. Perhaps even fewer bought into his protestation, repeated on several occasions, that he would 'rather abandon political life' than alter his standpoint on India. Undeterred, he persisted in that diehard, isolated and reputation-damaging course of action. His BBC address of 30 January 1935 sums up this phase and reveals the fallacy of his *idée fixe*. The BBC publication *The Listener* carried a transcript, entitled 'The Great Betrayal', in which he called the India Act a 'monument of shame' (in parliament he had actually said a 'monument of sham'[16]); he portrayed India as a land of '40 different nations', speaking in twenty tongues and professing an equal number of religions. He was wrong on the language count; eighty years later the Census of India noted that more than 121 languages are spoken by more than 10,000 people and there are 19,500 dialects.[17] What Churchill could not understand or accept was that behind that heterogeneity lay an abiding sense of Indianness that has permeated the people of this land over millennia, despite huge diversities, or perhaps because of its multifaceted syncretic culture.

Churchill's obsession with India distracted attention from his other loud refrain: the growing German menace which threatened all of Europe. For him that meant Britain needed the Empire more than ever before. The problem was that establishing provincial assemblies in India, the central goal of the legislation he was opposing, was hard to connect with dismantling the Empire. Indeed, the true intention of the Government of India Act was, as Lord Linlithgow said, 'to hold India to the Empire'.[18] Nehru called it a charter of slavery. Thus Churchill's alarm bells rang hollow and were not heeded.

The 1935 General Election saw the Conservative Party once again dominating the national government, initially under Baldwin and then Chamberlain, but Churchill was not given any ministerial position. Some have speculated that he also lost out on a possible bid for the prime ministership. Certainly, he discredited himself. In net terms, his dogmatic campaign against the 1935 India Act helped to delay its passage by at least three years and his actions left the leaders of the Indian independence movement embittered, indirectly contributing to Hindu–Muslim polarisation.

Churchill, Gandhi and Jinnah

Three round-table conferences on India had been held in London (1930–2), with no concrete outcome, other than entrenching the communal constituency formula that became the bedrock of the India Act of 1935. However, they had two political consequences, the first of them significantly negative. On the side-lines of the second conference, Gandhi tried to meet Churchill, through a message conveyed to Churchill's son, then a journalist covering the event. He was rebuffed. Some years later

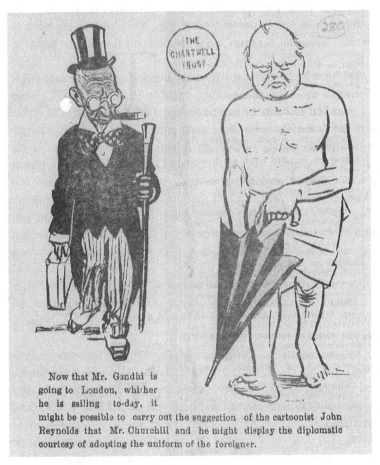

Now that Mr. Gandhi is going to London, whither he is sailing to-day, it might be possible to carry out the suggestion of the cartoonist John Reynolds that Mr. Churchill and he might display the diplomatic courtesy of adopting the uniform of the foreigner.

Figure 11.1 Cartoon parodying Churchill's description of Gandhi as a 'half-naked fakir', 1931 (Churchill Papers, CHAR 2/586C/280).

Churchill enigmatically told one of Gandhi's emissaries (Mira Behn, formerly Mary Slade) that he had wanted to meet Gandhi, but politically 'it would not have done'.[19]

The other outcome was that Jinnah opted to stay on in London after the first conference ended, in December 1930. He rapidly established a flourishing legal practice as a barrister at the Privy Council and the High Court, and remained until the end of 1934. That was a time of internal turmoil within the Muslim League which made a short self-exile politic. Jinnah wrote to one of his friends that 'the centre of gravity' on India's political future had shifted to London and it made sense to be there. This is but one instance of his well-calculated policy, both pragmatic and strategic. After 1934, Jinnah often travelled to London, ostensibly for court cases, but probably for political purposes as well.

The fluidity of the 1940s Jinnah–Churchill communications that survive in the archives, even their banality, suggests that these were not their first exchanges. But we do not find any documents of an earlier date in this thread, curious for a great public figure, famous for hoarding communications. Further, on leaving the premiership after his July 1945 election defeat, Churchill established with Jinnah a clandestine channel for exchanging telegrams in the names and addresses of their secretaries. At that time, when the privileges of high office were lost, Churchill did not create a comparable arrangement with anyone else. These and other bits of evidence, not definitive but suggestive, point to a unique degree of mutual collaboration, and a shared desire to cloak this.[20]

Certainly, Churchill's personal experiences in India and his writings on Indian affairs confirm his natural prejudices in favour of the Muslims and against the Hindus, and he made little distinction between the latter and the Congress Party.

As a consequence of the increasing congruence of interests between Jinnah and the raj, he came to identify Indian Muslims as pro-British and the Congress Party as anti-British. Ipso facto, Congress could only be the political party of the Hindus. It was difficult for Britons, and apparently impossible for Churchill, to acknowledge Muslims could support the Congress Party, and that an Indian political party could be 'secular' was unimaginable. Churchill placed the inhabitants of the subcontinent in rigid boxes.

This was in spite of the political reality on the ground. Remember, in the 1937 election to eleven Provincial Assemblies in British India (the only large voter-base election held in British India, if we exclude the hasty elections of 1946, held amid political turbulence), the Muslim League failed to capture power in any province. It won a mere 108 out of the 485 seats reserved for Muslims; in the strategic north-west frontier province adjoining Afghanistan, a Muslim affiliate of the Congress Party came to power. How then did Jinnah become the sole spokesman of the Muslims of India by 1941–2? This owed something to Churchill's favourable view of the Muslim League, the only major nationalist to support the British war effort, combined with Jinnah's acumen in positioning himself in New Delhi as the most articulate of spokesman of this community. Of course, it helped that Congress leaders had resigned their ministerial positions in 1939 and that many of them were in jail between August 1942 and mid-1945.

Second World War

As prime minister during the Second World War, Churchill tightly controlled Britain's response to the Indian independence movement, his firm opposition to Gandhi and the Congress Party tilting policy in favour of Jinnah, the Muslim League and therefore ultimately the creation of Pakistan.

In the opening months, as first lord of the admiralty, he opposed any attempt at religious reconciliation in India, cynically telling the War Cabinet on 31 January 1940 that he regarded the Hindu–Muslim feud 'as the bulwark of British rule in India'.[21] Churchill wrote to Neville Chamberlain on 20 February 1940 in the same vein, complaining about the Viceroy's policy of 'running after Ghandi [sic] and the Congress'.[22] An eyewitness to Churchill's satisfaction at the Congress–Muslim dissensions in India in those days was John Colville, shortly to become his private secretary. On 12 April 1940 Colville noted in his diary: 'Winston rejoiced in the quarrel that had broken out afresh between Hindus and Muslims, said he hoped it would remain bitter and bloody and was glad that we had made the suggestion of Dominion status which was acting as a cat among the pigeons.'[23]

After Japan's entry into the Second World War in December 1941 and its swift occupation of Singapore and Malaya, it seemed for a few months that India's fate might be in the balance. India suddenly became a major concern for the big two Allied leaders, Churchill and Roosevelt, but by mid-1942 that threat had receded, with Japan's offensive bogged down in south-east Asia and the USA now able to take the initiative in the Pacific War. The failure of the Cripps mission in April to May 1942, almost preordained because of the limited mandate given to him in London, produced huge disenchantment among the Indian nationalists, who reacted with the Quit India Movement of 8 August 1942. That played into British hands; from an Indian perspective, it was a major blunder. It produced a de facto near three-year suspension of the independence movement, right up to June 1945 when Nehru and other Congress leaders were finally released from jail, Gandhi having been released a year earlier after the death of his wife Kasturba, his fasts and his ill-health.

For Churchill it produced a near three-year hiatus in developing a cogent policy for exit from India. Some might argue that he was mentally unable to deal with that exit, despite its imminence and inevitability. The power vacuum also gave Jinnah the opportunity to establish himself as the only viable saviour of the subcontinent's Muslims. For three years there was little thought in London about India policy, much less any preparation for the future. The stasis contributed to the division of India. When followed by post-war British weakness, it made partition almost inevitable.

Race and Churchill

Eleanor Roosevelt, FDR's spouse and intellectual partner, a keen political observer, narrated a story about Churchill's stay at the White House at the end of December 1941, three weeks after Japan's attack on Pearl Harbor. Eleanor had just received a letter from her friend Pearl Buck (Nobel literature laureate, noted for her evocative novels set in China), which warned that 'a deep secret coloured solidarity is growing in the world'. Eleanor showed that letter to FDR, who responded that 'he would have to compel the British to give dominion status to India', adding that it was essential to enlarge 'Negro' rights in the USA. Eleanor wrote to a friend that when this was discussed with Churchill, he replied in terms of 'the English-speaking people' taking control after the war; Eleanor responded that those taking charge should include all the people that believed in democracy.[24]

Was there any other democratic leader, in Churchill's age or later, who treated the independence movements in the colonies gathering momentum in Asia and Africa as contemptuously as did Churchill? The catalogue of epithets he employed for Gandhi is lengthy, as is the list of aggressive actions he threatened. He suggested, for example, that Gandhi should be bound hand and foot at the gates of Delhi by an enormous elephant with the Viceroy seated on its back and trampled underfoot; he frequently suggested that the Mahatma should be exiled to a remote island.[25] Was there ever comparable hostility shown by a colonial power towards a national movement leader who was revered by an enormous proportion of his people?

Some will think it unfair to frame the Bengal Famine of 1942–3 in terms of race, but how else should we explain Britain's callousness in managing that human crisis? In both British India and London there was routine, bureaucratic laxity, bordering on indifference, in handling the tragedy. The famine resulted in the death of between 2 and 3 million people in Bengal and the neighbouring provinces. That equals almost half the number of Jews that perished in the Holocaust. This was not premeditated genocide, but it was symptomatic of systemic neglect and failure. Consider that the famine only figured for the first time in Secretary of State for India Amery's meticulous personal diary on 24 December 1942, several months after the development of extreme crisis in Bengal and nearby provinces.[26]

In hindsight, we can see that the famine resulted from a congruence of events. Japan's invasion of Burma in early 1942 meant that its regular rice supplies to Bengal were disrupted. Further, the Bengal administration had begun to stockpile food in anticipation of a Japanese attack on India (which materialised at Imphal in March 1944, as a last, vicious throw of the dice by a Japan then on the back foot). Those two factors were compounded by local administrative mismanagement, which, as Amartya Sen has pointed out, led to hoarding by traders, causing grave shortages and prices higher than the common consumer could afford.[27] In cascading fashion, the Bengal shortages led to food scarcity in the neighbouring provinces.

Viceroy Linlithgow (in office from 1936 until October 1943, when he handed over to Field Marshal Archibald Wavell), who was notoriously wooden and unimaginative, failed to confront that unfolding calamity. His administration, and Amery in London, pinned all hopes on getting ships released and switched from the transport of war materials to the delivery of food supplies, through the logistics management programme handled from Britain. Their appeals fell on deaf ears. Linlithgow's culpable inactivity is evident from the fact that he did not once visit Bengal during that crisis to spur the administration into decisive action.

Can Churchill as the leader of the British Empire evade responsibility for that gross instance of maladministration? Wavell's diary offers this: 'the Churchill Government's attitude to India [was] "negligent, hostile and contemptuous …. Apparently it is more important to save the Greeks and liberated countries than the Indians, and there is reluctance either to provide shipping or to reduce stocks in this country".'[28] Also noteworthy is the fact that the first debate in the British parliament on the Bengal Famine took place as late as 4 November 1943, when the Commons took up an adjournment motion.[29] What does that say of the Empire's sensitivity, and that of the British media and the country's body politic, in the face of such a colossal human tragedy?

Endgame in British India

After losing the July 1945 election, Churchill remained moderately active in Indian affairs. There was a meeting and correspondence with Jinnah. Churchill was occasionally testy in his replies. We find in the Churchill Archives a letter that Jinnah wrote to Churchill on 22 August 1946, in which he complained that 'even you do not have a grasp of the situation in India', the international press being dominated by the views of the Congress Party. He also alleged that the Cabinet mission of early 1946 had 'betrayed' the Muslim League and was being steamrollered by the Viceroy. Churchill drafted a revealing reply, though it looks as though it was not sent. In it he rebuked Jinnah for failing to make a distinction between criticising the British government and abusing the British nation. He added that Britain was actually shedding a burden by leaving India, and that the new countries were likely to face turmoil and anarchy due to both religious and political disputes.[30]

Visiting London in May 1947 for a final round of consultations before the partition that was just four months away, Viceroy Lord Mountbatten went to meet Churchill and spoke to him of his difficulty in pinning down Jinnah and securing his final agreement to the partition formula. According to US historian Stanley Wolpert, Churchill gave Mountbatten a verbal message for Jinnah: 'This is a matter of life and death for Pakistan, if you do not accept this offer with both hands.'[31] Mountbatten used this effectively on his return to India, and in early June 1947, during a series of meetings with leaders of the Muslim League and the Congress, he claimed to have pushed Jinnah into acquiescence.[32]

It is puzzling that besides Gandhi, no Indian independence movement leader reached out to Churchill. In London, Krishna Menon, long-time president of what was in effect a lobbying group, the India League, acted as the de facto resident representative of the Congress Party, but he mainly cultivated Labour Party leaders, besides one recorded meeting with Secretary of State Amery in 1940.

Nehru, Churchill's fellow-Harrovian steeped in the English way of life, might have built bridges to his fellow anti-Nazi. When Nehru visited Prague in 1938 as a gesture of solidarity towards a small country facing Hitler's irredentist demand over Sudetenland, Churchill sent him a message of appreciation, but Nehru did not reply. Thereafter, during the intense independence struggle following the outbreak of the Second World War, neither contacted the other. And during his near three-year jail incarceration, after the August 1942 arrest of virtually all Congress leaders, Nehru received no leniency or consideration. Even with the end of British rule in clear sight, Churchill persisted in a hostile stance; in a speech in parliament in March 1947 he called Nehru 'a caste Hindu' who could not be trusted as the head of a provisional government in India.[33]

Two years later, after the Commonwealth Conference and in the context of the developing Cold War, Nehru visited Churchill in April 1949, according to a 2010 account by an Indian official: 'Apparently Churchill was virtually in tears and said, "Mr. Prime Minister I have done you great wrong. You are like the prodigal whom we thought was lost. You have saved the legacy of the empire", or words to this effect.'[34]

Notes

1. R. Guha, 'The two faces of Winston Churchill', *The Hindustan Times*, 24 February 2019.
2. See, for example, CAC, CHAR 28/222/37, letter from Churchill to Lady Randolph Churchill, 23 December 1896. In the nineteenth century, the children of mixed marriages were called 'Indo-Britons' and 'Eurasians', but that changed around the first decade of the 1900s. They came to be called 'Anglo-Indians', first recognised as a distinct category in the decennial 1911 Indian Census. They were given preference in the railways, posts and telegraph and some other professions in British India. Numbering around 300,000 in 1947, a sizeable portion migrated to Australia Britain,

Canada, but over 100,000 remain in India, with their distinctive subculture, mores and ways of linguistic expression.

3. Dyer told the Hunter Commission in November 1919 that he had taken two armoured cars, and would have used machine guns, but the vehicles could not enter the Bagh. This was in response to questions by Sir Chimanlal Setalvad, vice-chancellor of Bombay University and an advocate. See www.dnaindia.com/india/report-would-have-used-machine-guns-when-general-dyer-explained-how-jallianwala-bagh-massacre-could-ve-been-worse-2201660. The key exchange is: 'Chimanlal Setalvad: "Supposing the passage was sufficient to allow the armoured cars to go in, would you have opened fire with the machine guns?" Dyer: "I think, probably, yes."'

4. *Hansard*, House of Commons Debates, vol. 131, cols. 1705–1819, 8 July 1920.

5. CAC, Churchill Papers, CHAR 17/10/21–2, Letter from Churchill to Montagu, 8 October 1921.

6. Letter from Churchill to Montagu, 8 October 1921.

7. N. Rose, *Churchill: An Unruly Life* (London: Simon & Schuster, 1994), p. 153.

8. A. Herman, *Gandhi and Churchill* (New York: Bantam Dell, 2008), p. 287.

9. A. Roberts, *Churchill: Walking with Destiny* (London: Allen Lane, 2018), p. 307.

10. W. S. Churchill, *India* (London: Butterworth, 1931).

11. Churchill, *India*. The dynamic growth of the Muslim population in post-independence India, outstripping the population growth rate, is proof enough of Churchill's bias and lack of understanding. See Pew Research Center, 21 September 2021: 'Between 1951 and 1961, the Muslim population expanded by 32.7%, 11 percentage points more than India's overall rate of 21.6%. But this gap has narrowed. From 2001 to 2011, the difference in growth between Muslims (24.7%) and Indians overall (17.7%) was 7 percentage points.' www.pewforum.org/2021/09/21/population-growth-and-religious-composition.

12. See, for example, CAC, Churchill Papers, CHAR 8/317/69A, W. S. Churchill, 'The real issue in India', *Daily Mail*, 30 June 1932.

13. 'British rule did little for India: as far as we know the economy barely grew at all for over a hundred years (from 0.38% growth p.a. between 1820–1870 it peaked at 0.97% between 1870–1913, but then declined to 0.23% between 1913 and 1950, an overall rate which barely kept pace with the growth in population in the same period).' A. Morrison, 'A plague on both your houses', www.academia.edu/149081/A—Plague—on—both—your—houses.

14. Rhodes James, *Complete Speeches*, vol. 5, pp. 5025–32; CAC, Churchill Papers, CHAR 9/94, Speech by Churchill, House of Commons, 13 May 1931.

15. Rhodes James, *Complete Speeches*, vol. 5, pp. 5467–8; CAC, Churchill Papers, CHAR 9/114/51, broadcast. Churchill, 'The great betrayal', *The Listener*, 30 January 1935.

16. It is rendered 'shame' in *The Listener* but, as Ronald Hyam has stated, Churchill meant 'sham' because his point was not that federal proposals were unworthy but that they were unworkable. See R. Hyam, *Britain's Declining Empire: The Road to Decolonisation, 1918–1968* (Cambridge: Cambridge University Press, 2006), p. 64.

17. *Indian Express*, 1 July 2018, https://indianexpress.com/article/india/more-than-19500-mother-tongues-spoken-in-india-census-5241056.

18. A. Read and D. Fisher, *The Proudest Day: India's Long Road to Independence* (London: Pimlico, 1998), p. 255; P. Brendon, *The Decline and Fall of the British Empire* (London: Jonathan Cape, 2007), p. 387.

19. Mira Behn's note to Gandhi on her meeting with Churchill, Mira Slade papers, cited in M. Gilbert, CV, vol. 5, part 2, p. 919.

20. This is examined further in the author's recent book, *Churchill and India: Manipulation or Betrayal?* (New Delhi: Routledge, 2022). This chapter was written prior to its publication.

21. Cabinet memo by secretary of state for India, Lord Zetland, 31 January 1940, cited in R. Moore, *Churchill, Cripps and India, 1939–1945* (Oxford: Clarendon Press, 1979), p. 28.

22. TNA, PREM 1/414, Letter from Churchill to Chamberlain, 20 February 1940.

23. J. Colville, *The Fringes of Power: Downing Street Diaries 1939–1955* (London: Hodder and Stoughton, 1985), p. 103.

24. J. Lash, *Eleanor and Franklin: The Story of Their Relationship, Based on Eleanor Roosevelt's Private Papers* (New York: Norton, 1971), pp. 863–4.

25. During the Second World War, after the Indian nationalists launched the Quit India movement, Churchill seriously considered externing Gandhi to Uganda or to Aden; wiser counsels in New Delhi prevailed. One may imagine the fury this exile would have evoked across India.

26. CAC, Leo Amery Papers, AMEL 7/36, Leo Amery diary, 1942.

27. A. Sen, *Poverty and Famines: An Essay on Entitlement and Deprivation* (Oxford: Clarendon, 1981).

28. B. Mukherjee, *Bengal and Its Partition* (New Delhi: Rupa, 2021), p. 146: Wavell's diary has been edited by P. Moon, *The Viceroy's Journal* (London: Oxford University Press, 1973), p. 19.

29. *Hansard* House of Commons Debate, vol. 393, cols. 887–970, 4 November 1943.

30. CAC, Churchill Papers, CHUR 2/42/242. Letter from Jinnah to Churchill, 22 August 1946; CHUR 2/42/231–2, draft reply from Churchill to Jinnah, n.d.

31. S. Wolpert *Jinnah of Pakistan* (Oxford: Oxford University Press, 1984), p. 326.

32. A. von Tunzelmann, *Indian Summer: The Secret History of the End of an Empire* (London: Simon & Schuster, 2007), pp. 197–200; she gives a graphic account, sourced from a variety of material, of the way Mountbatten handled that final obstacle to agreement.

33. Roberts, *Churchill: Walking with Destiny*, p. 898.

34. Note to the author by the late Jagat S. Mehta, former Indian foreign secretary (the civil service head of the ministry of external affairs), who was on the Indian PM's delegation, 2010.

Further Reading

P. Brendon, *The Decline and Fall of the British Empire, 1781–1997* (London: Vintage, 2008)

W. S. Churchill, *India* (London: Butterworth, 1931)

A. Herman, *Gandhi and Churchill* (New York: Bantam Dell, 2008)

M. Mukerjee, *Churchill's Secret War: The British Empire and the Ravaging of India During World War II* (London: Basic Books, 2010)

K. S. Rana, *Churchill and India: Manipulation or Betrayal?* (New Delhi: Routledge, 2022)

A. von Tunzelmann, *Indian Summer: The Secret History of the End of an Empire* (London: Simon & Schuster, 2007)

12

Churchill's Campaign against Appeasement

The many stages of the life of Winston Churchill are well known, with his period as prime minister, from 1940 to 1945 during the Second World War, being the most influential in shaping his historical reputation.[1] It could be argued that the decade or so leading up to his replacing Neville Chamberlain in 10 Downing Street were also some of the most important in his career in public life. An ironic fact perhaps, because for much of this period, during the 1930s, Churchill was firmly out of office, with very little power; these were what are often referred to as his 'Wilderness Years'. At this time, he was often seen as a warmonger by his political peers and the press barons, in an era where so much hope was placed on the ability of the twin policies of disarmament and appeasement to defuse the growing tension in international relations that seemed to suggest that a second global conflict in the space of a generation was imminent. Memories of the horrors of the First World War were still fresh and the passionate desire of the peacemakers to learn the lessons of that conflict remained uppermost in the minds of the majority of British politicians and diplomats. Public opinion was also firmly opposed to Britain being drawn into yet another dispute between her European neighbours. With so many factors stacked against him, it can be argued that his appointment as prime minister was all the more remarkable. This chapter examines Churchill's opinions and actions during the 1930s that ultimately resulted in this extraordinary change in his political fortunes. It explores the tactics he used to voice his opinions, including through his other career as a journalist and historian. From this, the extent to which Churchill's views were unique or distinctive will be examined, as will the way in which his hostility to appeasement evolved, especially during the later 1930s. Such an assessment would be unbalanced, of course, if it did not also consider the alternative strategies to that which he favoured, and why his views ultimately prevailed. Finally, this chapter discusses how and why Churchill became prime minister in May 1940.

The Roots of Churchill's Opposition to Appeasement

Although the policy of appeasement is most closely associated with the governments of Stanley Baldwin (1935–7)[2] and, more famously, Neville Chamberlain (1937–40),[3] its roots lie much deeper in a wider tradition within British foreign policy. During the 1930s, appeasement was the policy of making territorial and other concessions to the fascist dictators in Germany and Italy in order to placate their bellicose foreign policy ambitions and thus preserve international peace.[4] Its ultimate failure led to those most closely associated with it, including Chamberlain and his foreign secretary, Lord Halifax, being dubbed 'The Guilty Men'.[5] Thus, for many decades to follow, those who had supported appeasement were seen as having dragged Britain into yet another European war by failing to take a more robust stand against the fascist dictators.[6] The policy was seen as one not befitting a country of Britain's standing in world affairs; as being a sign of a lack of resolve, of political, military and diplomatic weakness. It was this perception of appeasement that formed the principal basis of Churchill's opposition to the policy.

That said, there was more to Churchill's views than opposition to the granting of territorial concessions to aggressor powers in order to prevent war. To him, appeasement also indicated the presence of excessive liberal flabbiness in British foreign policy. The British historian Martin Gilbert has argued that the roots of appeasement can be traced back to the aftermath of the First World War, and to the ideas that underpinned the Allied peace settlements drawn up in Paris in 1919–20.[7] During the negotiation of these treaties, the then British prime minister, David Lloyd George, had been one of the most in favour of offering Germany a conciliatory rather than punitive peace settlement.[8] He believed that the most effective way of nurturing the fledgling Weimar democracy and rehabilitating Germany back into the company of nations was through cooperation and goodwill, and that the victorious powers should lead the way towards lasting peace by showing their commitment to the work of the League of Nations and through promotion of international disarmament and the banishment of war. These ideas gained widespread support among a British public shaken and scarred by the First World War, and had wider international support, especially from the American president, Woodrow Wilson.[9] However, Churchill believed that such ideals, although commendable, were excessively idealistic and showed a dangerous disregard for what could be called the track record of the rogue states in Europe (he also included the Soviet Union in his analysis) when it came to a long-term commitment to peace. To him, the German love of war and the military life was so deeply hardwired into their culture and way of thinking that the lofty ideals of the peacemakers were unlikely to change it. The states of Europe, led by Britain and France with support from the United States, should therefore be in a state of preparedness for the challenges posed to peace by an inevitably resurgent Germany. Churchill also believed that it was incumbent on Britain, as the world's most influential Great Power, to lead the necessary emasculation of the vanquished – and that Britain should not be magnanimous to a former enemy whose ambitions in 1914 had led to a war that had cost several hundred thousand British lives.

Out of office throughout most of the 1930s, Churchill used a variety of tactics to express his opposition to appeasement. One of the most effective was through his evocative use of history. His notion that Germany would never abandon militarism permanently was based on his reading of the past; the ambitions of Kaiser William II had shared the same bellicose Prussian nationalism of Frederick the Great and Otto von Bismarck, and it was only a matter of time before another German leader moulded in that tradition would emerge. Being reminded of the lessons of the past and the connection between past and current events was at the heart of Churchill's writing of the histories of the two world wars, as well as explaining and justifying his own role in those conflicts.[10]

The study of history to Churchill was also about using the lessons of the past to provide a united common cause in the present. Britain's heritage and ancestry was shared by everyone, and was thus something that all strands of public opinion would understand and embrace. During a period of growing international tension and the threat of war, British history, especially those events that paralleled the contemporary, offered comforting reassurance that all would eventually be well and that Britain would prevail; but only if the threat was faced down, if necessary on the battlefield, as it had been in the past. This method of thinking was deeply personal to Churchill and was part of his long-held view that he too was destined to make his mark in British public life. In particular, he liked to draw parallels with his own life and that of his eighteenth-century ancestor and hero, the 1st Duke of Marlborough, the victor of Blenheim.[11] His swashbuckling, fearless, confident forebear had stood up to tyrants and possessed a profound sense of moral purpose that Churchill believed he shared. As the British historian Professor David Reynolds has argued, Churchill believed himself to be in command of history.[12]

Churchill's use of what could be termed the weapon of history to express his hostility to appeasement was not confined to his blockbuster written accounts of the recent past. They reached an even wider audience through his embrace of a more modern method of popular communication: the moving picture. This was facilitated by Churchill's perhaps unlikely friendship with the Hungarian-born film director living in Britain, Alexander Korda.[13] During the 1930s, Korda made a series of movies about famous figures in British history, such as Henry VIII and Queen Elizabeth, and the key events that shaped their reigns. Anxious to capture this view of a heroic Britain accurately, Korda enlisted Churchill's advice on the historical content of some of the screenplays.[14] Churchill's response was fulsome and enthusiastic. He lost no time in using these films as a vehicle to convey his anti-appeasement message; that Britain must now stand up to aggressors to be worthy of the legacy of, for example, Queen Elizabeth's resolve in the face of the threat posed by the Spanish Armada.

Into the Wilderness

The end of the 1920s began auspiciously for Churchill, when he retained his parliamentary seat as MP for Epping in the 1929 General Election. However, the Conservatives were not blessed with the same good fortune, losing overall power to Ramsay MacDonald's Labour Party. This was a landmark victory for MacDonald because it enabled Labour to form a majority administration, the first in the history of the Party; this lasted until 1931.[15] The Labour victory also placed MacDonald personally at the heart of British politics as prime minister for a total of six years, including as the first leader of the coalition National Government, 1931–5. This was a position Churchill envied: being at the locus of political power, as he entered what was to become almost a decade out of political office, in what were later termed his 'Wilderness Years'.

During the Wilderness Years, Churchill's life progressed along two parallel channels; one as an author, the other as a politician agitating for power and influence. While Churchill's love of extravagant living partly explains his need to generate income through writing, it is by no means true that the co-existence of the two strands was a random happen-chance. During the early months of his exile from political office, Churchill began his long-planned biography of his forebear, John Churchill, the 1st Duke of Marlborough.[16] The start of work on what became a four-volume biography coincided with plans to create a Conservative–Liberal coalition to respond to the growing socio-economic crisis caused by the Great Depression. Churchill believed that the new Labour administration simply lacked the experience and ability to survive, and predicted that MacDonald's days as prime minis-ter were likely to be numbered.[17] However, while Stanley Baldwin, the leader of the Conservative Party, welcomed the idea, the Liberals were less enthusiastic. And while the initiative came to nothing, it does reveal something about Churchill's political thinking; that he was a natural coalitionist. He was part of a generation of patrician, Anglican, Conservative politicians who were interested more in the politics of the expedient; what needed to be done to produce results rather than political ideology.[18] This is somewhat at odds with his more famous image as an implacably staunch critic of the politics and diplomacy of compromise associated with appeasement. While Churchill has often been viewed as a man of many contradictions, it could be argued that there was a concrete reason on this occasion for this apparent paradox. His opposition to appeasement was always underpinned by a sense of moral outrage. This stemmed in part from the reaction of many to the increasing persecution of the Jews and other minorities in Germany, and the growing bellicose nature of the regimes of the fascist dictators, and from a fear and hatred of war. But it also had a much more primal dimension to it; that one does not give in to bullying, an old schoolyard lesson that applied equally in the realms of international diplomacy.

The prospect of taking swift, decisive action against those who were not deemed to be acting in Britain's best interests was also evident in Churchill's response to the Labour government's proposal to grant dominion status to India in autumn 1930.[19] Churchill believed that such a step would encourage Indian nationalists to push for full independence from the British Empire.[20] Churchill anticipated that independence would be disastrous for India because he felt that the country's political leaders lacked the knowledge and experience necessary to govern such a vast, multicultural state.[21] He also feared that greater independence would encourage exercises in what today would be referred to as ethnic cleansing, with the dominant Hindu-Brahmin caste persecuting the so-called Untouchables and other minority groups. When civil unrest broke out in Cawnpore in March 1931 between Muslims and Hindus, Churchill gave a speech warning about the dangers of civil war and the effects of militaristic nationalism in India. He was openly critical of the actions of Mohandas Gandhi and his Indian National Congress, urging the British government to ban it. However, when Churchill learned that the British Viceroy in India, Lord Linlithgow, was endeavouring to broker a deal with Gandhi, and that his actions had the support in London of Stanley Baldwin, he decided to resign from the shadow Cabinet. But that was not the end of the matter for Churchill. When, in December 1931, the House of Commons finally debated the proposal to grant dominion status to India, Churchill made a final attempt to thwart the bill but lost by more than 300 votes. It could be argued that British government dealings with Gandhi and his Indian National Congress Party were a form of appeasement. Consequently, it is important to view Churchill's response to British policy as a strand in his opposition to that policy, even if appeasement is more usually associated with European diplomacy. The crisis over the future status of India in 1930–1 nevertheless is part of a significant narrative in Churchill's thinking that opposed displays of aggressive nationalism. Churchill's views on Indian nationalism are also at variance with his views on British nationalism, especially in the form embodied by the Empire. At the heart of his thinking was the primacy of British diplomatic and strategic interests. Consequently, he would not have recognised the fundamental paradox in his thinking and in the thinking of many of his generation of imperialists; that the forms of nationalism that bolstered British international power were legitimate and acceptable, while those that did not were not.

Churchill's opposition to granting India dominion status ensured that he remained firmly in the public eye. Coverage of the debates in the House of Commons in *The Times* especially ensured that Churchill's views on the need to offer a firm and robust response to challenges to British influence in the international arena were well known. To capitalise on his media profile further, and in order to recoup some of the financial losses he had suffered as a result of the Wall Street Crash in October 1929, Churchill decided to embark on a lecture tour of the United States. He arrived in New York on 11 December 1931, accompanied by his wife Clementine and his daughter Diana. While in the city, he was hospitalised briefly after being hit by a car, an experience about which he wrote in an article in the *Daily Mail*, resulting in an avalanche of goodwill messages from the newspaper's readership.[22] Although Churchill's sojourn to the United States in 1931 did not offer overt opportunities for him to express his opposition to the growing culture of militaristic nationalism in the world, it did set the seal on another aspect of his historical reputation. That was courage in the face of adversity, and a kind of indestructibility of body, soul and will; a bloody-minded indefatigability and courage of conviction that increasingly set him apart from many of his British contemporaries. Although Churchill's actual political identity was often difficult to define throughout his life, being a blend of conservatism and liberalism, and, as has already been suggested, he was often a man of paradox, his hostility to the rise of nationalism in the 1930s was consistent and unambiguous. Some critics have argued that his stance was often just party political, especially in regard to his opposition to dominion status for India, but that is to take that episode too much out of context. As it is, it was during these first Wilderness Years that he started to articulate a set of ideas and principles that would culminate in confrontation with Neville Chamberlain and, ultimately, in his election as prime minister.

Campaign against Appeasement

The parallel lives of Churchill the politician and Churchill the historian and author continued in 1932 and 1933. Much of 1932 was taken up with writing his biography of the 1st Duke of Marlborough, an experience he later claimed did more than any other to convince him of his destiny as a future political leader. Writing the book also consolidated his views on the rightness of the use of military force to defeat an aggressor; that there were occasions when its use was unavoidable and necessary. This was not simply a romantic vision. It was based in this case on his own first-hand experiences of walking the battlefields of Marlborough's greatest victories,

Figure 12.1 Churchill contesting the General Election, 1935. CAC, Churchill Press Photographs, CHPH 1A/F2/30.

including Blenheim. It was on one such tour of Europe, in August 1932, that Churchill met Ernst Hanfstaengl, a friend of Hitler. This almost resulted in a direct encounter between Churchill and Hitler.[23] Although Hitler had yet to secure power in Germany, his views on anti-Semitism were well known to many foreign politicians, including Churchill, who lost no time denouncing his prejudices. Several weeks later, while convalescing after a bout of paratyphoid fever, Churchill met the German chancellor, Franz von Papen, in the Austrian city of Salzburg.[24] Von Papen informed Churchill that his government intended to ask Britain and France to accept Germany's right to re-arm. When reported to the Foreign Office, this request was refused by the British foreign secretary, Sir John Simon, on the grounds that Germany was still bound by the disarmament clauses of the Treaty of Versailles.[25] Churchill agreed with Simon because he believed that if granted such latitude, Germany would use it immediately to pursue wars of conquest with its neighbours. Churchill's encounter with von Papen demonstrates that Churchill's concerns about the probable bellicose nature of German foreign policy were not simply based on antipathy to the Third Reich but stemmed from a closer, deeper reading of what could be termed the German 'mental map'. Consequently, when Hitler assumed power in Germany on 30 January 1933, Churchill lost no time in warning the House of Commons about the likely threat to international peace that the new German regime posed. He also spoke with equal vigour on German domestic politics, especially the escalating persecution of the Jews. Indeed, during the early days of the Third Reich, Churchill spoke about social and economic conditions within Germany at least as much as he did about the likely course of German foreign policy.

This balance of emphasis on domestic and foreign affairs was also evident in Churchill's approach to the British government. He believed that it was vitally important for the National Government led by Ramsay MacDonald to abandon all plans to engage in any form of disarmament, a strategy that did not chime well with the official British commitment to the efforts of the League of Nations to abandon all means of waging war.[26] Indeed, the British government was closely embroiled in the long-running international disarmament negotiations that had taken place in Geneva intermittently since the end of the First World War. Abandonment of disarmament would have been political suicide to a government determined to respect the wishes of British public opinion that was firmly hostile to any foreign policy that could result in armed conflict. Nonetheless, in November 1934, Churchill gave a radio broadcast in which he warned that the Third Reich was likely to pursue an aggressive programme of military rearmament and intended to prepare for war. His message, once again, was that it would be foolish for Britain and France to do anything other than to match that programme of rearmament. However, in this analysis of Churchill's Wilderness Years and how his fortunes in public life eventually changed, such speeches had another importance. They kept him in the public eye.

What is more, while the 1930s may have been Churchill's Wilderness Years, his was not a voice in the wilderness.[27] He had important allies in Whitehall, especially through the good offices of two civil servants, Desmond Morton and Ralph Wigram.[28] Morton was an officer in the British army who also provided the British government with military intelligence, while Wigram was head of the Central European Department of the Foreign Office that dealt with diplomatic traffic between Britain and Germany. He was thus privy to the opinions of senior diplomats based in the German capital, Berlin, especially the British ambassador, Sir Eric Phipps. Of greatest significance to Churchill was the data they provided on the size and rate of expansion of the German air force, the Luftwaffe. This information was supplied by clandestine means. But it was very high-grade intelligence, and meant that certainly in the mid-1930s Churchill knew as much about German economic and military planning as anyone in the British government. It is difficult to determine how far this covert attempt to undermine the official British commitment to international disarmament and to appeasement went within Whitehall, but the willingness of senior civil servants to take such personal risks on Churchill's behalf demonstrates that his views were respected in the higher echelons of government. This credibility would be vital in later years in establishing his credentials as an opponent of appeasement and thus a politician equipped to enable Britain to fight a war against Germany and her allies.

However, scholars of the British and French policy of appeasement during the 1930s usually begin their detailed analysis of the motives behind it not so much with an analysis of the military capability of the Third Reich but through a discussion of German diplomatic motive and intention;[29] that is, the reasons why specific regions of Europe were targeted and the rationale for that, together with a discussion of the Anglo-French response. The first key event cited is the reoccupation of the Rhineland in March 1936.[30] Today, the Rhineland is part of Germany's industrial heartland; during the 1930s that was also the case. Furthermore, the Rhineland was very close to the frontier with France. Under the terms of the Treaty of Versailles, concluded in 1919, the Rhineland was to become a demilitarised zone, a status that was reaffirmed by the Treaty of Locarno six years later.[31] Consequently, the German decision to remilitarise this border region that was vitally important for the production of munitions was a contravention of not one international treaty brokered by Britain and France, but two. The decision by the British and French governments not to oppose the remilitarisation with a military response has been seen as a sign of weakness in the Anglo-French relationship that was to gather momentum in the years that followed, culminating in the Munich crisis and ultimately war with Germany.[32] Defenders of British and French diplomatic thinking during this period have argued that the German reoccupation of the Rhineland was in reality of little consequence; that all it amounted to was a return of German territory to Germany. However, a more widely made argument is that Britain and France lacked the military capability to rebuff the German invasion, and so had little choice but to let the incident pass. Yet, as far as Churchill was concerned, the Rhineland Crisis offered the first concrete proof of Hitler's bellicose military aspirations. He did not accept that there was insufficient Anglo-French capability to see down the German challenge. In a conversation with the French foreign minister, Pierre-Etienne Flandin, a week after the crisis began, Churchill argued that the military of both countries had the wherewithal as well as the will to take action, but had been stymied by the spinelessness of their political masters. Furthermore, Churchill believed that the failure of Britain and France to stand up to German military was proof that the much-vaunted League of Nations, an organisation devoted to the promotion of international peace, was a toothless tiger. Consequently, any attempt to broker a lasting peace with Germany through diplomatic negotiation would always be doomed to fail. Thus, by spring 1936, the opposing positions adopted by Churchill and by the government in Whitehall to the threat to peace posed by the fascist dictators were in place. They were to remain largely unaltered for more than three years.

In May 1937, Stanley Baldwin was succeeded as prime minister by Neville Chamberlain. Initially, Churchill was optimistic about Chamberlain's appointment, hoping that he might be more receptive than his predecessor had been to his calls for British rearmament. To underline this point, Churchill once again made recourse to the press to promote his views on the growing threat to European peace and the need for a robust, militarily strong response to it by the British government. For several years, he had written fortnightly articles on current politics and international relations for the London-based daily newspaper, the *Evening Standard*. Many of these were syndicated to the major European press agencies, especially in France. As part of this series, Churchill published a direct appeal to Hitler to abandon the persecution of the Jews in September 1937. In the same year, and to underline his credibility as a commentator on recent history and current affairs, he published a series of twenty-one of his articles, including some pen portraits of key political figures of the time, in a book, *Great Contemporaries*.[33] Among their number was a study of Hitler. That Churchill saw fit to include him indicates how important he believed the German dictator was to understanding the contemporary world. Churchill's love of biography as a genre had strong links to the nineteenth-century tradition of 'Great Man' biographical writing, popularised by writers such as Thomas Carlyle.[34] Their emphasis was focussed only on exploring the lives of those men whose actions and thoughts had fundamentally shaped the fate of their generation.

There were other important divisions emerging about the advisability of the policy of appeasement, this time at the heart of the British government. In February 1938, the British foreign secretary, Anthony Eden, resigned in opposition to the Chamberlain government's desire to appease Mussolini and Hitler. Until this point, the principal focus had been on preventing the Italian dictator from collaborating with his German counterpart. The British desire to remain on good terms with Mussolini also had deeper roots. During the 1920s, he had been seen as a stabilising force in Italian politics and economics, and proved to be a willing ally in the negotiation of the Treaty of Locarno in 1925. However, Mussolini's commitment to long-term European peace and to a harmonious relationship with the British and French government had been undermined by the Italian invasion of Abyssinia in 1935. The realisation that it was difficult to predict where Mussolini's loyalties lay was further evident when the *Duce* failed to condemn the *Anschluss* between Germany and Austria in 1938. To Eden, it was thus evident that an Anglo-French policy of tolerance and appeasement had failed to rein in the territorial aspirations of Mussolini; consequently, there was little reason to believe that the same approach would placate Hitler.

At the time of the *Anschluss*, in March 1938, the *Evening Standard* ceased publication of Churchill's fortnightly articles about contemporary affairs, although the *Daily Telegraph* rapidly offered him an alternative home for his column. On 14 March, Churchill delivered a speech in the House of Commons in which he urged the British government to issue an immediate statement condemning the *Anschluss*. A delayed response, he argued, would make Britain look weak. It was clear that Hitler was bound on a programme of aggression that must be halted through decisive action by the British and French governments. Unless stopped in its tracks, the German army would be stronger than that of France within two years. Furthermore, the credibility of Britain and France as the dominant powers within the League of Nations would be irreversibly damaged unless a robust response was made to the policies of the German government. Such would be the likely extent of this loss of face that the members of the League, who looked to Britain and France for diplomatic protection, would probably leave and join forces with Hitler and his allies. Churchill was also mindful of the wider diplomatic consequences of the *Anschluss*. Churchill viewed the Austrian capital, Vienna, as a fulcrum of European diplomacy, whose heritage, prestige and geographical location made it a vital barometer of the politics and culture of central Europe. The creation of an axis between Berlin and Vienna dominated by Germany would fundamentally alter that dynamic. Churchill's solution was the creation of a mutual defence pact between those states most at risk of acts of aggression from the German military. This strategy is often dismissed as of limited relevance by historians because of the context in which it was made, and especially because of what happened next, when the German government began to turn its sights on Czechoslovakia. However, the plan is worthy of additional comment in that in his plan Churchill was, in effect, advocating a scheme of collective security. This was the modus operandi of the League of Nations, an organisation for which, as already indicated, Churchill had very little time. Furthermore, while Churchill had criticised the British and French governments for not standing up to Hitler regarding the annexation of Austria, his plan, with its emphasis on a collaborative diplomatic response, meant that he no longer believed that Britain and France could face down German aggression alone. In future, as far as Churchill was concerned, for Britain at the very least, there was safety in numbers. Maintaining French support was vital, and so increasingly was gaining that of the greatest economic and military powerhouse in international relations in the 1930s, the United States.

Yet while Churchill's strategic thinking was evolving, his opposition to the policy of appeasement to which the British and French governments were so wedded continued with unrelenting vigour. When German forces prepared to occupy the Sudetenland, the German-speaking region of Czechoslovakia, in September 1938, Churchill visited Chamberlain in Downing Street, urging him to declare war on Germany if Czech territory was invaded. However, Chamberlain was not willing to give him such an undertaking, instead brokering a deal with Hitler in Munich on 30 September, which ceded the Sudetenland to Germany. Six days later, on the third day of the House of Commons debate on the details of the Munich Agreement, Churchill delivered one of his most scathing condemnations of the policy of appeasement. He described the Agreement as a total and unmitigated defeat for British and French diplomacy and a fundamental betrayal of the Czechs, not least because Czechoslovakia was a member of the League of Nations and thus entitled to the protection of that organisation.

Churchill also used his Commons speech to extend his analysis of German expansionist foreign policy that had also been a feature of his response to the Rhineland Crisis and to the *Anschluss*.[35] He accused Chamberlain of smoothing Hitler's path, not barring it. He also viewed the Munich Agreement as a further erosion of the crucial diplomatic equilibrium in central Europe that had already been seriously undermined by the *Anschluss*. The ultimate containment of German territorial expansion could only be achieved if the dominant powers surrounding Germany collaborated in the act. Consequently, Churchill criticised Chamberlain for not including the Russians, alongside the French, during the Munich negotiations. He also repeated his warnings that if Britain, France and the Soviet Union did not act decisively in dealing with German aggression, the danger remained that the smaller European powers might decide to throw their lot in with Germany. It was vitally important for the future independence and stability of central Europe that countries such as Romania and Bulgaria were not tempted or coerced into allying themselves with Germany. What was left of the Little Entente should be shored up and protected, especially by Britain and France. Churchill used his speech in the Munich Agreement debate to reiterate his views on the need for British rearmament. A programme of rapid expansion of Britain's military capability remained vital. He expected his statements on rearmament to fall on deaf ears, as they had appeared to do in the past. However, the mood of British public opinion had been changed by the Munich Agreement as it appeared to suggest that the chances of Britain being drawn into a European war had now substantially increased, and that Hitler and his allies were indeed bent on war.

A further reason why Churchill's warnings began to have greater credibility was because there was deep dissent within the British Cabinet about the advisability of the Munich Agreement. The most high-profile critic was Alfred Duff Cooper, the secretary of state for war, who resigned on 3 October 1938, arguing that instead of pursuing a policy of peace with dishonour, Britain should prepare to fight a war with honour.[36] Duff Cooper's decision was widely acclaimed by other critics of appeasement in the Conservative Party, notably Vyvyan Adams. The *Manchester Guardian* also joined in the condemnation of the Munich Agreement, viewing it as the latest step in a litany of British diplomatic weaknesses in dealing with the aggressive foreign policies of the fascist dictators that stemmed back to the Rhineland Crisis in 1936. Yet, despite these encouraging developments, none had the effect of bringing Churchill closer to a position of political power. And, indeed, the action of Duff Cooper and others made little impact. The bill to endorse Chamberlain's actions in Munich was passed by the House of Commons by a vote of 366 to 144.

Path to Power

It was not until war broke out in Europe in September 1939 that there was any change in Churchill's fortunes. When Britain declared war on Germany on 3 September 1939, Chamberlain appointed Churchill first lord of the admiralty, and in so doing he became a member of the War Cabinet. In his book *The Gathering Storm*, Churchill later wrote that the news of his return to government had been announced to the British fleet by the signal 'Winston is back.' Churchill believed that he was now not only back where he wanted to be but also where he belonged. This was reflected in the enthusiasm and energy he exhibited in boosting morale in the Royal Navy. While the majority of the British military and civilian population braced themselves for a conflict that seemed slow to start, in the so-called Phoney War, Churchill found himself in the thick of one of the few theatres of action. The Battle of the River Plate in December 1939 was the first salvo in what became the Battle of the Atlantic and was concerned with the search and ultimate destruction of the German heavy cruiser, the *Admiral Graf Spee*, by three Royal Navy cruisers, the *Exeter*, the *Achilles* and the *Ajax*, near to the Uruguayan capital, Montevideo. Although the British ships were damaged in the attack, the sinking of the German cruiser was seen as a major victory and one from which Churchill was eager to make capital. The Battle of the River Plate placed Churchill in the spotlight nationally and in Whitehall, and the fact that it resulted in a victory for the Royal Navy did much to enhance his credibility as a Cabinet minister. His reputation was further enhanced when, in February 1940, under his direct orders, the British destroyer *Cossack* successfully intercepted the German supply ship *Altmark* off the Norwegian coast. The result was the liberation of 300 British prisoners that the *Altmark* had earlier picked up from the stricken *Graf Spee*.

The episode confirmed Churchill's view that naval warfare was likely to be as important to the outcome of the Second World War as it had been to the First. In spring 1940, he became increasingly concerned by German naval activity in the Baltic. His initial plan to send a naval task force was rapidly expanded to a much more ambitious plan, codenamed Operation Wilfred, to lay mines along most of the Norwegian coast, and to halt the transport of iron ore from Narvik to Germany.[37] With a German invasion of Norway believed to be imminent, HMS *Renown* sailed from Scapa Flow to Vestfjorden, accompanied by twelve destroyers, on 4 April 1940. Five days later, the British and German navies engaged at the Battle of Narvik while a force of British soldiers landed at Andalsnes on 13 April.[38] However, when the much-anticipated large-scale German invasion of Norway began on 9 April, Operation Wilfred rapidly became seen as too ineffective to curb the sweep of the invading forces. Although the campaign continued for a further two months, Operation Wilfred did little to combat the effect of the German invasion of Norway.

Indeed, the failure of the Norwegian campaign cast doubt on the government's handling of the war as a whole. On 7 May 1940, the House of Commons began a three-day debate on the conduct of the Norway campaign. The Norway Debate, as it became known, proved to be one of the most significant in Churchill's career and in British parliamentary history in the first half of the twentieth century.[39] On 8 May, a cohort of Labour MPs called for what was, in effect, a vote of no confidence in the Chamberlain government. As a member of the Cabinet, Churchill felt compelled to support the prime minister and was called upon to make a speech winding up the debate.[40] This placed him in a very difficult position. Although he had been a long-time critic of the government's policy of appeasement, and had distanced himself from it through open criticism, he had personally been central to the planning and execution of the Norwegian campaign. Consequently, any criticism that could be made of the Chamberlain's government policy towards the defence of Norway could equally be made of him, if not more so.[41] But, fortunately for Churchill, the government won the Norway Debate, albeit by a narrow margin. The real political damage was inflicted on Chamberlain.

Once again, however, the escalation of the war in Europe intervened, but on this occasion placing Churchill in a much less ambiguous position. The day after the Norway Debate, German forces invaded the Low Countries, with the clear intention of moving on to occupy France. Chamberlain's response was to create a coalition of leadership of the war effort with the Labour Party. Clement Attlee, the Labour leader, was unwilling to enter into such an arrangement as long as Chamberlain remained prime minister, but was prepared to serve with a different leader of the Conservative Party.[42] The only two possible candidates were Churchill and the foreign secretary, Lord Halifax, two leading members of the Conservative Party who were also existing members of the War Cabinet.[43] On 9 May 1940, they, along with Chamberlain and David Margesson, the government chief whip, met to resolve who the king should be advised to send for to form the new government. It is important to realise that on 9 May 1940, in the eyes of many, Halifax was the favoured candidate. Indeed, much of the historical literature on those crucial weeks in early May has focussed more on Halifax than on Churchill. Halifax himself believed that his ability to lead the government during a period of international emergency would be fundamentally undermined because he sat in the House of Lords and not in the House of Commons; he wrote of being an 'absentee prime minister'. Like Chamberlain had been, it was vital for the prime minister to be in the thick of parliamentary debates regarding the conduct of the war. Other scholars have suggested that Halifax objected to being a wartime leader because of deeply held Christian, pacifist beliefs, while others have argued that he was deemed unsuitable by his contemporaries because he was too tainted by his association with the policy of appeasement. By spring 1940, hostility to those who had lent their support to that strategy that had so disastrously failed to prevent another European war was reaching its head. This was the era of 'Cato' and the so-called Guilty Men thesis that stemmed from a group of journalists with Labour Party sympathies that was to shape Chamberlain's historical reputation and that of the policy of appeasement for many decades. It was primarily for these reasons that the decision about what advice should be given to the king went in Churchill's favour. It could be argued that, far from being a triumph of opportunity, in May 1940 there were simply no other suitable candidates for the post of prime minister. Indeed, it was from this inauspicious start that began the extraordinary five-year period that cemented Churchill's personal and historical reputation that has so profoundly influenced the way the British contribution to the Second World War has been seen ever since.

Notes

1. Within the vast literature on Churchill and the origins and course of the Second World War, the work of his official biographer, Martin Gilbert, continues to dominate the historical landscape. M. Gilbert, *OB*, vol. 5 (London: Heinemann, 1976); *Winston Churchill: The Wilderness Years* (London: Macmillan, 1981); *Churchill: A Life* (New York: Henry Holt & Co., 1991).

2. J. Barnes and K. Middlemas, *Baldwin* (London: Macmillan, 1970); P. Williamson, *Stanley Baldwin: Conservative Leadership and National Values* (Cambridge: Cambridge University Press, 2007).

3. A useful survey of Chamberlain's historical reputation as prime minister can be found in D. Dutton, *Neville Chamberlain* (London: Edward Arnold, 2001).

4. A. Cassells, *Mussolini's Early Diplomacy* (Princeton, NJ: Princeton University Press, 1970); P. M. Kennedy, The Tradition of Appeasement in British Foreign Policy. *British Journal of International Studies*, vol. 2, no. 3 (1976), pp. 195–215; R. Powell, Uncertainty, Shifting Power and Appeasement. *American Political Science Review*, vol. 90, no. 4 (1996), pp. 749–64; S. R. Rock, *Appeasement in International Politics* (Lexington: University of Kentucky Press, 2014).

5. *Guilty Men* was a polemic attack on fifteen members of the British government who had supported appeasement during the 1930s that was published in July 1940 by Victor Gollancz. The book was written by 'Cato', the nom de plume of three political journalists, Michael Foot, Frank Owen and Peter Howard. It argued that Britain had been drawn into war in Europe because of the ineffective and morally bankrupt nature of appeasement as a diplomatic strategy. The 'Guilty Men thesis' has done much to shape Neville Chamberlain's historical reputation as prime minister. See also J. V. Gottlieb, *Guilty Women, Foreign Policy and Appeasement in Interwar Britain* (London: Palgrave, 2015).

6. M. Beloff, Churchill and Europe. In R. Blake and W. R. Lewis (eds.), *Churchill* (New York: W. W. Norton, 1992), pp. 443–56.

7. M. Gilbert, *The Roots of Appeasement* (London: Heinemann, 1966).

8. A. Lentin : *Guilt at Versailles: Lloyd George and the Pre-History of Appeasement* (London: Routledge, 1985).

9. For a general assessment of the international history of the 1920s, see Z. Steiner, *The Lights That Failed: European International History 1919–1933* (Oxford: Oxford University Press, 2007).

10. This is most evident in the first volume of his history of the Second World War, *The Gathering Storm* (London: Houghton Mifflin, 1948).

11. F. Wood, *Artillery of Words: The Writings of Sir Winston Churchill* (London: Lee Cooper, 1992).

12. D. Reynolds, *In Command of History: Churchill Fighting and Writing the Second World War* (London: Allen Lane, 2004).

13. C. Drazin, *Korda: Britain's Only Movie Mogul – The Definitive Biography* (London: Sidgwick and Jackson, 2002).

14. For example, *The Private life of King Henry VIII* (1933), *The Reign of King George V* (1935) and *Fire over England* (1937).

15. D. Marquand, *Ramsay MacDonald: A Biography* (London: Jonathan Cape, 1977).

16. W. S. Churchill, *Marlborough* (London: George Harrup, 1947).

17. See especially J. Ramsden, *An Appetite for Power: A New History of the Conservative Party* (London: Harper Collins, 1998).

18. The connection between Anglicanism and the political beliefs of members of the Conservative Party is explored at length in the work of Philip Williamson; for example, in his biography of Stanley Baldwin, cited in n. 2 of this chapter.

19. S. Gopal, Churchill and India. In R. Blake and W. R. Lewis (eds.), *Churchill* (New York: W. W. Norton & Company, 1993), pp. 97–112.

20. A. Muldoon, *Empire, Politics and the Creation of the 1935 India Act* (London: Routledge, 2009).

21. P. E. Tetlock and A. Tyler, Churchill's Cognitive and Rhetorical Style: The Debates over Nazi Intentions and Self-Government for India. *Political Psychology*, vol. 17, no. 1 (March 1996), pp. 149–70.

22. This is discussed at length in M. Gilbert, *CV*, vol. 5 (London: Heinemann, 1982), pp. 456–9.

23. E. Hanfstaengl, *Hitler: The Missing Years* (London: Eyre and Spottiswoode, 1957).

24. L. E. Jones, Franz von Papen, Catholic Conservatives and the Establishment of the Third Reich, 1933–1934. *The Journal of Modern History, vol.* 18, no. 2 (2011), pp. 272–318.

25. See D. Dutton, *Simon: A Political Biography of Sir John Simon* (London: Aurum, 1992).

26. C. J. Kitching, *Britain and the Problem of International Disarmament, 1919–1934* (London: Routledge, 2002); F. S. Northedge, *The League of Nations: Its Life and Times* (Leicester: Leicester University Press, 1986).

27. See, for example, L. Olsen, *Troublesome Young Men: The Rebels Who Brought Churchill to Power and Helped Save England* (London: Farrar, Straus and Giroux, 2007) and C. Bryant, *The Glamour Boys: The Secret Story of the Rebels Who Fought for Britain to Defeat Hitler* (London: Bloomsbury, 2020).

28. A compelling account of Churchill's relations with Morton and Wigram is depicted in the film *The Gathering Storm* (2002), with Albert Finney as Churchill.

29. M. Thomas, *Britain and France and Appeasement: Anglo-French Relations in the Popular Front Era* (London: Berg, 1996).

30. R. Miller, Britain and the Rhineland Crisis, 7 March 1936: Retreat from Responsibility or Accepting the Inevitable. *Australian Journal of Politics and History, vol.* 33, no. 1 (1987), pp. 60–77.

31. G. Johnson (ed.), *Locarno Revisited: European Diplomacy 1920–1929* (London: Routledge, 2004).

32. The most rounded assessment of the Munich crisis is E. Goldstein and I. Lukes, *The Munich Crisis, 1938: Prelude to War* (London: Frank Cass, 1999).

33. An additional four essays were added to a reprinted version in 1939.

34. For example, T. Carlyle, *Frederick the Great* (Cambridge: Cambridge University Press, 1884).

35. A. Danchev, The Anschluss. *Review of International Studies*, vol. 20, no. 1 (2009), pp. 97–106.

36. J. Charmley, *Duff Cooper: The Authorised Biography* (London: Weidenfeld and Nicolson, 1992).

37. G. Rhys-Jones, *Churchill and the Norway Campaign, 1940* (London: Pen and Sword, 2008); A. Dix, *The Norway Campaign and the Rise of Churchill 1940* (London: Pen and Sword, 2014).

38. H. O. Lunde, *Hitler's Pre-Emptive War: The Battle for Norway, 1940* (Drexel Hill, PA: Casement Press, 2008).

39. S. Lawlor, *Churchill and the Politics of War, 1940–1941* (Cambridge: Cambridge University Press, 1994).

40. G. Stewart, *Burying Caesar: Churchill, Chamberlain and the Battle for the Tory Party* (London: Weidenfeld and Nicolson, 1999).
41. I. Colvin, *The Chamberlain Cabinet: How the Meetings in 10 Downing Street Led to the Second World War* (London: Gollancz, 1971).
42. T. Bouverie, *Appeasement: Chamberlain, Hitler, Churchill and the Road to War* (London: Tim Duggan, 2020).
43. A. Roberts, *The Holy Fox: A Biography of Lord Halifax* (London: Phoenix, 2011).

Further Reading

T. Bouverie, *Appeasement: Chamberlain, Hitler, Churchill and the Road to War* (London: Tim Duggan, 2020)
P. Brendon, *The Dark Valley: A Panorama of the 1930s* (London: Jonathan Cape, 2000)
M. Gilbert, *The Roots of Appeasement* (London: Heinemann, 1966)
Z. Steiner, *The Lights That Failed: European International History 1919–1933* (Oxford: Oxford University Press, 2007)

13
—————

Churchill As War Leader

And so he became the greatest leader in war this country has ever had. Everything had prepared him for it: he had been head of all the fighting services and knew more about it as a whole than the service chiefs. In the conduct of the war and in its over-all strategy, no chiefs of staff would have objected to his overruling their advice … Churchill had an absolutely united country behind him from beginning to end. The Labour Party accepted the leadership of the most uncompromising of anti-socialists with complete confidence; for they knew that under him no sectional or private interest would be allowed to come before the safety of the nation.[1]

These words were written in 1953 by the distinguished Oxford historian A. L. Rowse as the conclusion to a book of essays called *Churchill by His Contemporaries*. Churchill was back in 10 Downing Street as peacetime prime minister and the newspaper editor Charles Eade had been given the task of collating this tribute. The title was surely a deliberate nod to Churchill's own work *Great Contemporaries*, first published in 1937, in which he had identified the greatest national and international figures of his age and contributed an essay on each.[2] The inference in the Eade publication was clear: Churchill had now entered this pantheon himself. This was not history but hyperbole.

In the public consciousness, especially in Britain and the United States, Winston Churchill has become the archetypal embodiment of the modern war leader. Whether wearing his trademark spotted bowtie, frock coat and top hat or his tailored zip-up siren suit, his distinctive appearance, complete with bulldog scowl, V for Victory salute and omnipresent cigar, has been the subject of almost endless reproduction in every conceivable medium.

It is a reputation that was secured with the Allied victory in Europe in May 1945, but one which was also quickly reinforced by Churchill's own bestselling six-volume *The Second World War*, published between 1948 and 1954 in fifteen different countries and serialised worldwide.[3] Churchill had always used his pen to finance and support his political career; now he had used it to secure his legacy. By drawing primarily from his own minutes, speeches and telegrams and by focussing on the war in Europe and the Mediterranean, Churchill put himself firmly at the heart of his narrative. He wanted to show that he was not just the roaring lion, famous for delivering a series of morale-boosting speeches in summer 1940, but also the architect of victory who 'made all the main military decisions'.[4]

This chapter and those that follow it seek to put Churchill the war leader back in context and perspective; to examine how he approached his task; and to assess his success in meeting his key strategic and political objectives on the national and international stage.

The Reality of 1940

If we strip away the layers of hindsight, it immediately becomes apparent that, despite his feelings of 'walking with destiny', Churchill was never in full control of his fate.[5] As Gaynor Johnson has already shown in Chapter 12, he was not elected prime minister. His assumption of the premiership was the result of a Westminster rebellion by members of parliament against Prime Minister Neville Chamberlain. The debate on the Norwegian campaign in May 1940 had dramatically illustrated a widespread loss of confidence in Chamberlain's leadership, prompting him to conclude that a wider coalition government was needed. His fate was sealed when the Labour opposition refused to serve under him. The Conservatives remained the largest party in the House of Commons and it was therefore clear that the next prime minister should be drawn from their ranks. The only real contenders in terms of both their public profiles and government offices were Lord Halifax, the foreign secretary, and Churchill, the first lord of the admiralty. In essence this was a choice between a dove (Halifax) and a hawk (Churchill) and the foreign secretary stepped aside, almost certainly realising that the mood in parliament now favoured a more aggressive war leader who could direct efforts from the Commons chamber.

Churchill had already established himself as the most vocal opponent of Hitler and the most bellicose member of Chamberlain's War Cabinet, but huge doubts remained among the political elite about his suitability for the highest office. The contemporary diaries of many leading civil servants, military commanders and politicians reflect concerns about his rashness, instability and lack of judgement.[6] It was his commitment to the fight that enabled Churchill to form a coalition, bringing the Labour and Liberal parties into government, but, never having been a loyal party man, he lacked his own political powerbase and knew that his grip on the top office depended on maintaining the public resolve and political will to continue the struggle. He was supremely confident in his own abilities and his first address to parliament as prime minister on 13 May 1940 was an unequivocal call to arms, offering nothing but 'blood, toil, tears and sweat' and pledging himself to a policy of waging war, 'by sea, land and air', with the single aim of victory.[7]

This aim was immediately put to the test. On the very day that Churchill entered Downing Street (10 May 1940), Hitler launched his blitzkrieg offensive against the Low Countries. The first few weeks of Churchill's premiership were marked by military disaster. By the middle of June, the British Expeditionary Force had been evacuated from the beaches of Dunkirk and France, Britain's main ally, had sought terms with Germany. The planned war strategy of using the larger French army assisted by smaller British forces to check the enemy advance in northwestern Europe, while the Royal Navy blockaded Germany by sea, had unravelled.

Britain was certainly not alone.[8] The country was still able to draw on the vast resources of the Dominions and its Empire, but it was now on the front line, isolated in Europe, vulnerable to enemy blockade by sea and air, with its cities and industrial centres exposed to direct attack. Moreover, there were very real fears that Italy, Spain and Japan might all seize the moment to join the fight and move against British interests around the world. On 26 May 1940 Churchill received a memorandum from his chiefs of staff. He had asked them whether Britain could fight on given 'a certain eventuality' (the fall of France). The military commanders felt that the Royal Navy could only defend the islands if air superiority could be maintained and that this in turn depended upon guaranteeing aircraft production. The factories were vulnerable to night attack by the Luftwaffe and dependent upon the morale of the civilian workforce. If the Germans were able to make a successful landing, and secure a foothold, then Britain did not have sufficient land forces to resist a serious invasion. Their verdict was sobering:

> To sum up, our conclusion is that prima facie Germany has most of the cards; but the real test is whether the morale of our fighting personnel and civil population will counter balance the numerical advantages which Germany enjoys. We believe it will.[9]

The day before they had confirmed that Britain would only be able to fight on if the 'United States of America is willing to give us full economic and financial support, *without which we do not think we could continue the war with any chance of success.*'[10] The italics are in the original document and their significance would have been obvious to the new prime minister.

Churchill was under no illusions as to the scale of the challenge, but he did not believe that Britain was yet beaten. His knowledge of history told him that an invasion was not easy to mount. He had faith in the ability of the navy to hold the seas, confidence in the support of the Empire and the English-speaking world and a belief that there was no point seeking terms form a position of weakness. He was a gambler but not a reckless one and he now set about trying to strengthen his hand.

The Structures of Power

To streamline decision-making at the centre, the new prime minister initially restricted his War Cabinet to a small group of just five, bringing in his predecessor, Neville Chamberlain, still the leader of the Conservative Party; his main rival for the premiership, Lord Halifax, the foreign secretary; and the Labour leaders Clement Attlee and Arthur Greenwood. These were leaders of the majority parties in the coalition and their presence secured the support of parliament. With the exception of Halifax, they were also ministers without departmental responsibilities and therefore freer to concentrate on the big strategic questions. Yet they were not close colleagues and natural allies for Churchill and there was to be no honeymoon period for this new War Cabinet, which was immediately engulfed in a rapidly escalating crisis that threatened to undermine Churchill's whole policy of waging war.

This then was the challenge facing Churchill. He had been chosen by his contemporaries because he was felt to be a war leader, but he was not waging war from a position of his political or military choosing. To shore

ARRIVING AT No. 10 ACCOMPANIED BY OFFICER CARRYING CHARTS.
6.9.39.

Figure 13.1 Though taken while he was still first lord of the admiralty, this image captures the dynamism of Churchill's early war leadership, striding purposefully into Downing Street armed with the latest information supplied to him by his own statistical unit (CAC, Broadwater Collection, BRDW V 3/3).

up his own position, Churchill made himself not just prime minister but also minister of defence. He believed that one of the reasons for the failure of the Dardanelles operation in the First World War had been the division of political and military command, with no one person having overall responsibility for the operation. He was not going to make the same mistake again and refused to delegate control of strategy and operations to others. The chiefs of staff now reported directly to him and he insisted on control of the key Defence Committee. The three service ministers, the first lord of the admiralty and the secretaries of state for war and for air, were kept out of the War Cabinet and effectively demoted, attending meetings at Churchill's request.

These changes put Churchill at the heart of the war effort but also brought together the key civil and military secretariats and forged them into one body, an inner circle to which Churchill added his own team. He was the first British prime minister to have a permanent scientific adviser, in the form of his close friend, the Oxford-educated physicist Frederick Lindemann. It was Lindemann who helped create a dedicated statistical unit, designed to gather, sift, review and present information to the prime minister. To this Churchill added a personal map room and a direct channel to the security services, thereby creating a larger and more powerful centralised decision-making apparatus within 10 Downing Street. It was a clever power grab which had the effect of creating a core team around him for driving through his wishes. These were issued in a stream of dictated minutes, letters and telegrams, put into writing so that his intentions could not be misunderstood, and with the useful side effect of creating an archival record for posterity.[11]

While the new structures gave Churchill more power than his immediate predecessor, and indeed any modern prime minister, he was still heavily constrained: he was dependent on the support of his War Cabinet and ultimately of parliament for the continuation of his coalition, and reliant on others to run the domestic and economic aspects of the war while he focussed on the high-level political and military issues. The British and imperial state was a huge bureaucracy. General John Kennedy, who became assistant chief of the imperial general staff, described it as 'essentially a government of committees ... Winston is of course the dominating personality .... Yet Winston's views do not often prevail if they are contrary to the general trend of opinion among the service staffs.'[12] Churchill was presiding over a complex web of personalities, parties, departments, committees and interests. His success in navigating and influencing them was constantly shifting and his power inevitably waxed and waned as the war progressed.

Leadership Style and Oratory

Churchill's eccentric dress code and sense of theatre, combined with his obvious enjoyment of visits to the troops or to the scene of any action, helped to put him centre-stage in the British war effort. In 1940, most of the British media was working to support a mood of national unity and this led naturally to the creation of a personality cult around the prime minister, which in turn strengthened his position while also helping to foster the Churchillian bulldog image which forms such an integral part of his legacy.

His was certainly a very visual and vocal leadership. He understood the importance of communications in building and maintaining morale. This was the pre-television age when people got their news from the papers, from weekly visits to the cinema and from their wireless sets. The new prime minister set out to utilise all available media. He deliberately cultivated key newspaper magnates, bringing Lord Beaverbrook into his administration as minister of aircraft production and insisting that his close aide Brendan Bracken become a privy councillor and later minister of information. He gave interviews and press conferences (especially to American journalists), and when travelling would often be accompanied by specially selected reporters, official photographers and film camera crews. Churchill did not just watch films to relax; he knew their propaganda value. He actively encouraged productions like *That Hamilton Woman* (1941), about Nelson, or Laurence Olivier's *Henry V* (1944), which projected his vision of British history and defiance to a global, and especially American, audience.[13] Such dramas were the visual accompaniment to his oratory.

The key vehicles for Churchill's direct communication with the general public were his speeches, and especially his broadcasts over the radio, then a virtual BBC state monopoly. These were not the creation of committees or speech writers. The information for a major speech would be collated by his office from the relevant ministers and departments and sections of the draft text would often be sent out to concerned individuals for verification. Advice might be sought on content, but the language used was Churchill's own, thereby giving the speeches their distinctive voice. His style was old-fashioned and dramatic, conforming to rhetorical conventions that he had identified as early as 1897, and using key quotes from British history and literature.[14] In his selection of content, he managed to walk the tightrope between admitting the scale of the problem and promising a solution, thereby creating good copy for both the press and government information posters and establishing himself as the voice of his administration.

Churchill produced his speeches at quite short notice and in spite of the host of other pressures upon him. In the words of one of his secretaries, when 'an egg was to be laid', its gestation would dominate life in the office with dictation taking place in all locations and at all hours.[15]

Recurring allegations that some of his speeches were delivered by the actor Norman Shelley have been repeatedly disproved.[16] The survival of comprehensive drafts and notes in his archive prove his authorship. His speeches in the House of Commons were delivered in front of large gatherings of his contemporaries, while many of his public appearances outside the parliament chamber were filmed. It is true that some of his broadcasts over the BBC were criticised by some contemporaries for poor delivery, but this is probably because they lacked the excitement and spontaneity of a live audience and often involved repeating speeches he had already delivered in the Commons. It is also true that some of his most famous parliamentary speeches were not broadcast at the time and were only recorded for purposes of commercial release after the war.

Churchill's most famous phrases have become synonymous with the events of 1940. The events of that summer are routinely described as Britain's 'finest hour' and it is rare to find popular references about the Battle of Britain that do not mention his tribute to the airmen, 'never in the field of human conflict was so much owed by so many to so few'.[17] These speeches were unquestionably made more resonant by victory.[18] Nevertheless, there is no doubt that they were widely read and listened to, not just nationally but also internationally, and gave their author an incredible platform and profile.

Churchill was certainly aware of this and key passages of his oratory in 1940 and 1941 were deliberately aimed as much at the American audience as the British. On 20 August 1940, at the height of the Battle of Britain, he compared increasing Anglo-American cooperation to the Mississippi, 'inexorable, irresistible, benignant' and leading to 'broader lands and better days'.[19] His response to the Blitz on 11 September 1940 was to call for the 'Old World – and the New' to 'rebuild the temples of man's freedom and man's honour'.[20] And when President Roosevelt sent him a letter quoting the Longfellow verse 'The Sailing of the Ship', written out by hand on his third inauguration day in January 1941, Churchill broadcast his response back across the Atlantic, 'Give us the tools and we will finish the job.'[21] His words were part and parcel of his international courtship of the United States.

Strategy and Actions

However, Churchill was clear that he did not want to be judged on his speeches alone. When recalling his wartime oratory on his eightieth birthday in 1954, he talked of his luck at being called upon 'to give the roar' of the lion but pointedly expressed his hope that he had also 'sometimes suggested to the lion the right place to use his claws'.[22]

In May and June 1940, Churchill was fighting on two fronts. He was desperately trying to stem the tide of military defeat in France while also shoring up British resolve and ability to fight on in the increasingly likely event of a French collapse. These aims pulled in different directions. To deal with the former, he increased British air support over France in spite of the growing concerns of his air staff, urged the forlorn defence of Calais by its British garrison, returned British forces across the Channel after Dunkirk and was ultimately prepared to offer a union of Britain and France to enable the French to go on fighting even after their homeland had been lost, though perhaps primarily as a way of securing the powerful French fleet and as much men and material as possible. Ultimately, he welcomed de Gaulle to London and hosted the Free French forces. At home, he had to win a crucial debate within his own War Cabinet against Halifax's proposal that Britain should start to explore possible peace terms, while also preparing the country for the possibility of direct attack. In public, he was resolute and defiant; in private, his communications to President Roosevelt were increasingly frank about the risk of a British defeat or his own fall from office.

There is no doubt that tensions were running extremely high. John Martin, one of Churchill's private secretaries, later called it 'a time of agony piled on agony'.[23] Clementine Churchill felt it necessary to write her husband a letter passing on fears that he had become 'sarcastic, rude and overbearing' and calling on him to demonstrate 'Olympic calm'.[24] During the Dunkirk evacuation, when the War Cabinet was debating whether or not to fight on, Lord Halifax complained that he could no longer work with Winston, and Sir Alexander Cadogan accused the prime minister of being 'theatrically bulldoggish'.[25] At moments, the relationship between Churchill and his foreign secretary, the two most powerful men in the government, clearly came close to breaking down and at one point they had to have a private conversation in the Downing Street garden to defuse the tension. Nor was there complete harmony among the chiefs of staff. General Ironside was quickly replaced by General Dill and Air Chief Marshal Portal soon supplanted Cyril Newall as chief of the air staff.

Yet, overall, Churchill's new structures and the wider system held up under the pressure. He did allow the big issues to be fully debated by the War Cabinet and ultimately deferred to his chiefs of staff on withdrawing British soldiers and fighters from France. He was forceful in his views but also careful to take his colleagues with him. His inner circle, including men like Private Secretary Jock Colville, who had initially been highly sceptical, were bonded to the new prime minister by the emergency and the sense of shared purpose and urgency he was able to instil.[26]

However, it was only once he had weathered the immediate crisis and survived the fall of France that Churchill was able to truly consolidate his grip on power. This was helped by two deaths. When Neville Chamberlain succumbed to illness, Churchill gave a powerful eulogy but also took the opportunity to assume the leadership of the Conservative Party. Then the death of Lord Lothian, the British Ambassador to the United States, allowed him to appoint Halifax to the vacancy in Washington, DC. These changes established his personal control over the Conservative Party and therefore, by virtue of it being the largest party, over parliament and the War Cabinet, where he now enjoyed a generally closer working relationship with his new foreign secretary, Anthony Eden.

With Britain now in the front line, Churchill's actions were still heavily constrained. A lot of his time was occupied by overseeing the logistics of aircraft production and shipping supplies, using his convening power to bring together the different civilian and military departments and the status of his office to force through change. But he hated being on the defensive and was constantly looking for ways to take the fight to the enemy. Bombing raids against Germany were endorsed from the moment he took office (for a more detailed exploration of this, see Chapter 16 in this volume by Victoria Taylor).[27] After the fall of France, he was a keen proponent of commando raids and special operations against targets in occupied Europe.[28] Yet it was clear that he itched to do something bigger. His actions against the French fleet, including the sinking of several ships at Mers El Kébir, against the instincts of his own naval commanders, were an important statement of intent, signalling to the Americans that Britain would fight. But it was also born of weakness and the fear that combined German, French and Italian forces could overwhelm Britain in the Mediterranean, leading to the loss of crucial bases in Gibraltar, Malta and Egypt, severing links with the Empire in the east and further weakening British prestige and morale worldwide.

While the United Kingdom was able to survive the aerial onslaught of the Luftwaffe and German attempts to cut off supplies by sea in the Atlantic, the Allied armies were driven out of Norway, France and

Greece. Meanwhile, the campaign in North Africa see-sawed back and forth across the western desert, with Allied advances repeatedly forced back to the Egyptian border. The fear that British armies could not fight and win was a constant refrain within his inner circle and challenged Churchill's own historical assumptions of British racial and cultural superiority.[29]

Churchill took the important decision to reinforce the Mediterranean, even at the expense of the British homeland, which was still under threat of invasion. In part, this was because he was a lifelong imperialist and was fighting to preserve the British Empire of 1939. In part, it was because he felt victory could be achieved against the Italians and this was a theatre in which Britain already had the troops and a fleet to take the fight to the enemy. By opening up another front, which could be reinforced from the Empire, he also sought to stretch and wear down the Axis powers. Ultimately, his view was always that it was better to do something than sit on the defensive, but increasing involvement in the Mediterranean came at a price. Crucially, it restricted the reinforcement of the Far East, where Britain was now reliant on the protection of the American Pacific Fleet should Japan enter the war. General Dill, the chief of the imperial general staff, pointed out the risk to Singapore, Australia and New Zealand, provoking the prime minister's wrath and ultimately Dill's removal and replacement by General Brooke.[30]

Securing greater American involvement remained a central British war aim and a Churchillian charm offensive was launched to court President Roosevelt's emissaries: men such as Averell Harriman, Harry Hopkins and the new Ambassador to Britain, Gilbert Winant. Yet behind the scenes there was huge frustration with the pace of the American response. In 1940, Churchill privately compared the actions of the Americans in stripping British gold reserves to that of a 'Sheriff collecting the last assets of a hapless debtor' and was forced to give up British bases in return for old American destroyers.[31] The Lend Lease Act of March 1941 provided a much-needed lifeline in terms of equipment but Roosevelt could only go so far. Churchill crossed the ocean to meet the president and helped draft the Atlantic Charter as a common statement of aims. Although he downplayed and denied it, he must have known the declaration weakened the British case for empire. In the short term, he knew he needed the American alliance more.

The German invasion of the Soviet Union in June 1941 brought Churchill an unexpected ally, and one that, despite his strong anti-Bolshevik credentials, he embraced. The subsequent entry of the United States into the war, following the Japanese attack on the American Pacific Fleet at Pearl Harbor in Hawaii, transformed the international scene, creating an alliance that did have the potential to defeat the Axis powers. Yet, while it may have been better than not having allies, it clearly came with its own set of challenges.

Pearl Harbor resulted in an initial reduction in American lend lease supplies, as the United States prioritised its own war machine and sought to support China and Russia as well as the United Kingdom. Unfortunately for Churchill, this occurred just at the moment when Britain desperately needed extra resources to respond to the escalation of the war into a truly global conflict. The fall of Singapore and Hong Kong to the Japanese signalled the beginning of the end of empire in the Pacific, damaged relations with Australia and ceded naval operations in the theatre to the Americans. It also led to the creation of conditions in India which contributed to the subsequent Bengal Famine. Churchill's literary assistant recalls him admitting to 'a veil over my mind about the Japanese war. All the proportions were hidden in the mist.'[32] His prioritisation of the Mediterranean, his underestimation of the Japanese and his overreliance on American naval supremacy now came back to haunt him, and yet it is difficult to see what more he could have done earlier without risking defeat elsewhere. His despatch of HMS *Prince of Wales* and HMS *Repulse* to Singapore, done before the attack on Pearl Harbor as a deterrent, only made matters worse when they were exposed to Japanese air attack and sunk: a loss that was more personal than most to Churchill, as he had travelled to meet Roosevelt on the *Prince of Wales* just four months earlier.

Far from being a moment to sleep '*the sleep of the saved and thankful*' (as Churchill later described Pearl Harbor and the American entry into the war), this was a real low point.[33] He endured two confidence votes in early 1942, which, while he won them easily, were indicative of growing discontent in the British press and parliament. He was forced to restructure his government but resisted all calls to strip him of the defence portfolio.

America was now in the war and Churchill moved quickly to coordinate policy with the president. There was agreement on the primacy of the European theatre but Churchill and the chiefs of staff had to work hard to convince the Americans to support them in the Mediterranean, with the American chief of staff, General Marshall, favouring a direct attack on France. Churchill likened patient British diplomacy on the issue to '*the dripping of water on a stone*'.[34] In the short term it led to action in North Africa and then Sicily and Italy, but it was clear that America did not share Britain's long-term interests in the theatre. The complex 'special relationship' with the United States is explored in more detail by David B. Woolner in Chapter 14 in this volume.

The creation of the Anglo-American combined chiefs of staff in Washington, DC and joint commands in key theatres established an extremely close military alliance, but they also transferred much of the control of operations away from London. Consequently, the hands-on decision-making so relished by Churchill largely disappeared in the second half of the war. When it came to the invasion of North Africa in 1942, Italy in 1943 or France in 1944, the real planning and power lay with General Eisenhower in the field and General Marshall in the Pentagon. As the war widened, Britain's scope for independence diminished and Churchill's leadership became more about diplomacy and negotiating a joint Allied strategy. The challenges he faced on the international front are ably documented by David Reynolds in Chapter 15 in this volume.

Churchill may have constantly prodded his chiefs of staff but they were in basic agreement in terms of the overall strategy: Britain's interests were best served by gradually wearing the enemy down on as many fronts as possible, by seeking to recover and preserve the Empire and by preventing the emergence of unstable or potentially hostile communist governments in Europe and the Mediterranean. But this involved an increasingly complex balancing act between military and political considerations. As the end of the war neared, Churchill began to worry about a Soviet-dominated Europe, though he continued to believe in his own ability to do business with Stalin.[35]

After 1942, there were no real challenges to his personal authority on the domestic front, but his coalition government lost several by-elections to the left-wing Common Wealth Party or to independents. Though not opposed, he was slow in his response to the Beveridge Report, which recommended a huge expansion of state social welfare provision, preferring to delay implementation until after the end of the war. When, in January 1944, the government suffered its only wartime defeat in the Commons on an amendment to the Education Act voting for equal pay for female teachers, Churchill insisted on a confidence vote to reverse the decision. To many on the left he now seemed increasingly out of touch and dictatorial. Leading Labour figures such as Aneurin Bevan and Harold Laski were consistent and vociferous critics. By late 1944, Churchill found himself faced with both Conservative opposition over his failure to do more to defend Polish independence and large-scale Labour discontent over his decision to intervene in Greece. It is clear from personal correspondence between Churchill and Attlee that these party tensions were starting to fracture the unity of the War Cabinet. Such divisions can only have been exacerbated by Churchill's faltering health.

Physical and Mental Strain

The strain of leadership inevitably took a personal toll on Churchill, with complications intensifying from 1942 onwards. He suffered with potentially lethal bouts of pneumonia in February and December 1943 and August 1944.[36] These episodes can be linked to the rigours of his increased international travelling, though ironically it was on these trips that Churchill was clearly at his happiest, often described by his contemporaries as being like a child let out of school. He liked nothing more than being at the centre of international affairs, engaging in high-level summit diplomacy or visiting the front line. Conversely, what he hated most were the periods of enforced waiting and impotency.

The deterioration in Churchill's health in the last years of the war was remarked on by his contemporaries, many of whom were equally exhausted. In the run-up to the D-Day landings, Cadogan felt that Churchill was 'not the man he was 12 months ago', while General Brooke felt that the prime minister was 'failing fast' and had 'lost all balance'.[37] The effect of years of pressure combined with the frustrations of managing political alliances at home and abroad led to increasing outbursts in meetings against those individuals Churchill saw as seeking to thwart his policies. The Indian nationalist leader Mohandas Gandhi, the leader of the Free French General de Gaulle and the Labour Party Chairman Harold Laski were all prominent recipients of Churchill's wrath and invective, expressed privately but consistently and recorded by those around him. His remarks about Indians being a 'beastly people' at the time of the Bengal Famine are frequently cited as evidence of his racism.[38]

His outbursts were violent but often short-lived, and there are many examples of Eden and others delaying telegrams and papers dictated by the prime minister in the heat of the moment before later persuading him to moderate his tone.[39] He was given to showing and expressing his emotions, which made him easier to read than either Roosevelt or Stalin, but also easier to understand. Alcohol and tobacco certainly played a role in sustaining him, but the accounts from those around him suggest that his image as a hard drinker and smoker was exaggerated, both at the time and since, and one suspects with his tacit approval. He may have told the teetotal, non-smoking General Montgomery that he drank, smoked and was 200 per cent fit, but the reality was that his health was increasingly fragile and he probably needed his comforts to help him deal with the physical and mental toll of high office.[40]

By the end of the war, he could and did still rise to the big occasion, but it was becoming harder. For this reason, Clementine felt his election defeat was a 'blessing in disguise'.[41] Churchill did not agree.

Strengths and Weaknesses

There is no doubting Churchill's personal self-belief, determination and courage. This, coupled with a natural bellicosity, a flair for theatre and a gift for communication, allowed him to assert his authority over the British political and military machine in 1940. These characteristics have been emphasised because they were made highly visible through propaganda channels at the time, and they have since formed part of the Churchill legend.

However, they are not the whole story. Churchill may have been seen by many contemporaries as rash and opportunistic, but he was also very experienced. He had held most of the major offices of state and he had a good understanding of the structures of power and patronage and how to use them. As a backbencher or subordinate minister, his restless energy, tendency to dominate and desire to interfere with matters outside his brief had caused frictions. As prime minister, he was able to put himself at the centre of the machine and create a powerful central instrument in Downing Street for driving forward political policy and military strategy. That is not to say he did not drive his chiefs of staff and War Cabinet colleagues mad. He did. But he saw it as part of his role to challenge them. Debate and discussion were almost constant, including during weekends at his country residences of Chequers or Ditchley Park. The prime minister convened the meetings, often at unsociably late hours, and used his central secretariat to chase actions and ensure the flow of information, with Churchill taking a special personal interest in the 'most secret' information delivered to him from the intercepted enigma decrypts.[42] He saw himself as a prod.

In terms of his grand strategy, Churchill was proved right in his belief that Britain could fight on after the fall of France. He was also correct in his assertion that ultimate victory lay with the United States, but underestimated the political difficulties and willingness of President Roosevelt to bring America fully into the war. He showed foresight and pragmatism in embracing the Soviet alliance, while his decision to prioritise the offensive in the Mediterranean inevitably led to the exposure of India and the Far East. He was a consistent advocate of taking the offensive to the enemy but favoured a peripheral strategy that sought to fight on multiple fronts above the large-scale invasion of France. This was about protecting British interests worldwide, wearing the enemy down and waiting for the decisive moment.

But Churchill was often frustrated by his room for manoeuvre: in the early years of the war he largely lacked the resources to take the offensive, especially against Germany, and in the later years his freedom to do so in the way he wished was often constrained by his increasingly powerful allies.

He certainly did not get everything right. Not that there were always right decisions to make, especially as the war became wider and more complex. Believing himself to be a military expert, and often over-confident in his use of privileged intelligence information, he tended to try and micro-manage his commanders in the field. His desire for action led him to promote unsuccessful operations, like the Anglo-French attack on Dakar in 1940 or the Allied campaign in Greece in 1941, which have been criticised for diverting resources from key theatres. He often thought of armies only in terms of their front-line troops and navies in terms of their capital ships, leaving him frustrated at the logistical requirements of moving a modern army and failing to fully appreciate the importance of air power at sea.

Despite his protestations to the contrary, he frequently criticised his military commanders, favouring and advancing individuals such as Mountbatten and Alexander who fulfilled his stereotype of the dashing fighting man and dismissing those such as Wavell and Auchinleck whom he saw as too cautious. He believed in the importance of morale in influencing victory and did all he could to instil it, using words and film to create a heroic narrative, but he allowed his strong views on race to blind him to the scale of the Japanese threat and the impact of the war in weakening the bonds of Empire and Commonwealth.

The official records show that Rowse was wrong to say that there was always unity at the top. The chiefs of staff did sometimes overrule Churchill, the politicians often argued, parliament and press were frequently critical. But Churchill did hold together a national coalition government for over five years. There is no doubt that this became increasingly difficult as the war progressed and as the finish line of victory in Europe came in sight. It was a two-way process and relied on the contribution of the Labour leaders, but Churchill's personal role in sustaining it should not be underestimated. He always sought balance in his War Cabinet and from 1942 onwards, Clement Attlee was his deputy and chaired when Churchill was overseas. Collective government was maintained and key decisions were debated and ratified by the War Cabinet and the chiefs of staff, sometimes at great length.

Churchill also played a vital role in constructing and maintaining the international alliance against the Axis powers. Both at home and abroad, he showed himself prepared to compromise, albeit sometimes grudgingly – partly because the nature of his position meant he had to, but also partly because his approach to victory was an inherently practical one. His focus was simple. As a leader he was not interested in complex war aims and perhaps inevitably, given the temporary coalition nature of his government, he preferred to deflect difficult questions about post-war construction at home or abroad until after victory had been achieved.

Like his life as a whole, Churchill's war premiership was full of contradictions and ironies. He was pledged to preserving the imperial Britain of pre-1939 but was unable to fulfil his promise to preserve the Empire. His vision of British history and commitment to the past fuelled his oratory in 1940 but it ultimately lost him the election in 1945. After years of war, the British people were keener on a brave new world than he was but were still prepared to give him his place in their pantheon.

Notes

1. A. L. Rowse, The Summing Up: Churchill's Place in History. In C Eade (ed.), *Churchill by His Contemporaries* (London: Hutchinson, 1953), p. 501.
2. W. S. Churchill, *Great Contemporaries* (London: Thornton Butterworth, 1937).
3. W. S. Churchill, *The Second World War* (London: Cassell, 1948–54), 6 vols. For the story behind the production of this work, see D. Reynolds, *In Command of History: Churchill Fighting and Writing the Second World War* (London: Allen Lane, 2004).

4. Lord Moran, *Winston Churchill: The Struggle for Survival 1940–1965* (London: Constable & Company, 1966), pp. 291–2.
5. Churchill, *The Second World War*, vol. 1, pp. 526–7. For Churchill on his sense of destiny, see A. Roberts, *Churchill: Walking with Destiny* (London: Allen Lane, 2018), pp. 1–3.
6. See, for example, J. Colville, *The Fringes of Power: Downing Street Diaries, 1939–1955* (London: Hodder & Stoughton, 1985), pp. 29, 108 and 122; R. Self, *The Neville Chamberlain Diary Letters*, vol. 4 (Aldershot: Ashgate, 2005), pp. 179, 311 and 438.
7. CAC, Churchill Papers, CHAR 9/139B/194, *Hansard* extract for Churchill's address to parliament, 13 May 1940.
8. See D. Edgerton, *Britain's War Machine: Weapons, Resources and Experts in the Second World War* (London: Allen Lane, 2011).
9. TNA, CAB 80/11/3, COS (40) 397, Chiefs of Staff Committee Memoranda, 26 May 1940.
10. TNA, CAB 80/11/3, COS (40) 390, COS Committee Memoranda, 25 May 1940.
11. On how Churchill organised his inner circle, see J. Wheeler-Bennett, *Action This Day* (London: Macmillan, 1968) or M. P. Schoenfield, *The War Ministry of Winston Churchill* (Ames: The Iowa State University Press, 1972).
12. Cited in M. Hastings, *Finest Years: Churchill as Warlord 1940–1945* (London: Harper Press, 2009), p. xx.
13. J. Fleet, Alexander Korda: Churchill's Man in Hollywood. *Finest Hour*, vol. 179 (winter 2018), pp. 12–15.
14. CAC, Churchill Papers, CHAR 8/13, unpublished typescript article by Churchill entitled *The Scaffolding of Rhetoric*, 1897.
15. E. Nel, *Mr Churchill's Secretary* (London: Hodder & Stoughton, 1958), pp. 36–7, 51–4.
16. R. Toye, *The Roar of the Lion* (Oxford: Oxford University Press, 2013), p. 11.
17. For a published edition of Churchill's wartime speeches, see W. S. Churchill, *Never Give In!* (London: Hachette, 2004).
18. See Toye, *The Roar of the Lion*, for a detailed analysis of how the speeches were received.
19. CAC, Churchill Papers, CHAR 9/141A/68, address to the House of Commons, 20 August 1940.
20. CAC, Churchill Papers, CHAR 9/144/66, broadcast, 11 September 1940.
21. CAC, Churchill Papers, CHAR 9/150A/75, broadcast, 9 February 1941.
22. CAC, Churchill Papers, CHUR 5/56B/235, speech in Westminster Hall, 30 November 1954.
23. Churchill Archives Centre, Martin Papers, MART 1.
24. Churchill Archives Centre, Baroness Spencer-Churchill Papers, CSCT 1/24, published in M. Soames, *Speaking for Themselves: The Personal Letters of Winston and Clementine Churchill* (London: Doubleday, 1998), p. 454.
25. Dilks, *The Diaries of Sir Alexander Cadogan*, pp. 290–2.
26. Colville, *Fringes of Power*, p. 136.
27. TNA, CAB 65/13, WM (40) 119C, War Cabinet minutes, 12 May 1940.
28. See G. Milton, *The Ministry of Ungentlemanly Warfare* (London: John Murray, 2016).
29. Dilks, *The Diaries of Sir Alexander Cadogan*, pp. 430, 432–3. See also Max Hastings, *Finest Years*.
30. A. Packwood, *How Churchill Waged War* (Barnsley: Frontline Books, 2018), pp. 72–3.
31. TNA, PREM 4/17/1/ 86–94, cited in W. Kimball, *Forged in War* (London: HarperCollins, 1997), p. 76.
32. CAC, Kelly Papers, DEKE 1, letter from Denis Kelly to Sir Martin Gilbert, 1988.
33. Churchill, *The Second World War*, vol. 3, p. 540.

34. CAC, Jacob Papers, JACB 1/19, Sir Ian Jacob's diary for the Casablanca Conference, January 1943.
35. See Chapter 15 in this volume by David Reynolds.
36. For the latest research on Churchill's health during the war, see A. Vale and J. Scadding, *Winston Churchill's Illnesses 1886–1965* (Barnsley: Frontline Books, 2020).
37. Dilks, *The Diaries of Sir Alexander Cadogan*, p. 621; A. Danchev and D. Todman, *War Diaries 1939–1945: Field Marshal Lord Alanbrooke* (London: Weidenfeld & Nicolson, 2001), pp. 528 and 542.
38. J. Barnes and D. Nicholson, eds., *The Empire at Bay: The Leo Amery Diaries 1929–1945* (London: Hutchinson, 1988), p. 832.
39. For example, see D. Charlwood, *Churchill and Eden: Partners through War and Peace* (Barnsley: Pen & Sword, 2020), p. 82.
40. B. Montgomery, *The Memoirs of Field Marshal Viscount Montgomery of El Alamein* (London: Collins, 1958), p. 69.
41. M. Soames, *Clementine Churchill*, revised edition (London: Doubleday, 2002), p. 424.
42. See D. Stafford, *Churchill and Secret Service* (London: Abacus, 1999), pp. 222–6.

Further Reading

W. S. Churchill, *The Second World War*, 6 vols (London: Cassell, 1948–54)

J. Colville, *The Fringes of Power: Downing Street Diaries, 1939–1955* (London: Hodder & Stoughton, 1985)

A. Danchev and D. Todman, *War Diaries 1939–1945: Field Marshal Lord Alanbrooke* (London: Weidenfeld & Nicolson, 2001)

D. Dilks, *The Diaries of Air Alexander Cadogan* (London: Cassell, 1971)

M. Gilbert, [OB] *Winston S. Churchill*, vol. 6, *Finest Hour 1939–1941* (London: Heinemann, 1983)

M. Gilbert, [OB] *Winston Churchill*, vol. 7, *Road to Victory 1941–1945* (London: Heinemann, 1986)

M. Hastings, *Finest Years: Churchill as Warlord 1940–1945* (London: Harper Press, 2009)

Lord Moran, *Winston Churchill: The Struggle for Survival 1940–1965* (London: Constable & Company, 1966)

D. Reynolds, *In Command of History: Churchill Fighting and Writing the Second World War* (London: Allen Lane, 2004)

A. Roberts, *Churchill: Walking with Destiny* (London: Allen Lane, 2018)

M. P. Schoenfield, *The War Ministry of Winston Churchill* (Ames: The Iowa State University Press, 1972)

R. Toye, *The Roar of the Lion* (Oxford: Oxford University Press, 2013)

A. Vale and J. Scadding, *Winston Churchill's Illnesses 1886–1965* (Barnsley: Frontline Books, 2020)

J. Wheeler-Bennett, *Action This Day* (London: Macmillan, 1968)

14

Churchill, The English-Speaking Peoples and the 'Special Relationship'

In the preface to volume 1 of his *History of the English-Speaking Peoples*, Winston Churchill justifies his decision to write a book based on this linguistic theme by taking note of the important influence that those who share the common bond of the English language have had upon the world. Inspired by this conviction, Churchill had nearly completed a first draft of his four-volume account when work on this project was suddenly interrupted by the onset of the Second World War. Given his wartime responsibilities, and his focus in the immediate aftermath of the conflict on the writing of his war memoirs, it would be nearly twenty years before he had the chance to complete his study of the English-speaking peoples. He then observes – writing from the perspective of 1956 – that if there was a need for the work prior to the war, the necessity for such an account became even greater in the wake of the great convulsions that shook humanity between 1939 and 1945.[1]

Indeed, from Churchill's perspective, the Second World War made it obvious that the peace and stability of the world had become dependent in large measure on the drawing together of what he refers to in volume 3 of his study as the two separate 'branches' of the English-speaking peoples: the British Empire and Commonwealth and the United States, which, although it had broken away from the 'mother country in 1775', still remained 'fundamentally united' to the former by language, tradition and adherence to common law.[2]

Churchill famously encapsulated his belief in the need for the transatlantic element of this unity by his use of the term 'special relationship', which made its first appearance in instructions he sent to British post-war planners in September 1943, informing them that nothing they did should prejudice 'the natural Anglo-American special relationship'. Five months later, in a minute to the Foreign Office, he made known his 'deepest conviction' that 'unless Britain and the United States are joined in a special relationship, including Combined Chiefs of Staff organization and a wide measure of reciprocity in the use of bases – all within the ambit of a world organization – another destructive war will come to pass'.[3]

Churchill's first public use of the phrase did not come until after the war, however, in November 1945, when he spoke in the House of Commons about the need to preserve the 'special relationship' between the United States and Great Britain, and in March of 1946, during his famous Iron Curtain speech in Fulton, Missouri, when he warned that 'peace could not be preserved without the fraternal association of the English-speaking peoples. This means a special relationship between the British Commonwealth and Empire and the United States.'[4]

As the child of an American mother and British father and a great believer in the destiny of the English-speaking peoples, Churchill had always harboured a great deal of affection and admiration for the United States. He also recognised – long before Hitler's armies crossed the frontiers into Poland in September 1939 – that Great Britain's future security might well depend on its relationship with America. During the First World War, in a memo that Churchill penned to the War Cabinet just a week before the German army launched its final offensive in March 1918, Churchill argued that quite apart from the 'supreme priority' that must be given to the

> rapid augmentation by every conceivable means of the numbers of American soldiers in France ... the intermingling of British and American units on the field of battle ... may exert an immeasurable effect upon the future destiny of the English-speaking people, and will afford us perhaps the only guarantee of safety if Germany emerges stronger from the war than she entered it.[5]

It seems clear then, that one reason Churchill clung tenaciously to his belief in the importance of the Anglo-American special relationship stems from the simple fact that by the middle of the twentieth century Great Britain's national security depended on it. The fall of France in June 1940 and the subsequent rise and threat posed by the Soviet Union to Western Europe post-1945 – to say nothing of the possibility of a resurgent Germany – made this a reality that any responsible British statesman who lived through this era could hardly ignore.[6]

Equally important, however, was his desire to maintain Great Britain's status as a world power, which in Churchill's mind meant not only a close association with the United States – and, with luck, the concomitant ability to influence American foreign policy – but also the preservation of the British Empire. This would of course bring him into direct conflict with the one other great statesman associated with the birth of the 'special relationship', Franklin Roosevelt, whose antipathy for British imperialism was perhaps matched only by Churchill's correspondingly vehement assertion that he had 'not become the King's First Minister in order to preside over the liquidation of the British Empire' (see also Piers Brendon in Chapter 10 of this volume).[7]

Given these differences of opinion, which in Roosevelt's case were shared by a broad swathe of the American populace, it seems right to ask just how 'special' the 'special relationship' was. Did Great Britain really possess any ability to influence American policy? And is there any real substance to the idea that the English-speaking peoples hold a special responsibility for the maintenance of the peace and prosperity of the world?

Roosevelt's Initial Overture

To begin, we must first acknowledge that the construction of the Anglo-American alliance during the Second World War is unique in the annals of military history. It is also unusual in that its foundations rested on the extraordinary personal relationship that Churchill and Roosevelt (FDR) cultivated with each other over the course of the war – nurtured by the unprecedented level of communication that the two leaders shared, from FDR's first missive to Churchill when he was first lord of the admiralty in September 1939 to the last message Churchill sent to Roosevelt on the evening of 11 April 1945, less than twenty-four hours before the president's sudden death the following day.

The mere fact that Roosevelt – as president of the United States – should reach out to a specific member of British Prime Minister Neville Chamberlain's Cabinet at the beginning of the crisis is quite telling in and of itself. Churchill, after all, had spent the past ten years in the political wilderness, and was widely regarded in Whitehall and the British press as something of a loose cannon. Yet even at this early date, FDR sensed there was a strong possibility that Churchill might become Great Britain's next prime minister.[8]

FDR also pursued a relationship with Churchill out of his firm belief in the importance of naval power – reinforced by FDR's experience as assistant secretary of the navy in the First World War – and out of his recognition that the Atlantic might well become America's first line of defence in the emerging struggle with Hitler's Germany.

Knowing full well how thrilled Churchill must have been at his return to the Admiralty – a position Churchill held at the opening of the First World War – FDR began by expressing 'how glad' he was to see Churchill back at the helm.[9] And in a further indication of how he hoped to establish a personal relationship with the first lord, he closed the letter with a reference to Churchill's four-volume biography of his ancestor, John Churchill, the Duke of Marlborough, noting his satisfaction that Churchill had completed the volumes 'before this thing started' as he 'much enjoyed reading them'.[10]

FDR also urged Churchill to 'keep me in touch personally with any information you want me to know about' and, consistent with FDR's preference for bypassing the State Department, indicated that he could send sealed letters directly to him through the American Embassy's diplomatic pouch.

This casual, almost breezy tone – typical of FDR's interactions in person and in print – masks the serious nature of this highly unusual diplomatic overture. For reasons of protocol, FDR was careful to mention Prime Minister Chamberlain in the letter, indicating how he wanted both of them to know how he would welcome being kept informed, but the letter is unmistakably directed to Churchill. It is Churchill – not Chamberlain – that the president is reaching out to at this vital moment, and Churchill that he hopes to hear from as the conflict begins to deepen and take shape.

Viewed from this perspective, one could argue that in some respects it is Roosevelt, not Churchill, who initiated the 'special relationship'. This may seem surprising in light of Churchill's well-known efforts to draw the United States into the war, but a deeper examination of Roosevelt's thinking reveals that, like Churchill, FDR understood that American security was closely tied to the security of the United Kingdom. This is not to say that FDR did not share many of the prejudices his fellow countrymen exhibited in their attitudes towards the British. As noted, his hostility towards imperialism was well established. He also harboured a deep suspicion of the financial titans of the City of London, whom he regarded as synonymous with the 'economic royalists' of Wall Street that had helped bring about the Great Depression through their greed and wanton disregard for the wellbeing of the average citizen.

Yet it must also be said that FDR maintained a sincere appreciation for British institutions and culture and, like many of his generation, was raised on the notion that the 'Anglo-Saxon race' possessed a distinctive character and unique responsibilities. In this sense, FDR's view of the English-speaking peoples was not so different from Churchill's, with one over-riding caveat: Roosevelt had no intention, as he said to an aide shortly after his famous quarantine speech of 1937, of seeing the United States become 'a tail on the British kite'.[11]

Given Churchill's view that Great Britain, as the wellspring of the English-speaking peoples, possessed a unique ability to provide the leadership required to fashion a better world out of the ruins of the war, the critical question at the heart of their wartime relationship, therefore – and the relationship of their two nations – centred on the issue of who was going to be the 'kite' and who the 'tail'. The answer to this question may seem obvious today. But in the dark days of 1939, when the United States possessed an army of fewer than 200,000 men and when the British navy still ruled the seas with the largest war-fleet in the world, the question of which power would play the predominant role in the emerging Anglo-American alliance was by no means certain.

Nor was it certain that the United States – still dominated by an isolationist Congress and public – would even enter the war. But for the Japanese attack on Pearl Harbor, it is entirely possible that FDR may have pursued a far more cautious level of support for the British effort to defeat Hitler, providing the UK with US naval and air forces but sticking to his October 1940 promise of not sending American soldiers 'into any foreign wars'.[12]

Hence, the question of just how 'special' the 'special relationship' would become was very much up in the air in October 1939, when Churchill circulated FDR's initial letter to the War Cabinet with the suggestion that he maintain the 'sealed' correspondence that Roosevelt suggested. In light of this reality, Churchill deserves a great deal of credit for the role he played in nurturing the special bond that would develop between Great Britain and the United States over the course of the war. This is especially true during the first phase of what might best be described as the three phases of the Anglo-American wartime relationship, from the outbreak of the war in September 1939 until the Japanese attack on Pearl Harbor on 7 December 1941.

Getting Mixed Up Together

The first phase of the wartime special relationship was perhaps the most difficult – and the most important. It was during this critical period that the two leaders and the two nations laid the basis for the close association that would become the hallmark of the Western Alliance. Yet, as Allen Packwood notes in his account, *How Churchill Waged War*, the over-riding sentiment among Churchill's contemporaries about the prospects for Anglo-American comity during this difficult first phase of the conflict was one of failure. As the Germans went from one stunning victory to the next, and the prospects for British survival deteriorated, Churchill's attention naturally turned towards securing the United States' entry into the war. Having already established a solid rapport with the president during his tenure as 'Naval Person' – the moniker Churchill chose for himself during his time as first lord of the admiralty – Churchill intensified his outreach to the president as 'Former Naval Person', the name he chose for himself following his assumption of the office of prime minister on 10 May 1940. Moreover, from this day forward, Churchill's correspondence with Roosevelt increased not only in volume but also in stature. By appointing himself Great Britain's first minister of defence, Churchill purposely combined in one person 'the oversight of the political and military direction of the war and had deliberately put himself at the heart of the British war machine'.[13] This placed Churchill on a more or less equal footing with Roosevelt who, as president and commander-in-chief, also possessed the power to orchestrate the political and military direction of the war.

Churchill's assumption of these new powers certainly increased his authority, but as Packwood adroitly points out, it also increased his political vulnerability, as it meant he ran the risk of being identified as the source of any failure in the field.[14] This was surely the case with respect to Churchill's unsuccessful effort to convince the American president to declare war on Germany in the weeks and months that followed the fall of France in June 1940. Yet, given the steady increase of American support for the British war effort that materialised over this precarious period, is it really fair to characterise Churchill's attempts to secure an American declaration of war as a failure?

Here, we must remember that the collapse of French resistance to Hitler in spring 1940 was widely viewed as an unmitigated disaster in Washington. For most Americans, the Nazi war machine seemed unstoppable; the fear now was that Britain would be next and should Hitler gain access to the British and French fleets as a consequence of his military prowess, the Atlantic would prove small comfort to an unprepared and under-armed America.[15] This hard reality led FDR's military advisors to coalesce around a strategy based on unilateral hemispheric defence, augmented by the rapid expansion of America's vastly inferior armed forces and the abandonment of the established policy of allowing the British to purchase 'surplus' US weapons under the cash-and-carry provision of the 1939 Neutrality Act.[16]

This shift in US policy placed Churchill – who had just assumed office as prime minister – in a very difficult position. By this point, his chiefs of staff – watching the French collapse in late May and early June – had already concluded that it would be impossible for Great Britain 'to continue the war with any chance of success' without the full financial and economic support of the United States.[17] At the same time, Churchill's foreign secretary, Lord Halifax, responded to the events in France with the recommendation that Churchill entertain the prospect of a negotiated settlement with Hitler through an approach to the Italian government (not yet in the war) about possible terms.

We now know that behind the scenes Churchill gave serious consideration to Halifax's suggestion but, after reflection, decided that all such thoughts should be put off until the outcome of the Battle of Britain had been determined. Churchill also understood that even the slightest hint in the public's mind that his government had considered a negotiated settlement with Hitler at this vital moment might prove fatal to British morale.[18]

As such, Churchill's response to the French catastrophe was essentially twofold: first, he had to convince the British public and his Cabinet colleagues that Great Britain should carry on the struggle against Germany no matter the costs; and second, he did all he could to convince his special correspondent in the White House to throw America's support behind the British war effort.

In Churchill's mind, his ability to influence Roosevelt stemmed largely from his decisive leadership and not from the memorable rhetoric he used to rally the British people at their moment of greatest peril, when the battle for France was over and the battle for Britain was about to begin. Reflecting on this after the war, Churchill once complained to his physician, Lord Moran, that 'People say my speeches after Dunkirk were the thing. That was only part, not the chief part', he grumbled. 'They forget I made all the main military decisions.'[19]

To say that Churchill made *all* the main military decisions is an exaggeration, of course, as most of the critical moves taken during the war were decided in council with the War Cabinet and the British chiefs of staff. Still, there is no question that Churchill, as prime minister and minister of defence, possessed the power to over-ride his military chiefs, and did at times issue critical orders that greatly influenced the outcome of the war.

It is also inaccurate to downplay the importance of Churchill's efforts, as Edward R. Murrow famously put it, 'to mobilise the English language and send it into battle'. Indeed, Churchill's ability to inspire an entire generation to 'never surrender' and stand up to what he rightly called a 'monstrous tyranny' in the weeks and months following the British evacuation at Dunkirk came at a critical moment (see Allen Packwood in Chapter 13 of this volume on how Churchill tailored his speeches for an American audience).

Churchill's leadership was most powerful, however, when he combined words with action. Perhaps the most significant example of this combination can be found in Churchill's decision to issue orders for the forcible seizure of the French fleet less than two weeks after the French signed the Armistice with Germany on 22 June 1940. This included an operation to seize a number of powerful French warships stationed in French North Africa to prevent them from falling into German hands. At one installation near Oran, after the French commander refused the British demand that he scuttle or surrender his ships, the British admiral on the scene opened fire, killing 1,297 French sailors.[20]

Speaking in the Commons the next day, Churchill justified his decision to order the Royal Navy 'to turns its guns on former brothers-in-arms' as a necessary act of 'self-preservation ... to prevent the French Fleet falling into enemy hands through the "malevolent" peace that Marshal Henri Philippe Pétain had made with Chancellor Hitler'. Churchill also insisted that any talk of the British following the same course of action – as rumoured in the United States and elsewhere by 'German propagandists' – was a lie. Indeed, 'All idea of that should be completely swept away by the very drastic and grievous action we have felt ourselves compelled to take. On the contrary', he declared, 'Britain is determined to prosecute the war until the righteous purposes upon which we entered upon it have been in all respects fulfilled.'[21]

Churchill's decision to seize the French fleet was taken in large part as a means to convince the United States that Great Britain was serious about continuing the war. It also came at a critical moment in Washington, where FDR and his military advisors were engaged in an intense debate over how best to fashion American military strategy now that Great Britain stood alone against the Axis. At the centre of this debate stood an earlier request that Churchill had made in his private correspondence with FDR for the loan of forty or fifty older US destroyers to assist in the defence of the British Isles.[22]

Still convinced that Great Britain's chances of survival were slim at best, and that the United States should husband its military resources so as to establish 'fortress America', FDR's military advisors remained adamantly opposed to the idea of transferring these vessels to the Royal Navy.

FDR shared in these anxieties. Yet, in spite of his own uncertainty about the British will to fight, he refused to give up on the notion that Great Britain might be able to hold on. Part of this stemmed from his conviction that a strategy of hemispheric defence – as advocated by his chiefs of staff – was simply not possible without the presence of the Royal Navy in the Atlantic.[23] As such, anything that FDR could do to bolster the strength of Great Britain and the British fleet made sense. At the same time, FDR also had to consider the fact that 1940 was an election year, and if he was to have any chance of successfully gaining the White House for an unprecedented third term, it was critically important to convince the American people that he was not scheming to find a way to drag the United States into the war in Europe. He also had to consider the possibility that these ships might well end up in the hands of the Germans should Great Britain fall or surrender.

All of these factors weighed heavily on FDR's mind as he tried to determine whether or not he should continue to offer Great Britain a measure of American support in the wake of the French defeat. It is for this reason that Churchill's decision to convert his words into action and seize the French fleet on 3 July 1940 is significant. For as FDR's personal emissary, Harry Hopkins, put it to a member of the prime minister's staff some months later, 'it was Churchill's action at Oran that convinced Roosevelt that Britain would continue the fight'.[24] Moreover, Churchill's move on the French fleet was taken in consultation with FDR, who, when asked, informed the British ambassador to Washington on 1 July that his government would fully support such an operation. As Hopkins indicated, these confidence-building steps proved vital. By August, FDR had decided to pursue a dual-track policy insofar as the German threat to the Americas was concerned: do all he could to strengthen hemispheric defences in both Latin America and Canada, while simultaneously providing all possible aid to Britain. To coordinate this effort, FDR sent a secret three-man military mission to London to initiate what in effect represented the first staff conversations between senior British and American military personnel. The signing of the Destroyers for Bases deal followed in short order, but under terms that fit neatly within the ambit of FDR's dual-track policy. The ships would be given in exchange for the USA being granted ninety-nine-year leases to British bases in Newfoundland, Bermuda, and five other locations in the Caribbean – a move that would both strengthen the US position in the Atlantic and provide additional American protection of the Western hemisphere. FDR also insisted that the British government issue a public statement guaranteeing that if Great Britain should fall, the British fleet would not be sunk or surrendered but turned over to the Empire to carry on the struggle.[25]

The terms of the Destroyers for Bases deal clearly favoured the United States – so much so that many of Churchill's advisors urged the prime minister to take a harder line in the negotiations with the Americans, particularly over FDR's insistence on a public statement on the fleet. In the end, however, Churchill decided to give way to Roosevelt's demands, in large part – as he said to the House of Commons near the end of August – because of the symbolism involved in seeing 'these two great organizations of the English-speaking democracies, the British Empire and the United States, mixed up together ... for mutual advantage'. As for the hard bargain the Americans drove over the talks, Churchill insisted that he 'did not view the process with any misgivings' and, in words that presaged the increasing Anglo-American cooperation that would flow from this moment, insisted that he could not stop the process of mutual support even if he wished to: 'no one can stop it', he said. 'Like the Mississippi, it just keeps rolling along. Let it roll on – full flood, inexorable, irresistible, benignant, to broader lands and better days.'[26]

Becoming More and More Provocative

By September 1940, then, Churchill's assertion that the two great English-speaking democracies had become 'mixed up together for mutual advantage' was not far off the mark. Autumn 1940 did in fact represent something of a watershed in Anglo-American relations, as by this point FDR's military chiefs felt confident enough in Great Britain's survival that they abandoned their previous demand for unilateral hemispheric defence and instead developed military plans more in keeping with FDR's insistence that American security was directly linked to the security of Great Britain and the Royal Navy.[27]

This new approach found expression in the host of measures FDR took in support of the British war effort throughout the first half of 1941. These included the passage of the Lend Lease Act in March, which granted the president the authority to provide war material to Great Britain or any other nation deemed vital to the defence of the United States without the need for payment; the extension of US 'naval patrols' to the mid-Atlantic in April; and the occupation of Iceland by US troops in July.

None of these moves was taken in a vacuum. All of them were the result of the close and ongoing communication between Churchill and Roosevelt. The president's decision to turn the United States into 'the great arsenal of democracy' and establish the lend lease programme, for example, came as a direct response to a ten-page missive that Churchill sent to Roosevelt in December 1940, which laid out in stark terms the two great dangers that threatened Great Britain's ability to continue the war: 'the steady and increasing diminution of sea tonnage' lost to German submarine attacks and the fact that the moment was fast approaching when the British government would 'no longer be able to pay cash for shipping and other supplies'.[28]

This sense of mutual cooperation also found expression in the decision of the two powers to embrace the Germany First strategy that US military planners developed in autumn 1940. This policy reflected the growing concern in Washington and London about further Japanese aggression in Asia, particularly after Japan signed the Tri-partite Pact with Germany and Italy on 27 September 1940. To deter Japan, FDR moved the US fleet to Pearl Harbor, and placed an embargo on the sale of scrap iron and high-octane fuel to Japan, but in light of Japan's decision to join the Axis, US military planners had to consider the possibility that the United States might soon find itself confronted with a two-front war. To meet this challenge, FDR's military chiefs developed a strategy that in the event the United States found itself simultaneously involved in a war with Japan and Germany, it should stand on the defensive in the Pacific and focus on the defeat of Germany first.[29]

The terms by which Great Britain and the United States would adhere to the Germany First strategy were worked out in secret Anglo-American staff talks that took place in Washington in February and March 1941. These high-level conversations – known as the ABC1 talks – coupled with the other measures FDR initiated in spring 1941 add credence to the notion that the establishment of the Anglo-American 'special relationship' was driven just as much by US security interests as it was by the security interests of the United Kingdom.[30]

The increasing American support for the British war effort that took place in the first half of 1941 was of course welcome in London. But the deterioration of the British position on the battlefield that took place at roughly the same time – marked by the setbacks in the Western Desert in March, the loss of Yugoslavia and Greece in April, and the relentless destruction of merchant shipping in the Atlantic, to say nothing of the intensification of the bombing raids against London and other cities – raised serious questions not only about Churchill's leadership – and a confidence vote in the Commons – but also about Great Britain's ability to continue the war.[31]

These fears became acute in May 1941 as the strategic island of Crete fell to German paratroopers and as the prospect of a renewed German attempt to invade the British Isles suddenly seemed a real possibility. In response to this 'May crisis', Churchill renewed his effort to convince FDR to enter the war, sending the president an explicit request for the United States 'to range herself with us as a belligerent power'.[32] But thanks to the strength of isolationist sentiment in the USA – spearheaded by the America First movement – the most FDR would do at this point was take to the airwaves to declare an 'unlimited National emergency'. This muted response came as a great disappointment to Churchill and his colleagues in London, who were becoming increasingly frustrated with what they regarded as FDR's unwillingness to get ahead of American public opinion. Moreover, even though the German attack on the Soviet Union in June removed the immediate threat of a German invasion of Great Britain, neither Churchill nor Roosevelt held out much hope that the Red Army would be able to survive this onslaught – even with the proffered material support of both the British and American governments.

It was in the midst of this rapidly evolving situation that FDR issued his invitation to meet with Churchill at Placentia Bay off the coast of Newfoundland in August 1941. The dramatic encounter that took place at this first summit meeting between the two leaders represents the climax of Churchill's long-standing effort to secure US involvement in the war. Thrilled at the prospect and convinced that FDR's presidential summons meant that American declaration of war was imminent, Churchill embarked for the Atlantic Conference in a buoyant mood. But the Conference that resulted in the famous Atlantic Charter was best characterised in the mind of one British official as the Atlantic 'flop'.[33] Yes, the joint statement of guiding principles that FDR and Churchill issued was significant and would take on ever-greater importance as the war dragged on, but the fact that Great Britain and the United States made clear their intention not to use the conflict as a means to seek any aggrandisement, territorial or other, and had issued this important document did nothing to alleviate the precarious situation on the battlefield in summer 1941.[34] Indeed, with the Red Army still reeling from the launch of Hitler's devastating attack on Russia in June, and with German U-boats still inflicting alarming losses on British merchant ships in the Atlantic, to say nothing of the increasingly aggressive posture of the Japanese in the Far East, the British Cabinet was gripped by what Churchill called 'a wave of depression' following the Atlantic Conference.[35]

But is this sentiment justified? At the Atlantic meeting FDR informed Churchill that 'he would wage war but not declare it'; that he would 'become more and more provocative. If the Germans did not like it', he said, 'they could attack American [naval] forces.' FDR also made clear that 'he would look for an "incident" that would justify his opening hostilities'.[36] These avowals may have fallen short of the full commitment the British were looking for, but they nevertheless represent an extraordinary assertion on FDR's part, especially given the strong residue of isolationism within the US Congress. Just two days after the Atlantic Conference ended, in fact, FDR's efforts to gain Congressional approval for an extension of the 1940 Selective Service Act only passed the US House of Representatives by a single vote.[37]

And yet, not only did FDR issue a promise 'to become more and more provocative' and to look for an 'incident' that might justify the opening of hostilities, he also informed Churchill of his intent to order the US navy to provide British convoys with armed escorts as far as Iceland, even though how he would announce such 'a bold step remained a problem'.[38] The fact that Churchill had been pressing the president to take such a step since at least December 1940 may have rendered

FDR's remarks somewhat anti-climactic for Churchill and the British chiefs of staff.[39] But within a matter of weeks, the rather exaggerated encounter between the US destroyer *Greer* and German U-boat U-652 provided FDR with the pretext he needed to issue his famous 'shoot on sight' order to the US navy on 11 September 1941. Six days later, off the coast of Newfoundland, a fifty-ship convoy shepherded by Canadian warships was handed off to five US destroyers, who safely escorted the merchantmen across the North Atlantic and into the hands of a Royal Navy squadron just south of Iceland. The armed escorts that FDR had promised were now operational. Given the subsequent U-boat attack on the USS *Kearny* on 17 October and the sinking of the USS *Reuben James* two weeks later, there can be little doubt that insofar as the US navy was concerned, the United States was now engaged in the undeclared war against Germany that FDR had promised.[40]

The 'shoot on sight' order represents the pinnacle of the 'all aid short of war' policy that FDR had been slowly cultivating over the past year. This policy may have been less than the British wanted, but it nevertheless makes clear that the 'special relationship' so sought after by Churchill was already in place even before the Japanese launched their surprise attack on the US naval base at Pearl Harbor. This was in keeping with FDR's long-standing inclination to see the Atlantic – protected in part by the Royal Navy – as the key to American security. Nevertheless, it is hard to imagine that these developments would have taken place without the concerted effort to gain Roosevelt's confidence that Churchill had been engaged in since his assumption of power on 10 May 1940.

The United Nations versus the Grand Alliance

The Japanese attack on Pearl Harbor and the subsequent German and Italian declaration of war on the United States ushered in the second phase of the Anglo-American wartime relationship. It was during this eighteen-month period, which ran from roughly December 1941 until July 1943, that the Churchill–Roosevelt relationship reached its high-water mark. Unlike the first phase of the 'special relationship', it was Churchill who initiated this segment, with his much-celebrated – and self-invited – visit to Washington over the course of the 1941–2 holiday season.

Code-named Arcadia, this sojourn was marked by an historic address Churchill delivered to a joint session of the US Congress, where, after

Figure 14.1 In the shadow of the United States? Churchill at the White House, December 1941 (CAC, Baroness Spencer-Churchill Papers, CSCT 7/2 B).

commenting on how comfortable he felt in a democratic assembly where English is spoken, and warning his audience about the many trials and tribulations that the British and American people faced in their common struggle against fascism, he nevertheless assured his listeners that he remained confident in the final outcome. 'Provided', he said, that 'every effort is made, that nothing is held back, that the whole manpower, brain power, virility, valor and civic virtue of the English-speaking world with all its galaxy of loyal, friendly or associated communities ... is bent unremittingly to the ... supreme task.'

Churchill then set forth a plea for the continuation of the fraternal association between the British and American people which the war had brought about, and which presaged the remarks he made in his 1946 Fulton speech on the same theme, when he observed that if the United States and Great Britain had taken common measures for the two nations' safety, the renewal of the curse of a world war need never have fallen upon the two states. 'Do we not owe it to ourselves, to our children, to tormented mankind', he said, 'to make sure that these catastrophes do not engulf us for the third time?'

Five or six years ago, he admonished, 'it would have been easy, without shedding a drop of blood, for the United States and Great

Britain to have insisted on the fulfilment of the disarmament clauses of the treaties which Germany signed after the Great War'. The two states could also have ensured that Germany was given access to the raw materials which, as declared in the Atlantic Charter, 'should not be denied to any nation, victor or vanquished'. But the chance has passed, he said; 'it is gone'.

Nonetheless, Churchill could not help but discern that perhaps 'some great purpose and design' had brought the two countries together at this vital moment, which led him to avow his 'hope and faith, sure and inviolate, that in the days to come the British and American peoples will, for their own safety and for the good of all, walk together in majesty, in justice and in peace'.[41]

As Churchill left the Senate Chamber, to thunderous applause, many members of Congress remarked that the speech was among the finest they had ever heard. And in an indication of the shift in attitude about US involvement in the wider world that came in the wake of Pearl Harbor, a number of US Congressmen remarked on the perspicacity of the prime minister's suggestion that the two nations could have easily put a stop to Hitler if they had worked together in the past, and should not allow a recurrence of what transpired during the 1930s. The *Washington Post* even went so far as to interpret Churchill's remarks as tantamount to a call for an Anglo-American alliance 'after victory is won'.[42]

Churchill was not being presumptuous when he alluded to the idea of using the circumstances of the war as a means by which Great Britain and the United States might establish a long-term Anglo-American alliance. The first step in this direction came about in the creation of the combined chiefs of staff (CCOS). Composed of the British chiefs of staff and the newly created US joint chiefs of staff, the primary responsibility of the CCOS was to coordinate military strategy and logistics for what had suddenly become a global war. At Arcadia, the two powers also agreed to create an integrated command structure, whereby a single officer in each theatre would command the military forces of both the United States and Great Britain. Behind the scenes, they also came to an understanding over the sharing of the signals intelligence gleaned from the British 'Ultra' project and the American 'Magic' intercepts, and by this point had also taken the first tentative steps towards the joint development of the atomic bomb. The creation of the CCOS and establishment of unified commands, coupled with the intelligence sharing and scientific cooperation, tied the Anglo-American war effort together in a manner that is unique in the annals of military history. Given the scope of the war, and the geopolitical realities confronting the two nations, the creation of this war-fighting structure made sense. But it is hard to imagine that these developments would have occurred without the strong sense of cooperation and common purpose that the personal relationship between Churchill and Roosevelt helped foster.[43]

This is not to say, however, that the drawing together of the British and American military chiefs was not without its difficulties, for unity of command at the theatre level also required unified strategic direction.[44] One of Churchill's primary goals in making the trip to Washington was to reaffirm the Germany First strategy that the two powers had agreed to in the ABC1 talks. A second was to convince FDR and his military chiefs to embrace what Churchill often referred to as his 'peripheral strategy' – weakening the German hold on the continent through bombing, special operations and taking the war to the Wehrmacht in areas such as North Africa where the British army could meet the Axis forces on relatively equal terms. As Churchill would soon discover, gaining American support for both these objectives turned out to be far more complicated in light of the hard realities the two powers faced in the weeks and months that followed the US entry into the war. FDR's chief of staff, General George C. Marshall, remained adamantly opposed to Churchill's peripheral strategy. As such, he regarded Churchill's December 1941 proposal for an Allied landing in north-west Africa as a distraction from what he regarded as the main task at hand: marshalling the forces needed to launch a successful invasion of north-west Europe as soon as possible.

Marshall's push for this far more direct approach to the defeat of Germany was further complicated by the Japanese sweep across much of south-east Asia in the wake of the attack on Pearl Harbor. Here, the loss of such key outposts as Singapore and the Philippines rendered the policy of 'standing on the defensive in the Pacific' meaningless, leaving US military planners no choice but to call for reinforcements to halt the growing Japanese threat to Australia and New Zeeland, while the British sent reinforcements to stop the Japanese advance from Burma into India. These demands impeded the much-needed effort to build up the forces required to take on Hitler's 'fortress Europe' at the very moment when the US and British chiefs of staff were engaged in critical conversations about the future direction of the war. What's more, given the relatively small size of the British army, and the time it would take for the United States to assemble the forces needed to launch a successful invasion of the continent, there was no realistic possibility that such an invasion could be launched in 1942.

This placed FDR in something of a dilemma, for if the United States was to pursue a policy based on defeating Germany first, it was important to get the American public – still furious over the Japanese attack on Pearl Harbor – engaged in the war in Europe. Like Churchill, FDR also had to consider Stalin's urgent demand that the Allies open a second front as a means to take the pressure off the Red Army. Taken together, these factors made the prime minister's suggestion of a move into North Africa an attractive proposition, and after many months of debate with his chiefs of staff over the merits of the proposal, FDR finally made the decision to support Churchill's recommendation.[45]

The decision to launch Operation Torch – as the invasion was known – had a profound impact on the course of the Second World War, for, as General Marshall feared, clearing North Africa took far longer than anticipated; first, because the initial landings in Morocco and Mers El Kébir would not get underway until 8 November 1942; and second, because Hitler's decision to send German forces into Tunisia – where British forces advancing from the east were meant to link up with the largely American forces advancing from the west – rendered the battle for that mountainous country a long and bloody drawn-out affair that would not end until 13 May 1943. This made it all but impossible to launch an invasion of France in 1943.

Unwilling to see their forces sit idle until such time as a move into north-west Europe could be organised, Churchill and the British chiefs of staff pressed ahead with their earlier recommendation for a peripheral approach to the war, through the invasion of Sicily in July and the invasion of Italy in September. This 'Mediterranean strategy', which the Anglo-Americans agreed to at the Third Washington Conference of May to June 1943, and which delayed the proposed invasion of France until spring 1944, infuriated Stalin, who, like Marshall, regarded the Anglo-American push into the North African/ Mediterranean theatre as little more than a side show.[46]

By this point, the Red Army's victory at Stalingrad had rendered the question of Soviet survival much less of a concern to Churchill and Roosevelt. But this did not entirely eliminate their apprehensions over the ability and/or willingness of the Soviets to continue the struggle.

The scope and ferocity of the Russo-German war made it obvious that the final defeat of Hitler's forces remained a gargantuan task – even with the help of the Anglo-Americans. In light of this, the two leaders were never quite able to shake their fear that an exhausted Soviet Union might opt for a negotiated separate peace along the lines of the 1939 Nazi-Soviet Pact. Paradoxically, they also had to consider just how the concomitant rise in Soviet power might impact the post-war world. These twin factors not only placed the two men under tremendous pressure as they struggled to cope with Stalin's vociferous demand for a second front but also exposed a growing divergence of opinion between them about the purpose of the war, and the structure of the world to follow.[47]

In many respects, we can trace the origins of this divergence to the terms the two leaders used to describe the anti-Axis coalition that materialised in the wake of the Japanese attack on Pearl Harbor in early December 1941. For Roosevelt, this association of powers was best represented by the use of the phrase 'United Nations', an idiom that stemmed from the gathering of representatives of twenty-four nations at the White House on 1 January 1942, there to sign a common pledge – what FDR called a 'Declaration by United Nations' – through which they agreed to adhere to the principles of the Atlantic Charter; to make no separate armistice or peace with the Axis; and to employ their full military and/or economic resources in the common struggle to see the Axis powers defeated. The Declaration represented the first official use of the term 'United Nations', a phrase coined by FDR that would go on to become the official name of the Allied forces fighting the Axis and eventually the official name of the 'United Nations organisation' that he hoped would emerge after the war.

FDR's interest in creating a world organisation that would maintain the peace and promote a universal set of values was long-standing. So too was his conviction that it was the economic crisis of the 1930s that led to the rise of fascism in Europe and Asia and hence the war. As such, FDR viewed the construction of the Allied coalition in the Second World War as an opportunity for the United States to use its wartime leverage as a means to secure the peace and reorder the world's social and economic conditions. This effort first manifested itself in January 1941 with FDR's call for a world founded on four fundamental human freedoms – freedom of speech and expression, freedom of worship, freedom from want and freedom from fear. These fundamental principles – including the all-important concepts of 'freedom from want' and 'freedom from fear' – were further articulated in the Atlantic Charter, which signalled the rights of all peoples to choose the form of government under which they would live; identified the need to secure improved labour standards, economic advancement and social security for all; and dedicated the United States and its allies to what was referred to as a 'permanent system of general security'. Taken as a whole, these concepts not only point towards the creation of what would become the United Nations, they also reference the need to establish a new international economic order, built – in FDR's mind – on an American foundation.[48]

Churchill was certainly not averse to signing the 'Declaration by United Nations' – in fact, it was the prime minister, during the Arcadia Conference, who first suggested the idea of bringing together a group of representatives to sign a common pledge against the Axis. Nor was he opposed to the general principles articulated in the Four Freedoms and Atlantic Charter – so long as the latter's call for self-determination was interpreted to refer only to states under German occupation. But unlike FDR, Churchill's conception of the anti-Axis coalition is best captured by his use of the phrase 'Grand Alliance', which he utilised in a conscious attempt to tie the British, American and Soviet efforts to defeat the Axis with the coalition that would go on to defeat Louis XIV in the 1701–14 War of the Spanish Succession under the leadership of his ancestor, the 1st Duke of Marlborough.

Technically speaking, the 'Grand Alliance' and 'United Nations' both refer to the association of nations that was brought together to defeat the Axis. But in practice the two appellations came to embody two separate – and at times, quite different – entities, with the Grand Alliance most often referring to the military coalition among the 'Big Three', while the 'United Nations' referred to the much broader affiliation of anti-Axis powers represented in the 1 January 1942 declaration. Viewed from this perspective, the two entities represented two separate wartime realities and two separate visions for the future: the first placing a greater emphasis on the perpetuation of Great Power prerogatives; the second placing a greater emphasis on the democratisation of power and the reduction – or repurposing – of those prerogatives to promote a new world order under American leadership.[49]

Hence, while FDR saw America's involvement in the war as an opportunity to draw the English-speaking peoples together to create a new, multilateral world order that rejected imperialism and the tenets of economic nationalism, Churchill saw the war as a means to restore the British Empire and re-dedicate the English-speaking peoples to the perpetuation of British power and influence in the world. Perhaps the most tangible example of this fundamental difference in interpretation can be seen in the ordering of signatories in the initial draft of the 'Declaration of United Nations' that Churchill and FDR sketched during Churchill's visit to the White House in December 1941. Both Churchill and Roosevelt – along with the Soviet and Chinese ambassadors to Washington – agreed that the first four powers listed for signature under the declaration should be the United States, China, the Union of Soviet Republics and the United Kingdom of Great Britain and Northern Ireland – what FDR by this point was beginning to call 'the Four Policemen'. Thereafter, Churchill and his foreign secretary, Anthony Eden (who had cabled his views from London), favoured listing the four British Dominions plus India (which was included as a separate state at the insistence of FDR) under the United Kingdom, after which the remaining signatory nations would be listed in alphabetical order. FDR initially agreed to this, but when the time came for the various representatives to sign the document, he had changed his mind and, taking out his pencil, insisted – as illustrated by the edits he made to his original hand-written draft – that the British Dominions and India should be incorporated alphabetically into the list of other signatory nations (see Figure 14.2).[50]

It was these two separate visions that ultimately led to a fundamental shift in the relationship between the two men. For in spite of their close personal relationship, FDR remained wary of British motives and, like many in his administration, had no desire to fight the war on behalf of the British Empire. Moreover, as the war progressed, and the reality of Soviet power became ever more apparent, FDR became increasingly convinced that for his vision to work it was critically important to draw the Soviets into what he sometimes referred to as 'the family of nations'. Indeed, FDR saw the maintenance of Great Power cooperation – particularly the continuation of US-Soviet cooperation – as a vital component of his effort to establish the post-war international order, and by spring 1943 he was most anxious to impress this view upon his Soviet counterpart. This led FDR to seek out an opportunity to meet Stalin one on one without informing Churchill. This move deeply wounded Churchill, who, upon learning of it, made clear his adamant

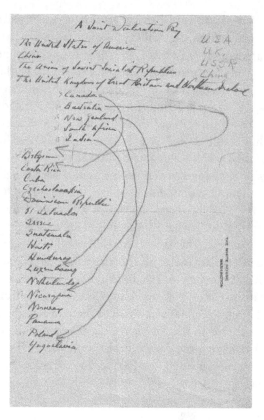

Figure 14.2 Roosevelt's draft of the United Nations Declaration, December 1941 (courtesy of the FDR Presidential Library).

opposition to the idea in a conversation with FDR's personal envoy to London, Averell Harriman, near the end of June 1943. Churchill also sent a less vehement telegram to Roosevelt, where he cautioned the president about the use that enemy propaganda would make of a meeting between the president and Stalin, 'with the British Commonwealth and Empire excluded'. Such a development would be 'serious and vexatious', he wrote, and might cause a good deal of bewilderment and alarm. Churchill may have closed this message by reassuring FDR that he would go along with whatever the president decided, but Churchill's angst over FDR's pursuit of a bilateral relationship with Stalin led to real tensions between them, and signalled

Churchill's growing frustration over his realisation that Great Britain was becoming the junior partner in the Anglo-American alliance.[51]

Towards a New World Order

It was this tension that initiated the third and final phase of the wartime special relationship, which ran from the moment Churchill made plain his opposition to FDR's attempt to arrange a bilateral meeting with Stalin in late June 1943 until FDR's untimely death in April 1945 and the final victory over Germany and Japan which followed. In light of Churchill's feelings, FDR dropped his plans for a private summit with the Soviet leader. In lieu of this, however, Roosevelt made a point of showing his independence from Churchill when the 'Big Three' finally did meet at the Tehran Conference near the end of 1943. Here, the three leaders reached general understandings about such issues as the future borders of Poland and the establishment of a European Advisory Commission to produce plans for the occupation of Germany. But FDR's behaviour both before and during the Conference made it clear that his relationship with Churchill – like the relationship between London and Washington – was undergoing a change.

The president, for example, refused Churchill's repeated requests for a pre-Tehran discussion to develop an Anglo-American approach to the summit when the two met in Cairo prior to travelling to the Iranian capital. Moreover, once at Tehran, FDR avoided long meetings with Churchill, while seeking out private conversations with Stalin. It was during one of these private conversations that FDR introduced Stalin to his thoughts about the creation of the United Nations, including his conception of what would become the Security Council, where 'the four policemen' – the USA, UK, USSR and China – would maintain the peace of the world.

In the meantime, during the tripartite discussions, Roosevelt also refused to back Churchill's ardent desire to maintain and enhance Anglo-American operations then underway in Italy and the eastern Mediterranean (offshoots of the North African invasion), and instead agreed with Stalin that the focus of the Anglo-American war effort must now be geared towards the long-awaited landings in France. The imperative, in short, was Operation Overlord (the Normandy invasion), which must occur no later than May 1944.[52]

By the time the Tehran Conference had ended, it was clear that FDR was serious when he said the United States had no intention of becoming a tail on the British kite. Hence, in the months that followed, the US effort to fashion a new post-war world took on a much more tangible form; first, through the economic accords achieved at the Bretton Woods Conference in July 1944 – which led to the creation of the International Monetary Fund and World Bank – and second, through the crafting of the basic structure of the United Nations organisation that was hammered out at the Dumbarton Oaks Conference shortly thereafter.

The post-Tehran period also brought about a subtle-yet-important indication of the change in the personal relationship between Churchill and Roosevelt: the cessation of the two men's use of the moniker 'Former Naval Person'.[53] Perhaps they had simply grown tired of this form of address, but it is interesting to note that their shift to more formal language coincides with the heightened state of tension that had crept into the Anglo-American alliance as the end of the war drew nearer. Here, questions over the continuation of lend lease; the issue of freer trade; the future of Greece; and how best to settle the political make-up of liberated Poland and other territories in eastern and central Europe all created their own set of challenges. So too did the question of how best to prosecute the war in the Far East.

Given Churchill's concern over the diminution of British power within the 'Grand Alliance' and the potential loss of British influence that would result as a consequence, it is perhaps not surprising that the Anglo-American victories in France in summer 1944 tended to increase – rather than diminish – his anxiety about the shape of the post-war world. It was this anxiety that led to his insistence on a meeting with Roosevelt in Quebec in September 1944 and with Stalin a month later. At Quebec, Churchill did his best to hammer out understandings with FDR over the British and American zones of occupation in defeated Germany; the continuation of lend lease after victory; and participation of the Royal Navy in the final push against Japan.[54] In Moscow, Churchill sought to further secure the British position in the eastern Mediterranean through the negotiation of the so-called percentages agreement, by which Stalin and Churchill approved a formula that gave Britain the upper hand in Greece; split British and Russian influence in Yugoslavia and Hungary; and ceded Russian preponderance in Romania and Bulgaria.[55]

Churchill kept Roosevelt informed about his activities in Moscow, but like FDR's decision to distance himself from the prime minister in his negotiations with Stalin at Tehran, what emerges from all of this activity is the clear sense that Churchill had reached the point in the war where he was determined to do what he could to assert British interests.[56] Churchill's efforts in this regard are certainly understandable. Yet in an indication of the shift in the power dynamic that had occurred by this point, FDR sent a message to Stalin prior to his meeting with Churchill to remind the Soviet leader that he regarded whatever understandings the men reached as preliminary, and that 'in this global war, there is literally no question, political or military, in which the United States is not interested'.[57]

Still, it is important to remember that Churchill pursued his nation's aims within the context of the wartime alliance, as did his Russian and American counterparts. Indeed, it is this often-overlooked determination to keep the alliance together that is perhaps the most remarkable aspect of the relationship not only between Churchill and Roosevelt but also between the two of them and Stalin.

This brings us to the last of the 'Big Three' summit meetings attended by Roosevelt – the Yalta Conference of February 1945. Of all the wartime conferences, Yalta remains the most prominent – and controversial. The truth, however, is that much of what took place at Yalta merely represented the final touches on what had already been agreed to at Tehran over a year earlier. We must also remember that the reality that the Soviet regime would hold a predominant position in eastern Europe following the war was decided not at Yalta, but long before: on the battlefields of Russia in 1942–3 and by the Allied failure to land in France until June 1944.[58] Both Roosevelt and Churchill recognised this and, as such, what the two men sought to accomplish at Yalta was not the elimination of Soviet influence in eastern Europe but its amelioration. This led to the Declaration of Liberated Europe and the Declaration of Poland, both of which called for adherence to the right of all people to choose the form of government under which they would live and which, in the case of Poland, specifically called for 'the holding of free and unfettered elections as soon as possible on the basis of universal suffrage and secret ballot'.[59] Roosevelt was also anxious to confirm Stalin's earlier promise to commit Russian forces to the war against Japan, as well as to secure Soviet participation in the United Nations organisation, both of which were accomplished. Most important, of course, was the continuation of wartime cooperation, which Roosevelt in particular saw as critical to future peace and to the success of the new world organisation that he and his administration had worked so hard to achieve.

Sadly, Franklin Roosevelt would not live to see either the end of the war or the birth of the United Nations. He died at his Warm Springs cottage on 12 April 1945 while resting after the physical exhaustion that was brought on in part by the demands of the Yalta Conference. The news of FDR's death sent shockwaves around the world. Churchill described the news as a 'physical blow' and in a letter to King George VI observed that with FDR gone, 'ties have been torn asunder which years have woven'.[60] Churchill also delivered a moving eulogy to FDR in the House of Commons where he recounted not only their mutual friendship but also FDR's determination to help Great Britain at its critical hour, inspired by 'the beatings of that generous heart which was always stirred to anger and to action by spectacles of aggression and oppression by the strong against the weak'.[61]

Uniting the Western Democracies

Roosevelt's death and Churchill's fall from power shortly thereafter may have altered the personal nature of the special relationship, but even before these two towering figures disappeared from the wartime stage, it was already clear that the affiliation between the United States and Great Britain was largely framed in American terms. The post-war economic and security infrastructure that emerged during and after the war certainly reflects this. Great Britain may have held the most prominent non-American seat at the wartime Bretton Woods and Dumbarton Oaks conferences, for example, but the institutions that arose from both of these gatherings reflect a largely American design. The same might be said about the global trading arrangements that materialised in the 1947 General Agreement on Tariff and Trade, or GATT. Here, Great Britain's dependency on the USA for war materiel, which led to the development of the lend lease programme – and which did not require the recipients of US aid to pay for the goods received – may have appeared extraordinarily altruistic, but it did not come without a price. Under the terms of what became the Lend Lease Consideration Agreement signed in 1942, the USA all but demanded that Great Britain do away with the 1932 system of Imperial Preference whereby commodities traded within the British Empire were largely exempt from import duties and tariffs. By the end of the war the preponderance of US economic power – and continued British dependence on US financial aid – left Whitehall no choice but to abandon these Depression-era arrangements and sign on to American-designed multilateral system of freer trade that came out of GATT.[62]

It is also the case that while in some respects the outbreak of war in September 1939 strengthened the bonds of the Empire, the rapid advance of the Japanese in spring 1942 and inability of the British government to provide adequate security for Australia and New Zealand meant that this role was increasingly usurped by the United States.

In a similar fashion, the successful development of the atomic bomb, which might not have been possible without the important and early contributions of British science, did not necessarily lead to the sharing of atomic secrets. By 1945, most senior American officials involved in the management of the Manhattan Project had already endorsed a policy of limiting Great Britain's access to the nuclear secret and, with the successful test of the bomb in July of that year, pushed the Truman administration not to share the keys to this new-found source of military and economic power with the United Kingdom. This trend ultimately found expression in the passage of the McMahon Act on 1 August 1946, which formally severed the atomic partnership between London and Washington.

Churchill, who was no longer in power when most of these developments took place, certainly viewed these changes with misgivings, yet we should not let the clear preponderance of the American side of the special relationship that emerged over the course of the war obscure the fact that the habit of staying all 'mixed up together' was not so easily discarded. In many respects this is because the 'mutual advantage' that both nations gleaned from the establishment of the wartime alliance did not disappear at the moment of victory. Here, the recognition of the Atlantic as the lynchpin of Anglo-American security would soon find expression in the establishment of the North Atlantic Treaty Organization (NATO); similarly, the wartime intelligence-sharing arrangements would find renewed life under the 1946 United Kingdom–United States Communications Intelligence Act, which established the 'Five Eyes' signals intelligence network among the five Anglophone countries of Australia, New Zealand, Canada, the United

States and the United Kingdom. The use of American economic power to help lift a struggling Britain and Europe from its knees re-emerged in the Marshall Plan. And while the United States may have insisted on maintaining a monopoly over the atomic bomb in the immediate post-war period, the detonation of Russia's first atomic bomb in 1949 and the advance of Soviet science through the launch of the Sputnik satellite ultimately led the USA to abandon most aspects of the McMahon Act, provide the UK with nuclear-armed Polaris submarines and renew much of the scientific collaboration that existed during the war.

Nor did the sense of common purpose among what Churchill called the English-speaking peoples necessarily disappear with the end of the war. Perhaps this is the most important legacy of the special relationship, for as Churchill penned in the preface to his four-volume history, the drawing together of the British and American people in their joint struggle against fascism involved far more than simply adherence to a common language. It also involved a shared belief in democracy and the rule of law, customs which evolved over time and which 'afforded a unique foundation' upon which the two peoples might dedicate themselves to the concerted task of shaping a better future for the wider world. In this sense, Churchill's 1918 observation that 'the intermingling' of British and American troops 'on the field of battle' might exert 'an immeasurable effect upon the future destiny of the English-speaking peoples' proved prescient, except that by the time that war ended, the notion of a fraternity among the British Commonwealth and the United States had been superseded by the idea that it was the 'Western democracies' acting within the structure of the United Nations, as he said in his 1946 Fulton address, that possessed 'a common duty' to help maintain the principles he and Franklin Roosevelt had first articulated in their meeting off the coast of Newfoundland in 1941, and which had found renewed expression in the United Nations' founding documents.[63]

Given Churchill's Victorian sensibilities and somewhat anachronistic view of the British Empire, his support for these principles may seem somewhat paradoxical. But as the historian Richard Toye notes, Churchill's view of empire is more complex than the public image he adopted.[64] And while the special relationship that emerged with the war would ultimately become far more important in Great Britain than in the United States, the determination of the two peoples to resist the advance of totalitarianism in the Second World War and the Cold War that followed owed far more to the two peoples' shared belief in preserving the principles of democracy than simply a self-serving desire for survival. Viewed from this perspective, Churchill was surely correct when he reflected on the occasion of his being bestowed honorary citizenship of the United States in 1963 that in spite of the 'storm and tragedy' that marked much of the twentieth century, he could not help but regard 'the constant factor of the interwoven and upward progress' of the British and American people with anything but profound satisfaction. 'Our comradeship and our brotherhood in war were unexampled', he observed. 'We stood together, and because of that fact, the free world now stands.'[65]

Notes

1. W. S. Churchill, *A History of the English-Speaking Peoples*, Volume 1: The Birth of Britain (London: Bloomsbury Academic, 2016), p. xi.
2. W. S. Churchill, *A History of the English-Speaking Peoples, Volume 3: The Age of Revolution* (London: Bloomsbury Academic, 2016), p. xi.
3. D. Reynolds, Rethinking Anglo-American Relations. *International Affairs (Royal Institute of International Affairs)*, vol. 65, no. 1 (Winter 1988–9), p. 94; TNA, PREM 4/27/10, Churchill, Minute M. 125/4, 16 February 1944.
4. TNA, PREM 4/27/10, Churchill, Minute M. 125/4, 16 February 1944.
5. W. S. Churchill, *The World Crisis*, vol. 4 (New York: Scribner & Sons, 1955), pp. 194–5.
6. For more on this, see D. Reynolds, 1940: Fulcrum of the Twentieth Century? *International Affairs* (Royal Institute of International Affairs), vol. 66, no. 2 (April 1990), pp. 325–50.
7. Winston Churchill, Speech to Mansion House, 10 November 1942.
8. W. Kimball, *Churchill and Roosevelt: The Complete Correspondence*, vol. 1 (Princeton, NJ: Princeton University Press, 1984), p. 7.
9. Churchill's initial tenure as First Lord of the Admiralty ran from October 1911 to May 1915. He relished holding this all-important Cabinet position but was forced to resign in the wake of the failed mission in the Dardanelles in spring 1915.
10. FDR Library, Hyde Park, NY, Map Room Papers, Box 1, FDR to Churchill, 11 September 1939.
11. D. Reynolds, *The Creation of the Anglo-American Alliance: A Study in Competitive Cooperation* (Chapel Hill: University of North Carolina Press, 1981), pp. 23–5; Library of Congress, Norman Davis Papers, Box 4, Record of Conversation between Franklin Roosevelt and Norman Davis, 19 October 1937.
12. FDR Library, Master Speech File, Box 55, FDR Speech in Boston, Massachusetts, 30 October 1940.
13. A. Packwood, *How Churchill Waged War: The Most Challenging Decisions of the Second World War* (Barnsley: Frontline Books, 2018), p. 11.
14. Packwood, *How Churchill Waged War*, p. 20.
15. D. Woolner, Churchill and the Special Relationship. In R. Toye (ed.), *Winston Churchill: Politics, Strategy and Statecraft* (London: Bloomsbury Academic, 2017), pp. 155–6.

16. M. Stoler, *Allies and Adversaries: The Joint Chiefs of Staff, the Grand Alliance, and U.S. Strategy in WWII* (Chapel Hill: University of North Carolina Press, 2000), pp. 25–6.
17. TNA, CAB 66/7, WP (40) 168, 'British Strategy in a Certain Eventuality', 25 May 1940.
18. D. Reynolds, *In Command of History: Churchill Fighting and Writing the Second World War* (London: Allen Lane, 2004), pp. 169–71.
19. Packwood, *How Churchill Waged War*, pp. x–xi; Lord Moran, *Winston Churchill: The Struggle for Survival 1940–1965* (London: Constable, 1966), p. 292.
20. On 22 June 1940, France signed an Armistice agreement with Germany that divided the country into two zones, a German occupation zone which included the north and west of the country, including the entire Atlantic seaboard, and an unoccupied zone in the south of France where a newly established government was formed in the French city of Vichy. The Vichy government also controlled French North Africa and other French colonial possessions, including Indochina. Under the terms of the Armistice, the French fleet, then scattered in various ports around the world, was to sail home to metropolitan France for the duration of the war, with the understanding that French warships would remain out of action except for coastal patrols and mine sweeping. See CAC, The Churchill Papers, CHAR 20/14, printed copies of personal telegrams from Churchill, May to December 1940.
21. 'Churchill grieved: Explains fleet had to fight erstwhile Allies to thwart the Nazis', *New York Times*, 5 July 1940, p. 1.
22. FDR Library, Map Room Files, Box 1, Churchill to FDR, 15 May 1940.
23. M. Mattloff and E. M. Snell, Strategic Planning for Coalition Warfare, 1941–1942. *United States Army in World War II*, series 4, vol. 3 (1953), pp. 13–14.
24. M. Gilbert, *Churchill and America* (New York: Free Press, 2005), p. 198.
25. Reynolds, *Competitive Cooperation*, pp. 121–9. FDR's efforts strengthen the defensive ties between the United States, Canada and the Latin American republics found expression in the Ogdensburg Agreement of August 1940, which established the US-Canadian Permanent Joint Board of Defense, and in the Act of Havana of July 1940, which stated that 'any attempt on the part of a non-American state against the integrity, sovereignty or political independence of an American state' would be considered an act of aggression by the signatory powers.
26. Rhodes James, *Complete Speeches*, vol. 6, p. 6268.
27. In October 1940, for example, US chief of naval operations Admiral Harold Stark wrote that the preservation of the territorial, economic and ideological integrity of the United States and the rest of the hemisphere 'depended on a strong British navy and empire to check any military incursion by a hostile Continental power'. Stoler, *Allies and Adversaries*, p. 30.
28. CAC, Churchill Papers CHAR 23/4/11, Churchill to Roosevelt, 7 December 1940.
29. Stoler, *Allies and Adversaries*, pp. 29–34; FDR Library Hyde Park, Safe Files, Navy Department, Plan Dog, Memorandum by Harold Stark, Chief of Naval Operations, to the Secretary of the Navy, 12 November 1940.
30. During the ABC1 talks the British pressed the Americans to send a US naval squadron to Singapore as a corollary of FDR's policy of deterrence. But convinced that the Atlantic remained the decisive theatre, and not wanting to do anything that might be interpreted by the US public as support for the British Empire, Roosevelt steadfastly refused to do so – agreeing instead to the reinforcement of the US naval position in the Atlantic so that the British might then send their own naval reinforcements to the Pacific. Mattloff and Snell, *Strategic Planning*, pp. 34–6; R. Dallek, *Franklin Roosevelt*

and American Foreign Policy, 1932–1945 (New York: Oxford University Press, 1995), p. 272; FDR Library, PSF Box 175, Public Opinion Polls, 1935–41.

31. D. Reynolds, *From Munich to Pearl Harbor: Roosevelt's America and the Origins of the Second World War* (Chicago, IL: Ivan R. Dee, 2001), pp. 123–5.

32. FDR Library Map Room Papers, Box 1, Churchill to Roosevelt, 3 May 1941. This represented only the second time since the start of the war that Churchill sent FDR an explicit request for the USA to enter the war; the first occurred on 15 June 1940, on the eve of the final capitulation of the French army. The fact that Churchill felt the need to do so in May 1941 speaks to the equally grave situation in which Great Britain found itself at this period in the war.

33. Alexander Cadogan, the permanent undersecretary of the British Foreign Office who was present at the meeting, recorded in his diary that the conference that resulted in the famous Atlantic Charter was best characterised in his mind as the Atlantic 'flop'. CAC, Cadogan Papers, ACAD 1/10 and 7/2. Alexander Cadogan diary, 19 August 1941.

34. W. Kimball, *Forged in War: Roosevelt, Churchill and the Second World War* (New York: William and Morrow, 1997), p. 99.

35. CAC, Churchill Papers, CHAR 20/42A/35, Churchill to Harry Hopkins, 28 August 1941.

36. TNA, CAB 65/19, WM 84 (41) I, annex, Minutes of 19 August 1941.

37. '2½ year draft by one vote! House passes bill to extend term 203–202', *Chicago Tribune*, 13 August 1941, p. 1.

38. D. M. Kennedy, *Freedom from Fear: The American People in Depression and War* (New York: Oxford University Press, 2005), p. 496.

39. FDR Library, Map Room Files, Churchill to FDR, 7 December 1940.

40. Kennedy, *Freedom from Fear*, pp. 496–9.

41. Rhodes James, *Complete Speeches*, vol. 6, pp. 6536–41.

42. 'Churchill's speech hailed in Congress', *New York Times*, 27 December 1941, p. 3; 'Alliance of U.S. and Great Britain is forecast after victory is won', *Washington Post*, 27 December 1941, p. 1.

43. Woolner, Special Relationship, p. 160; Kimball, *Forged in War*, p. 130.

44. Kimball, *Forged in War*, p. 129.

45. For more on FDR's decision to invade North Africa, see A. Buchanan, *American Grand Strategy in the Mediterranean during World War II* (New York: Cambridge University Press, 2014), chapter 2, pp. 33–52.

46. M. Matloff, Strategic Planning for Coalition Warfare, 1943–1944. *United States Army in World War II*, series 4, vol. 4 (1953), p. 134; M. Howard, *The Mediterranean Strategy in the Second World War* (London: Greenhill, 1968), pp. 35–7.

47. D. Reynolds and V. Pechatnov, *The Kremlin Letters: Stalin's Wartime Correspondence with Churchill and Roosevelt* (New Haven, CT: Yale University Press, 2018), pp. 272–3.

48. D. Woolner, *The Last 100 Days: FDR at War and at Peace* (New York: Basic Books, 2017), pp. 294–5.

49. D. Woolner, The United Nations and the Grand Alliance. In G. K. Piehler (ed.), *The Oxford Handbook on World War II* (Oxford: Oxford University Press, 2023).

50. Declaration by United Nations, President's Secretary's Files; Subject Files, United Nations 1942–5, Box 168, FDR Library, Hyde Park, NY.

51. D. Woolner, Epilogue: Reflections on Legacy and Leadership. In D. Woolner, W. Kimball and D. Reynolds (eds.), *FDR's World: War, Peace and Legacies* (New York: Palgrave Macmillan, 2008), p. 229; FDR Library, PSF, Great Britain, 1943, Box 36, Averill

Harriman to FDR, 5 July 1943; CAC, Churchill Papers, CHAR 2/470, Churchill to Roosevelt, 25 June 1943.

52. Woolner, Special Relationship, p. 162.

53. Kimball, *Complete Correspondence*, p. 17.

54. At the Second Quebec Conference, US Treasury Secretary Henry Morgenthau, Jr. put forward a plan calling for the pastoralisation of Germany. D. Woolner, Coming to Grips with the German Problem. In D. Woolner (ed.), *The Second Quebec Conference Revisited* (New York: St. Martin's Press, 1998), pp. 65–101.

55. W. S. Churchill, *The Second World War, vol. 6: Triumph and Tragedy* (Boston, MA: Houghton & Mifflin, 1981), p. 227.

56. CAC, Churchill Papers, CHAR 20/173/30–1, Churchill to Roosevelt, 11 October 1944.

57. FDR Library, Map Room Files, Box 9, FDR to Stalin, 4 October 1944; FDR to Harriman, 4 October 1944.

58. D. Reynolds, *Summits: Six Meetings That Shaped the Twentieth Century* (London: Allen Lane, 2007), pp. 148–50.

59. The United States Department of State, *Foreign Relations of the United States, Conferences at Malta and Yalta, 1945* (Washington, DC: Government Printing Office (GPO), 1955), p. 973.

60. Woolner, *The Last 100 Days*, p. 292.

61. CAC, Churchill Papers, CHAR 9/167, Churchill to the House of Commons, 17 April 1945.

62. The British system of Imperial Preference drastically reduced tariffs and other impediments to trade within the British Empire. The system was set up in part as a reaction to the establishment in 1930 of the US Smoot-Hawley Tariff, the highest tariff in American history. FDR's Secretary of State Cordell Hull was adamantly opposed to both the Smoot-Hawley Tariff and the British system of Imperial Preference and would use lend lease and Britain's dependence on US aid as a lever by which he hoped to convince the British to abandon the system. For more on this, see R. B. Woods, FDR and the New Economic Order. In D. B. Woolner, W. F. Kimball and D. Reynolds (eds.), *FDR's World War Peace and Legacies* (New York: Palgrave Macmillan, 2008).

63. Churchill, *English-Speaking Peoples*, vol. 1, p. xi.

64. R. Toye, *Churchill's Empire: The World That Made Him and the World He Made* (New York: Henry Holt, 2010), pp. xiv–xix.

65. Rhodes James, *Complete Speeches*, vol. 8, pp. 8709–10.

Further Reading

W. S. Churchill, *The Second World War*, 6 vols. (London: Cassell & Co. Ltd, 1948–54)

W. Kimball, *Churchill and Roosevelt: The Complete Correspondence*, 3 vols. (Princeton, NJ: Princeton University Press, 1984)

W. Kimball, *Forged in War: Roosevelt, Churchill and the Second World War* (New York: William and Morrow, 1997)

A. Packwood, *How Churchill Waged War: The Most Challenging Decisions of the Second World War* (Barnsley: Frontline Books, 2018)

D. Reynolds, *The Creation of the Anglo-American Alliance: A Study in Competitive Cooperation* (Chapel Hill: University of North Carolina Press, 1981)

D. Reynolds, *In Command of History: Churchill Fighting and Writing the Second World War* (London: Allen Lane, 2004)

D. Reynolds and V. Pechatnov, *The Kremlin Letters: Stalin's Wartime Correspondence with Churchill and Roosevelt* (New Haven, CT: Yale University Press, 2018)

D. Woolner, Churchill and the Special Relationship. In R. Toye (ed.), *Winston Churchill: Politics, Strategy and Statecraft* (London: Bloomsbury Academic, 2017)

D. Woolner, *The Last 100 Days: FDR at War and at Peace* (New York: Basic Books, 2017)

15

Churchill As International Statesman

'There is only one thing worse than fighting with allies', Churchill liked to say during the Second World War, 'and that is fighting without them.'[1] An international coalition was essential to wage global war against the Axis powers, yet the interests of the allies often clashed with those of Britain. Churchill had experienced some of these strains in 1914–18, albeit at a ministerial level. From 1940 he had to manage alliances at the very top. Worse still, the list of allies changed dramatically over time, in the process diminishing Britain's influence and leverage. The conflict started in September 1939 with Britain and France in a close and equal relationship. When it ended in May 1945 Britain was the junior partner in what Churchill called the 'Grand Alliance' with the emerging superpowers: the United States and the Soviet Union. The fulcrum of this story is the collapse of France in May 1940, just as Churchill finally gained the job for which he had yearned.

1939–1940: 'Thank God for the French Army!'

'Thank God for the French army!' was Churchill's mantra for much of the 1930s. He saw French power as the best protection against German revanchism. By 1938, he was calling for a Franco-British Treaty of 'mutual defence against aggression', backed by 'arrangements' between their military staffs.[2] He envisaged a loose division of labour, with Britain providing the sea power and France the land power, backed by up their combined air forces. That's why in May 1940 there were only 10 British divisions alongside 104 French, 22 Belgian and 8 Dutch on the Western Front. British public opinion was still haunted by memories of the Somme and Passchendaele, and rearmament in the 1930s – encouraged by Churchill himself – concentrated on airpower in view of the new threat from the bomber to a country that had hitherto felt secure in the naval age.

During the winter of 1939–40, Churchill was relatively complacent about the Western Front. Unlike Prime Minister Neville Chamberlain, he had no doubt that the Germans would attack in force, but he did not ask a lot of questions about French strength or strategy. Pre-occupied by the bomber, he was dismissive of tactical airpower – planes used in close support of ground troops – and, despite being a pioneer of the tank during the Great War, he now doubted that it would be effective against modern anti-tank guns. In early 1940 he was sufficiently confident about the robustness of the Western Front to press for offensive action in the Baltic. The Norway campaign, poorly planned and badly executed, was still in progress when Hitler began his Western offensive on 10 May 1940, the day Churchill became prime minister.

Absorbed in the construction of his new coalition government, Churchill did not pay close attention to the news from the Western Front, and it was not until 15 May that the full gravity of the crisis hit him, as he recalled later in chapter 2 of *Their Finest Hour* (the second volume of his war memoirs). At 7.30 a.m. (a grossly un-Churchillian hour) he was woken by a phone call from Paul Reynaud, the French prime minister, who shouted in English, 'we are beaten; we have lost the battle'. Next day Churchill flew to Paris for a crisis meeting in the Quai d'Orsay, France's foreign ministry. There General Maurice Gamelin, the French army commander, explained that German tanks had made a surprise breakthrough across the Meuse river at Sedan and were thrusting towards the Channel, around the back of the French and British armies in Belgium. 'Ou est la masse de manoeuvre?' demanded Churchill in his best Franglais. With a Gallic shrug, Gamelin uttered just one word: 'Aucune.' No strategic reserve! Churchill was dumbfounded. Struggling to think, he walked over to the grand windows. In the garden below he saw elderly gentlemen pushing wheelbarrows full of official papers onto great bonfires. Already the evacuation of Paris was being prepared. In his memoirs, Churchill called this 'one of the greatest surprises I have had in my life'.[3]

Over the next few weeks, Churchill tried to sustain the French will to fight – providing additional fighter squadrons even though the RAF was now warning him that every plane could be vital for the defence of Britain. But on 25 May the chiefs of staff submitted a formal assessment entitled 'British Strategy in a Certain Eventuality' – Whitehall's euphemism for the fall of France. Although the Dunkirk evacuation saved the bulk of the British Expeditionary Force (without most of its heavy weaponry), France's surrender was now clearly only a matter of time. 'Thank God for the French army!' rang pretty hollow in June 1940.

1940–1941: Seeking New Partners

France's new government under Marshal Philippe Pétain signed an armistice on 22 June. Churchill had already declared in the Commons on 4 June that Britain would fight on – 'if necessary for years, if necessary alone'.[4] But even in 1940, Britain was not strictly 'alone' – being still the centre of a vast and supportive empire. A Canadian division was already along the North Downs, part of the defence of London against invasion, and, despite German U-boats, vital imports were still flowing to Britain from its colonies. Churchill was at pains to promote Charles de Gaulle, a renegade French officer, as the embodiment in London of 'Fighting France', and in October 1940 Mussolini's botched invasion of Greece added another country to the Allied cause. But none of this counted for much in the scales now that Hitler was in control of much of continental Europe from the Pyrenees to Poland. What Britain desperately needed was the support of major international powers.

The chiefs of staff made it clear in their 'Certain Eventuality' appraisal that, without 'full economic and financial support' from the United States, 'we do not think we could continue the war with any chance of success'.[5] But America, disillusioned by the Great War, was deeply isolationist and 1940 was a presidential election year, so bold gestures were unlikely – especially towards a country that seemed on the rocks. As shown in other chapters of this volume, Churchill wooed Roosevelt assiduously and the president gradually increased material aid but on a scale that London considered woefully inadequate, and he evaded any talk of declaring war. To the east, the USSR seemed a de facto enemy after the bombshell Nazi-Soviet Pact of August 1939. Deeply suspicious of Britain, Stalin grudgingly met Churchill's new ambassador, Sir Stafford Cripps, on 1 July 1940 but then did not see him for a whole year. That was after the war had been totally transformed.

In the early hours of 22 June 1941 Hitler unleashed a massive surprise attack on the Soviet Union, 'Operation Barbarossa', involving some 3 million men along a front of 1,800 miles. Under the Nazi-Soviet Pact of August 1939, Stalin had connived with Hitler in the brutal partition of Poland in September; he then occupied the Baltic states of Estonia, Latvia and Lithuania in June 1940. The Soviet leader also maintained supplies of food, raw materials and slave labour to the Third Reich right up to the start of Barbarossa, turning a blind eye to the ample intelligence about what Hitler was preparing. Churchill, however, was not surprised. That night at 9 p.m. he broadcast to the world, castigating Hitler as 'a monster of wickedness' and pledging that 'any man or state that fights on against Nazidom will have our aid'. Churchill admitted that, for a quarter of a century, he had been a vocal opponent of Bolshevism – adding, 'I will unsay no word.' But, he insisted, 'all this fades away before the spectacle which is now unfolding'. He also warned that Barbarossa, if successful, was 'no more than a prelude to an attempted invasion of the British Isles'.[6] Geopolitically, Churchill had no choice but to embrace Stalin. Yet doing so tarnished the moral clarity of the Allied cause.

A year earlier, as France crumbled, Churchill had seen clearly that Britain's fate depended on a partnership with the United States. That was a natural reflex for one who was himself, as he liked to say, the product of an Anglo-American alliance. In June 1941 – with equal clarity but against all past instincts – he reached out to the Soviet Union as Britain's other vital partner, at a time when many anti-communists in Britain and America believed that their countries should stand aside and let the two totalitarians fight themselves into exhaustion. Churchill would spend the rest of the war wooing, in very different ways, FDR and 'Uncle Joe' (the nickname for Stalin).

But that was far from clear in mid-1941. The USA was still not a belligerent, and it seemed doubtful how long the Red Army would survive. Many in British and American intelligence, mindful of what Germany had done to France, gave the Soviets only four to six weeks. Churchill, like Roosevelt, was more hopeful but the limited aid either could offer that summer made little difference as Soviet soldiers surrendered in their hundreds of thousands and Hitler's forces lunged on towards Leningrad and Moscow. On 1 July Churchill told Roosevelt sombrely that he had ordered Britain's defences to be 'at concert pitch for invasion from September 1st'.[7]

At least the American scene seemed more encouraging for Churchill. From 9 to 12 August he and Roosevelt met in Placentia Bay, Newfoundland – their first encounter since 1918. The prime minister had hoped that this 'Atlantic Meeting' might presage a US declaration of war; instead he got a declaration of war aims, the 'Atlantic Charter'. Given American neutrality, it was a remarkable step that Roosevelt was aligning himself with Britain in this way, and the PR effect was immense – accentuated by photos and film of the two leaders talking together and of sailors from both navies sharing in worship on HMS *Prince of Wales*. But the Charter was double-edged: affirming common values but also indicating that on issues such as empire and trading blocs America had a different agenda. Nor was Roosevelt encouraging on the question of American belligerency. He told Churchill that if he took the issue of peace or war to Congress, they would debate it for three months, so he intended to wage war but not declare it, becoming more and more provocative in the Atlantic. This was indeed what happened – in mid-September, for instance, the US navy assumed responsibility for escorting convoys to Britain in the western half of the Atlantic – but occasional incidents with German U-boats that autumn did not escalate in the way Churchill hoped.

Meanwhile, Hitler's armies continued to surge across Russia. In early December advance units could see the pale sun glinting on the domes of the Kremlin. But then, over the next week, the war was totally transformed. Taking advantage of his neutrality pact with Japan, Stalin moved dozens of divisions from Siberia. On 5 December they crashed into the exhausted Germans around Moscow, relieving the capital and driving the enemy back a hundred miles or more during the following month. And on 7 December the Japanese mounted a daring and devastating air raid on the US naval base at Pearl Harbor, Hawaii, destroying much of America's Pacific fleet and leaving 2,400 dead. On 11 December Hitler followed suit with his own declaration of war on America, thereby resolving FDR's continuing equivocations about Congress.

Churchill was jubilant. He immediately set out for Washington, determined to keep US strategy focussed on Germany despite the crisis in the Pacific. Meanwhile, his foreign secretary Anthony Eden travelled to Moscow in an attempt to address Stalin's demands for greater aid and a formal treaty. The Grand Alliance was now a reality, but holding it together would require all Churchill's energy and skill over the next three and a half years.

1942–1945: Juggling Roosevelt and Stalin

Churchill's visit to Washington was a major step forward. During the Arcadia conferences that he and Roosevelt held with their military advisors (22 December 1941 to 14 January 1942), they created the

Figure 15.1 The 'Big Three': Russian President Joseph Stalin, American President Franklin D. Roosevelt and British Prime Minister Winston Churchill at the Yalta Conference, February 1945. American Secretary of State Edward R. Stettinius appears to be proposing the toast (CAC, Kinna Papers, KNNA 1/5).

combined chiefs of staff to oversee military policy, together with a network of combined boards to harmonise the handling of munitions, shipping, supply and the like. The two allies also affirmed that their top priority was the defeat of Germany, after which it was assumed that Italy and Japan would succumb. Confirming this Germany First strategy had been Churchill's prime objective for Arcadia. Behind the scenes, the British and Americans were pooling their programmes to develop an atomic bomb and also sharing signals intelligence gleaned from code-breaking through the British 'Ultra' project and US 'Magic' intercepts. In all these ways, the alliance between Washington and London blossomed into perhaps the closest in the history of warfare. This anecdote captures the mood. During the prime minister's visit he was given a suite in the White House. On one occasion Roosevelt dropped by, only to find his guest emerging wet, glowing and naked from the bath. Embarrassed, FDR started to withdraw, but Churchill beckoned him back: 'The Prime Minister of Great

Britain', he boomed, 'has nothing to conceal from the President of the United States.'

Although overshadowed by Churchill in Washington, Eden's visit to Russia (15–22 December 1941) was also a milestone in relations between the two countries – the first time a British foreign secretary had visited the USSR. The main topic of discussion was the signing of a Treaty of Alliance, but Stalin suddenly extended the agenda by demanding that the Treaty include agreement about the USSR's post-war borders. In order to stake out the Soviet position for a future peace conference, he wanted recognition of USSR's borders before the German attack in June 1941. These had been established under the Nazi-Soviet Pact of 1939 – giving the USSR control of eastern Poland, parts of Romania and the three Baltic states – so Stalin's demand aroused intense transatlantic debate over the next few months. In London, Eden was sympathetic and Churchill gradually came around, except on Poland, but Roosevelt and the State Department were strongly opposed to any breach of the Atlantic Charter. The British felt caught between their two allies. In the end, American opposition and the crisis caused by the German spring offensive caused Stalin to drop his territorial demands and he accepted a general treaty with Britain, pledging twenty years of friendship. This was signed on 26 May when Vyacheslav Molotov, the Soviet foreign minister, was visiting in London.

Meanwhile, the Pentagon tried to hold the line on the Germany First strategy against those in the US navy and army who wanted to concentrate on the crisis in the Pacific. In March 1942, military planners formulated outlines for a full-scale invasion of northern France in spring 1943 (codenamed 'Roundup'). In case of imminent Soviet defeat or a 'sharp weakening' of Germany in summer and autumn 1942, a smaller landing was conceived involving six to eight divisions (Operation 'Sledgehammer'). But any cross-Channel attack in 1942 would have to depend mostly on British and Canadian troops, and this gave Churchill almost a veto power. His preference was a 'peripheral strategy' of gradually closing the ring on Germany through operations in the Mediterranean backed by the bombing, blockade and subversion of Hitler's 'Fortress Europe'.

By this time the war in North Africa had reached a critical stage. The British surrender of Tobruk on 20 June to Rommel's inferior forces left the road to Cairo open. Adding insult to injury for Churchill, he received the news from Roosevelt himself while conferring in the White House.

It was another humiliation to follow the capitulation of Singapore to Japanese forces in February. Desperate to win a desert victory and shore up his beleaguered premiership, Churchill stuck to his guns about no suicide mission across the Channel in 1942. Eventually Roosevelt over-ruled his joint chiefs of staff and committed the USA to joint American-British landings in Algeria and Morocco (Operation 'Torch') in the autumn.

This diplomatic victory, however, left Churchill in a difficult position with Stalin, who renewed his demands for a second front as the Germans cut their way towards the Caucasus. Speaking to Molotov on 10 June, the prime minister had tried to dampen any such hopes in 1942 but, as a counter-balance, he talked up the prospects for 1943 in a way that created hostages to fortune. To make matters worse, on 17 July he sent the Soviet leader a long telegram regretfully announcing postpone-ment of Arctic convoys during the summer months of the midnight sun, after two-thirds of the ships in convoy PQ17 had been lost to U-boats and the *Luftwaffe*. Stalin – his back to the wall for the second time in a year – sent an irate reply about the convoys and the second front, virtually accusing the prime minister of betrayal. Churchill decided that he must go in person to Moscow in order to reinforce the alliance.

The trip was no picnic: 10,000 miles in an unheated, unpressurised bomber, flying via West Africa, Cairo and Tehran to avoid enemy air-space. And the prime minister did not expect a warm reception. As reflected in his memoirs, the message he was bearing – 'No Second Front in 1942' – seemed like 'carrying a large lump of ice to the North Pole'.[8] Once in Moscow, he was also the victim of Stalin's frequent one-two-three treatment of foreign visitors – a friendly first meeting, a nasty follow-up and then a more harmonious final encounter – all designed to keep them off balance. After round two, when Stalin accused the British of being scared to fight the Germans, a furious Churchill was ready to fly home immediately. But by the end of a boozy farewell dinner in Stalin's Kremlin apartment, the prime minister left with a serious hangover and, more significantly, an indelible impression of the dictator's stra-tegic acumen and personal magnetism. The rough second session he put down to pressure on Stalin from shadowy colleagues, such as the 'Council of Commissars'. This, as is now clear, was nonsense – Stalin ran a team, but everyone knew who was boss – yet the 'two Stalins' trope allowed Churchill to conclude that he could do business with the Soviet leader, man to man, despite those dark forces in the Kremlin. That said, he never abandoned his long-standing suspicions of the USSR, writing to Eden in October 1942 that it would be 'a measureless disaster if Russian barbarism overlaid the culture and independence of the ancient States of Europe'[9] – but Stalin was now seen almost as a moderate, holding the hardliners at bay.

In January 1943, Churchill and Roosevelt met at Casablanca to plan strategy for 1943 but 'Uncle Joe', as they now called him, would not attend – pleading the demands of 'the Front' (this was the endgame of Stalingrad). Although Rommel, defeated at Alamein, was now in retreat westward and the 'Torch' landings had been successful, Hitler had reinforced German forces in Tunisia and Allied progress was slow. (Tunis did not fall until May.) At Casablanca, the Western Allies made the best of things by talking up the bombing offensive on Germany as their central strategy for the moment, and the Americans reluctantly agreed that Sicily would be next on the list after North Africa had been won. Churchill and Roosevelt sent several deceptive telegrams to Stalin, trying to jolly him along, until on 24 June 1943 the Soviet leader replied with a forensic dissection of their messages since January, declaring that these challenged the USSR's basic 'confidence' in its allies.[10] Churchill was stung by that word, and also disconcerted by Stalin's sudden decision to recall his ambassadors in London and Washington for 'consultations'. Even more unsettling was the silence from Moscow all through July. Churchill and Roosevelt received no replies to their messages.

One reason was Stalin's desire to keep his allies on the wrong foot. But he was also immersed in the planning and execution of the epic Soviet counter-offensive at Kursk. From then on, the Red Army was rolling inexorably west across the Ukraine towards Berlin. And in July, after the British-American landings in Sicily, Mussolini was toppled in Italy. Although German troops moved rapidly to take control of most of Italy and hold Rome, eventual Allied victory was now in sight. This posed new challenges for the Big Three. It was clear what they were *against* – Hitler's bid for European domination – but less clear what they were *for*. Trying to agree on that became urgent. Between 19 and 30 October, the three foreign ministers met in Moscow for surprisingly positive discussions, including an agreement to establish a European Advisory Commission in London to start serious planning.

Moscow paved the way for Tehran. Churchill had met Stalin alone in August 1942; Roosevelt tried to do the same (behind the prime minister's back) in spring 1943. Eventually, from 28 November to 1 December the three leaders met for the first time in the Persian capital, which Stalin insisted was as far as he could go while still remaining in secure communication with Moscow. Knowing Churchill and Roosevelt's desire to meet, he could dictate his terms and, with the Red Army on the attack, he was in a much stronger bargaining position than in 1942. Tehran was not a good conference for Churchill. The president, determined to foster relations with Stalin, chose to stay in the Soviet Embassy, and during the meetings he often deliberately distanced himself from the prime minister to show Stalin that he was not facing an anti-Soviet bloc. What's more, the political dynamics of a threesome were very different from the bilateral diplomacy that Churchill had practised hitherto. On the question of a cross-Channel attack, the prime minister was now outvoted by Stalin and FDR, who pinned down the British to May 1944 and made clear that Italy was definitely a secondary theatre to France. The Americans also blocked Churchill's desire to pre-empt the Germans to islands in the Aegean.

Despite these intimations of the shifting balance of power, the conference confirmed Churchill's confidence from August 1942 that he could work with the Soviet leader. 'If only Stalin and I could meet once a week, there would be no trouble at all', he assured a friend in January 1944. 'We get on like a house on fire.'[11] And although still chafing at the 'tyranny' of Overlord, he confessed he was 'hardening' on the operation, despite nagging fears of what could go wrong. In the final weeks before D-Day, the intrepid warrior inside him displaced the wary strategist, and only a direct order from the king stopped him from witnessing the landings from one of the bombarding warships.

June 1944 marked the apogee of Big Three cooperation. The Soviets played their part in the elaborate deception operation to persuade the Germans that the assault would not be directed on Normandy, and Stalin sent an unusually warm message on 11 June congratulating his allies on the success of their 'grandiose' plan to cross the Channel: 'History will record this deed as an achievement of the highest order.'[12] As he had promised at Tehran, the Red Army's summer offensive in Byelorussia – Operation 'Bagration' – opened two weeks later. In June 1944, for the first time, the Third Reich was under attack on the continent of Europe from west as well as east.

Yet this moment of success created new alliance tensions for Churchill. That summer saw his fiercest strategic argument with the Americans, who were determined to close down the British-led Italian theatre and concentrate resources on southern France to reinforce the campaign in the north. Not only did Churchill fail to prevent this, but the success of the US landings around Marseilles and the speed of their advance up the Rhone Valley made his dire warnings look ridiculous. In north-west Europe, too, he was unable to exert much influence on the American preference for a 'broad front' strategy, involving all the Allied armies, rather than London's call for a (British-led) thrust across northern Germany. As the prime minister admitted to his old friend Jan Smuts, the South African leader, in December 1944, 'our armies are only about one-half the size of the American and will soon be little more than one-third', so 'it is not as easy as it used to be for me to get things done'.[13]

Meanwhile, the dramatic success of 'Bagration' and other Soviet offensives that summer was transforming the map of Europe. The crunch point for Churchill was an independent Poland, for which Britain had officially gone to war in 1939. But Stalin wanted eastern Poland, part of the Tsarist Empire, and he also considered the whole country to be vital for Soviet security as the gateway for another German attack. The Polish question had reared its head in spring 1943, when the Nazis unearthed mass graves of Polish officers in the Katyn forest near Smolensk. They and the exiled Polish government in London blamed Stalin (rightly, as we now know). But, with breath-taking chutzpah, he blamed the Germans and used the opportunity to sever diplomatic relations with the London Poles and to create a rival communist government-in-waiting in Moscow. Both Churchill and Roosevelt had little doubt who had been responsible for Katyn but they said nothing, to avoid straining the alliance. In the months after Tehran, the prime minister really focussed on Poland, devoting much time to trying to craft a deal between Stalin and the London Poles on two key issues: Poland's future borders and the construction of a coalition government.

Yet his efforts were undermined in August 1944 when the Red Army, having reached the edge of Warsaw, stood by while the Germans ruthlessly suppressed the uprising within the city. The Polish Home Army, working with the London Poles, wanted to gain control before the Russians arrived. Soviet inertia partly reflected the exhaustion of the Red Army after fighting its way 400 miles west in five weeks, but Stalin was perfectly happy for the Germans to eliminate the Polish resistance before he took Warsaw himself. On this issue, too, America and Britain were at odds. Roosevelt's priority was to maintain the alliance with Moscow in the interests of post-war cooperation, whereas Churchill was much more concerned with the fate of Poland – both as a 'debt of honour' after 1939 and because Poland mattered to the balance of power in Europe. He took the lead in pleading with Stalin to provide aid to the Polish resistance and to let British and US relief planes use nearby Soviet airfields for refuelling. But Stalin denounced the Warsaw Rising as the work of 'criminals' and provided little aid until it was on its last legs. Meanwhile, his Polish communist client government was installed in Lublin.

Poland was only part of the East European jigsaw. By October the Red Army had conquered Romania and Bulgaria, while Tito's communist partisans were taking over Yugoslavia. Fearful that his worst nightmares about the Bolshevik tide were now becoming reality, Churchill nevertheless continued to place his faith in Stalin the moderate. He invited himself to Moscow in an effort to reach agreement on eastern Europe before it all fell to the Red Army. In the Kremlin on 9 October 1944 he presented Stalin with what he jocularly called a 'naughty document' setting out which of them would take the lead in specific Balkan countries. He was trying to avoid the term 'spheres of influence', to which Washington was allergic. Churchill's main concern was with Greece – regarded as a vital bulwark in the Mediterranean – where he allocated Britain 90 per cent. Conversely, against Romania, he wrote 90 per cent for Russia, while Yugoslavia was marked 50:50, to suggest a joint policy. Over the next couple of days, Eden and Molotov finessed the precise figures across the Balkans, even though the British foreign secretary had no firm idea what Churchill really meant by his arithmetic.

What is now known as the 'percentages deal' had come out of the blue, and the prime minister never repeated the ploy. But at its core, the document was intended to secure Stalin's prior agreement to the planned British intervention in Greece, where the German pull-out intensified the struggle between pro-royalist forces and communist partisans backed by Yugoslavia and Albania. The use of British troops in Greece, coupled with the prime minister's surprise trip to Athens at Christmas, prompted an anti-imperialistic outcry in the American press, but Churchill would always insist that Stalin kept his promise about Greece. Despite the prime minister's efforts in Moscow, however, no agreement was reached on a 50:50 deal over Poland, even though he had the London and Lublin Poles brought to the Kremlin in the hope of banging heads together.

The prime minister's solo mission to Moscow strengthened the president's determination to arrange another full conference of the Big Three and their advisors. Once again, Stalin dug in on the venue, forcing Churchill and Roosevelt (now seriously ill with heart disease) to undertake a laborious journey to Yalta in the Crimea. The conference (4–11 February) later became notorious in the West: a sell-out of eastern Europe to Moscow in the view of the American right; a cynical superpower partition of Europe according to French Gaullists. In reality Yalta was a complex negotiation, resulting in a series of compromises from which each of the Big Three came away with something.

Roosevelt firmed up Soviet commitments on the two issues that topped his agenda – to join the new United Nations organisation and to enter the war against Japan within three months of Germany's surrender. On the latter, FDR – fearful of the cost in American lives of invading Japan and not yet sure about the potency of the atomic bomb – was ready to offer a sweetener by approving Stalin's demands for Chinese and Japanese territory. Churchill agreed, overruling Eden's argument that Soviet entry into the Asian war did not need to be bought. Much to Stalin's irritation, the prime minister was successful in blocking Russian demands for immediate agreement on massive reparations from Germany. Britain feared post-war dislocation of Europe's economy similar to the aftermath of the Great War. He also secured the reluctant consent of both his allies that France should share in the occupation of Germany and have a seat on the post-war control commission. This British concern to rebuild the continental balance of power was a reaction to FDR's warning that, politically, he could not keep US troops in Europe for more than a year or two. Eden and the Foreign Office were particularly keen on creating a western European bloc, centred on France and allied to Britain.

As for Stalin, in addition to achieving most of his territorial demands in Asia, he also got his way on Poland. Churchill had tried hard to secure a new Polish government and free elections, supervised by Allied ambassadors, but – with Roosevelt's mind on Japan and the United Nations – this got watered down to a commitment that the Lublin government would be 'reorganised on a broader democratic basis'. On the issue of elections, Stalin merely promised that his allies would be 'kept informed about the situation in Poland' once their ambassadors had been accredited to the government in Warsaw. (This, of course, would only happen once Britain and America had recognised that government.) The prime minister did secure, in return for Poland's loss of (Ukrainian) lands to the USSR in the east, a pledge that it 'must receive substantial accessions of territory in the north and west' from Germany. The Americans placed their faith in Stalin's endorsement of a general 'Declaration on Liberated Europe' which stated that the principles of 'sovereign rights and self-government' should prevail in all countries freed from Nazi rule.[14]

Churchill and Roosevelt had travelled to Yalta with few illusions about their leverage over Poland. The 'concessions' they made there to Stalin on this issue were the result not of credulous diplomacy in 1945 but of strategic decisions in 1942–3 when they delayed their invasion of France until 1944. This meant that, if the Red Army eventually defeated the Wehrmacht, the Soviets would end the war in control of eastern Europe. Yet Churchill and Roosevelt did not (choose to) see Yalta in this way. Each was pleased with what he had achieved in the conference and especially by the atmosphere of the talks – more fluid and cordial than at Tehran. Despite the mounting imbalance within the Big Three, Churchill hoped – as he put it picturesquely – that it was the small British lion which 'knew the way', not the 'huge Russian bear' or the 'great American elephant'.[15]

Once back home, both Western leaders went out on a limb in talking up the significance of Yalta for post-war peace. With the deals on United Nations voting and Soviet gains in the Far East still secret for the moment, public attention focussed on Poland. Churchill faced a Commons motion deploring 'the decision to transfer to one ally the territory of another ally', which he was able to defeat on 1 March by 396 votes to 25. But that huge margin concealed the depth of opposition within his own Party: eleven government ministers abstained and one resigned. During the debate, the prime minister admitted the deficiencies of the Polish settlement but told the House he was sure that the Soviet leaders wished to 'live in honourable friendship and equality with the Western democracies', adding 'I feel also that their word is their bond.' Printing these words in his memoirs, Churchill stated: 'I felt bound to proclaim my confidence in Soviet faith in order to procure it.' But when addressing a special meeting of government ministers, he made the remarkable statement that 'Poor Neville Chamberlain believed he could trust Hitler. He was wrong. But I don't think I'm wrong about Stalin.'[16]

Within a few weeks, however, the prime minister was worried about what was happening behind the 'veil' or 'curtain' now coming down over eastern Europe. He told FDR that Poland was 'the test case between us and the Russians of the meaning which is to be attached to such terms as Democracy, Sovereignty, Independence, Representative Government and free and unfettered elections'. But Roosevelt rebuffed Churchill's plea to put Polish issues 'squarely to the Soviet Government' in a joint message to Stalin. Though ailing, he focussed as usual on the Big Three relationship as a whole – especially ahead of the founding conference of the United Nations in April – and hoped to resolve matters at the ambassadorial level. The joint message was not sent until 31 March.[17]

By then Stalin was accusing Roosevelt and Churchill of trying to arrange a German surrender in the West, behind the USSR's back, through secret talks in Bern, Switzerland. In a very rare display of anger with Stalin, on 4 April FDR expressed his 'bitter resentment' at 'such vile misrepresentations of my actions'. But after Stalin backed off, Roosevelt dropped the matter – having made his point. Unlike Churchill, he did not flare up about every dispute with the Soviets because, as he wrote late on 11 April, 'these problems, in one form or another, seem to arise every day as in the case of the Bern meeting. We must be firm, however, and our course thus far is correct.'[18] Those were FDR's last words to Churchill. The following day, the president dropped dead from a cerebral haemorrhage.

1945–1953: From World War to Cold War

Churchill titled the final volume of his war memoirs *Triumph and Tragedy*. The 'triumph' was clear: on 8 May 1945 Britons celebrated the end of the war in Europe, almost five years since he had assumed the premiership. But victory seemed bittersweet: the wartime coalition ended on 23 May, before the defeat of Japan, and the country faced an election campaign that summer. Worse still for Churchill, Harry S. Truman, Roosevelt's successor as president, refused to have things out with the Soviets, and in June he fixed up a deal over Poland's government with only cosmetic changes to communist dominance. Grudgingly the prime minister acquiesced. The Polish soldiers who had fought across Europe for a 'free Poland' felt utterly betrayed, and Churchill knew it – painfully.

In mid-May, the gloomy prime minister had even asked the chiefs of staff to explore the possibility of using force to get a 'square deal for Poland'. The possible start date was 1 July. The astounded planners labelled the idea 'Operation Unthinkable'. It seemed inconceivable a couple of weeks after victory to imagine turning against one of Britain's two great wartime allies, in the process rearming the former German enemy. Moreover, there was no chance of success. The planners explained that a surprise attack by forty-seven British and US divisions around Dresden might force Soviet concessions over Poland, but the conflict would escalate into a world war in which victory was 'quite impossible'.[19] That Churchill could entertain such an amazing idea – apparently totally oblivious to the story of the Eastern Front in 1941–5 – surely reveals his total exhaustion after five years of war leadership.

Having rejected the unthinkable, the prime minister reverted to his default position: to resolve matters with another Big Three meeting. For all his sombre talk of an 'iron curtain' coming down across Europe, a phrase he used in a cable to Truman on 12 May, Churchill had not abandoned his faith in Stalin. Like other British policy-makers, he blamed recent problems on Molotov or the 'Party Bosses' or the 'Army Marshals'.[20] But when the Potsdam Conference finally convened on 17 July, Churchill found himself marginalised by the Americans. Keen to extricate themselves from Europe, they stitched up another deal with the Soviets over German reparations and Poland's western border. Even more devastating, Churchill was then marginalised by British voters. When the results of the election were made public on 26 July, the Tories had suffered their worst defeat since 1906. The 'tragedy' had become very personal.

Churchill was deeply hurt by what had happened. But, characteristically, he treated humiliating defeat as yet another challenge and the roots of Churchill the Cold Warrior are to be found in these years as war leader. Most famously, his faith in a 'special relationship' with the United States was the bedrock of future British foreign policy. But he also hoped that the rift with Moscow could be bridged by another meeting with Stalin, conducted in Anglo-American solidarity to ensure negotiation from a position of strength. And he was convinced that 1939–45 had been part of a modern 'Thirty Years' War',[21] which could only end when France and Germany buried the hatchet. These ideas – outlined during 1946 in world-resonating speeches at Fulton and Zurich – heralded his political resurrection and would guide his final decade in public life.

The acclaim he won in the West for those two clarion calls encouraged him to stay on as Tory leader, silencing backbench mutters that it was time for the old warhorse to give way to Anthony Eden and inject new blood into the Party's hardening arteries. As his old crony Brendan Bracken remarked colourfully in October 1946, Churchill was now 'determined to continue to lead the Tory party till he becomes Prime Minister on earth or Minister of Defence in Heaven'.[22] One motive was simply 'to stay in the pub till closing time': like most political veterans, he found it hard to imagine life without power. But he also convinced himself that he was a man with a mission: to help save his country and humanity from the horror of a third world war in the nuclear age.

On 4 November 1951, little over a week after returning to Downing Street for a second term, he cabled the Soviet leader: 'Now that I am again in charge of His Majesty's Government, let me reply to your farewell telegram from Potsdam in 1945, "Greetings. Winston Churchill."' Stalin responded next day with a short note of thanks, whereupon Churchill cabled Truman, 'we are again on speaking terms'. On 6 November he promised MPs 'a supreme effort to bridge the gulf between the two worlds, so that each can live its life, if not in friendship at least without the fear, the hatreds and the frightful waste of the "cold war"'.[23] The wartime meetings were fresh in his mind from writing his war memoirs, and his message to Stalin was almost saying: 'Let's resume from where we were so rudely interrupted six years ago.'

In February 1950, while still leader of the opposition, Churchill called for another 'parley at the summit' with the USSR – coining yet another slogan for the diplomatic lexicon to complement 'iron curtain' and 'special relationship'.[24] Summitry became the over-riding passion of the old man's second term and on several occasions in 1952 he spoke privately of his desire for an Anglo-American approach to Stalin, leading perhaps to a modern Congress of Vienna at which the Potsdam Conference would be reopened and then properly concluded. But he never met Stalin again. On 5 March 1953 the dictator died following a massive stroke. Churchill hoped that the new collective leadership in Moscow might be ready for a thaw in relations with the West and he wrote to Truman's successor Dwight D. Eisenhower, another wartime colleague, urging joint or parallel approaches to the new regime. He even sent 'Ike' the draft of a letter he planned to send to the Politburo inviting himself to Moscow 'so that we could renew our own war-time relation'. An incredulous Eisenhower warned against anything the Kremlin could 'misinterpret as weakness or over-eagerness on our part'. Discouraging the idea of Churchill's 'solitary pilgrimage', he stated firmly that renewed conference diplomacy should await 'some evidence, in deeds, of a changed Soviet attitude'.[25]

Indignant at the rebuff, Churchill went public on 11 May, telling the Commons and the world that, given the 'change of attitude' and the 'amicable gestures' from the new Soviet government, 'a conference on the highest level should take place between the leading Powers without long delay', conducted 'with a measure of informality and a still greater measure of privacy and seclusion'.[26] But his grand design got nowhere. In part this was because on 23 June 1953 he, too, suffered a severe stroke – not fatal, but sufficient to undermine the rest of his second premiership. In any case, whatever the prime minister's state of health, neither Eisenhower nor the new Soviet leadership had any intention of reprising the roles of Roosevelt and Stalin for Churchill's gratification in an era very different from wartime. When Churchill's family finally persuaded him to let go of the reins of power in April 1955, one of the prime minister's last 'Dear Friend' messages to the president contained the striking lament that now 'we shall never meet on a Top Level confrontation of our would-be friends'.[27]

Churchill's final attempts at summitry are, in one sense, a sad footnote to his wartime glory days. But they also show that the man who had dreamed all his life of being a great military leader never saw war as an end in itself. As he murmured sadly soon after being 'kicked out' of Downing Street in 1945, 'I wanted . . . I wanted to do the peace too.'[28]

Notes

1. A. Danchev and D. Todman (eds.), *War Diaries, 1939–1945: Field Marshal Lord Alanbrooke* (London: Weidenfeld & Nicolson, 2001), 1 April 1945, p. 680.
2. *Hansard*, House of Commons Debates, vol. 333, cols. 99–100, 14 March 1938.
3. W. S. Churchill, *The Second World War* (London: Cassell & Co., 1948–54), vol. 2, pp. 38, 42, 43.
4. *Hansard*, House of Commons Debates, vol. 361, col. 795, 4 June 1940.
5. TNA, CAB 66/7, WP (40) 168, 25 May 1940.
6. Radio address of 22 June 1941, in Eade (ed.), *The Unrelenting Struggle*, pp. 176–80.
7. Message C-103x in Kimball (ed.), *Churchill and Roosevelt: The Complete Correspondence*, vol. 1, p. 216.
8. Churchill, *Second World War*, vol. 4, p. 428.

9. TNA, PREM 4/30/11, Churchill to Eden, 21 October 1942.
10. D. Reynolds and V. Pechatnov (eds.), *The Kremlin Letters: Stalin's Wartime Correspondence with Churchill and Roosevelt* (London: Yale University Press, 2018), pp. 267–70.
11. M. Gilbert and L. Arnn (eds.), CV, vol. 19, p. 1534.
12. Reynolds and Pechatnov, *The Kremlin Letters*, p. 429.
13. CAC, CHAR 20/176/53-54, Churchill to Smuts, 3 December 1944.
14. Conference protocol, in US Department of State, *The Conferences at Malta and Yalta, 1945* (Washington, DC: Government Printing Office, 1955), quoting pp. 980, 977.
15. J. Colville, *The Fringes of Power: Downing Street Diaries, 1939–1955* (London: Hodder & Stoughton, 1985), 24 February 1945, p. 564.
16. Churchill, *Second World War*, vol. 6, p. 351; B. Pimlott (ed.), *The Second World War Diary of Hugh Dalton, 1940–1945* (London: Jonathan Cape, 1986), p. 836.
17. Kimball (ed.), *Churchill and Roosevelt: The Complete Correspondence*, vol. 3, pp. 547–51, 553–9.
18. Reynolds and Pechatnov (eds.), *Kremlin Letters*, pp. 572–3, 581. Message sent at 02:13 on 12 April.
19. TNA, CAB 120/691, Joint Planning Staff, 'Operation Unthinkable', 22 May 1945; Danchev and Todman (eds.), *War Diaries*, p. 693.
20. See D. Reynolds, *In Command of History: Churchill Fighting and Writing the Second World War* (London: Allen Lane, 2004), p. 470.
21. A phrase he used after Yalta in the Commons: *Hansard*, House of Commons Debates, vol. 408, cols. 1276–7, 27 February 1945.
22. Bracken to Beaverbrook, 16 October 1946, Beaverbrook papers, House of Lords Record Office, C/56.
23. Gilbert, OB, vol. 8, p. 659; Rhodes James, *Complete Speeches*, vol. 8, pp. 8296–7; John W. Young, *Winston Churchill's Last Campaign: Britain and the Cold War, 1951–5* (Oxford: Oxford University Press, 1996), pp. 46–7.
24. Speech in Edinburgh, 14 February 1950, in Rhodes James, *Complete Speeches*, vol. 8, p. 7944.
25. Messages of 4 and 5 May 1953 in Peter Boyle, ed., *The Churchill-Eisenhower Correspondence, 1953–1955* (Chapel Hill: University of North Carolina Press, 1990), pp. 48–50.
26. Rhodes James, *Complete Speeches*, vol. 8, pp. 8475–85, quoting pp. 8484–5.
27. Churchill to Eisenhower, 18 March 1955, in Boyle, ed., *Correspondence*, p. 200.
28. Gilbert, OB, vol. 8, p. 126.

Further Reading

W. S. Churchill, *The Second World War*, 6 vols. (London: Cassell & Co., 1948–54)
J. Colville, *The Fringes of Power: Downing Street Diaries, 1939–1955* (London: Hodder & Stoughton, 1985)
A. Danchev and D. Todman (eds.), *War Diaries, 1939–1945: Field Marshal Lord Alanbrooke* (London: Weidenfeld & Nicolson, 2001)
D. Dilks (ed.), *The Diaries of Sir Alexander Cadogan, O.M. 1938–1945* (London: Cassell, 1971)
M. Gilbert, [OB] *Winston S. Churchill*, vol. 6, *Finest Hour 1939–1941* (London: Heinemann, 1983)
M. Gilbert, [OB] *Winston S. Churchill*, vol. 7, *Road to Victory* (London: Heinemann, 1986)

W. Kimball (ed.), *Churchill and Roosevelt: The Complete Correspondence*, 3 vols. (Princeton, NJ: Princeton University Press, 1984)

D. Reynolds, *In Command of History: Churchill Fighting and Writing the Second World War* (London: Allen Lane, 2004)

D. Reynolds and V. Pechatnov (eds.), *The Kremlin Letters: Stalin's Wartime Correspondence with Churchill and Roosevelt* (London: Yale University Press, 2018)

16

Churchill and the Bombing Campaign

'In an aerial war the greatest form of defence will undoubtedly be offense. Does the House think that the Air Service will get its chance if it is separated into two parts and one mutilated fragment handed over to the Navy and the other handed over to the Army?'[1] Addressing the House of Commons on 21 March 1922, Winston Churchill passionately advocated for the Royal Air Force (RAF) to maintain its budding independence. Having overseen the establishment of the Royal Naval Air Service (RNAS) on 1 July 1914, he had briefly flirted with merging the nascent RAF with the Royal Navy after the First World War.[2] Yet, enraptured by the future offensive possibilities of British airpower, Churchill ended up protecting a cause he remained tightly affiliated with for much of his political career: the independent development of Britain's bomber arm. In the First World War and beyond, he explored using aerial bombardment to subdue belligerent powers and insurgent movements alike. He wrote in 1928 of how death and terror had been 'carried far behind the lines of the actual armies, to women, children, the aged, the sick' during the war – knowing that such horrors would lurk again in future conflicts.[3]

When British cities came into the bombsights of the Luftwaffe during the Second World War, Churchill's interwar campaign to bolster the RAF's bomber strength appeared to pay dividends. Yet, as Richard Overy writes, 'the major question remains Churchill's part in approving and sustaining the bombing of German cities and civilians'.[4] In particular, he controversially distanced himself from the Anglo-American fire-bombing of Dresden between 13 and 15 February 1945 – condemning Bomber Command to being, in Mark Connelly's words, 'the black sheep of the British popular memory of World War II'.[5] Through pinpointing how Churchill's perceptions of aerial bombardment evolved across his political career, this chapter highlights the ambivalence and incongruence that dogged his bombing policy from its earliest days. Ultimately, it argues that his vacillating approach towards the Allied bombing campaign – and his eventual calculated detachment from it – was not out of character. The chapter begins by establishing Churchill's preliminary beliefs about aerial bombardment; next, it traces how his bombing theory converted into destructive reality, from 'aerially policing' the British Empire in the 1920s to the Combined Allied Strategic Bomber Offensive; and finally, it examines how Churchill attempted to reconcile his incriminating role in the German firestorms with a war-scarred Britain after 1945.

Churchill's Early Perceptions of Aerial Bombardment

Winston Churchill's fascination with aviation was almost as old as powered flight itself. In 1909, just six years after Wilbur and Orville Wright completed the first successful flight in a heavier-than-air-powered aircraft, he enquired as a member of the Committee of Imperial Defence whether their invention could be used in a military context.[6] Appointed as first lord of the admiralty in 1911, Churchill was quickly imbued with a fervent curiosity about aviation after Commander Spenser Gray gifted him a flight in a seaplane.[7] He took up flying lessons in 1913 despite the acute misgivings of his friends and especially his wife, Clementine, while even the Royal Navy was keen to curb the first lord's obsession with flying. Rear-Admiral Arthur Limpus reminded Churchill on 7 June 1915 that others 'can do the flying quite as well as you. You may be needed for things that others cannot do.'[8] Churchill eventually stopped taking flying lessons in 1919 after several aviators in his inner circle died from plane crashes. Nevertheless, what he had learnt from venturing into the air could not be so easily discarded: his early airborne experiences inspired the creation of the RNAS during summer 1914.

The RNAS was assigned to protect Allied ships, dockyards, harbours and oil reserves. However, with the rising threat of the German zeppelins to the British fleet, Churchill approved a series of RNAS long-range bombing raids in autumn 1914 on German airship manufacturing plants and maintenance sheds.[9] He had quickly recognised that airpower could take the fight more directly to the enemy across new distances and in different ways: now, zeppelin infrastructure in Cologne, Düsseldorf, Cuxhaven and Friedrichshafen was in reach of the RNAS. Yet his most painful learning of this lesson came when German zeppelin and Gotha bomber raids began to intensify over Britain – from London and Great Yarmouth to Hull, across Tyneside and even up to Rosyth and the Forth Bridge – despite him being responsible for organising the country's air defences. The *Daily Mail* ridiculed the future possibility of Churchill becoming an air minister on 28 June 1915, arguing that his broken promise in March 1914 that any hostile aircraft 'would be promptly attacked in superior force by a swarm of very formidable hornets' illustrated 'the unwisdom of leaving a matter of this kind in the hands of politicians'.[10]

Another incident which pressed home early to Churchill the importance of having strong aerial offensive capabilities was the Dardanelles campaign. Attempting to ease Turkish pressure on the Russians in the Caucasus, Churchill was implored by the secretary of state for war, Lord Herbert Kitchener, to launch an operation against the Dardanelles Strait which snaked below the Gallipoli peninsula. Churchill had initially argued for a combined armed forces offensive, a proposal through which, as Paul Addison has noted, 'he might have become the hero of 1915'.[11] However, Kitchener's initial refusal to spare infantry for the campaign meant Churchill planned an entirely naval manoeuvre: when this stalled, it led to separate military landings that killed 46,000 Allied soldiers.[12] To help remedy the situation, Churchill had called for 'seventy aeroplanes and seaplanes' in his Minute from May 1915, among which 'the heaviest seaplanes capable of carrying and dropping 500-lb. bombs are to be included'.[13] That only an average of five aeroplanes and seaplanes were available per day by July 1915 constituted, according to Churchill, 'a failure on the part of the Air Department to grasp the importance of the aviation services at the Dardanelles'.[14]

The Dardanelles campaign heralded Churchill's fall from political grace; he was not redeemed until David Lloyd George appointed him as minister of munitions on 16 July 1917, after the first Dardanelles report had partly alleviated him of the blame. However, the roots had already been firmly planted for Churchill's future bombing policy. During the Dardanelles campaign, he had envisioned 'half a dozen seaplanes working in the Marmara in conjunction with our submarines: scouting for them, making bomb attacks on Constantinople, on the munition factories, on bridges, and on the railways supplying Constantinople'. He theorised that 'the 100-lb bombs would be very effective for smashing up railway bridges', while he also claimed that 'there is a reference in the Foreign Office telegrams to the important effect which would be produced by a bomb attack on Constantinople'.[15] He later served on the Aerial Operations Committee and the Air Raids Committee from autumn 1917, compiling a 'Munitions possibilities of 1918' memorandum that called for long-range attacks on enemy industrial centres.[16] His detailed hypotheses demonstrated his early belief that aerial bombardment of the enemy's beating heart and wartime lifelines was now an indispensable means of waging modern warfare.

Churchill and Airpower after the First World War

Following the General Election of December 1918, Churchill joined the Cabinet as the secretary for war – but he was soon persuaded by Lloyd George to combine this with his other appointment as secretary of state for air from early 1919 until 1921. He quickly installed Major-General[17] Hugh Trenchard as the RAF's chief of the air staff, with whom he came to share a common vision of guaranteeing the young air force's independence. Appointed as secretary of state for the colonies on 13 February 1921, Churchill became further convinced that the RAF should remain separate: he believed its bomber arm could fulfil army counterinsurgency roles more cheaply within the unsettled Middle East.[18] He frequently lobbied for boosting the RAF's resources to secure the 'aerial policing' of the British Empire, having previously agitated for bombing Sinn Fein members in Ireland.[19] As Richard Langworth details, he had 'no compunction against the use of bombing'[20] to suppress insurgent activities in the British Empire. This culminated in his support of the RAF's sustained bombing campaign over Mesopotamia – which, after a recent uprising against British rule, became the Kingdom of Iraq under British administration on 23 August 1921, – and Palestine in the early 1920s.

Churchill's anti-Middle Eastern prejudices unapologetically shaped his offensive aerial policy. In February 1920, he had proposed using a 'non-lethal' gas that caused 'discomfort or illness but not death' to subdue the unrest rippling through the region – even before the Iraqi revolt against British rule had fully ignited.[21] Yet, in an early representation of how Churchill's attitude towards aerial bombardment could lurch from savage to sanctimonious, he was aghast at reports that RAF aircraft had strafed women and children hiding from the aerial campaign in a lake. In July 1921, he told Trenchard of his surprise 'that you do not order the officers responsible for it, to be tried by court martial' and that 'by doing such things we put ourselves on the lowest level'. At the same time, however, he warned Trenchard that 'if such a thing became public it would ruin the air project which you have in view'.[22] Thus, as would later be epitomised by the bombing of Dresden in the Second World War, it was the threat of negative public opinion towards his bombing policy which festered most strongly in Churchill's subconscious – even if he did have fleeting moments of genuine reflection on its morality.

The International Threat of Aerial Bombardment

Nevertheless, Churchill's expansion of British airpower was widely recognised by the early 1920s. On 24 November 1924, the editor of *The Aeroplane* magazine, Charles Grey, sent Churchill an issue and a letter which praised his work as secretary of state for air. He signed off with his sincere wish that 'you may do as good work for the nation as you did when as First Lord of the Admiralty you laid the foundations of British Air Power'.[23] Grey's words were rendered even more heartfelt given the mounting apprehension in Britain at the future of aerial bombardment, which spiked with Stanley Baldwin's assertion on 10 November 1932 that 'the bomber will always get through'.[24] After Adolf Hitler pulled Nazi Germany from the League of Nations in October 1933, Churchill pressed for a rigorous comparison of British and German air strength during the various Air Estimates of 1933–5. Admittedly, pushing the agenda of British airpower did have an ulterior political motive in his self-deemed 'wilderness years'. His relentless striking of frayed British nerves regarding aerial bombardment bestowed him with elevated relevance for a backbencher who had held no ministerial positions since being chancellor of the exchequer from 1924 to 1929.[25]

Yet Churchill was also genuinely frustrated with the sluggish progress made towards expanding Britain's airpower capabilities by all sides of the Commons, witheringly describing the Labour prime minister Ramsay MacDonald as a 'hopeless twister'[26] on air defence in January 1935. Once Stanley Baldwin replaced MacDonald as the Conservative prime minister from June 1935, Churchill endlessly picked fault with *his* rearmament policy. Despite their 'disputes about various things',[27] however, he appreciated Baldwin's invitation for him to join the Air Defence Research Sub-Committee in July 1935. 'Of course', the prime minister had assured Churchill on 8 July, 'you are free as air (the correct expression in this case!) to debate the general issues of policy, programmes, and all else connected with the Air Services.'[28] Once more, Churchill threw himself into aviation discourse with his characteristic verve. Britain watched nervously as the Nazi Party publicly unveiled its new Luftwaffe in March 1935, with Churchill's insistence that the Germans possessed a clandestine air force having been dismissed often enough that his friend Sir Reginald Barnes wrote to him in May about how 'you must be tempted to say to the govt "I told you so", over the German Air Force'.[29]

Moreover, Italy's merciless use of aerial bombardment and poisonous gas by the *Regia Aeronautica* against the Ethiopians in the Second Italo-Ethiopian War (1935–7) demonstrated how other European nations were also using aerial bombardment to prop up their imperial ambitions; a fearsome means of waging modern aerial warfare which was already being brought closer to home in the Spanish Civil War (1936–9). In addition to Italy's *Aviazione Legionaria* assisting General Francisco Franco's nationalists during the conflict, *Kampfgeschwader* (bomber wings) from the Condor Legion – a combined *Wehrmacht* (armed forces) unit also sent to Franco by the Nazis – had started bombing Spanish cities in quick succession. Churchill even had a personal link to the damage wreaked in Spain: his son Randolph, who had gone to Spain as a war correspondent in February 1937, wrote to him of having 'inspected the ruins of the Casa del Campo'[30] near Madrid, which had been constantly bombarded by the Condor Legion in late 1936. International howls of outrage were provoked by the Legion's aerial destruction of Guernica on 26 April 1937, which the *Dundee Courier* claimed 'will rank as the most completely a-moral action yet recorded in connexion with the modern war'.[31]

Even before these wars, however, Churchill was being inundated with concerned letters from the public about British air defences. On 19 June 1935, he even wrote to the secretary of state for air, Sir Philip Cunliffe-Lister, and requested that they be passed onto him as 'I am afflicted with many letters from people who have inventions or ideas about Air Defence in its various branches. I cannot deal with them.'[32] Time, then, was of the essence when it came to equipping Britain with a powerful bomber arm. Reflecting his active involvement in British airpower discourse, Churchill penned several memoranda on the subject. One from 1936 claimed that 'the Germans have already, including their convertible civil-aviation fast-bombers, from 1500 to 2000 modern military machines'.[33] On 12 March 1938, Churchill sent another memorandum to Prime Minister Neville Chamberlain in which he asserted that of the Metropolitan Air Force's 123 squadrons now formed, 'more than half are still armed with obsolete types'. Among them he highlighted two light bombers, the Hawker Hind and Hart, and the twin-engine Handley Page Heyford bomber, which were being delivered to RAF bomber squadrons despite lacking 'essential armament and equipment, namely, Browning guns, turrets, sights and modern blind-flying equipment'.[34]

Growing Dissatisfaction within Bomber Command, 1936–1938

Churchill's long-standing proactivity in campaigning for the expansion of British airpower won him considerable support in certain circles. 'What bothers me, between ourselves, is the lack of enterprise shown by the Air Ministry. What I would like to see would be a man of your calibre put in charge',[35] wrote H. A. Gwynne, the editor of *The Morning Post*, to Churchill on 21 May 1935. Ralph Wigram, a contact of Churchill's in the Foreign Office, told him of hoping the latter's recent speech on German air strength that same month would 'make the Government push on all the faster with the air programme'.[36] Yet Churchill's incessant crusade for British rearmament, as Overy has noted, also earnt him 'a reputation as a warmonger amongst a largely anti-war public'.[37] By late 1935, *The Aeroplane* – having sung Churchill's praises for strengthening British airpower a decade ago – claimed he had 'made himself ridiculous by his Germano-phobia and his air panic effort'.[38] Part of his paranoia regarding German rearmament had been stoked by the inaccurate and misleading information of the former RAF Group Captain Malcolm Christie, who fed the Foreign Office questionable statistics that Wigram and Michael Creswell relayed to Churchill.[39]

Yet, the fact that Wigram, Creswell and Desmond Morton – the director of the Industrial Intelligence Centre – broke the Official Secrets Act for Churchill highlighted their considerable disillusion surrounding Britain's aerial rearmament.[40] This extended to the Air

Ministry and Bomber Command, the RAF's new dedicated striking force from 14 July 1936. Despite 'Scheme F' aiming to 'increase the striking power of the bomber squadrons',[41] it was claimed in correspondence between Group Captain Lachlan MacLean and Wing Commander Charles Anderson on 29 January 1937 that 'if we have a war forced on us in the next three, possibly five years, we shall be powerless to retaliate'.[42] Squadron Leader Herbert Rowley commented two months beforehand:

> It is my sincere and considered opinion, as an Air Staff Officer, as an Engineering Officer, and as an Officer with over 20 years' experience of Air Force operations at Home and Abroad, in fighters and bombers, that, out of all these aircraft there are only two which are superior bombing weapons to the German Heinkel and the Junkers. These two are the Vickers B 9 and the Blenheim. All the others, except possibly the Handley-Page, of which I know little, are inferior to the German weapons and some of them, for example the Whitley and Hendon, are merely deathtraps if sent to war.[43]

Admittedly, such reports were possibly over-exaggerated to secure governmental resources more quickly for the new bomber arm. Yet the despondency in Bomber Command was potent enough that MacLean handed in his resignation to the Air Officer Commanding, No. 3 (Bomber) Group at RAF Mildenhall, on 17 November 1938 because of 'a steady process of disenchantment and foreboding, which reached its culmination in a profound horror at the situation disclosed by the recent International [Munich] crisis, with regard to the readiness of the Air Force and its ability to take any part in the active defence of this country'.[44]

Escalation of Aerial Bombardment in Europe

Once Britain and France descended into war with Nazi Germany on 3 September 1939, rectifying these stark inadequacies became of paramount importance. As Richard Toye writes, Churchill's combative spirit 'helped establish him in the public mind as a potential alternative to Chamberlain',[45] who had postponed a decision on attacking the militarily legitimate, industrial Ruhr Valley in Germany even as France was facing Nazi attack on the last day of his premiership.[46] This was partially because of his scrupulous adherence to a plea from Franklin

D. Roosevelt, the president of the United States, for all nations in the new conflict to refrain from bombing civilians. Churchill, on the other hand, had possessed a more unflinching and pragmatic appraisal of the Luftwaffe's potential bombing war since the mid-1930s. On 23 July 1935, he had noted the strong likelihood of attempts being made 'to burn down London, or other great cities within easy reach, in order to test the resisting will-power of the Government and people under these terrible ordeals'.[47] Not long afterwards, he recognised that 'the more serious danger is probably the small incendiary bomb ... whose action, since it spreads, might result in the complete destruction of London or any other large city'.[48]

After succeeding Chamberlain as prime minister on 10 May 1940, Churchill had no qualms about sending out Bomber Command to attack German military, economic and industrial targets. From July until October 1940, Bomber Command and its maritime brother, Coastal Command, spent much of the Battle of Britain attempting to strike German invasion barges, embarkment points and industrial targets to disrupt Hitler's planning for Operation Sea Lion – the amphibious Wehrmacht invasion of Britain. Privately, Churchill was alarmed at Bomber Command's increasing losses. On 11 July 1940, he fretted in his Personal Minutes to Sir Archibald Sinclair – his secretary of state for air and close friend – that 'the losses in the Bomber force seem unduly heavy'.[49] Yet, in his famous 'The Few' speech on 20 August 1940, Churchill declared that:

> We must never forget that all the time, night after night, month after month, our bomber squadrons travel far into Germany, find their targets in the darkness by the highest navigational skill, aim their attacks, often under the heaviest fire, often with serious loss, with deliberate careful discrimination, and inflict shattering blows upon the whole of the technical and war-making structure of the Nazi power. On no part of the Royal Air Force does the weight of the war fall more heavily than on the daylight bombers, who will play an invaluable part in the case of invasion and whose unflinching zeal it has been necessary in the meanwhile on numerous occasions to restrain.[50]

For Churchill to dedicate far more lines to Bomber Command than their counterparts in Fighter Command demonstrated the immense value he assigned to the 'Bomber Few'. That he amended an early draft of the iconic speech to add that 'our bomber and fighter strength now, after all this fighting, are larger than they have ever been'[51] also displayed the equal worth he placed on both Commands, despite the swift etymological hijacking of 'The Few' to refer to the fighter pilots alone in British mythology. That Churchill had finished his Minute to Sinclair with the claim that it was 'very important to build up the numbers of the Bomber force, which is very low at the present time'[52] illustrated his ongoing commitment to boosting Bomber Command.

The Blitz over Britain

On the night of 24–25 August 1940, stray German bombs accidentally fell onto two civilian boroughs in London during a Luftwaffe air raid. Churchill immediately greenlit a retaliatory blow against Berlin by Bomber Command, but – as Overy has noted – 'approval of bombing was a decision that came at a high price. Bomber Command achieved negligible results against German targets and invited German retaliation'.[53] Switching away from grinding down Fighter Command in the Battle of Britain, the commander-in-chief of the Luftwaffe – *Reichsmarschall* Hermann Göring – hoped to bring the British to the negotiating table by pounding their cities instead. On 7 September 1940, 650 German bombers killed 448 civilians and injured a further 1,337 people in London alone during the first day of the Blitz.[54] For nine months afterwards, the Luftwaffe's high-explosive, incendiary, fragmentation and delay-action bombs seared through buildings, human flesh and livelihoods across Britain. Downing Street, the Treasury and the House of Commons all suffered bomb damage to varying degrees, while on 8 June 1941, Churchill even informed his son Randolph that 'your Mother [Clementine] is now insisting upon becoming a fire watcher on the roof'[55] after a hefty 4,000-pound bomb had fallen near Randolph's flat in Westminster Gardens.

Churchill and his War Cabinet were anxious at the prospect of the nation turning their backs on them for the Blitz, but the prime minister was relieved to meet certain members of the British public who were as grimly resolved to see out the war as he was. After an impromptu trip to inspect some heavy bomb damage in Peckham, Churchill alleged that the watchful crowd had brayed for him to 'give it 'em back' and 'let them have it too'.[56] In an evocation of the transcendent 'Blitz Spirit', defined by Mark Clapson as 'the alleged mood of wartime unity across the class divide',[57] he soon repeated this in the House of Commons on 8 October 1940: 'on every side, there is the cry, "we can take it." But with it, there is also the cry, "give it 'em back"'.[58] He used this pithy refrain, as Allen Packwood explains, to defend 'the British policy of bombing military targets'[59] and to circumvent the morality of such reprisals. Yet, although he tended to be favourably received when visiting Blitzed cities across the North and Midlands, his London-centric perspective arguably resulted in him overstating the nation's appetite for retaliation.

Indeed, according to a December 1940 survey, 48 per cent of respondents from the rest of the country 'disapproved [of reprisals] and six per cent did not know'[60] how they felt. The Bombing Restriction Committee – founded as the Committee for the Abolition of Night Bombing just after the Blitz – was especially critical of the reprisals against Germany. It controversially advertised its leaflets such as 'Stop Bombing Civilians!' and 'Bomb, Burn and Ruthlessly Destroy' in newspapers such as the *Liverpool Daily Post*.[61] This did not, however, prevent Churchill's immortalisation in British wartime culture as the redeemer of the Blitz. A farcical example of this was his depiction in two artistic window displays during the War Weapons Week at Tunbridge Wells in December 1940. One drew Hitler as Humpty Dumpty while Churchill edged closer towards dropping a bomb on the Führer's head, depending on how many donations were made to the war effort. Another presented 'Hitler and Göring as bed partners in a house with a snowy setting . . . awaiting the arrival of Father Christmas. Father Christmas takes the sinister form of Mr. Winston Churchill holding a huge bomb over the chimney pot bearing the greeting "A present from Tunbridge Wells".'[62]

Mid-War Criticism of Bomber Command and the Rise of Arthur 'Bomber' Harris

The *Kent & Sussex Courier*'s coverage of the displays assured its readers that 'Bombers may come and bombers may go, but we will deal the fatal blow'.[63] Despite Bomber Command's perilous ventures above occupied Europe each night, however, it was struggling to land any blow at all by summer 1941. On 18 August, the statistician David Butt presented the infamous 'Butt Report' to Bomber Command, which claimed only one in four of its aircraft came within five miles of its target – decreasing to just one in ten over the Ruhr. In addition, the Luftwaffe killed more than ten times as many civilians as Bomber Command did during the Blitz.[64] Nevertheless, the policy of military reprisals was proving favourable in Britain, with *The Sphere* writing on 26 April 1941 that:

> Whenever weather conditions permit, the heavy bombers set off to attack military objectives in Germany – and Berlin itself. More and bigger bombers of the R.A.F., carrying larger and more powerful bombs, are striking harder each week, hitting the enemy where it hurts most in his own country. Each new raid on Britain sends our own air-crews out determined to 'give it to them back' – with interest.[65]

In January 1937, Bomber Command had identified the need to 'reach those "centres" in the enemy's country which are vital to his existence and the attack on which will react immediately on his will or ability to continue the war'.[66] Combined with Churchill's subtle caveat in his 'The Few' speech that 'it has been necessary in the meanwhile on numerous occasions to restrain'[67] Bomber Command, this demonstrated an early flexibility as to the intensity, scope and – most fatefully – targets of Britain's bombing policy. Its commander-in-chief, Air Marshal Sir Richard Peirse, had attempted to rectify the Command's poor accuracy over Germany through commissioning multiple reports and acquiring more reconnaissance cameras for his bombers.[68] Yet, with Bomber Command haemorrhaging its aircrews for little gain, Peirse's days were numbered.

On 22 February 1942, he was replaced by the irascible yet resolute Air Marshal Arthur Harris. Harris' plan to rectify Bomber Command's inaccuracy was to pursue 'area bombing' – where the vulnerable giblets of a city were broadly targeted – over the more specialised 'strategic bombing' of industrial and military targets on the outskirts. He sought to 'de-house' the German population by striking directly at the homes, families and morale of the industrial workers. This concept was advanced by the divisive physicist Lord Cherwell, Churchill's trusted scientific advisor and friend, who used incomplete data from the Blitz in Hull and Birmingham to persuade the prime minister on 30 March 1942 that '[de-housing] would break the spirit of the [German] people'.[69] Churchill soon forwarded Cherwell's report to the War Cabinet despite it constituting, as Daniel Todman notes, 'a political document rather than a decision over strategy'.[70] Moreover, as Tami Davis Biddle outlines, Cherwell's assertions were strongly misguided: 'loss of production was caused almost entirely by direct damage to factories, and that loss had been only about 5 percent'.[71] Nevertheless, Cherwell's aggressive proposal suited Harris down to the ground, who had declared that the Germans had 'sowed the wind, and now they are going to reap the whirlwind'.[72]

Casablanca, 'Total War' and the Combined Allied Strategic Bomber Offensive

As Richard L. Blanco states, Harris' command 'coincided with improvements in aircraft, formations, navigational aids and bombing techniques'.[73] Lübeck was the first major casualty of Harris' appointment, with half of the city destroyed at little cost to Bomber Command on 28 March 1942.[74] Rostock was next on 23 April, with only 40 per cent of the city left standing.[75] Churchill's imagination was particularly enraptured, however, by the commander-in-chief's proposed thousand-bomber raid on Cologne in Operation Millennium. After Bomber Command had destroyed 600 acres of the cathedral city on 30 and 31 May 1942 – killing 1,000 civilians, injuring 15,000 more and making 45,000 homeless[76] – Harris claimed: 'I knew at once that [Churchill] was satisfied then ... he wanted above all to get on with the war.'[77] Churchill did not share Harris' view that Bomber Command alone could win the war, but he did hope it would at least afford one 'of the surest, if not the shortest of all roads to victory'.[78] Britain's improving success in the bombing war came at a fortunate time for Churchill, as it allowed him to illustrate the nation's continued usefulness to the war in the eyes of Roosevelt and Joseph Stalin, the demanding premier of the USSR.

Between 14 and 24 January 1943, Churchill and Roosevelt met during the Casablanca Conference to discuss the next phase against the Axis powers. Two days later, Stalin's request for a 'second front' to be opened in the West was formally approved by Churchill and Roosevelt. The United States VIII Bomber Command and the RAF's Bomber Command were to collaborate even more tightly so that 'an increased tempo and weight of daylight and night attacks will lead to greatly increased material and morale damage in Germany and rapidly deplete German fighter strength'.[79] The subsequent 'Casablanca Directive' demanded the 'undermining of the morale of the German people to a point where their capacity for armed resistance is fatally weakened'.[80] That Churchill approved the directive illustrated once more his significant culpability in shaping British bombing policy during his premiership. Furthermore, his adherence to the Allied policy of securing 'unconditional surrender'[81] from the Axis powers set the tone for a further hardening of the bombing war. Thus, when Joseph Goebbels – Hitler's propaganda minister – called for a war 'more total and radical than anything [Germany] can imagine today'[82] on 18 February 1943, the prime minister had already primed Britain to 'take the gloves off' in the Combined Allied Bomber Offensive.

Churchill, as Packwood points out, was 'determined to take the fight to the enemy and was frustrated by his lack of ability to command the whole scene'.[83] Indeed, as Toye notes, he kept his generals up 'late at night, often indulging in what they regarded as rambling irrelevancies, and putting forward plans for action they regarded as hare-brained'.[84] They were obliged to listen, too, seeing as the prime minister retained the ultimate say on the bigger picture of British bombing policy despite not micromanaging it at the operational level. Nevertheless, as John Keegan has stated, Churchill 'warned and advised, encouraged and occasionally excoriated. He appointed and removed commanders. But he did not presume their job.'[85] This was evidenced in his rejection of Lord Hankey's suggestion to reassign aircraft from Bomber Command to British sea power in May 1942, telling him 'the decision must necessarily be left to those who bear the responsibility'.[86] Even in the most emotive circumstances, Churchill's bombing policy was capable of yielding to professional military opinion. He had initially been staunchly in favour of honouring the Jewish Agency for Palestine's call to bomb the railway lines at Auschwitz-Birkenau in summer 1944, imploring his foreign secretary, Anthony Eden, to 'get anything out of the Air Force you can' on 7 July. Yet he soon recognised the dangers that such precision bombing posed to both the camp inmates and Allied bomber crews, later heeding the Air Ministry's assertion that bombing Treblinka and Auschwitz-Birkenau 'would cost British lives and aircraft to no purpose'.[87]

'Are We Beasts?': The German Firestorms

Nevertheless, as Overy writes, 'bombing was a useful tool [for Churchill] even when its effects were open to criticism'.[88] As Churchill attempted to pacify Stalin, Bomber Command was making slow but steady progress in the Battle of the Ruhr from March to July 1943. Then, the combined Allied firebombing of Hamburg in Operation Gomorrah during the last week of that July – in which 45,000 civilians were killed – was especially played up by the British prime minister. A year later, despite Bomber Command's substantial losses in the aerial Battle of Berlin campaign from November 1943 until March 1944, Churchill spoke animatedly to the House of Commons on 6 July 1944 about 'the terrific destruction by fire and high explosives with which we have been assaulting Berlin, Hamburg, Cologne, and scores of other cities and other war manufacturing points in Germany'.[89] Five months before-hand, however, the Lord Bishop of Chichester had given a speech to the House of Lords:

> There are old German towns, away from the great centres, which may be subjected – which almost certainly will be subjected – to the raids of Bomber Command. Almost certainly they are on the long list. Dresden, Augsburg, Munich are among the larger towns . . . . After the destruction of the ancient town centres of Cologne, with its unique Romanesque churches, and Lübeck, with its brick cathedral, and Mainz, with one of the most famous German cathedrals, and of the old Gothic towns, the inner towns, Nuremburg, Hamburg and others . . . it must surely be apparent to any but the most complacent and reckless how far the destruction of European culture has already gone. We ought to think once, twice, and three times before destroying the rest.[90]

The Bishop of Chichester's speech unequivocally expressed his discomfort at Churchill's bombing campaign. Even more fatefully, it illustrated how some British contemporaries considered Dresden to be different compared to the 'great centres' of Nazi Germany, though it also showed the city was not an entirely unexpected target. Yet it was not just the bishop and men like the Labour MP Richard Stokes who had their doubts: even Churchill himself had one of his occasional wobbles just before Hamburg, asking gravely after viewing footage of the bombed-out German cities, 'are we beasts? Are we taking this too far?'[91] However, as Stephen A. Garrett has noted, the pressure for the bombing campaign to succeed meant 'the turn to indiscriminate bombing followed almost as a matter of course'.[92] By 1944–5, further German firestorms allowed Churchill to keenly demonstrate to the British people – now trudging into nearly half a decade of constant fighting – that the raining down of Hitler's *Vergeltungswaffen* (vengeance weapons) on Britain would not go unpunished.

Two main controversies surround Bomber Command and the Eighth Air Force's firebombing of Dresden between 13 and 15 February 1945, in which an estimated 25,000 people were killed.[93] The first is the long-standing debate over whether Dresden was a 'war crime' – or, given the nebulous legal definitions of a 'war crime' by February 1945, if its destruction constituted an unreasonable breach of the existing Laws and Customs of War and Hague Conventions. Proponents of this argument include Donald Bloxham, Jörg Friedrich and the British rifleman Victor Gregg, who saw the inferno for himself as a prisoner of war in Dresden.[94] This school of thought points to the fact that the deliberate staggering of the bomber waves, perfected after multiple Allied firestorms over Germany, sought to maximise human suffering by catching out any civilians re-emerging from their shelters.[95] Other facets of this argument include the fact that Dresden's wartime industrial output hardly rivalled cities such as Hamburg, Berlin or Chemnitz; that the city was 'defenceless' by February 1945, although the Allied bomber crews were unaware that its last heavy flak battery had been reassigned to bolster German defences in the East by mid-January 1945;[96] and that the Allies knew attacking Dresden would create further disarray among the refugees who had fled there from other bombed-out cities. Moreover, the obliteration of Dresden's priceless historical landmarks as the conflagration devoured the city's impuissant wooden centre – such as the Frauenkirche, the Residenzschloss and the Zwinger – rubbed salt into the city's gaping wounds, signifying a complete disregard for the capital of Saxony's immense cultural and historical value.

Other scholars, most notably Addison, Biddle and especially Frederick Taylor, have given a more moderate interpretation of the raid that acknowledges its bloodcurdling horrors while pointing out that, in Biddle's words, it 'followed routines that were well established by that point in the European theatre'.[97] Such circles have argued that Dresden was an important communications and transportation hub, with Colonel General Heinz Guderian having classed the city as a *Verteidigungsbereich* (defensive area), akin to a temporary fortress, by February 1945.[98] Moreover, in contrast to Goebbels' claim that Dresden produced only 'toothpaste and baby-powder',[99] the city manufactured a variety of *Feinarbeit* (precision work) wartime equipment – from the Cartonnagenindustrie paper factory churning out shell linings for munitions[100] to the specialised work of the camera and lenses expert Zeiss Ikon A.G.[101] Most worryingly for the Allies, though, Dresden's

Chemische Fabrik Gehe A.G. was suspected of manufacturing poison gas.[102] Notwithstanding the presence of these military targets, the unremitting brutality of the bomber raids greatly unsettled contemporary observers on all sides. Thus, the second main controversy surrounding Dresden arose: who was ultimately responsible for its destruction?[103] For one German newspaper, the *Leipziger Neueste Nachrichten*, the perpetrators were obvious: 'the Anglo-American air pirates sent by the mortal enemies of European civilisation, by Roosevelt and Churchill'.[104] Then, on 20 February 1945, another issue of the newspaper reported how 'Air Marshal Harris stated on 29 July 1942: "we are bombing Germany city by city in an increasingly terrible way. We will punish the Germans from one end [of the country] to the other."'[105]

Strike Hard, Strike Unsure? Post-War Relations between Churchill and Bomber Command

In Britain, however, the blame game for Dresden was starting to brew. Churchill – who, as Biddle writes, 'always had one eye toward posterity' – immediately distanced himself from the growing international criticism surrounding Dresden. He accused Marshal of the Royal Air Force Sir Charles Portal of having ordered the raid 'simply for the sake of increasing the terror'. 'The destruction of Dresden', he lectured the offended Portal, 'remains a serious query against the conduct of Allied bombing'.[106] After the war, Harris implicated Churchill by claiming Dresden was 'at the time considered a military necessity by much more important people than myself'.[107] Indeed, Portal and Harris had seen Dresden as a continuation of Churchill's enquiry to Sinclair on 26 January 1945 as to 'whether Berlin, and no doubt other large cities in East Germany, should not now be considered especially attractive targets'.[108] It is true that Churchill had a direct input into the nation's bombing policy, such as informing the House of Commons on 6 July 1944 that 'the Commander-in-Chief, Bomber Command, has been instructed to include [the V-1 weapons sites] on a high priority in his current bombing programme'.[109] Even before the Blitz, Churchill had secretly claimed to Sinclair that only 'an absolutely devastating, exterminating attack by very heavy bombers'[110] would bring Hitler to his knees.

Thus, the call for Dresden was an argument of semantics which Churchill used, in Connelly's words, to 'make Harris a scapegoat for agreed wartime policy by implying that he was the sole architect of the strategy'.[111] Churchill's fraught relationship with Harris directly after the war over the latter's proposed book on the bombing campaign may well have contributed to this. On 15 May 1945, he gushed to Harris that Bomber Command's wartime service 'will long be remembered as an example of duty nobly done'.[112] In June 1946, however, Churchill was 'shocked by the style of the extracts from your book which ill consort with your splendid services to our country' and that 'if these extracts are typical ... I personally will be forced to repudiate your quotations'.[113] The friction between the pair, preceded by Churchill's omission of Bomber Command from his victory speech of May 1945, had largely dissipated by the 1950s: Harris accepted Churchill's offer of a baronetcy in 1953.[114] Nevertheless, for Bomber Command's veterans – who smarted at not receiving the dedicated campaign medal or bar they had anticipated, and whose ostracisation by Churchill had left them susceptible to being painted as murderers – the damage had been done.

Warmonger? Churchill and the Allied Bombing Campaign in Post-War Memory

Churchill later claimed in his six-volume history of the Second World War that Bomber Command 'made a decisive contribution to victory'[115] – yet, despite covering the heavy wartime bombing raids on Lübeck, Rostock, Cologne, Hamburg and Berlin, he failed to mention Dresden. Historians have correctly interpreted this as a further airbrushing of his association with the raid, but it is important to fully contextualise his editorial choice. Volume 5 of his war memoirs, *Closing the Ring* (1951), mentioned the Allied bombing campaign in more detail, but Dresden remained a sore diplomatic point for the Western Allies after the Soviets had occupied the city. It was published just a year after the *Belfast News-Letter* reported that 'German Communists [were accusing] Winston Churchill of bombing Dresden to slow the Red Army's advance on Berlin' and that 'Eastern newspapers and Soviet-controlled Berlin radio called the attack "militarily completely senseless" and "planned in cold blood to secure the profits of the British armament magnates up to the very end"'.[116] Thus, Churchill's diplomatic choice to sidestep the issue – having previously disclaimed that 'I have softened many of the severities

Figure 16.1 Churchill watching a Flying Fortress, June 1941 (CAC, Broadwater Collection, BRDW V 3/3).

of contemporary controversy'[117] in the series – and to avoid inflaming Cold War tensions was arguably more justified than is often argued.

Despite attempting to control the narrative of the bombing campaign, however, Churchill's old label of 'warmonger' partially cost him the General Election of July 1945. That he was dubbed as 'Warmonger No. 1'[118] five years later by the *Daily Herald* demonstrated how, as Kenneth W. Thompson put it, the hot-headed Churchill continued to seem more likely to 'plunge the world into conflict'.[119] Just two years after his death on 24 January 1965, *The Soldiers* – a play by the German playwright Rolf Hochhuth – demonstrated Churchill's enduring synonymity with the bombing campaign. Among other controversies, it included a scene where Harris was depicted 'extolling the virtues of a butterfly to Sir Winston Churchill while the bombing of German cities is portrayed on a screen. Sir Winston, in the play, likens the butterfly to a city being bombed.'[120] The Board of the National

Theatre's refusal to run the play incurred the chagrin of its literary manager and its founding director, Sir Laurence Olivier. However, in an era of loosening British theatre censorship by the late 1960s, this controversy illustrated how the national memory of Churchill remained sacrosanct for some and irrevocably tainted for others in post-war Britain.

Even more importantly, it demonstrated how Churchill's association with the bombing campaign had the eternal power to split opinion. Although he typically deferred to his advisors and commanders on the minutia of the airborne offensive over Germany, his bombing policy was frequently a reflection of himself. He was committed, but prone to unpredictability and stark moments of contradiction; he was ruthless and sometimes even reckless in avenging the Blitz, but had notable incidences of reflection and anxiety. Having taken a keen interest in the future of offensive airpower and its application from the earliest stages of flight, he quickly grasped during the First World War – from the Dardanelles campaign to the Gotha and zeppelin raids over Britain – that aerial bombardment could potentially hit a belligerent's centres with renewed efficiency and versatility. In the interwar period, he correctly identified how aerial bombardment would be deployed in ever-terrible ways during a future war and crucially helped to prepare Britain for this pressing threat, though he was not averse to unleashing such methods himself to 'aerially police' the British Empire. Throughout his early political life and leading up to his wartime premiership, then, Churchill had a sporadic yet significant level of input into all aspects of Britain's bombing policy.

Once he became prime minister in May 1940, Churchill was determined, as Packwood writes, to 'get his hands dirty and take direct personal control of the day to day running of military policy'.[121] Yet, as the dirt on his hands turned to blood with the German firestorms, he gradually became more uncomfortable at 'giving it 'em back' a little too brutally. Though Churchill's admiration for the bomber arm was genuine – having passionately described himself as 'a champion of Bomber Command'[122] to Trenchard on 4 September 1942 – his opportunistic deflection of international criticism surrounding Dresden onto Harris, Portal and others illustrated why he was a master politician instead of a military commander. His insistence on placing the blame for Dresden squarely on their shoulders constituted a cynical political manoeuvre to exonerate himself from the bombing policy he helped to escalate through years of fiery rhetoric and vengeful sentiment, sullying Bomber Command's reputation in a sly attempt to save his own. Ultimately, the ends of Churchill's bombing campaign – to shorten the Second World War – were undeniably justified. The means, however, remain far more contentious.

Notes

1. *Hansard*, House of Commons debates. 'ROYAL AIR FORCE (CONTROL)', vol. 152, cols. 342–94, at 384, 21 March 1922.
2. R. Overy, *The Birth of the RAF* (London: Allen Lane, 2018), p. 85.
3. W. S. Churchill, *The Second World War*, vol. 1, *The Gathering Storm* (London: Penguin, 1985), p. 36.
4. R. Overy, Churchill and Airpower. In R. Toye (ed.), *Winston Churchill: Politics, Strategy and Statecraft* (London: Bloomsbury, 2017), pp. 127–37, p. 127.
5. M. Connelly, The British Debate. In I. Primoratz (ed.), *Terror from the Sky: The Bombing of German Cities in World War II* (New York: Berghahn, 2014), pp. 181–202, p. 198.
6. K. Ruane, Churchill and Nuclear Weapons. In R. Toye (ed.), *Winston Churchill: Politics, Strategy and Statecraft* (London: Bloomsbury, 2017), pp. 171–86, p. 172.
7. Overy, Churchill and Airpower, p. 128.
8. CAC, CHAR 2/66/64. Letter from Rear-Admiral Arthur Limpus (HM Dockyard, Malta) to Churchill commending the article in the *Observer* of 30 May, 7 June 1915.
9. Overy, Churchill and Airpower, p. 128.
10. CAC, CHAR 2/69/19. Cutting from the *Daily Mail*: 'More Aeroplanes?; Yes! But Of What Kind?', Monday 28 June 1915.
11. P. Addison, *Churchill: The Unexpected Hero* (Oxford: Oxford University Press, 2005), p. 76.
12. M. Thornton, Churchill as First Lord of the Admiralty. In R. Toye (ed.), *Winston Churchill: Politics, Strategy and Statecraft* (London: Bloomsbury, 2017), pp. 23–34, p. 31.
13. CAC, CHAR 2/74/118. Minute by Churchill stating that the Dardanelles operations could easily develop into a great siege, 14 May 1915.
14. CAC, CHAR 2/74/129. Letter from Churchill to Arthur Balfour (later Lord Balfour) on the need for aircraft and 12-inch monitors in the Dardanelles, 22 July 1915.
15. Letter from Churchill to Balfour, 22 July 1915.
16. Overy, Churchill and Airpower, p. 128.
17. One of the RAF's first reforms under Trenchard as chief of the air staff was making its proposed officer ranks more distinct from those of the British army. Thus, his original army rank of major-general later changed to air vice marshal. He proceeded to rise through the new RAF ranks before he was made a marshal of the Royal Air Force in January 1927.
18. Y. Tanaka, British 'Human Bombing' in Iraq during the Interwar Era. In Y. Tanaka and M. B. Young (eds.), *Bombing Civilians: A Twentieth-Century History* (New York: New Press, 2009), pp. 8–29, p. 18.
19. R. Langworth, *Churchill by Himself* (London: Ebury, 2008), p. 204.
20. Langworth, *Churchill by Himself*, p. 204.
21. Langworth, *Churchill by Himself*, p. 22.

22. W. Dockter, *Churchill and the Islamic World: Orientalism, Empire and Diplomacy in the Middle East* (London: I. B. Taurus, 2015), p. 119.

23. CAC, CHAR 2/136/85–6. Letter from Charles Grey to Churchill congratulating him [on his appointment as Chancellor of the Exchequer] and enclosing a copy of the 'Aeroplane' in which he praises Churchill's promotion of aviation, 24 November 1924.

24. *Hansard*, House of Commons debates. 'INTERNATIONAL AFFAIRS', vol. 270, cols. 525–641, at 632, 21 March 1922.

25. Overy, Churchill and Airpower, p. 129.

26. CAC, CHAR 2/243/8. Letter from Churchill to F. A. Lindemann (later Lord Cherwell), on letter from the prime minister [Ramsay MacDonald] on air defence, 21 January 1935.

27. CAC, CHAR 2/236/108. Letter from Churchill to the prime minister [Stanley Baldwin] assuring him that he recognises his gesture of friendliness, 09 July 1935.

28. CAC, CHAR 2/236/106. Letter from Stanley Baldwin [the prime minister] (10 Downing Street, Whitehall) to Churchill, saying how glad he is that Churchill is willing to serve on the [Air Defence Research Sub-Committee], 08 July 1935.

29. CAC, CHAR 1/271/20. Letter from Sir Reginald Barnes to Churchill, asking if he would be able to attend 4th Hussars dinner on 4 June, and commenting on Churchill's views on the German air force, 14 May 1935.

30. CAC, CHAR 1/301/10–14. Letter from Randolph Churchill to Churchill, news from Spain, account of visit to the front line 5 km from Madrid, 22 March 1937.

31. The British Newspaper Archive, *Dundee Courier*, 'The Guernica Massacre', Thursday 29 April 1937, p. 6.

32. CAC, CHAR 2/243/121. Letter from Churchill to Sir Philip Cunliffe-Lister [later Lord Swinton], secretary of state for air, on the number of letters he received on the subject of air defence, 19 June 1935.

33. CAC, CHAR 2/268. Memorandum by Churchill on air defence, 14 February 1936 to 26 October 1936.

34. CAC, CHAR 2/336. Memorandum on aircraft types by The Rt. Hon. Winston S. Churchill to Neville Chamberlain, 12 March 1938.

35. CAC, CHAR 2/243/89–90. Letter from H. A. Gwynne, *The Morning Post*, Tudor Street, London, EC4, to CHURCHILL, on British and German air strength, 21 May 1935.

36. CAC, CHAR 2/235/67. Letter from Ralph Wigram (Southease Farm, Lewes, Sussex) to Churchill, congratulating him on his speech [on German air strength], 3 May 1935.

37. Overy, Churchill and Airpower, p. 130.

38. CAC, CHAR 2/238/106–7. Letter from Churchill to Spenser Grey, regretting that he could not preside at airmen's luncheon as he was leaving for a long holiday in Majorca. Asking Grey to comment on cuttings from recent issues of *The Aeroplane*, 7 December 1935.

39. Overy, Churchill and Airpower, p. 130.

40. Addison, *Churchill: The Unexpected Hero*, p. 141.

41. CAC, CHAR 2/271. Correspondence and notes from Wing-Commander Charles Anderson, Director of Training, Air Ministry, later commander of RAF Hucknall, Nottinghamshire, May to 24 November 1936.

42. CAC, CHAR 2/303. Public and Political: General: Air Defence: Wing Commander Anderson, 29 January 1937.

43. CAC, CHAR 2/271. Memorandum by Squadron-Leader Herbert Rowley on his visit to Germany, October 1936.

44. CAC, CHAR 2/339. Public and Political: General: Air Defence: Group Captain Maclean. From: Group Captain L. L. MacLean. To: Air Officer Commanding, No. 3 (Bomber) Group, Mildenhall, 17 November 1938.

45. R. Toye, Introduction. In R. Toye (ed.), *Winston Churchill: Politics, Strategy and Statecraft* (London: Bloomsbury, 2017), pp. 1–11, p. 5.

46. A. Packwood, *How Churchill Waged War: The Most Challenging Decisions of the Second World War* (Barnsley: Pen & Sword, 2018), p. 59.

47. Churchill, *The Gathering Storm*, p. 137.

48. CAC, CHAR 2/270. Churchill on British and German air strength, 21 July 1936 to 21 January 1937.

49. CAC, CHAR 20/13/4. The Prime Minister's Personal Minutes, 11 July 1940.

50. CAC, CHAR 9/141A/37–68, 'The Few', 20 August 1940.

51. CAC, CHAR 9/141A/37–68, 'The Few', 20 August 1940.

52. CAC, CHAR 20/13/4. The Prime Minister's Personal Minutes, 11 July 1940.

53. R. Overy, *The Bombers and the Bombed: Allied Air War over Europe, 1940–1945* (New York: Penguin, 2013), p. 53.

54. R. L. Blanco, *The Luftwaffe in World War II: The Rise and Decline of the German Air Force* (New York: Julian Messner, 1987), p. 71.

55. CAC, CHAR 1/362/18–25. Letter from Churchill (Ditchley House, [Dytchley] Oxfordshire) to Randolph Churchill, 8 June 1941.

56. W. S. Churchill, *The Second World War, Volume 2: Their Finest Hour* (London: Penguin, 1985), p. 308.

57. M. Clapson, *The Blitz Companion: Aerial Warfare, Civilians and the City since 1911* (London: University of Westminster Press, 2019), p. 125.

58. *Hansard*, House of Commons debates. 'WAR SITUATION', vol. 365, cols. 261–352, at 292, 8 October 1940.

59. Packwood, *How Churchill Waged War*, p. 54.

60. Connelly, The British Debate, p. 197.

61. The British Newspaper Archive, 'Stop Bombing Civilians!', Bombing Restriction Committee advert, *Liverpool Daily Post*, Saturday 16 October 1943, p. 3.

62. The British Newspaper Archive, 'Tunbridge Wells war weapons week; town is aiming at £500,000 target', *Kent & Sussex Courier*, Friday 13 December 1940.

63. 'Tunbridge Wells war weapons week'.

64. Overy, *The Bombers and the Bombed*, p. 69.

65. The British Newspaper Archive, 'We are giving it back', *The Sphere*, Saturday 26 April 1941, p. 105.

66. CAC, CHAR 2/303. Public and Political: General: Air Defence: Wing Commander Anderson, 29 January 1937.

67. CAC, CHAR 9/141A/37–68, 'The Few', 20 August 1940.

68. Overy, *The Bombers and the Bombed*, p. 69.

69. T. D. Biddle, *Rhetoric and Reality in Air Warfare: The Evolution of British and American Ideas about Strategic Bombing, 1914–1945* (Princeton, NJ: Princeton University Press, 2002), p. 200.

70. D. Todman, *Britain's War: A New World, 1942–1947* (Oxford: Oxford University Press, 2020), p. 171.

71. Biddle, *Rhetoric and Reality in Air Warfare*, p. 200.

72. Blanco, *The Luftwaffe in World War II*, p. 129.

73. Blanco, *The Luftwaffe in World War II*, p. 129.

74. C. Everitt and M. Middlebrook, *The Bomber Command War Diaries: An Operational Reference Book, 1939–1945* (Barnsley: Pen & Sword, 2014), p. 26.

75. M. Bowman, *Bomber Command: Reflections of War* (Barnsley: Pen & Sword, 2011), p. 189.

76. S. A. Garrett, The Bombing Campaign: The RAF. In R. Toye (ed.), *Winston Churchill: Politics, Strategy and Statecraft* (London: Bloomsbury, 2017), pp. 19–38, p. 30.

77. Garrett, The Bombing Campaign, p. 30.

78. CAC, CHAR 9/141A/37–68, 'The Few', 20 August 1940.

79. W. S. Churchill, *The Second World War, Volume 4: The Hinge of Fate* (London: Penguin, 1985), p. 665.

80. Churchill, *The Second World War, Volume 5: Closing the Ring* (London: Penguin, 1985), p. 458.

81. Churchill, *The Second World War, Volume 4: The Hinge of Fate*, p. 612.

82. J. Goebbels, 'Total War', address to the Nazi Party (Berlin, 18 February 1943). In R. L. Bytwerk (ed. and trans.), *Landmark Speeches of National Socialism* (College Station: Texas A&M University Press, 2008), pp. 112–39.

83. Packwood, *How Churchill Waged War*, p. 6.

84. Toye, 'Introduction', p. 7.

85. J. Keegan, Introduction. In W. S. Churchill, *The Second World War, Volume 1: The Gathering Storm* (London: Penguin, 1985), pp. ix–xii, p. xi.

86. CAC, CHAR 20/57B/157–83, 185. Letter from 1st Lord Hankey [Paymaster-General] to Churchill enclosing memoranda on the use and techniques of Bomber Command, 27 May 1942.

87. M. Gilbert, *Auschwitz and the Allies: A Devastating Account of How the Allies Responded to the News of Hitler's Mass Murder* (London: Pimlico, 2001), p. 270.

88. Overy, 'Churchill and Airpower', p. 133.

89. CAC, CHAR 9/199A-D. Speeches: House of Commons: 'Prime Minister's Statement, "Flying Bombs", House of Commons', 6 July 1944.

90. *Hansard*, House of Lords debates. 'BOMBING POLICY', vol. 130, cols. 737–55, at 743, 9 February 1944.

91. Addison, *Churchill: The Unexpected Hero*, p. 193.

92. Garrett, The Bombing Campaign: The RAF, p. 28.

93. This figure was established by German historians in 2010 as part of a five-year review by the Dresden Historians' Commission into the historical evidence surrounding the Allied raids on the city between 13 and 15 February 1945. While still recognising the shocking destruction wreaked, the findings demonstrated how Joseph Goebbels' initial propagandic claims of 200,000-plus dead were considerably over-exaggerated. See M. Neutzner et al., *Abschlussbericht der Historikerkommission zu den Luftangriffen auf Dresden zwischen dem 13. und 15. February 1945* (Landeshauptstadt Dresden, 2010), www.dresden.de/media/pdf/infoblaetter/Historikerkommission—Dresden1945—Abschlussbericht—V1—14a.pdf.

94. See V. Gregg, *Dresden: A Survivor's Story, February 1945* (London: Bloomsbury, 2013); J. Friedrich, *The Fire: The Bombing of Germany, 1940–1945*. Translated from German by A. Brown (New York: Columbia University Press, 2008); and D. Bloxham, Dresden as a War Crime. In P. Addison and J. Crang (eds.), *Firestorm: The Bombing of Dresden, 1945* (London: Pimlico, 2006), pp. 180–208.

95. F. Taylor, *Dresden: Tuesday 13 February 1945* (London: Bloomsbury, 2005), p. 8.

96. S. Neitzel, The City Under Attack. In P. Addison and J. A. Crang (eds.), *Firestorm: The Bombing of Dresden, 1945* (London: Pimlico, 2006), pp. 62–77, p. 68.

97. T. D. Biddle, Wartime Reactions. In P. Addison and J. Crang (eds.), *Firestorm: The Bombing of Dresden, 1945* (London: Pimlico, 2006), pp. 96–122.

98. Taylor, *Dresden: Tuesday 13 February 1945*, p. 258.

99. A. W. Cooper, *Target Dresden* (Bromley: Independent Books, 1995), p. 201.

100. TNA, AIR 34/602. 'Dresden: Cartonnagenindustrie – Paper Factory' [Target Information Sheet], 4 January 1943.

101. Taylor, *Dresden: Tuesday 13 February 1945*, p. 65.

102. S. Cox, The Dresden Raids: Why and How. In P. Addison and J. Crang (eds.), *Firestorm: The Bombing of Dresden, 1945* (London: Pimlico, 2006), pp. 18–61, p. 54.

103. It has often been alleged that Stalin directly called for the city's bombardment, but Overy has dismissed this as 'one of the myths of Cold War history'. Although the Soviets wanted Dresden to be included in the Allied bombing line running through Berlin, Vienna and Zagreb, Harris recalled that Stalin had only verbally enquired about attacks on Leipzig – and not Dresden – during the Yalta Conference held between 4 and 11 February 1945. See R. Overy, The Post-War Debate. In P. Addison and J. Crang (eds.), *Firestorm: The Bombing of Dresden, 1945* (London: Pimlico, 2006), pp. 123–42; Taylor, *Dresden: Tuesday 13 February 1945*, p. 218.

104. Staatsbibliothek zu Berlin, *Leipziger Neueste Nachrichten*, DerTerrorangriff auf Dresden, Friday 16 February 1945.

105. Staatsbibliothek zu Berlin, *Leipziger Neueste Nachrichten*. 'Ein zynisches Dementi zum dem Terrorangriff gegen Dresden', Tuesday 20 February 1945.

106. Biddle, *Rhetoric and Reality in Air Warfare*, p. 256.

107. Taylor, *Dresden: Tuesday 13 February 1945*, p. 244.

108. Biddle, *Rhetoric and Reality in Air Warfare*, p. 254.

109. CAC, CHAR 9/199A-D. 'Prime Minister's Statement, "Flying Bombs", House of Commons', 6 July 1944.

110. Overy, Churchill and Airpower, p. 131.

111. Connelly, The British Debate, p. 198.

112. CAC, CHAR 20/229C/329. Telegram from the Air Ministry to Bomber Command passing on a message from Churchill to [Commander in Chief] Air Chief Marshal Sir Arthur Harris praising the 'decisive contribution' of Bomber Command, 15 May 1945.

113. CAC, CHUR 2/150A-B. Telegram from Churchill to Sir Arthur Harris, June 1946.

114. Addison, *Churchill: The Unexpected Hero*, p. 197.

115. Churchill, *The Second World War, Volume 5: Closing the Ring*, p. 456.

116. The British Newspaper Archive, *Belfast News-Letter*, 'Dresden bombing: "Churchill's plan to delay Reds"', Tuesday 14 February 1950, p. 5.

117. Churchill, *The Second World War, Volume 1: The Gathering Storm*, p. xvi.

118. *Hansard*, House of Lords debates. Marquess of Salisbury, 'The King's Speech: Address in Reply', vol. 166, at col. 40, 7 March 1950.

119. K. W. Thompson, *Winston Churchill's World View: Statesmanship and Power* (Baton Rouge: Louisiana State University Press, 1983), p. 21.

120. The British Newspaper Archive, *Daily Mirror*, B. McConnell, '"Ban" row over Churchill plan; Sir Winston maligned, says Board', Tuesday 25 April 1967.

121. Packwood, *How Churchill Waged War*, p. 11.

122. Churchill, *The Second World War, Volume 4: The Hinge of Fate*, p. 496.

Further Reading

T. D. Biddle, *Rhetoric and Reality in Air Warfare: The Evolution of British and American Ideas about Strategic Bombing, 1914–1945* (Princeton, NJ: Princeton University Press, 2002)

R. L. Blanco, *The Luftwaffe in World War II: The Rise and Decline of the German Air Force* (New York: Julian Messner, 1987)

M. Bowman, *Bomber Command: Reflections of War* (Barnsley: Pen & Sword, 2011)

C. Everitt and M. Middlebrook, *The Bomber Command War Diaries: An Operational Reference Book, 1939–1945* (Barnsley: Pen & Sword, 2014)

S. A. Garrett, The Bombing Campaign: The RAF. In R. Toye (ed.), *Winston Churchill: Politics, Strategy and Statecraft* (London: Bloomsbury, 2017), pp. 19–38

R. Overy, *The Bombers and the Bombed: Allied Air War over Europe, 1940–1945* (New York: Penguin, 2013)

R. Overy, Churchill and Airpower. In R. Toye (ed.), *Winston Churchill: Politics, Strategy and Statecraft* (London: Bloomsbury, 2017), pp. 127–37

R. Overy, *The Birth of the RAF* (London: Allen Lane, 2018)

K. Ruane, Churchill and Nuclear Weapons. In R. Toye (ed.), *Winston Churchill: Politics, Strategy and Statecraft* (London: Bloomsbury, 2017), pp. 171–86

F. Taylor, *Dresden: Tuesday 13 February 1945* (London: Bloomsbury, 2005)

D. Todman, *Britain's War: A New World, 1942–1947* (Oxford: Oxford University Press, 2020)

17

The Influence of Clementine Churchill

On the morning of 12 September 1948, in a villa at Cap d'Antibes in the south of France, a note was pushed under the bedroom door of a distinguished houseguest. Sent by Winston to his wife Clementine on the occasion of their fortieth wedding anniversary, the victorious war leader had decided it was time to pay tribute on paper. He wrote lovingly about how she had given him 'so much happiness in a world of accident and storm' but perhaps his most telling line was: 'I send this token, but how little can it express my gratitude to you for making my life & any work I have done possible.'[1]

As more books on the subject of Winston Churchill's family appear, it becomes ever more evident how his wife Clementine was a key to his greatness and ultimate success.[2] Indeed, he himself knew all too well just how much he owed to a woman whose exceptional role in history has until recently been largely overlooked or misunderstood.

She Who Commands

This was no mere dutiful gesture but a genuine recognition that Churchill would likely not have achieved greatness without his wife as his closest advisor and greatest influence. The extent of Clementine's role may not have been obvious to many outside the Churchills' innermost circle. After all, Winston had presented neither doubt nor weakness to a world watching his every move in June 1940. Since he had declared that Britain would 'never surrender', his had become the voice of defiance, strength and valour and a beacon of hope. Stalin, no natural admirer or friend, conceded that he could think of no other instance in history when the future of the world had so depended on the resolve of one man.[3]

And yet Winston's road to such historic stature was pitted with blunders and setbacks that more than once looked almost certain to wreck his career. Clementine steered him through his crises and stuck by him when he was out of office and out of favour, forever plotting his way back into power, always believing, as she put it, in 'his star'. And just as the prospect of the 'call of honour' thrilled his 'being'[4] when Britain declared war on Germany in 1939, he noted with pride that his wife was equally 'braced'[5] for whatever the future held. As soon as the then Prime Minister Neville Chamberlain summoned Winston to Downing Street to appoint him first lord of the admiralty, Clementine also sprang into action.

She called together a large group of supporters, set about transforming his office into a modern command centre and, fully briefed about the navy's engagements with the enemy, was soon accompanying Winston to Plymouth when the ships sailed in. It was her idea, when the crews from the battle of the River Plate were being honoured, to set up a special enclosure on Horse Guards Parade for the families of the bereaved to show them respect and consideration. Of course, she was an old hand with the navy from Winston's time at the Admiralty in the Great War – when she had also broken with convention to accompany him to inspect battleships, advise on appointments and personally congratulate admirals on their victories, rewarding them with invitations to lunch.

These touches and many more were a reflection of her total involvement in Winston's career and how she constantly protected and projected her husband. She counselled but also challenged him, consoled but also chided him. He depended on her utterly at the peak – and the troughs – of his powers and throughout their sometimes tempestuous marriage.

She was no easy touch. She intervened to try to steer him on another course and, when she thought it absolutely necessary, privately took the side of staff or colleagues against him. She was often the only member of his inner circle to argue against his opinion – and he always listened and quite often conceded with the words, 'I see you were right'. It was not unknown for him to call his wife 'She whose commands must be obeyed' – only partly in jest.

Clementine shored up his inadequacies (particularly his impetuosity and sentimentality) and moderated his extremes (forever reminding him to curb his temper and to help those outside his gilded circle). She was in some ways his ultimate authority; certainly his conscience and the nearest he (as an aristocrat born in a palace who never took the bus and only once ventured on the Tube) had to a direct line to the people. The way Clementine managed a character described by his wartime deputy prime minister and successor Clement Attlee as 'fifty per cent genius, fifty per cent bloody fool' was itself a kind of genius.[6]

And yet, particularly in the early days of their marriage, she had been the object of scorn for her rackety background and ridicule for her shyness. The unflattering chatter about her uncertain paternity, relative poverty (she made some of her own clothes despite being the granddaughter of an earl) and tendency to blush rose to the point that her husband would exclaim in frustration that there was more to his new bride 'than meets the eye'.

Her occasional sternness, her willingness to challenge her husband and her dislike of his male cronies – notably the three 'Bs', Brendan Bracken and Lords Beaverbrook and Birkenhead – have often seen her written off (as shrewish) or written out (the index of Nigel Knight's 405-page tome is titled *Churchill: The Greatest Briton Unmasked* but does not mention her once).[7]

Clementine was hardly raised for such a role: she was born into cash-strapped Victorian aristocracy in 1885 and raised to marry a rich peer. Like Winston, she did not attend university and her mother Lady Blanche was (also like Winston's) often absent, more preoccupied with entertaining her lovers. And yet Clementine achieved an understanding and intuition about events and people that made up for Winston's own shortcomings (particularly in understanding other people) and maximised his gifts. Since she did not seek attention, she has hitherto largely not been granted it.[8] But as we will see, she was a fully engaged partner in her husband's political career, especially during both wars.

Closer reading of the diaries, memoirs and letters of those who saw the Churchills in action at close range reveal how she was consigliere, speech-editor, spin-doctor (before the term was invented), personal pollster (through her enormous mailbag and frequent tours of streets and air-raid shelters) and even a sort of chief of staff. It is for this reason that recent on-screen portrayals by leading actresses have beefed up her role. Harriet Walter in *The Crown* and Kristin Scott Thomas in *Darkest*

Hour both fought for Clementine to be given at least part of her due, with some success. We are perhaps edging towards a consensus that Clementine should not be relegated to the long-suffering observer depicted in the past, but recognised as a vibrant and essential figure.

The Churchills' partnership – she remained a solid Liberal even when he re-ratted to the Tories – was perhaps the ultimate political coalition. Who else could have persuaded a man who railed against 'cocksure' women to go on to vote for limited female suffrage in 1918 (even if it was in part out of self-interest, believing that many would vote for him)? A decade later he earned a rebuke from his wife for 'naughtily' abstaining in a bill designed to give women the same voting rights as men, but she continued to work on him and unsuccessfully pushed for Churchill College to be made co-educational from the time of its foundation in the late 1950s.

Perhaps her greatest success on this was convincing him that while the Second World War was to be fought by men, it could only be won with the endurance and strength of women. She, like many others, had discovered what she was capable of – not least setting up and running vast canteens for munitions workers and fronting a campaign on gas masks – when called to action in the First World War. Now with Britain facing an even greater crisis, she made it clear to Winston that women would be more vital than ever. He still remembered his rough treatment at the hands of the suffragettes – one of whom tried to push him in front of a train until Clementine pulled him back by the coat-tails – and was initially unenthused by the idea of women serving in auxiliary military roles. But she persevered and he became one of the first to appreciate that the country could not win through the sacrifice of its menfolk alone.

By January 1940 Winston was aiming to draft a million women to work in munitions and aircraft factories. With her help – and the example of her three adult daughters, Diana, Sarah and Mary, who each donned military uniforms during the war – the government enlisted women to man anti-aircraft guns, analyse intelligence, fly aircraft from factories to airfields and monitor fires from roof-tops during air-raids. Both Winston and Clementine were proud of their daughters serving the war effort in this way – particularly Mary, who rose to the rank of a junior officer in the anti-aircraft batteries of the Auxiliary Territorial Service and Sarah, who became a valued photographic interpreter at RAF Medmenham. Their service and those of many of their female compatriots in these most untraditional roles were noticed by visiting Americans, who came away with the belief that 'it is the spirit of the women that is carrying this country'.[9] Winston too was struck by how essential their contribution had become.

Clementine's own role was, however, the most vital of all. Let us consult Lord Moran, both Winston's doctor and semi-permanent companion during the Second World War, for his view on the Clementine effect. While tending his exceptional patient, Moran came to the conclusion that Winston's famous conviction that led a nation to victory against impossible odds began 'in his own bedroom'. His strength, Moran noted, drew on another's, one whom her husband depended on entirely and who was inextricably involved in every aspect of his career.

This national saviour and global powerhouse was after all also human, and far from the emotional island devoid of the need for personal sustenance, as many historians have depicted him. Another Churchill intimate – Violet Asquith, who adored Winston all his life and as a young and brilliant woman had dreamed of marrying him – noted that he was 'armed to the teeth for life's encounter' but was 'strangely vulnerable' and in need of 'protection'.[10]

It was to Violet's eternal sadness that she could not provide that 'protection' and that the role fell to Clementine, whatever the challenge, whatever the occasion. As Violet admitted later in life to her once bitter rival – whom she at first held in open contempt – she would never have done as Winston's wife. The less competitive Clementine alone had a 'private line' through to her exceptional life companion.[11]

Take 5 June 1944, the night before D-Day, a tortured evening given the uncertainties and dangers about to confront so many thousands of young men. Clementine had already intervened, helped by the king, to stop Winston's plan to watch the battle unfold from the bridge of the cruiser HMS *Belfast*. Such a move would have been a distraction and a folly on behalf of the prime minister, who had refused to listen to anyone else's pleas to drop the idea. Now, however, he had agreed to count down the final hours back in London. But during that tense summer's evening only she knew the particular torment in which Winston found himself just as huge convoys of Allied ships were moving through the darkness towards their battle stations off the coast of Normandy.

Wearing an elegant silk housecoat that covered her nightdress, with her face still fully made up and looking immaculate as ever, she walked past the royal marine guards into the Downing Street Map Room. She looked serene at this late hour but the atmosphere around her at the heart of British military command was anything but. A team of grave-faced 'plotters' were busily tracking troops, trucks and ships on their charts. A central table buzzed to the sound of several phones ringing at once.

Over in the far corner she saw, as she expected, Winston, with shoulders hunched, his jowly face cast in agonised brooding. She went to him as she always did and knew she must, because no aide, no general, no minister or friend, however loyal, could help him now. Clementine was one of a tiny group privy to the years of top-secret preparations of what would be the largest seaborne invasion in history. She knew only too well the unthinkable price of failure. Millions would remain under Nazi tyranny, their hopes of liberation dashed perhaps indefinitely.

Clementine also understood, however, what others perhaps could not know. Winston was haunted by the loss of the thousands of men he had sent to their deaths in the Dardanelles campaign of the First World War and feared another, even bloodier catastrophe on the beaches of Normandy. She alone had sustained him through that disaster – and encouraged him to take up painting as a distraction – and endured with him the lion's share of the blame for the devastating bloodshed (and the social Siberia that ensued).

Clementine had also supported him through the horrors of his time serving in the trenches on the Western Front, even as she set about enacting a brilliant strategy to resurrect his good name and political career back home via a one-woman lobbying campaign that drew in the prime minister, newspaper editors and proprietors, and military chiefs. It had been her idea that he stay in the trenches – despite the evident risk a 'wicked bullet' might find him – long enough to acquire what she called a 'military halo' and consequent political redemption back home. It was not the only time she stepped in to rescue his rollercoaster of a career or risked his wrath for arguing against him.[12]

Now, thirty years later in June 1944, tens of thousands more young men were to risk their lives in northern France on his orders (although of course under the direct command of US General Dwight Eisenhower). Winston had long had misgivings about Operation Overlord, fearing British, Canadian and American lives might be sacrificed on a hastily conceived European incursion merely to meet Stalin's demands for a second front. He delayed it for as long as he could to ensure the greatest chance of success in the hope of minimising casualties. But now thousands of Allied troops were in a few short hours to attempt to take a heavily fortified coastline defended by what were regarded as the world's best soldiers.

Earlier in the evening, Clementine had discussed the prospects of the invasion's success again, at length and alone over a candle-lit dinner. Winston no doubt poured out his fears and Clementine no doubt sought to stiffen his resolve, as she had so often done before. She was fully aware of the details as well as the dangers, but there was no way back. Now, as she approached him in the Map Room, he turned to his wife and asked rhetorically: 'Do you realise that by the time you wake up in the morning twenty thousand men may have been killed?'[13]

First Lady

On D-Day itself, Winston lunched with the king while they waited for news and Clementine ate with the head of the British army, General Alan Brooke. The arrangement was nothing unusual and reflected her pivotal involvement in Winston's conduct of the war and close relationship with the military top brass. Despite the fact her position as a mere prime minister's wife was poorly defined and resourced compared to the heavily staffed Office of the First Lady in the USA, Clementine arguably played a far greater role in the Second World War than the greatest of American First Ladies and her direct contemporary Eleanor Roosevelt.

Eleanor long remained a more public and famous figure than Clementine. She had become much-loved for her approachability and pioneering work during the 1930s for the New Deal and had evidently done much to help propel her husband Franklin to the White House. Yet when America entered the war, she found herself more and more excluded by the president. In fact, Roosevelt waited right up until the evening before D-Day, just as Eleanor was retiring to bed, to brief her for the first time on the invasion. This reticence with her led to a feeling of redundancy and Eleanor began to describe her reduced role as that of a 'plain citizen'[14] who had to 'allow the important people' to take the decisions.

She was, however, an adept politician in her own right, even if mostly away from the White House – most productively as advocate for the rights of Black servicemen, who at the time were segregated. And she remained a key role model for Clementine to step further into the public eye.

The difference in their respective roles at the centre of power was brought into stark contrast by the Quebec Conference between Churchill and Roosevelt in August 1943, which had been called to discuss the imminent landings in Italy and the next steps in Europe. Some 200 people joined the prime minister for this most crucial meeting, and for the first time the entourage included Clementine, who was accustomed to advising her husband on his wartime meetings with foreign leaders but had not travelled with him to one before.[15]

Her inclusion was a bold, pioneering move – but also reflected the exhausted Winston's dependence on his wife in so many ways. Her advice was regularly sought or offered on how best to protect key alliances. On this occasion, she intended to take a more active part as Winston sensed his influence over Roosevelt was waning. Knowing full well the power of personal chemistry, Clementine was to use her considerable charm in an attempt to woo the president to the Churchill way of thinking, just as she had previously so adeptly made supporters of his most influential advisors Gil Winant (the American ambassador to Britain), Harry Hopkins (Roosevelt's right-hand man) and Averell Harriman (another of his key envoys).

Such conferences were traditionally all-male events, but the Churchills' daughter Mary was also to attend as her father's aide-de-camp. When Roosevelt was notified by Winston that the two women would be key members of his official team, the president cabled back, 'I am perfectly delighted.'[16] In truth, it set an awkward precedent to which the president responded by dispatching Eleanor to visit American troops in the Pacific. He did invite his cousin Daisy Suckley – but merely in a limited and traditionally feminine role of hostess.

On an earlier wartime visit to the White House, Winston had been aghast at Eleanor's exclusion. 'You know I tell Clemmie everything', he told Roosevelt, who replied, 'Well, I don't do that.'[17] It is all the more remarkable given that Clementine, who had no official staff, role model or guidebook, invented her wartime role from scratch, eventually persuading an initially reluctant government machine to help her.

Her role in editing and rehearsing Winston's speeches was a long-standing one that she had honed over time, sending him a prompt by handwritten note if he was tardy in sending her the draft. By the time the Churchills entered Downing Street in 1940, she was to be found suggesting words (she urged him at the beginning of the Second World War to use simple vocabulary that someone with only an elementary education would understand without recourse to a dictionary), urging him to remove unnecessarily provocative comments, rehearsing his delivery and suggesting valuable additions that would rouse popular support or cement the bond between the Allies. It was her approval that Winston sought after he delivered a speech, asking, 'Was that alright?'

Gil Winant, the shy but effective American ambassador, was just one of the circle of Churchill intimates to come to recognise this as just one of many of her quiet achievements. He wrote to her on one occasion to ask her to congratulate Winston on 'one of the greatest [speeches] of its kind ever made'. He knew that she had played her part in its success and added: 'I especially liked the references to [the Free French leader General] de Gaulle and France and felt that perhaps you had had something to do with it.'[18]

It was a classic Clementine intervention, for brokering peace between the dominant and fractious egos leading the Allies was both fraught and essential. As Winston himself remarked at Chequers on 1 April 1945, 'there is only one thing worse than fighting with allies, that is fighting without them'.[19] Her work was helped by the respect she inspired in the other leaders.

Charles de Gaulle never forgot the experience when he came to lunch in the small white dining room at Downing Street in mid-summer 1940, shortly after Winston had ordered the Royal Navy to open fire on the French fleet anchored at Oran in North Africa. It had been a brutal decision, leading to 1,300 deaths and considerable fury among the French, but an undeniably necessary one to stop much of the well-armed French navy from falling into enemy hands. France had now capitulated to the Nazis and the battleships might have been commandeered by the Nazis or their allies.

The conversation inevitably turned to the future of the remaining French fleet and Clementine said she hoped it would rally behind the British. The famously prickly de Gaulle replied that it would provide the French with more satisfaction to turn their guns on the British instead. She bristled at what she considered an unacceptable response and in stately French upbraided him for comments ill suited to an ally, let alone a guest. Winston intervened at this point to placate the general: 'You must forgive my wife. *Elle parle trop bien le français.*'

Most political spouses would have been chastened and perhaps retreated at this point. But Clementine was unafraid of the great men around the table and would fight her corner against both if necessary. Glaring at her husband, she retorted again in French: 'Winston, it's not that at all. There are certain things that a woman can say to a man which a man cannot say, and I am saying them to you, General de Gaulle!'

The Frenchman apologised repeatedly to his hostess and the following day sent her a huge bouquet of flowers. The Churchills' daughter-in-law Pamela witnessed the spat, seeing it as just one of many examples of Clementine's unique ability to say 'no' to Winston. 'She did that often, often, often . . . .'[20] Clementine was not only hard on herself to succeed but also on occasion her husband. In one sitting, however, Clementine had faced down not only Winston but another of the most powerful men in the fragile alliance against Germany. She earned in the process the undying respect of both of them, which would again and again come in useful.

By early 1944, Roosevelt's loathing of de Gaulle was obvious, as was the utter indifference on behalf of Stalin as to the fate of the French as a whole. The Free French leader's mercurial temperament – not least arranging and cancelling meetings with Winston apparently at whim – had driven even the prime minister (a great lover of France and supporter of its cause) to distraction. He had even considered placing de Gaulle under house arrest at one point for 'insubordination'. Now the Frenchman had caused Winston apoplexy with a 'boorish' and unappreciative message that took no account of the special pleading that Britain constantly exercised for its ally.

De Gaulle was now finally on his way to see the prime minister in what promised to be a stormy confrontation in Morocco, where Winston was only just recovering from being gravely ill. With Roosevelt increasingly ready to tread roughshod over Winston's wishes and Stalin's often outright hostility, Clementine knew full well just how important de Gaulle's continuing support was as the war reached its culminating stages. 'I am trying to smooth Papa down', Clementine reported to her family, although she was also lecturing him on the need to avoid antagonising de Gaulle unnecessarily. 'I hope there will be no explosions!'[21]

She was waiting to pounce as soon as the French leader arrived. Quickly separating him from his aides and steering him into the garden, she knew she needed to speak to him in all frankness and alone. Another of the Churchills' daughters, Sarah, overheard at least part of the conversation, however, during which Clementine was heard to remark pointedly: '*Mon Général*, you must take care not to hate your allies more than your enemies.'[22]

Details of the remainder of their encounter remain unknown, but de Gaulle reappeared shortly afterwards in a particularly good mood and the subsequent lunch and discussions with Winston played out far more amicably than expected. Most unusually, de Gaulle even insisted on speaking in English as a personal olive branch. The Franco-British alliance – like the others so dependent on the personal rapport of the principals involved – was in good hands. (Indeed, Clementine's friendship with de Gaulle survived the post-war years. On the first anniversary of Winston's death Clementine received only one commemorative letter, a warmly effusive handwritten note from the then President de Gaulle.)

Russian and American Diplomacy

Winston's relationship with Stalin was even more fraught. The Soviet leader was not only incensed at the lack of British military assistance when millions of Russians were dying but had also neither forgotten nor

Figure 17.1 The prime minister symbolically 'buying a flag' from his wife Clementine on Aid to Russia Day. Her chairmanship of the Red Cross Aid to Russia Fund was just the most visible way in which she assisted his premiership (CAC, Broadwater Collection, BRDW V 3/4).

forgiven Churchill's attempts to 'strangle Bolshevism at birth' by intervening on the side of the White Russians following the 1918 Armistice. It was clear to all that it was vital to defuse this history of antagonism and keep a suspicious Kremlin onside. After all, Stalin had started the war on the other side and could not be allowed to return to his old ally in Berlin by seeking a separate peace. It would be almost as disastrous if Moscow became too close to Washington and moved to shut Britain out.

Furthermore, by late 1941 public opinion in Britain had become deeply admiring of the Russians' stoic resistance bought at such a high price in blood. Thousands of people wrote every week to Clementine – who had become the human face of the entire Churchill wartime government – to say they were 'disturbed and distressed' at Britain's apparent inability or unwillingness to help. It was highly useful feedback from the home front, but Britain simply did not have the resources to send more military hardware to Russia. Another solution was needed to cement the alliance and head off the potential for trouble back home. Clementine suggested one and Winston agreed to it – but neither could have predicted the extent of her success.

Clementine had originally launched her Red Cross Aid to Russia Fund in October 1941 and by Christmas that year had already raised £1 million. Now the Fund was to be stepped up again and presented as a critical show of support for the Russian people. With a brilliant public relations campaign she galvanised factory workers, millionaires and widows; she organised auctions, flag days and galas and pioneered the idea of celebrity musicians giving fundraiser concerts and charity football matches. Soon hundreds of thousands of tons of medical supplies were on their way to Russia from a country itself struggling desperately with shortages. She appealed to schoolgirls to knit gloves, scarves and hats for the Russian forces and sent them letters of thanks that many kept for the rest of their lives.[23] In all, Clementine raised the equivalent of hundreds of millions of pounds, as well as attracting the right sort of attention in Moscow.

Stalin, who had so belittled her husband, was astonished by what she achieved. In April 1945 – even as relations between Soviet Russia and Britain were growing icier by the day over the Red Army's occupation of Poland – he sent word that he would like to honour her in person for her work. Initially Winston hesitated to let her go; some of his biographers such as Roy Jenkins have since criticised her for accepting the invitation.[24] But it was undoubtedly a singular honour and she hoped it would reap diplomatic dividends while the war was not yet won, particularly in the Pacific where Russian military support might be needed (as at this point the atom bomb remained an unknown and untested quantity).

Eventually she left, to be greeted at Moscow aerodrome by, among others, Foreign Minister Molotov. As she toured hospitals from Moscow to Stalingrad – all equipped by her Red Cross Fund – cheering crowds threw violets at her feet. Concerts and ballet performances were put on to celebrate her visit. In Leningrad, she received word that Stalin was to award her the prestigious Order of the Red Banner of Labour.

Reports of her popularity – and the fact that both American and British officials commented that she was the one bright spot in Anglo-Russian relations – made Winston burst with pride. Clementine was even – most unusually – invited to meet Stalin himself in his vast study in the Kremlin Senate, accompanied only by an interpreter and secretary. It was an extraordinary meeting at an exceptional time – for as her interpreter Hugh Lunghi noted, 'the alliance [with Russia] was about to break up so it was important to get every little clue as to what Stalin was thinking'.[25]

No other Western prime minister's or president's spouse can claim an encounter like it – Stalin welcoming a Western woman, and a Churchill, into the Kremlin, and in her own right. It also took place against the backdrop of a growing crisis between Moscow and London, which Winston described to Clementine in a letter as 'dynamite'.[26] Set against what is now considered to be the early stages of the Cold War, the meeting – and other aspects of the tour – remained largely unknown, even secret, for more than seventy years.

Receiving regular briefings from senior British military officers, Clementine also made use of her time in Moscow to engineer a meeting with Josip Tito, leader of the communist Yugoslav partisans, with the aim of gleaning intelligence on their behalf on his potential designs on the Italian city of Trieste. Separately Clementine remonstrated with Russian officials about Soviet atrocities now reported to be taking place in Poland. She believed that Britain had to stand up to the great Russian bear.

Stalin was obviously a tough nut to crack, but so was the other member of the Big Three, FDR. Clementine's personal goal of charming the American president – who typically adored the company of attractive women – was predicated on her exceptional success in recruiting his chief envoys as devotees as part of the Churchills' desperate pre-Pearl Harbor bid to bring America into the war as Britain's only true hope of long-term survival.

Known for his virulent Anglo-sceptic views, Harry Hopkins arrived in Britain in early 1941 as Roosevelt's emissary determined to resist the prime minister's legendary persuasiveness.[27] Instinctively an isolationist, he doubted whether Britain was even worth saving. Clementine set about changing his mind, choreographing every minute of his day to witness the spirit of the British people and the immediacy of the Nazi threat, and exercising her full personal magic to drive home the British cause.

By the time he was ready to return to Washington with his report, Hopkins was a convert, a fervent partisan to the British cause and a believer in Winston's greatness as a leader, but in no doubt at all that 'the most charming and entertaining of all the people' he had met on his extended six-week trip was 'Mrs Churchill'.[28] Back home he persuaded the once sceptical Roosevelt that America must do all it could to help Britain with military hardware but also urgent financial aid.

This double-handed Churchillian seduction of influential Americans continued apace with other Roosevelt envoys. Averell Harriman, sent to London to take charge of the lend-lease military aid, was literally seduced by their daughter-in-law Pamela, with certainly what appears to be the tacit approval of Clementine and Winston. They also frequently invited him to intimate Churchill dinners where excellent food, wine and conversation also weaved a certain memorable magic. When he returned home, Harriman was such a fervent Britain supporter some concluded he must have been 'bewitched'.

Clementine also befriended Janet Murrow, spotting the opportunity for Winston to get close to her husband, the phenomenally influential CBS journalist Ed (whose reports helped to turn American public opinion in Britain's favour and who is credited with coining the phrase that Churchill mobilised the English language and sent it into battle). Clementine's friendship with the US ambassador, Gil Winant, also paid dividends in American support. Watching her at close range touring bombsites, talking to people left with little of their lives beyond piles of rubble, he saw the particularly 'great appreciation' she stirred in middle-aged women, who seemed uplifted by her presence. He then noted how she sent officials scurrying off to give them shelter, food and clothes for them and their families, without fuss or a need for glory, and in so doing had become their quiet and trusted champion. He puzzled at how British newspapers and indeed the government made so little of what she did out on the streets and behind closed doors. 'If the future breeds historians of understanding', he wrote shortly after the return of peace, her 'service to Great Britain' will finally be 'given the full measure [it] deserves.'[29]

It is, then, perhaps even more surprising that Clementine and FDR himself never really hit it off; her famous charm was largely ineffective in his presence. When they first met at the conference in Quebec in August 1943, she in her turn was disappointed by the man whom her husband so adored. She thought him vain; he thought her reserved. She was more successful in winning over the American people, attracting gushing notices for her first ever press conference, after which she was hailed as 'Winston's greatest asset'.

Quebec was also an occasion when it became abundantly clear that the Americans were generally in the driving seat and that for all the Churchills' efforts, Britain's leading role in the war was now transparently over. Sensing Roosevelt's interest in Churchill and his ideas was waning, she advised her husband to be wary in his dealings with the president. She understood the strategic imperative of befriending Roosevelt – and later in the war insisted on Winston dropping his support for the return of the unpopular king in Greece not least because of the damage such a course would wreak on Anglo-American relations. She knew Britain depended on the USA for food as well as military muscle and would be financially sunk if the lend-lease aid programme was curtailed, let alone closed.

She considered Winston to be too sentimental and emotionally transparent and warned him to be more guarded with the president. Indeed, he soon discovered the true nature of his 'friendship' with Roosevelt at the Big Three conference in Tehran in December 1943, where the American openly chose Stalin over Winston, and even found it amusing when the Russian leader bullied his British ally.

Managing Winston

No-one knew Winston better than Clementine or indeed how he should – like so many political leaders – be best managed. During the war, he became, in her words, 'rather naughty' in all sorts of ways.

During night raids, while the bombs were falling and fires raging, he liked to go out with a torch and see the damage for himself. These excursions understandably prompted alarm in his private office and among his ministers and military top brass. Many a brave man tried and failed to stop the prime minister on his way to the front door of Downing Street.

As so often when all else failed, Clementine provided the backstop. Quietly asked to intervene, she was ready in coat and scarf to join him on his next expedition even while the raid was still underway. 'This time, concerned for *her* safety, he returned home before nightfall', recalled General 'Pug' Ismay, Winston's chief of staff. 'This was her technique. She knew perfectly how to handle him.'[30]

She saw it as her first duty to keep Winston alive for the sake of his country. His recklessness spurred her to establish what became known as her 'espionage' network, whereby his staff would tip her off if he was planning something unduly dangerous. When she was informed that he had refused to travel in his armoured car during a raid, she hid all his other vehicles so that he had no choice. On another occasion, she instructed his valet to remove his boots until Winston ordered him to fetch them at once and the poor man had no option but to obey.

That said, she knew too well when her husband had to face danger to do his job and was prepared to take a difficult decision when necessary. Since the early and accident-prone days of flight at the beginning of her marriage, she had always greatly feared her husband taking off in dangerous conditions. From the insouciance of his youth, Winston too had become a nervous flyer. Before the war she had always tried to dissuade him from taking to the air, but in June 1940 he resolved to fly to France through rough weather to try to convince its leaders to continue to fight.

Having run out of other avenues to persuade the prime minister it was too risky, the air staff petitioned Clementine. She listened and then asked: 'Is the RAF flying today?' 'Yes, of course, on operations', they responded. She came back with: 'Well, isn't Winston going on an operation?' Her decision, made in the national interest over her own, was final.[31]

Winston becoming prime minister of course brought out the best in him – his vision, his oratory, his single-mindedness. But it also perhaps brought out the worst. Never before or since has a British premier accrued such wide powers or exerted similar control over the operation of a conflict. He was not only the king's first minister but minister of defence as well and 'thus ... became virtually a dictator', as one close observer put it.[32] Like all dictators, he invoked fear, in his case in officials, ministers, military commanders and most everyone else. Even his family described his leadership style as tyrannical.

Drawing on her experience of her husband in the First World War, Clementine had seen the dangers of his tendency to browbeat opposition. His failure to bring colleagues onside with him on the ill-fated Dardanelles expedition had led to him becoming the scapegoat for others' failings as well as his own once the scale of the tragedy had unfolded. She had warned him then of the dangers of passive acquiescence and saw the urgency of doing so again. When he took office in May 1940 she took the trouble to invite key members of staff to take tea with her alone in her private retreat in Downing Street. She made them feel appreciated, won their trust and sounded them out for signs of trouble. It soon came.

One private session with an undisclosed member of Winston's entourage took place in mid-June when Britain's situation could barely have been more critical. France, Britain's only major ally, was on the point of capitulation and the British Expeditionary Force had retreated from Dunkirk, leaving huge loss of materiel. Meanwhile, Germany was massing vast numbers of bombers and fighters just across the Channel for what many feared would be imminent invasion. Winston was all too aware of the peril from the Nazis but seemed oblivious to the mounting dangers at home.

Clementine gleaned, however, that Winston's manner risked if not outright rebellion from his staff then a dangerous and hostile 'slave mentality'. She knew she had to calibrate her next move extremely carefully and so tore up her first letter to Winston to think again. Then she once more took to paper. The effect was incalculable in the way in which Winston went on to lead.

'I hope you will forgive me if I tell you something that I feel you ought to know', she began. There was a 'danger' of him being 'disliked' because of his increasingly 'rough, sarcastic and overbearing manner' which had led to his closest staff escaping as soon as they could 'from his presence'. Senior colleagues complained that he was 'contemptuous' of their ideas and now few dared to venture any, good or bad. He could exercise 'terrific power' and sack anybody, but with that came the need to 'combine urbanity, kindness and if possible Olympic calm. Besides you won't get the best results by irascibility and rudeness. They will breed either dislike or a slave mentality .... Your loving, devoted and watchful Clemmie.'[33]

No answer to her letter has been found but Winston did change. While his staff continued to find him impossible on occasion, dislike gave way to affection, with some even coming to view the boss as 'lovable'. One official remarked that the prime minister's 'ill-tempered phase' had been a passing one. Others were grateful for the conciliatory power of a small gesture, with one private secretary recalling him putting his hand on his shoulder after a fraught few hours and saying: 'I may seem very fierce, but I am fierce with only one man – Hitler.'[34] Winston remembered to show his gratitude from time to time and make life entertaining and colourful when he could, often over the dinner table or drinks and treating his staff almost as family.

Living onsite in Downing Street meant that Clementine could continue to monitor her husband's behaviour. As Pamela Churchill (who was living with them at the time) observed, her mother-in-law's intervention demonstrated to others 'that she was an enormously important component in the whole thing ... and a very important balance for him'. Clementine was rightly convinced that 'if anything happened to her, Winston might run amok'.[35]

It is perhaps no surprise, then, that Clementine's many roles in supporting her illustrious husband absorbed almost all her energy and time, leaving her little of either for herself or her family. It was a year after Winston died that a Labour prime minister, Harold Winston, finally formally recognised Clementine's very great talents as a politician by appointing her to the House of Lords in her own right. Her obvious excitement at the honour – which she marked by taking a seat on the non-partisan crossbenches – was, however, marred by the fact that she was by then eighty years of age with failing hearing. It was, despite all her efforts, really too late for her to make the renewed contribution to national life that she had so wanted to make. She nevertheless ensured that she did what she could to protect her husband's legacy – through the opening to the public of the family home, Chartwell in Kent, and her support for Churchill College, Cambridge, which also houses the rich treasures of the Churchill family archives.

The other great casualties of her devotion to Winston, of course, were most notably her relationships with her children – particularly the obstreperous Randolph and the troubled Diana – and her own health.

Both Winston and Clementine were absent and imperfect parents and their offspring – with the possible exception of Mary – plainly suffered as a result. Clementine was undoubtedly a better wife and political partner than mother, but whereas she tended Winston's afflictions including the famous 'Black Dog', he was usually at a loss as to how to help her with her recurrent nervous complaints and far more serious bouts of depression. She struggled alone, only a handful of close friends realising that the unceasing demands of her chosen vocation had taken a terrible toll.

Clementine nevertheless found the resources and strength to offer a much-needed countervailing force to her husband throughout their near fifty-seven years of marriage, all the while being his protector and mainstay. She maximised his strengths and bore down on his weaknesses. General Ismay – no feminist, he – was constantly struck by her effectiveness and purpose. After more than five years with the Churchills he concluded that Winston, the embodiment of British courage and resolve, took his strength 'from Clemmie'. Without her, he wrote, the 'history of Winston Churchill and of the world would have been a very different story'.[36]

Notes

1. M. Soames (ed.), *Speaking for Themselves: The Personal Letters of Winston and Clementine Churchill* (London: Doubleday, 1998), p. 549. For original letter, see CAC, Baroness Spencer-Churchill Papers, CSCT 2/37.
2. For the most recent biography of Clementine Churchill, see S. Purnell, *First Lady: The Life and Wars of Clementine Churchill* (London: Aurum Press, 2015); for recent books on the Churchill family, see C. Katz, *Daughters of Yalta* (London: William Collins, 2020); J. Ireland, *Churchill and Son* (New York: Dutton, 2021); and R. Trethewey, *The Churchill Girls* (Cheltenham: The History Press, 2021).
3. Lord Moran, *Winston Churchill: The Struggle for Survival* (London: Constable, 1966), p. 227.
4. W. S. Churchill, *The Second World War, Volume 1: The Gathering Storm* (London: Cassell & Co. Ltd, 1948), p. 320.
5. Churchill, *The Second World War*, p. 319.
6. Lord Moran, *Churchill: The Struggle for Survival*, p. 777.
7. N. Knight, *Churchill: The Greatest Briton Unmasked* (Newton Abbot: David & Charles, 2009).
8. One notable exception is Mary Soames' biography of her mother; see M. Soames, *Clementine Churchill*, rev. ed. (London: Doubleday, 1998).
9. Library of Congress, Harriman Papers, Box 159.
10. Violet Bonham Carter, *Winston Churchill As I Knew Him* (London: Eyre and Spottiswoode, 1965), p. 18.
11. CAC, Baroness Spencer-Churchill Papers, CSCT 3/111, letter from Lady Bonham Carter to Clementine, 1962.

12. From a selection of letters between Winston and Clementine during March and April 1916. See CAC, Churchill Papers and Baroness Spencer-Churchill Papers. See also M. Soames, *Speaking for Themselves*.

13. O. Pawle, *The War and Colonel Warden: Based on the Recollections of C.R. Thompson, Personal Assistant to the Prime Minister, 1940–1945* (London: G.G. Harrap, 1963), p. 302.

14. D. Kearns Goodwin, *No Ordinary Time: Franklin and Eleanor Roosevelt – The Home Front in World War II* (New York: Simon & Schuster, 1994), p. 82.

15. Though she had accompanied him to pre-war conferences, such as the Cairo Conference of 1921.

16. J. Meacham, *Franklin and Winston* (New York: Random House, 2003), p. 228.

17. Meacham, *Franklin and Winston*, p. 21.

18. CAC, Baroness Spencer-Churchill Papers, CSCT 3/43, dated 2 August but no year.

19. A. Bryant, *Triumph in the West: Completing the War Diaries of Field Marshal Viscount Alanbrooke* (London: Collins, 1959), p. 445. Diary entry, 1 April 1945.

20. Library of Congress, Pamela Harriman Papers, Box 3.

21. M. Soames, *Clementine Churchill*, rev. ed. (London: Doubleday, 1998), p. 385.

22. Soames, *Clementine Churchill*, p. 386.

23. The author Barbara Taylor Bradford presented one such note to the Churchill Archives Centre in Cambridge.

24. R. Jenkins, *Churchill* (London: Macmillan, 2001), p. 786.

25. CAC, Churchill Oral History. CHOH 3 CSCT, Hugh Lunghi interview, 12 September 2012.

26. M. Soames, *Speaking for Themselves*, p. 522; CAC, Baroness Spencer-Churchill Papers, CSCT 2/34, 6 April 1945.

27. R. Sherwood, *Roosevelt and Hopkins: An Intimate History* (New York: Harper & Bro., 1948), p. 232.

28. Sherwood, *Roosevelt and Hopkins*, p. 241.

29. G. Winant, *A Letter from Grosvenor Square* (London: Hodder & Stoughton, 1947), p. 46.

30. J. Fishman, *My Darling Clementine* (London: W. H. Allen, 1963), p. 153.

31. Fishman, *My Darling Clementine*, p. 151.

32. V. Cowles, *Winston Churchill: The Era and the Man* (London: Hamilton, 1953), p. 318.

33. CAC, Baroness Spencer-Churchill Papers, CSCT 1/24, letter of 27 June 1940.

34. J. Wheeler-Bennet (ed.), *Action This Day: Working with Churchill* (London: Macmillan, 1968), p. 140.

35. Library of Congress, Pamela Harriman Papers, Box 3.

36. Fishman, *My Darling Clementine*, p. 464.

Further Reading

J. Fishman, *My Darling Clementine: The Story of Lady Churchill* (London: W. H. Allen, 1963)

J. Meacham, *Franklin and Winston: An Intimate Portrait of an Epic Friendship* (New York: Random House, 2003)

S. Purnell, *First Lady: The Life and Wars of Clementine Churchill* (London: Aurum Press, 2015)

M. Soames (ed.), *Speaking for Themselves: The Personal Letters of Winston and Clementine Churchill* (London: Doubleday, 1998)

M. Soames, *Clementine Churchill*, rev. ed. (London: Doubleday, 2002)

18

Churchill and the 'United States of Europe'

Churchill's post-Second World War campaign for European unity was well publicised at the time and it led to significant results. It has been understandably overshadowed by his other activities and achievements, not least his campaign against the appeasement of Germany during the 1930s and his role as prime minister between 1940 and 1945. In his efforts to unite Europe he made full use of the credibility he had established as an opponent of the Nazis and a victorious wartime leader. Nevertheless, many of his statements on Europe were replete with ambiguity and deliberately lacking in detail. When he returned to office in 1951, his more enthusiastic pro-European supporters were disappointed by his apparent failure to live up to the agenda he had outlined when in opposition. In recent years, Churchill's views on Europe have become a point of reference in debates over Brexit. Both Leavers and Remainers have tried to recruit his memory to their cause. The specific circumstances in which he operated – and the complexities of his actual opinions – are too easily overlooked by those who wish to claim his European views in support of their own.

The campaign Churchill launched in Zurich was never totally forgotten, but this dimension of his thought, and his record on European integration during his second premiership, did not receive sustained academic attention until the 1980s.[1] More recently, Felix Klos has provided a lively and enthusiastic account of Churchill's post-war efforts.[2] Marco Duranti has explored in great detail Churchill's role in establishing the Council of Europe and the European Convention on Human Rights (ECHR), which are separate, of course, from the institutions of the European Union and its

I am grateful to Jon Danzig, Yuhei Hasegawa and Allen Packwood for valuable information and suggestions. Any errors are my own responsibility.

forerunners. Duranti suggests that Churchill's European battle was essentially about the quest for domestic political advantage, and that the ECHR itself could be seen as a mechanism for constraining socialist governments from carrying out policies (such as the weakening of property rights) which Conservatives believed were tyrannical.[3] In spite of these important advances in the scholarship, there remains scope for further analysis of the connections between Churchill's personal history and the political and intellectual climate in which he developed his European ideas.

Churchill had a great flair for articulating and popularising concepts which had been devised by others. So it was with the 'United States of Europe', a term he used in a famous speech in Switzerland in 1946, but which was by no means original to him.[4] By the time he spoke at the University of Zurich, the geopolitical context had changed radically from the first occasion he had used the phrase, in 1930, when Europe was in crisis but before the Nazis had seized power. Now Germany had been defeated, and the Cold War was in its confusing opening phase, at a time when the United States still had a monopoly on the atomic bomb. New international organisations were proliferating. Churchill – well aware of his own reputation as a Russophobe – simultaneously wanted to use Franco-German reconciliation as the basis for western European solidarity *and* to avoid being portrayed as an anti-Soviet hawk.

Context

The idea of a United States of Europe had a long nineteenth-century heritage. The London *Times* contains at least 190 mentions of the term prior to Churchill's Zurich speech, three of which were attributable to Churchill himself during 1945–6. Although there are earlier examples to be found elsewhere, the first of the *Times* references were connected to the International Peace Congress which took place in Geneva in 1867 and which resolved to found a journal called the *United States of Europe*.[5] The young Churchill, who made his name as a soldier and military writer, had little time for the well-meaning resolutions of pacifist conferences. However, the idea that the future would be dominated by large agglomerations or blocs of countries, rather than by smaller nation-states, was a pre-1914 commonplace.[6] In an unpublished article written a couple of years prior to the second Boer War (1899–1902), Churchill warned of the possible rise of 'An African United States' that would pose a threat to British supremacy in South Africa.[7]

As this suggests, he had a habit of playing with and adapting ideas and phrases across many decades.[8] Churchill did not start to use the language of 'the English-speaking peoples' – which, again, was not original to him – until a few years before the First World War.[9] This concept rested on an idea of White solidarity that transcended national boundaries and involved a willingness – as seen in Churchill's 1943 proposal for common Anglo-US citizenship – to pool some forms of sovereignty.[10] In this sense, Churchill's racism and imperialism should be seen as complementary to, rather than the antithesis of, his post-1930 ideas about European integration. His ideas should also be read in the light of fin-de-siècle thinking that blended beliefs about the power of communications technology with faith in the destiny of the 'white race'.[11] He spoke (in 1950) of the need for an 'all-powerful world order' and a 'world super-government', with a united Europe as one of its pillars. This belief in world government was in line with contemporary utopian thinking, of which, for decades, Churchill's friend H. G. Wells was one of the foremost exponents.[12]

Though the word 'globalisation' had not yet been coined, Churchill had an enthusiasm for technologies such as the telegraph and the aeroplane which compressed time and space. His parents, like many of their class, had treated the continent as their playground; he too gained considerable experience of leisurely and privileged European travel. The First World War tore this Europe apart, and when Churchill fought on the Western Front he witnessed the devastation first hand. Having disliked Latin at school, he was for a long time lukewarm towards the Classics but, during the 1940s, he came to perceive Greek and Roman culture as a crucial part of the heritage of the Christian West. This inheritance needed, in his view, to be preserved and restored as the foundation of future peace. Although he was not a conventional religious believer, the concept of 'Christendom' remained part of his geopolitical terminology. His faith in the superiority of the culture of Christian Europe was linked to his belief in a (somewhat flexible) hierarchy of civilisations.[13] He made this explicit in the opening of the Zurich speech: 'This noble continent, comprising on the whole the fairest and the most cultivated regions of the earth, enjoying a temperate and equable climate, is the home of all the great parent races of the western world.'[14]

The Evolution of Churchill's Thinking

In the Zurich speech, Churchill mentioned two figures who had done much to promote the cause of European federalism during the interwar years. The first of these was Count Richard Coudenhove-Kalergi (1894–1972), the Austrian founder of the Pan-Europa Movement and an effective propagandist, whom Churchill credited (in 1938) as 'the principal author of the idea of a United States of Europe'.[15] Churchill's ambivalence towards Kalergi is captured in the introduction he wrote to the Count's 1953 memoirs: 'The form of his theme may be crude, erroneous and impracticable but the impulse and the inspiration are true.'[16] The other figure Churchill cited was Aristide Briand (1862–1932), who headed eleven different French governments (many of them successive) during the twenty years after 1909. Inspired by Kalergi, Briand put forward a plan for European federation, enunciated initially at a meeting of the League of Nations in September 1929. Churchill first laid out his ideas about a United States of Europe in an article in the *Saturday Evening Post* (an American paper) in February 1930. He did not mention Briand by name, but his enthusiasm made a striking contrast with the cool reception the Briand plan had in London and other European capitals.[17]

Making no mention of the recent Wall Street Crash, Churchill set out in this article to explain why Europe was, in his assessment, prospering so much less than the United States, which had a smaller population and not many more resources. The answer was to be found in the tariff barriers that had proliferated on the continent since the Great War and the new national boundaries that had multiplied as a consequence of the peace treaties. Now that Europe was 'organized, as it never was before, upon a purely national-istic basis', it was much less economically efficient than it had been before 1914. European unity would lead to a 'vast increase of wealth' and 'the ceaseless diminution of armies' as war became less and less likely. Churchill was explicit that Britain should not be a member of the United States of Europe. 'We are with Europe, but not of it', he wrote. Its creation was, however, in line with British interests. 'The conception of a United States of Europe is right. Every step taken to that end which appeases the obsolete hatred and vanished oppressions, which make easier the traffic and recip-rocal services of Europe, which encourages its nations to lay aside their precautionary panoply, is good in itself, is good for them and good for all.' At the same time it was necessary, as Europe's unity progressed, that British

Empire solidarity should develop at the same rate, and that there should be 'also a deepening self-knowledge and mutual recognition among the English-speaking people'. Churchill saw no contradiction between decrying excess nationalism, arguing for a stronger British Empire and promoting the integration of a Europe which he took for granted would retain 'its African and Asiatic possessions and plantations'.[18]

Although the *Saturday Evening Post* piece is well known, two further articles, published in the *New York American* in 1931, have eluded the attention of scholars. The first of these offered amusing comment on the polite resistance Briand's plan had met from the different national representatives at Geneva: 'If they damn it is with faint praise; if they praise it is with faint damns.' Churchill was, however, certain that the pan-European idea would ultimately succeed: 'The wave may advance and recede, but the tide will keep coming in.'[19] The second article offered a response to the decision of the Austrian and German governments to create a customs union between the two countries.[20] Churchill's reaction to this plan – which within a few months proved abortive – needs to be read in the light of the Nazi Party's breakthrough at the previous year's elections. (Heinrich Brüning, of the Centre Party, remained chancellor of Germany.) Churchill recognised that the Austro-German demarche had caused shock and anger in other European countries, and that the customs union idea raised the spectre of an *Anschluss*. Yet he mocked Briand's rejection of the proposal which, Churchill argued, was actually in line with the Frenchman's ideal of a United States of Europe. Although reserving judgement to a degree, Churchill was on the whole remarkably positive:

> High hopes are placed in Chancellor Bruening. A success in the German foreign policy, an assertion of reviving power, will bring to the constitutional, and at present peaceful German forces, a prestige which will rob the much more dangerous Hitler movement of its mainspring. Will not the mastery of Hitlerism by constitutional forces in Germany be a real factor in the immediate peace of Europe?[21]

Churchill met Kalergi for the first time in February 1938. He invited him to Chartwell: 'I was gratified to feel that Churchill had remained faithful to the ideal of Pan-Europe, though for years he had ceased to write and speak about it.'[22] A few months later, in fact, Churchill republished an abridged version of his *Saturday Evening Post* article.[23] His primary motivation may have been monetary – he liked to shore up his finances by recycling old material. Even so, it seems that, in his view, the idea of a United States of Europe had not been rendered redundant by recent events (which by this point included Hitler's imposition of an *Anschluss* on Austria).

After Churchill became prime minister two years later, his government made the offer of Franco-British union in a desperate bid to keep the French in the war. He was not really the driving force behind the idea, which was the product of the deliberations of a wider group, and was likely interested in using it as a vehicle for securing as much French material as possible. As a symbolic gesture, the offer was also a potentially powerful propaganda weapon. Churchill may therefore not have imagined it would actually be accepted, but it does illustrate his taste for dramatic, if rather woolly, proposals for international cooperation and pooled sovereignty.[24]

By autumn 1942, Churchill had begun to give thought to the shape of the post-war world, in response to developing proposals for a future United Nations organisation. That October, he wrote to his foreign secretary, Anthony Eden:

> It would be a measureless disaster if Russian barbarism overlaid the culture and independence of the ancient States of Europe. Hard as it is to say now, I trust that the European family may act unitedly as one under a Council of Europe. I look forward to a United States of Europe in which the barriers between the nations will be greatly minimised and unrestricted travel will be possible.[25]

The Soviet Union was, of course, at this moment, Britain's ally. Russia – viewed as tyrannical and dubiously European, and with its apparently suspect Orthodox Christian heritage – held a liminal position in Churchill's hierarchy of civilisations. (The Germans appear to have stood higher in this hierarchy than the Russians, possibly even during the Second World War.)[26] If Russia had slipped back into barbarity as a consequence of the Bolshevik revolution, it might nevertheless one day become a healthy factor in the human commonwealth. This could even be possible under Stalin, whom Churchill perceived (in contrast to Trotsky) as a rational diplomatic actor in the Great Power/Concert of Europe tradition.[27] This was quite consistent with Churchill's continuing suspicions of the Soviets, whom he expected to be guided by Russian national interests, even though those interests overlapped with those of the British Empire for the time being.

While the war lasted, Churchill could not voice those suspicions publicly, and he at any rate thought that Stalin's human rights abuses, such as the notorious Katyn massacre, were best swept under the carpet.[28] In his 'Four Years' Plan' broadcast of 1943, Churchill suggested that a future world organisation should have a Council of Europe and a Council of Asia as subordinate bodies. The work represented by the creation of the League of Nations should not be thrown away. The Council of Europe should be made 'into a really effective League' with a High Court to settle disputes and armed forces to enforce the court's decisions and prevent future wars.[29] It is not unreasonable to argue, as Max Beloff does, that Churchill did not intend Britain to be a member of the new organisation; truly, the speech was not explicit on the point.[30] On the other hand, unlike in 1930, he did not rule it out either, and five years later he claimed that he had meant for Britain to be included.[31] One can at least say with certainty that, at a time when the British Empire was threatened by the rise of the USA and the USSR to superpower status, he regarded a powerful and independent Europe as crucial to his own country's security.

Defeated at the General Election at the war's end, Churchill was determined to demonstrate his continued relevance on the world stage. Europe was in deep economic distress; trade and currency restrictions impeded its nations from exchanging goods. The USA, which would take much of the burden of the relief effort, had a strong interest in the removal of these barriers so that the continent could be rehabilitated and no longer require aid. 'It is an open secret that President Truman has been considering the possibilities of a United States of Europe', wrote the American journalist George Creel in in *Collier's* magazine in December 1945. A copy of the article is preserved in Churchill's papers.[32] This may help explain why Churchill briefly contemplated the 'United States of Europe' as the theme for the address delivered in Fulton, Missouri that became the 'iron curtain' speech.[33] In fact, he had already used the phrase in a speech in Brussels (16 November 1945) and would do so again at The Hague (9 May 1946).[34] Leo Amery, Churchill's former Cabinet colleague, gave a speech on 26 November 1945 which contained ideas that were quite similar to those contained in the Zurich speech.[35] Amery was probably mistaken, though, to believe that this address had a major influence on Churchill.[36] It was simply another example of a discourse that was relatively common at the time.

The Zurich Speech

Why, then, did the Zurich speech – delivered when Churchill was receiving an honorary degree – come to be perceived as a world-historical pronouncement when his previous usages did not? Part of the reason may be that Churchill took active steps to ensure that the speech was broadcast.[37] But the speech also gained resonance from its explicit advocacy of Franco-German reconciliation: 'I am now going to say something that will astonish you. The first step in the recreation of the European Family must be a partnership between France and Germany.'[38] The verdicts at Nuremburg had yet to be handed down – but Churchill believed that once the guilty had been punished, the

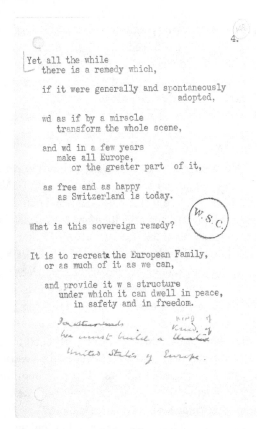

Figure 18.1 A key page from Churchill's speaking notes for his Zurich speech in which he calls for 'a kind of United States of Europe', September 1946 (CAC, Churchill Papers, CHUR 5/8).

process of retribution should come to an end. Yet, however remarkable his suggestion, it had a precedent.

On 6 September US Secretary of State James F. Byrnes had given a major speech in Stuttgart. In this he argued that the Allies should collectively clarify to the German people the basic terms of the post-war settlement which they were expected to observe, and that the Germans should then be allowed and aided to set up a democratic German government which could accept and observe those conditions. (Byrnes originally planned to call for a 'United States of Germany' but cut the line at the last minute.)[39] This intervention was a powerful indication to the Germans that they would not be treated indefinitely as pariahs, but it could also be read as an anti-Soviet move. Secretary of Commerce Henry A. Wallace lashed out at the Truman administration's increasingly hawkish line in his own speech in New York; he lost his conflict with Byrnes and the president forced his resignation, though not until the day after Churchill spoke in Zurich. Meanwhile, Soviet foreign minister Vyacheslav Molotov warned Western countries against attempting to devise a bloc that excluded the USSR.[40] At the time, the speeches of Byrnes, Molotov and Churchill were seen as signs that all three were 'seeking German support of their varying ideas for dealing with the future of that nation'.[41]

The Cold War dimension of the Zurich speech can also be seen in Churchill's treatment of nuclear issues. He warned that the USA's monopoly of the atomic bomb might only last a few years, and that the spread of the weapon could threaten the end of civilisation. The current 'breathing-space' should therefore be used for building a United States of Europe – a project which, then, was implicitly intended as a bulwark against the Soviet Union.[42] (Churchill, though he may never have given up hope of a rapprochement with the USSR, seems during his opposition years to have thought that Stalin could best be brought to reason through the issuance of blood-curdling nuclear threats.)[43] Back in the UK, the *Daily Mail* grasped the point. In its laudatory leading article on the speech, it noted that a United States of Europe that excluded the Russians 'would give an opportunity for Europe to find its soul apart from the distracting influences of the great semi-oriental land mass to the east'. Readers should remember, the *Mail* concluded, that 'The time is short.'[44]

Unsurprisingly, Soviet radio accused Churchill of 'pulling out of the dust bin the tattered flag of Pan-Europa and gathering around him shady businessmen who are clamouring for a new war'.[45] Moreover, as Churchill was supported by the *Daily Mail*, the *Observer* and other Conservative papers, it was 'evident that the reactionary and imperialistic circles of the Anglo-Saxon countries want to use the atom threat for their own purposes'.[46] Although, in France, some reacted angrily to Churchill's proposal of friendship with Germany, *Le Monde* gave a thoughtful if sceptical response. It argued that since the end of the war Europe had no longer been dominated by Franco-German relations but by relations between the Soviet Union, on one side, and Britain and the United States, on the other. The rivalry of the two camps now extended to Germany. If they reached an understanding on this point, peace could be assured, but if not, it was hard to see how the division of Europe could be avoided. 'Feigning forgetfulness of this situation, Mr Churchill reposes the future of Europe in a Franco-German *entente* that would, in his view, permit the creation of a federation of States on our continent.' The paper also noted that he had excluded neither Britain nor Russia from his envisioned organisation, although he did assign them a position apart.[47]

Specifically, Churchill had said that Great Britain and its Commonwealth, 'mighty America', and the USSR must all 'be the friends and sponsors of the new Europe'.[48] This passage is a powerful weapon in the armoury of those who argue he only ever wanted Britain to smile benevolently on an integrated Europe from the outside. However, Felix Klos has drawn attention to an account written by a Swiss diplomat, who asked Churchill just prior to the Zurich speech if the UK would be able to be a member of the United States of Europe. Churchill responded that he preferred not to emphasise this point, in order to leave to others the task of inviting Britain to join: 'One must not give the impression that we wish to control Europe, even though it is clear that England alone is capable of leading her properly today.' Moreover, if Russia were to be invited and refused, the way would be opened for British membership.[49]

Churchill believed that eastern Europe might one day come within the ambit of the new organisation. 'I am not attracted to a Western bloc as a final solution', he wrote in the aftermath of the speech. 'The ideal should be EUROPE. The Western bloc as an instalment of the United States of Europe would be an important step, but the case should be put on the broadest lines of a unity of Europe and Christendom as a whole.'[50] It is not quite clear where, for Churchill, the boundaries of Christendom lay, but he regarded Europe and 'Western Civilization' as coterminous, separated from Asia by a cultural frontier rather than a physical one.[51]

The United Europe Campaign and After

The United Europe Movement, founded in 1947, became the vehicle for Churchill's campaign; his son-in-law, the Conservative MP Duncan Sandys, was a leading light. The Movement's inaugural rally began with a hymn and was then addressed by the Archbishop of Canterbury. Cardinal Bernard Griffin of the Roman Catholic Church was unable to attend but sent a message of support; the Rev. J. R. Richardson, the Moderator of the Free Church Federal Council, was invited in his stead.[52] The involvement of the churches allowed a non-temporal emphasis which was helpful to Churchill; forced to deny that his movement was an anti-Russian plot, he sought to distance himself from the concerns of power politics.[53] But the Labour Party was keeping its distance from the movement, casting its non-partisan status in doubt. Securing Archbishop Fisher's collaboration thus required Churchill and his colleagues to stick to 'the broad conception' of European unity and to avoid committing themselves 'to any constitutional scheme'.[54] Churchill presented himself as a spiritual crusader working for the moral regeneration of the continent.[55] This was an image quite consistent with his desire – which also applied in domestic politics – to avoid being pinned down to detailed plans that would expose him to criticism or risk being falsified by events.

Churchill's efforts, though they served a political function, were based on sincere belief, and should be credited with helping inspire a broader transnational movement, which included Conservatives, Liberals and democratic socialists. The first Congress of Europe began in The Hague in May 1948, with Churchill as its honorary president. In his opening address, delivered with missionary zeal, he emphasised that 'In the centre of our movement stands the idea of a Charter of Human Rights, guarded by freedom and sustained by law.' He spoke of mutual aid in the fields of economics and defence, steps which he said 'must inevitably be accompanied step by step with a parallel policy of closer political unity'. He acknowledged – in response to pressure from Sandys and others at the drafting stage – that this would involve 'some sacrifice or merger of national sovereignty'.[56]

How can this be squared with his insistence the following year (at a private dinner with *New York Times* journalists) that he did not favour taking his country 'into a binding federation with the other states of Western Europe'?[57] It has been argued that Churchill had merely been telling the Europeans to pool *their* sovereignty.[58] This does not wholly convince, given his insistence that Great Britain was 'profoundly blended' with Europe, though it may be that he thought continental countries needed to sacrifice more sovereignty than Britain did.[59] It should also be noted that it was important for him to counter Labour's insinuation that he was seeking to entangle Britain in major commitments without first putting such proposals before the electorate.[60] Federalism had attracted a fair measure of popular support before the outbreak of war in 1939, but suspicion of it was now growing.[61]

Churchill therefore struck a balance between deprecating 'the tangles and intricacies of rigid constitution-making' and expressing enthusiasm for British involvement that stopped short of that.

> I cannot conceive that Britain would be an ordinary member of a Federal Union limited to Europe in any period which can at present be foreseen. ... Although a hard-and-fast concrete federal constitution for Europe is not within the scope of practical affairs, we should help, sponsor and aid in every possible way the movement towards European unity. We should seek steadfastly for means to become intimately associated with it.[62]

At the same time, Churchill supported forms of institutional cooperation, such as a European court to enforce human rights, which did involve some surrender of sovereignty but which fell far short of a 'binding federation'. He favoured Britain's membership of the Council of Europe, as established in 1949, and also ratification of the ECHR, which the Attlee government reluctantly approved.[63]

It is important not to conflate or confuse this with his attitude to British membership of a hypothetical federal Europe or of the European Economic Community as it eventually emerged. Moreover, Churchill's approach involved a strong element of strategic ambiguity (which was in part a means of dealing with American pressure for British involvement in European defence cooperation).[64] The Tory MP Bob Boothby once interrogated him as to the true meaning of his phrase 'a kind of United States of Europe'. Churchill, however, 'refused to be drawn. All he said was: "We are not making a machine, we are growing a living plant."'[65]

After Churchill returned to office, his more ardent Euro-enthusiast supporters were disappointed by what they saw as his failure to live up to the ideals he had promoted in opposition. According to his old friend Violet Bonham Carter, 'W. was too old to grasp the *practical* implication of his own idea.'[66] Whereas the Conservatives had criticised the Labour government for turning a cold shoulder on the 1950 Schuman Plan (which led to the foundation of the European Coal and Steel Community), his new administration showed no serious inclination to revisit the question. In a November 1951 memorandum, Churchill wrote: 'I never thought that Britain or the British Commonwealth should, either individually or collectively, become an integral part of a European Federation, and have never given the slightest support to the idea.'[67] As John Young has argued, the notion of a missed opportunity, or even a betrayal, became an orthodoxy promoted by Boothby, Harold Macmillan and others. Yet, in fact, Churchill's fundamental assumptions were shared not only by Labour leaders but also by the 'pro-Europeans' within the Cabinet themselves, who maintained unrealistic hopes of winning over other countries to their non-federalist vision.[68]

Assessment

In conclusion, it is clear that judging Churchill's views on European unity is no easy task. The fact that he advocated a United States of Europe as a cure for excess racial and national feeling runs counter to his standard, rather xenophobic, reputation. But his genuinely expansive vision of Europe's future did not trump his imperialism and had important limits when it came to determining the extent of Britain's practical involvement. To some degree, he simply wanted to have his cake and eat it, advocating positions that were simultaneously grandiose and vague, and more suited to the poetry of campaigning than the prose of government. He wanted Britain and the Empire to hold some very special and pivotal position with respect to Europe, as 'a separate closely- and specially-related ally and friend', without ever really knowing or explaining how that could be made to work.[69]

Yet it was not all simply hot air: the Council of Europe and the ECHR were concrete outcomes for which Churchill's efforts were partly responsible. The prosaic truth is that Churchill favoured less surrender of sovereignty than that involved in Britain's eventual membership of the European Union, but probably significantly more than many

Europhobes would today be willing to countenance. When passions over Europe rise, it is often tempting to start bandying rival Churchillian quotations. But on closer inspection, the nineteenth-century-inspired views of a twentieth-century statesman may be a problematic guide to the politics of the twenty-first.

Notes

1. Key contributions include J. W. Young, Churchill's 'No' to Europe: The 'Rejection' of European Union by Churchill's Post-War Government, 1951–1952. *Historical Journal*, vol. 28 (1985), pp. 923–37; M. Beloff, Churchill and Europe. In R. Blake and W. R. Louis (eds.), *Churchill* (Oxford: Oxford University Press, 1993), pp. 443–56; and J. Ramsden, *Man of the Century: Winston Churchill and His Legend Since 1945* (London: HarperCollins, 2002), chapter 6.
2. F. Klos, *Churchill's Last Stand: The Struggle to Unite Europe* (London: I. B. Tauris, 2017).
3. M. Duranti, *The Conservative Human Rights Revolution: European Identity, Transnational Politics, and the Origins of the European Convention* (Oxford: Oxford University Press, 2017).
4. It is sometimes suggested, wrongly, that Churchill coined the phrase. See, for example, W. R. Mauter, Churchill and the Unification of Europe. *The Historian*, vol. 61 (1998), pp. 67–84, at 67.
5. 'The Peace Congress', *The Times*, 19 September 1867.
6. A. Thompson, *Imperial Britain: The Empire in British Politics, c. 1880–1932* (Harlow: Longman, 2000), p. 24. In 1904 Churchill was sent a typescript translation of a German article on 'The United States of Europe', though there is no sign that he paid it any particular attention. W. Jameson to Winston S. Churchill, 12 October 1904, CAC, Churchill Papers, CHAR 2/18/36–42.
7. CAC, Churchill Papers, CHAR 1/19/1–21, Churchill, 'Our Account with the Boers', dated in the catalogue as November 1897.
8. See R. Hyam, Winston Churchill Before 1914. *Historical Journal*, vol. 12 (1969), pp. 164–73.
9. P. Addison, Winston Churchill's Concept of the English-Speaking Peoples. In A. Pók (ed.), *The Fabric of Modern Europe: Studies in Social and Diplomatic History* (Nottingham: Astra Press, 1999), pp. 103–17; P. Clarke, *Mr Churchill's Profession: Statesman, Orator, Writer* (London: Bloomsbury, 2012).
10. For the way that these ideas subsequently manifested themselves in Churchill's 'iron curtain' speech, see S. Vucetic, The Fulton Address as Racial Discourse. In A. Dobson and S. Marsh (eds.), *Churchill and the Anglo-American Special Relationship* (London: Routledge, 2017), pp. 96–115.
11. D. Bell, Cyborg Imperium, c. 1900. In A. O. Chapman and N. Chowe (eds.), *Coding and Representation from the Nineteenth Century to the Present: Scrambled Messages* (London: Routledge, 2021), pp. 48–70.
12. 'Four Pillars of World Peace', *The Times*, 12 October 1950; CAC, Churchill Papers, CHUR 5/38A-C/90, speech to Students Association and Danish British Society, Copenhagen, 11 October 1950.

13. For further discussions of these points, see R. Toye, 'This Famous Island Is the Home of Freedom': Winston Churchill and the Battle for 'European civilization'. *History of European Ideas*, vol. 46, no. 5 (2020), pp. 666–80. See also P. Addison, Destiny, History and Providence: The Religion of Winston Churchill. In M. Bentley (ed.), *Private and Public Doctrine: Essays in British History Presented to Maurice Cowling* (Cambridge: Cambridge University Press, 1993), pp. 236–50 and W. Dockter, *Churchill and the Islamic World: Orientalism, Empire and Diplomacy in the Middle East* (London: I. B. Tauris, 2015), pp. 42–3.

14. Speech of 19 September 1946. Unless otherwise indicated, all speeches and broadcasts cited are to be found in Rhodes James, *Complete Speeches*.

15. CAC, Churchill Papers, CHAR 8/594/111, Churchill to Thornton Butterworth, 28 June 1938.

16. Count Coudenhove-Kalergi, *An Idea Conquers the World* (New York: Roy Publishers, 1953), p. ix. See also M. Duranti, *The Conservative Human Rights Revolution: European Identity, Transnational Politics, and the Origins of the European Convention* (Oxford: Oxford University Press, 2017), p. 146.

17. W. Roobol, Aristide Briand's Plan: The Seed of European Unification. In M. Spiering and M. Wintle (eds.), *Ideas of Europe Since 1914: The Legacy of the First World War* (Basingstoke: Palgrave Macmillan, 2002), pp. 32–46.

18. W. S. Churchill, 'The United States of Europe', *Saturday Evening Post*, 15 February 1930; M. Wolff (ed.), *The Collected Essays of Winston Churchill, vol. 2: Churchill and Politics* (London: Library of Imperial History, 1976), pp. 176–86.

19. W. S. Churchill, 'No hope for U.S. of Europe NOW', *New York American*, 11 January 1931, copy in CAC, Churchill Papers, CHAR 8/303/13–17. Compare the quotation from the third marquess of Salisbury that Churchill used as the epigraph for his first book, *The Story of the Malakand Field Force* (London: Longmans, Green & Co., 1898): 'They (frontier wars) are but the surf that marks the edge and the advance of the wave of civilisation.'

20. On the plan, see A. Orde, The Origins of the German-Austrian Customs Union Affair of 1931. *Central European History*, vol. 13 (1980), pp. 34–59 and I. G. Aguado, The Creditanstalt Crisis of 1931 and the Failure of the Austro-German Customs Union Project. *Historical Journal*, vol. 44 (2001), pp. 199–221.

21. *New York American*, Churchill, 'Austro-German Union would Aid European peace', 5 April 1931, copy in CAC, Churchill Papers, CHAR 8/303/46.

22. Coudenhove-Kalergi, *An Idea Conquers the World*, p. 214.

23. It appeared in the *News of the World* on 29 May 1938.

24. On Churchill's taste for drama, see J. Rose, *The Literary Churchill: Author, Reader, Actor* (New Haven, CT: Yale University Press, 2014).

25. TNA, PREM 4/100/7, Churchill to Anthony Eden, 21 October 1942. Seven years later Churchill permitted Harold Macmillan to quote this document publicly. See *Gloucestershire Echo*, 'Churchill warned in 1942 of "Russian barbarism"', 5 September 1949.

26. Of the destruction of European Jewry, Churchill wrote: 'There is no doubt this is the most horrible crime ever committed in the whole history of the world, and it has been done by scientific machinery by nominally civilised men in the name of a great State and *one of the leading races of Europe*' (emphasis added). Prime minister's Minute of 11 June 1944, CAC, Churchill Papers, CHAR 20/153/1.

27. R. Toye, Churchill, Munich, and 'the European System'. In J. Gottlieb, D. Hucker and R. Toye (eds.), *The Munich Crisis, Politics, and the People* (Manchester: Manchester University Press, 2021), pp. 112–132.

28. G. Gorodetsky (ed.), *The Maisky Diaries: Red Ambassador to the Court of St James's, 1932–1943* (New Haven, CT: Yale University Press, 2015), pp. 505–11 (entry for 23 April 1943).

29. Broadcast of 21 March 1943.

30. Beloff, Churchill and Europe, p. 446.

31. Speech of 7 May 1948.

32. *Collier's*, G. Creel, 'The United States of Europe', 22 December 1945, copy in CAC Churchill Papers, CHUR 2/19/229.

33. Time Inc. Records, Box 260, F8, New York Historical Society, Walter Graebner, letter of 24 April 1947 (addressed to Andrew Heiskell but with the salutation 'Dear Bob').

34. See also his remarks at a press conference in Amsterdam on 10 May: 'Mr. Churchill on future of Germany', *The Times*, 11 May 1946.

35. L. S. Amery, *British Links with Europe* (London: University of London Press, 1945).

36. CAC, Amery Papers, AMEL 7/40, Leo Amery diary, 19 September 1946. A shortened version of this entry can be found in J. Barnes and D. Nicholson (eds.), *The Empire at Bay: The Leo Amery Diaries, 1929–1945* (London: Hutchinson, 1988), p. 1060.

37. CAC, Churchill Papers, CHUR 2/247/245, Elizabeth Gilliatt to Jo Sturdee, 9 September 1946. After Churchill had delivered the speech, which was broadcast by the BBC, the story led the radio news bulletins for the rest of the day. The bulletins can be consulted on microfilm at the British Library.

38. Speech of 19 September 1946.

39. 'New policy is acclaimed in U.S.', *Daily Telegraph*, 7 September 1946.

40. Lansing Warren, 'Molotov warns West not to try anti-Soviet bloc', *New York Times*, 15 September 1946.

41. Cutting headlined '"Friendly Stalin". Test seen on Reich issue', 26 September 1946, in Associated Press World News: Wire Copy and Clippings, 6–30 September 1946, Associated Press Collections Online.

42. Speech of 19 September 1946.

43. K. Larres, Churchill's 'Iron Curtain' Speech in Context: The Attempt to Achieve a 'Good Understanding on All Points' with Stalin's Soviet Union. *International History Review*, vol. 40 (2018), pp. 86–107; K. Ruane, *Churchill and the Bomb in War and Cold War* (London: Bloomsbury Academic, 2016).

44. 'A plea to Europe', *Daily Mail*, 20 September 1946.

45. Moscow, Soviet European Service in Rumanian, 6 October 1946, 2.00 p.m. EST, quoted in Daily Report: Foreign Radio Broadcasts, 8 October 1946, Foreign Broadcast Information Service (FBIS) database, FBIS-FRB-46-200.

46. Moscow, in German to Europe, 8 October 1946, 9.00 a.m. EST, quoted in Daily Report: Foreign Radio Broadcasts, 10 October 1946, FBIS-FRB-46-202.

47. 'Les idées de M. Churchill', *Le Monde*, 21 September 1946.

48. Speech of 19 September 1946.

49. Here I have offered some slight amendments to the translation given in Klos, *Churchill's Last Stand*, p. 83. The document in question is Albert Cuttat, 'Notice pour monsieur le Conseiller fédéral Petitpierre sur mes entretiens avec M. Churchill et M. Montag', 22 September 1946, available at https://dodis.ch/1659.

50. CAC, Churchill Papers, CHUR 2/23/1–2, Churchill to Lord Salisbury (draft). This was a response to Salisbury's letter of 14 October 1946, CHUR 2/23/3–6.

51. Speech of 14 May 1947. For further discussion, see Toye, 'This Famous Island'.
52. CAC, DNSD 9/1/1, Minutes of the Executive Committee of the United Europe Movement, 22 April 1947.
53. 'No power politics behind United Europe campaign', *Aberdeen Journal*, 15 May 1947; 'United Europe plot against Russia denied', *Dundee Courier*, 15 May 1947.
54. CAC, Churchill Papers, CHUR 2/25A/14, Leo Amery to Churchill, 10 January 1947.
55. P. M. Coupland, *Britannia, Europa and Christendom: British Christians and European Integration* (Basingstoke: Palgrave Macmillan, 2006), pp. 91–2.
56. Speech of 7 May 1948; Duranti, *Conservative Human Rights Revolution*, pp. 116–17.
57. New York Times Company Records: Arthur Hays Sulzberger Papers, Series I b. 12, New York Public Library, H. Bradford to Arthur Hays Sulzberger, 29 March 1949.
58. John Charmley to the editor of the *Daily Telegraph*, published 23 September 1996.
59. 'Four pillars of world peace', *The Times*, 12 October 1950; CAC, Churchill Papers, CHUR 5/38A-C/84, speech to Students Association and Danish British Society, Copenhagen, 11 October 1950.
60. 'Council of Europe and West Germany', *Financial Times*, 18 August 1949.
61. T. Haapala and T. Häkkinen, Debating Federal Europe in the British Parliament, c. 1940–49. *European Review of History: Revue européenne d'histoire*, vol. 24 (2017), pp. 801–16.
62. Speech of 27 June 1950.
63. Duranti, *Conservative Human Rights Revolution*, p. 252.
64. J. Q. Olmstead, 'A Second-Class Status': The Othering of Germany and Attempts at Alliance Building, 1950–1955. Paper delivered at the American Historical Association conference, 2020.
65. Lord Boothby, *Recollections of a Rebel* (London: Hutchinson, 1978), p. 217.
66. M. Pottle (ed.), *Daring to Hope: The Diaries and Letters of Violet Bonham Carter, 1946–1969* (London: Weidenfeld & Nicolson, 2000), entry for 8 June 1959, p. 208. Emphasis in original.
67. TNA, CAB 129/48, C (51) 32, 29 November 1951.
68. Young, Churchill's 'No' to Europe.
69. Churchill, United Europe.

Further Reading

M. Beloff, Churchill and Europe. In R. Blake and W. R. Louis (eds.), *Churchill* (Oxford: Oxford University Press, 1993)

M. Duranti, *The Conservative Human Rights Revolution: European Identity, Transnational Politics, and the Origins of the European Convention* (Oxford: Oxford University Press, 2017)

F. Klos, *Churchill's Last Stand: The Struggle to Unite Europe* (London: I. B. Tauris, 2017)

J. Ramsden, *Man of the Century: Winston Churchill and His Legend Since 1945* (London: HarperCollins, 2002)

R. Toye, 'This Famous Island Is the Home of Freedom': Winston Churchill and the Battle for 'European Civilization'. *History of European Ideas*, vol. 46, no. 5 (2020), pp. 666–80

J. W. Young, Churchill's 'No' to Europe: The 'Rejection' of European Union by Churchill's Post-War Government, 1951–1952. *Historical Journal*, vol. 28 (1985), pp. 923–93

19

Indian Summer or Conservative Winter?
Churchill's Final Fall from Power

Sir Winston Churchill undoubtedly occupies the mantle of the most famous modern British politician, if not the most famous international statesman of the twentieth century. Yet despite his enduring legacy, he presided over, and was at least partly responsible for, the historic and overwhelming Conservative defeat in 1945 to Clement Attlee's Labour Party, a humiliation which occurred only a few weeks after the allied victory in Europe. Many believed that this would signal the retirement of the old warrior and that the party leadership could pass, now that the war was over, to the much younger but experienced Anthony Eden. However, those that knew the tenacious Churchill well speculated that this was hardly likely to be the end. Lord Cranborne correctly evaluated the situation, writing in 1946 that 'I never shared the optimistic views of some of our friends that the old gentlemen would be willing to retire gracefully into the background. He has had too much of the limelight for that.'[1]

Churchill the great wartime leader was determined to be the great peacetime premier as well. He had become prime minister in May 1940 without having to fight an election and was adamant that he must now accomplish this most necessary of political tasks for a leader and win a mandate. This was finally achieved at the age of seventy-six in October 1951, heralding a major revival of his long career. While some hoped he would relinquish the seals of office soon after having achieved his electoral goal, this idea was quickly quashed by a prime minister who was convinced that his unique role in ending the war was now essential to preserving the peace, and that this could be ensured by his occupation of high office. This chapter is concerned with the last period of Churchill's premiership and leadership of the Conservative Party. It focusses not just on the last part of his 'Indian Summer'[2] when back in office but also on the tempestuous moves and motives of the Conservatives to compel his retirement in an age before party leadership elections. It also examines Churchill's manoeuvres to frustrate these ambitions and continue in power. While many studies have examined how British politicians gain the leadership of political parties,[3] there has been less analysis of their inevitable fall. The chapter is written primarily from the Conservative perspective since, until the 1965 Douglas-Home Rules which established leadership elections and procedures, so-called customary processes existed to enable, largely without public knowledge (and even beyond the engagement of many Conservative politicians themselves), the emergence and removal of leaders 'for the good of the party'.[4]

The Party had its suspicions and concerns as to whether Churchill could still deliver. But it was not only his party that wanted power. The vanity and comfort he derived from holding the reins of power gave much sustenance to Churchill's almost granite, yet emotional occupancy of the leadership. As Roy Jenkins explained:

> It is impossible to re-read the story of Churchill's life as Prime Minister of that second government without feeling that he was gloriously unfit for office. The oxymoron is appropriate to the contradictions of his performance. The splendour of his personality, which infused everything he did with style and interest, is not in doubt. Yet many of the faults of his conduct of business, to which Attlee had so devastatingly drawn private attention in the last months of the war, were present in if anything exaggerated form.[5]

Many senior Conservatives had been wary of Churchill's leadership ever since he had taken over from Chamberlain as prime minister in dramatic and far from celebrated circumstances at the beginning the war. Indeed, on becoming prime minister in May 1940 Churchill had not assumed the leadership of the Conservative Party, which remained firmly in Chamberlain's hands until just prior to his death in November that year.[6] Churchill's Conservative credentials were weak as he had visibly oscillated between parties in the past and had always preferred the label 'National' rather than Conservative government. Churchill, unlike most modern party leaders, had a 'National' appeal, which was reflected in his politics and Cabinet selection and which was not wholly to Conservative liking. The Party knew that Churchill would retire, but the question was when. The Party was faced with the predicament of how they could force this public hero away. Senior ministers such as Rab Butler, Harold Macmillan, Bobbety Salisbury (formerly Cranborne), James Stuart, Lord Woolton and Harry Crookshank applied as much pressure as possible. Yet the proclaimed successor, Anthony Eden, was not as forceful as he could have been, and Churchill was more dogged than he should have been. Churchill understood his international and domestic standing and therefore knew that if he exposed the dethronement machinations, it would damage the Party. This analysis will look primarily from 1953 onwards but will select necessary information from previous years that acknowledge the pressure and inclination to resign.

The Right Man?

Churchill was a larger-than-life figure throughout his leadership of the nation during the darkest times in the history of Britain, but was he the man capable of leading the Conservative Party into the post-war era, which demanded vigour, renewal and dynamism? Churchill was a titan on any stage and therefore the Conservatives would have to pay extra care in any attempt to dislodge this monumental figure. The dilemma was that Churchill, immersed in power and politics for more than fifty years, was loath to withdraw from its embrace and adamant to continue despite declining health, and unwilling to give way to the various alternative leaders of a younger generation, chief among whom was Eden. As Andrew Roberts argues, while Churchill in opposition had mocked the ageing Attlee government's hold of power, its 'tenacity paled beside that of the octogenarian Churchill' himself once he succeeded them in 1951.[7]

The reliable witness and Cabinet secretary Sir Norman Brook believed there were three key periods in Churchill's second premiership, from October 1951 to his June 1953 stroke, from June 1953 until late 1954, and from then until his retirement in April 1955. In the first, he was less energetic than during the war, he worked slowly, he was less absorbed by peacetime issues and his speeches were more of a burden, but he still rose to the occasion, had the full support of the Party and dominated the Cabinet. The second period was initially concerned with preserving his life and thereafter remaining in office. Churchill's vitality continued to fall, and he was less able to control the Cabinet, but he still did much of his own work. In the final period Churchill lacked physical and mental energy to give full attention to the demands of his position, and in these last six months his unfitness for office was undoubted.[8] Brook's analysis highlights Churchill's obstinacy, enhanced by age, and also illustrates the declining powers of a man who was beset by serious health concerns by the time he finally retired.

Neither the Conservative Party nor many others, save perhaps Churchill himself, believed he would hold on to power for almost four years. His continuance was made possible through his power to delay the inevitable and his ability to frustrate those who should have compelled his resignation. The Conservative Party never quite figured out how to deal with Churchill. The Chairman of the 1922 Committee in 1951, Derek Walker-Smith, wrote of this unique quandary from a backbench perspective towards a leader who bore little resemblance to his Conservative predecessors or successors, 'with Mr Churchill, a formidable, isolated and elevated figure, without at that time even a PPS [parliamentary private secretary] to bridge the gulf, it was obviously a different and more difficult matter'.[9] Dealing with the war hero was indeed a 'difficult matter' that had perplexed Party grandees since at least the 1945 defeat. From the Party's perspective, Churchill had lost two elections as Party leader in 1945 and 1950 and had only won the 1951 election with a seventeen-seat majority.

Within only nine months of returning to office, senior Conservatives such as Salisbury, Stuart and the chief whip Patrick Buchan-Hepburn gathered to discuss how to induce Churchill to retire at Crookshank's house as they had four years earlier.[10] Churchill gave a grave and terse response to his tense chief whip who brought the message to his leader. His popularity had been falling since the election, with only 51 per cent of the country satisfied with his performance in a Gallup poll of May 1952.[11] Churchill's intransigence frustrated the objective of these senior Conservatives by constantly citing reasons, such as the death of George VI in 1952 and the need to usher in the new queen, to stay on as leader despite telling intimates he would step down after a year.[12]

The Conservative Party was unsure as to how much the victory owed to a leader who had rarely been present in the Commons and had not provided a determined, organised programme while leader of the opposition. Churchill's leadership meant taking little part in the new policies that shaped post-war Conservative thinking, which was mainly left to younger leaders such as Butler. A confidential report on public opinion by the Party chairman, Lord Woolton, in 1949 concluded that

Churchill's departure would make no difference to the Conservatives' standing in opinion polls.[13] Indeed, Labour made light of some of Churchill's positions, which were sometimes seen as not wholly Conservative. When Attlee and Bevan were being criticised for visiting the Soviet Union and communist China in August 1954, Herbert Morrison replied, 'Well, one has to run jolly fast to keep to the left of Churchill nowadays.'[14]

The new Cabinet was not even particularly Conservative. Harking back to the days of the 'National War Government', Churchill invited old non-party figures from the war years such as Lord Alexander (who was serving as governor-general of Canada) and Lords Leathers, Ismay and Cherwell, as well as those whose origins were not even with the Conservative Party, such as Lords De la Warr, Simonds and Reading, Gwilym Lloyd George, Sir Walter Monckton and the economist Sir Arthur Salter. This satisfied the prime minister's wish for a broad government, and few Cabinets of the twentieth century have been such personal creations. The Cabinet headed by a seventy-seven-year-old had an average age of fifty-nine, with Peter Thorneycroft, at forty-two, by far the youngest.[15] Thus the Churchill Cabinet was a highly moderate one, and though not a group of sycophants, it was composed of a significant number of non-Conservatives that owed their place to the prime minister. The Liberal Party leader, Clement Davies, was even personally offered the Ministry of Education by Churchill, though his Party compelled him to refuse, which characteristically inspired tears in a man who had been a Liberal MP himself and served in the Liberal administrations of Asquith and Lloyd George.[16]

But how long would this rather non-partisan administration continue? Churchill had serious health problems which compelled party and government officials, loyal or disloyal, to contemplate leadership contingencies. Various party and establishment figures discussed in the shadows ways to deal with the situation. As early as February 1952, for example, after Churchill suffered an arterial spasm, the queen's private secretary, Sir Alan Lascelles, and Lord Salisbury created a plan whereby Churchill could remain prime minister until after the Coronation but be elevated to the Lords, while Eden would be in charge of the Commons.[17] The premiership was a gruelling role, but especially when the occupant was nearing eighty. This was illustrated between April and July 1953. Churchill took over the Foreign Office (Eden was in the United States in Boston for a bile duct operation), partook in the long Garter induction ceremony, dealt with the incessant demands of the Coronation and the accompanying panoply of duties, followed by exacting Commonwealth heads of government meetings, and then suffered a stroke at a banquet in June for the Italian prime minister, Alcide De Gasperi. But even this did not prevent a rather uncommunicative prime minister from chairing the Cabinet the next day.[18] Despite the stimulation of taking many amphetamines or 'Morans', as Churchill called them after his physician, even stalwart supporters despaired over his declining work rate. His assistant private secretary and close confidante, Jock Colville, recalled that 'He was ageing month by month ... reluctant to read any papers. More and more time was bezique and ever less to public business. It was becoming an effort even to sign letters and positive condescension to read Foreign Office telegrams.'[19]

Churchill was not senile but he did struggle with the necessities of high office. Cabinets were becoming more about history lessons, from a man who was a generation older than most of his colleagues, than the active apex of executive decision-making. Eden recorded in his diary that these crucial meetings were driven by Churchill's style, which meant 'drawling Cabinets, the failure to take decisions, the general atmosphere of "aprés moi le déluge"'.[20] Another Conservative successor and member of Cabinet, Macmillan, recorded in his diary in July 1954 that 'Churchill is now often speechless in Cabinet; alternatively, he rambles about nothing. Sometimes he looks as if he is going to have another stroke .... He was always an egoist, but a magnanimous one. Now he has become almost a monomaniac.'[21] These were not the most favourable impressions from two of his most senior colleagues. Despite the efforts of his son-in-law, the backbench Conservative MP Christopher Soames, and Colville to cover up their chief's decline and intractable idiosyncrasies, such information was known in the higher echelons of the Conservative Party and among senior diplomats based in London, who conveyed the information to their home capitals. The impression was not the most conducive for a party that hoped to create an image of modernisation and vitality for the post-war world.

Churchill and his supporters became more interested in surviving the trials of office than creating and fronting the policies that could assist the Conservative post-war image. As Jenkins accurately details, 'the most important milestones in [Churchill's] political year were the occasions when he could endeavour to show the Cabinet or the Americans, the Conservative Conference or the House of Commons, that he was fit to carry on. It was not so much what he said on these occasions, although he maintained his habit of meticulous preparation, as the fact that he was able to keep on his feet sufficiently long to say it at all.'[22] Though there was undisputed affection for Churchill, this trial of personal endurance did not arouse universal cries of admiration, respect or gratitude from the Conservatives. Though undoubtedly still capable of famed witticisms and panache, Churchill's performances were not always to be relied upon. During a parliamentary debate in April 1954 on atomic policy, he became wooden and was beset by cries of 'Resign!' from the Labour benches and despair and embarrassment from the Treasury (government) benches. It was not the heckling but his inability to combat it that drew complaint. To some it was a turning point where he showed his 'aged feebleness' and even one his loyal private secretaries, Anthony Montague Browne, recalled that it was the 'first time that I realised how much his powers had waned. In days gone by he would have put aside his notes and devastated the opposition.'[23]

The Changing Party

In 1950 the One Nation Group was formed by young Conservative MPs who would go on to influence and lead the Party, right up to the Thatcher era: men such as Robert Carr, Angus Maude, Enoch Powell, Iain Macleod and Edward Heath. This group of young Conservatives represented the new professional wing of the Party that rejected class and were compelled to action by the 'recognition of the persistent ineptitude of the Conservative frontbench when dealing with the Attlee government in matters of social policy'.[24] The group looked to Eden and Butler as leaders that could espouse new and pertinent social policy leadership. The One Nation Group were concerned with Churchill's hold of the party leadership since they doubted he understood the needs of Britain or had the ability to lead it. So alarmed were they by the damage of him being leader and prime minister that they held an emergency meeting with the heading 'Senility of the Prime Minister' which resolved that Churchill must retire, and passed this on to the 1922 Committee. As Robert Walsha astutely notes, 'apart from his deteriorating faculties, the very aloofness of the leader, not only from backbenchers but also from policy development, and his lack of interest in social policy in particular, could hardly have endeared him to the ONG [One Nation Group], whose affinity lay with the generation of leaders poised to take over'.[25] Such was the despondency of some Conservative MPs over Churchill's inactive leadership that it was reported that they praised in May 1954 the 'comparative decisiveness' in leadership of the seventy-one-year-old Labour leader of the opposition, Clement Attlee.[26]

Though social policy was not the prime minister's strongest claim to leadership, foreign affairs was where he believed he could continue to dominate and where he felt his knowledge was key to Britain's and his Party's interests. Churchill, like all other Conservative leaders, publicly or privately, considered their occupation as the queen's first minister essential to the success of the Party. Foreign policy and imperial affairs had always aroused the interest and passions of the Conservative Party and his was a unique reputation that gave him access to channels of admiration and respect internationally that could hardly be emulated. Churchill was able to utilise this respect for his international impact with his lustrous wit and charm (that had not dulled with age) to impress the wider Party. This was exemplified at the Margate Party Conference in August 1953 when Churchill needed to prove his fitness and credentials for office after his stroke a few weeks earlier. The almost seventy-nine-year-old leader ended his determined and highly applauded speech by saying, 'If I stay on for the time being bearing the burden at my age it is not because of love for power or office. I have had an ample share of both. If I stay it is because I have a feeling that I may through things that have happened have an influence on what I care about above all else, the building of a sure and lasting peace.'[27]

Despite the outward display of loyalty in almost panegyric proportions towards their elderly leader, the Party was generally far from satisfied with his supposed area of aptitude – foreign affairs. The Conservatives had since 1945 been wary of Churchill's pro-Europe stance as an electoral liability and others found it difficult to reconcile this with their leader's pro-Empire sentiments, which also alienated many new Conservatives.[28] The effectiveness of his often self-lauded diplomacy with the Americans and Russians, viewed from both sides, was of questionable relevance. Indeed, Churchill was sometimes admonished by the Cabinet for his 'personal diplomacy', including an almost censorious reprimand for ignoring Cabinet and sending despatches to the new Soviet leadership in March 1953.[29] Churchill's diplomatic ambitions were also now blighted by the fact that he was often unable to personally persuade the Americans to follow his advice on world affairs. This contributed to the prime minister's melancholy and frustrations since his powers as a world statesman were substantially constrained in peacetime. As Churchill told Butler, after failing to budge Eisenhower and Dulles on issues including North Korea, Indo-China, Egypt and Germany when meeting in Bermuda in December 1953: 'I feel like an aeroplane at the end of its flight ... in the dusk, with the petrol running out, looking for a safe landing.'[30]

The Party seemed closer to Eden's stance of being pro-Commonwealth, while wanting a firm but fair hand on colonial policy and not being greatly concerned with Europe. The 'Suez Group' with imperialist old school credentials, a crew of Churchillian sympathy, could only muster twenty-eight MPs to vote against a treaty with Egypt which signalled the withdrawal from the Canal Zone, while Eden was commended for successfully navigating the Bill through the House.[31] Eden's mastery and experience of foreign affairs even rivalled the curriculum vitae of his leader. The foreign secretary's successes in Indo-China, Trieste and Iran meant that 'never had his standing within the party in the country been higher',[32] while Churchill created '[b]ackbench dissatisfaction' by being surrounded by 'old cronies, giving little opportunity to post-war entrants ... [which] created a ripple effect onto the conduct of foreign policy'.[33]

A Lack of Killer Instinct

This growing and clandestine dissatisfaction has to be offset against Churchill's ability to present himself as the saviour of the nation. The displeasure of sections of the Party could not be channelled with force against Churchill unless the Cabinet was prepared to be a determined conduit of this opinion. The Cabinet in this case failed, not because of its desire to keep Churchill, but because of its own inertia and Churchill's knack of stymieing, through delaying tactics, their aspirations to see his retirement. The entire Cabinet bore responsibility for its lack of killer instinct; but it was Eden, especially, who claimed the desire to get rid of Churchill and yet allowed, through events and weary abnegation, the old leader to continue. As Macmillan reflected after another failed attempt to dislodge the prime minister, Churchill could still use his experience and dexterity in political arts in the face of the Cabinet's objection: 'it is remarkable with what skill and tenacity Churchill has played his hand . . . . He has refused ever (or practically so) to see any of us

Figure 19.1 Churchill with Clementine at the time of his final resignation as prime minister, April 1955 (CAC, Baroness Spencer-Churchill Papers, CSCT 5/8/124).

except separately. He has played off one against the other – and he has come off triumphant.'[34]

Eden had been the anointed dauphin since the war and was accepted as the next leader. Churchill realised that he had to tread delicately with the impatient Eden in regard to the succession. The battle between the prime minister and foreign secretary, with their twenty-three-year age difference, was wearisome, inopportune and unhelpful to both after years of working well together. They dominated the government. As such, 'Churchill's complex dealings with Eden proved a strain on the record of his peacetime administration' and was characterised by arguments over their shared leadership of foreign affairs and the timing of retirement.[35] Churchill had long tried to appease Eden's impatience as crown prince and in this he had been partly successful in at least being able to frustrate these long-simmering ambitions. Churchill tried to reason with Eden and his supporters that it would be best to avoid the example of 'brilliant figures' such as Lord Rosebery and Arthur Balfour getting a 'fag end' term of government after succeeding William Gladstone and Lord Salisbury. Churchill proposed instead that Eden could become 'managing director' responsible for the 'Home Front' and take over the party machine, but leave Churchill as a sort of 'chairman' prime minister until the next election. Eden, while wavering, did not take the bait.[36]

The meetings of senior ministers that had occurred at Crookshank's house soon after regaining office resolved that Churchill should retire as soon as was practicable and be succeeded by Eden. As mentioned previously, the prime minister did not receive this well. Salisbury urged Eden, after these meetings, to confront Churchill about his intentions, and if he received an unsatisfactory response, a group of senior ministers, not including Eden, would consider what action to take.[37] By early 1953 Churchill's procrastination was prompting Eden to have a 'show down' and the prime minister's indecision had made Eden so depressed that he sombrely considered resignation in February 1953.[38] Churchill on his part would not have liked seeing the acclamations towards Eden's foreign successes as they trespassed on his bastion. During Eden's successes there were nonetheless attacks on the foreign secretary from the Beaverbrook press, which close civil service sources such as Sir Evelyn Shuckburgh suspected were 'tacitly condoned, or even instigated, by Churchill himself, as a means of extending his time in Downing Street'.[39] As D. R. Thorpe illustrates, using Eden's diplomatic coup in welcoming Tito's Yugoslavia to the West, Eden by 'dipping his foot in the waters of détente . . . was showing that Churchill was not indispensable for that purpose'.[40] The pressure to resign now was growing with discontent from ministers and an aspirant successor who was proving his ability to the world, country and Party.

Then Churchill received two excuses for continuing. The death of Stalin in March 1953 required his presence to broker peace. The second, and more pertinent for the Conservative Party, occurred suddenly in April when Eden needed a serious and immediate operation on his gall bladder in Boston, which kept him from active politics for six months. Churchill, as earlier detailed, went on to have a stroke in June that year but recovered remarkably quickly, though his incapacity meant that for three weeks urgent government business such as that regarding the Korean War needed to be attended to without the prime minister, who, recuperating at Chartwell, had resulting difficulty with speech and mobility. As Andrew Roberts asserts, the fact that Churchill continued in office for nearly two more years after this serious stroke was extraordinary and equally incredible that neither the queen, Lady Churchill nor the Cabinet intervened to insist on Churchill's retirement from office after this debilitating condition, even when they knew his physician did not think he would survive.[41] The public had little details of either Churchill's or Eden's health, while extraordinarily these two infirm men were ostensibly governing Britain. This peculiar situation of double incapacity, or, as Jenkins calls it, 'compounding of invalidism', made the seventy-eight-year-old prime minister's continuance possible as the fifty-five-year-old foreign secretary was compelled to desist calls of resignation because of his own ill health.[42] Even Eden supporters had to concede Churchill's continuance since they did not want usurpation by Butler, who was enjoying a successful tenure at the exchequer.

Churchill's valiant recovery, compared to the slow, painful recuperation of Eden, allowed him to delay any plans of retirement. Propelled by a letter from Macmillan, complaining of the unsettled nature within the Party due to Churchill, Eden rushed back to England in July but recoiled from confronting his leader and acquiesced to Churchill's decision to continue until at least June 1954 when the queen returned from Australia.[43] Despite Eden's resistance to confrontation, other ministers took it into their own hands to register their discontent with Churchill. In September, Salisbury wrote subtly to Churchill of his concern over the high average age of the Cabinet and offered his own resignation, despite being almost twenty years Churchill's junior, to allow younger men in – Churchill, seeing the game, refused.[44] A year later, Lord Woolton, a minister and Party chairman, wrote after a Central Office report on electoral prospects of the unfavourable circumstances of continuing with the status quo and that 'an election now, under the present Government, would lead to a disaster, electorally .... Nothing can avoid this result next year, except a complete change in the structure of the Government under a new PM.'[45]

Churchill made an unsuccessful and limited attempt to reshuffle the Cabinet in October 1954. The Cabinet was growing restive with Churchill and some were even dismayed by Eden's lack of determination to clearly induce the old man's retirement. After refusing the Home Office in the reshuffle, Crookshank wrote to Eden (with copies sent to Butler, Macmillan and Salisbury), [since] I gather you have agreed to carry on with him as PM, it would be absurd to be more royal than the Prince of Wales, and stage a private one man abstention. If therefore he does ask me to stay on in the administration in my present post, I shall do so rather than rock the boat: but we are all I think taking upon ourselves very great responsibilities, for we all know that he is not fit to carry on . . .. We have a duty to the nation which we neglect at our and its peril.[46]

On several occasions Macmillan confided to his diary in 1954 his wish, shared by colleagues such as Salisbury, that the royal prerogative be used with the queen herself removing Churchill because of his perceived unfitness for office and on account of his age and conduct. However, the young monarch in her twenties, newly on the throne, would have found the task of removing her famous first prime minister, and her beloved father's last, an emotional as well as constitutional step too far. Macmillan believed that the Britain of the 1950s was 'missing an essential part of our constitutional mechanism – the effective working depends on the power and authority of the Sovereign being revived and used. A king or queen alone could say to Churchill what needs to be said in his interests as well as in ours.'[47] However, it was for the Party, not the Head of State, to decide who should lead the Conservatives.

In Conservative administrations the leader has always constantly been harangued by 'alternative leader(s)' to their throne. The second Churchill premiership had generally one lone accepted leader in Eden rather than a cohort of bickering barons vying for the crown. However, Eden was an alternative leader who, though he desired the leadership, failed to do more than berate Churchill, instead of more actively inducing his retirement like most parallel Conservative cases would have attempted. In Churchill we find a Conservative leader who all knew would soon retire after his appointment as prime minister in October 1951, thereby robbing some of that usual activism redolent in that clandestine and eponymous Conservative industry of dethroning its leader. Churchill was thus able to starve away the Conservative wolves with his tactful promises and even dates for his exit. Anthony Seldon records that 'above all there was the feeling in both the Cabinet and the Party as a whole of absolute stalemate: they did not see any way of forcing Churchill out without risk of splitting the Party'.[48] The speculation and uncertainty, however, were damaging for the Party, especially since they were heading into an election. Even the normally supportive *Times* reported in October 1954 that 'Above all, if the Conservatives are to retain their present impetus they should have some idea of the date of the change-over.'[49] In December 1954, a meeting of senior ministers discussed election dates on which Churchill's retirement would need to be known. Churchill announced that he would step down in June or July 1955. Eden immediately countered that this date was unacceptable since it gave insufficient time to prepare for an autumn election. Churchill replied with animus and stated to the assembled ministers that he knew that they were 'trying to get rid of me . . . and it is up to me to go to the Queen and hand her my resignation and yours – but I won't do it. But if you feel strongly about it you can force my hand by a sufficiently large number of Ministers handing in their resignations, in which case an Election will be inevitable; but if this happens I shall not be in favour of it and shall tell the country so.'[50] This stunned the gathering, and the Cabinet left on their Christmas break where senior ministers such as Macmillan, Salisbury, Crookshank, Stuart, Butler, Monckton, Buchan-Hepburn and Eden met and contemplated the same topic of dismissal. As Butler was reputed to have remarked: 'we've got the fish on the hook but he hasn't been gaffed yet'.[51] Macmillan, believed by Churchill to be 'Captain of the Praetorian Guard' and a staunch ally, told the prime minister's physician, Lord Moran, in January of the New Year to convince his patient that he was incapable of going on.[52] This perceived key defection might well have affected Churchill's thoughts of fighting on.

In February of the New Year, Eden tied Churchill down for a date before leaving for Bangkok and recorded that Churchill 'admitted he could not carry on & after discussion said I could base my plans on his departure during the last week of session before Easter [10 April 1955]'.[53] Churchill then contemplated reversing his decision as he had done on other occasions, threatening to frustrate Eden's ambitions one more time. This time Churchill's reasons to stay rested on the hope of a four-power summit in Paris with the Soviet Union, which he felt he could contribute to, especially since President Eisenhower proposed visiting Britain as well. Churchill discussed this proposal with the Cabinet on 14 March, to which a strained Eden asked, as Macmillan vividly recorded:

> 'Does that mean, Prime Minister, that the arrangements you have
> made with me are at an end?' Churchill, rattled, mumbled that the

national interest must come first. Eden then blurted out 'I have been Foreign Secretary for ten years. Am I not to be trusted?' Churchill replied, 'All this is very unusual. These matters are not, in my experience discussed in Cabinets'. There was a long & difficult silence ... [after Salisbury asked about the details of any agreement since many in Cabinet did not know] Churchill said, 'I cannot assent to such a discussion. I know my duty & will perform it. If any member of the Cabinet dissents his way is open'. After another pause, Butler made a useful intervention saying, 'It's not a question of loyalty to your leadership, Prime Minister. It's a question of whether an election may become necessary. You have always said that you wd. not lead the party at another election'.[54]

This tense Cabinet illustrated the gulf between the leader and the led. Churchill seemed more tranquil and accepting of his exit at the Cabinet the next day. He now knew his ministers did not accept their leader's personal objectives and view of indispensability. He must have realised that his personal summitry was no longer required, and he no longer relished the task, with his age and health, of leading unhappy Conservatives to another election. Interestingly, the Eisenhower visit did not happen; ministers covertly contacted the American ambassador, Winthrop Aldrich, after that taut Cabinet to persuade him to request the president to delay his visit until June, after the election – with Churchill gone.[55] Disgruntled and drained, the prime minister realised the difficulty in continuously delaying the unavoidable.

Churchill finally accepted, not without further doubts, his fate and after over five decades of political service, not always to the Conservatives, the octogenarian tendered his resignation on 5 April 1955 and finally signalled an almost acrid end to fifteen peerless and sometimes problematic years as leader of the Conservative Party. His final years in the party leadership and at Downing Street show a very different perspective of his career. Like almost all leaders, he was reluctant to voluntarily give up power and only did so when it appeared he had few realistic options left to retain it. Ultimately it is the Party that will exact from a leader the consequences of abusing, misusing or confusing the colossal power that is prominently placed on the head of the Conservative Party. Churchill articulated this multifarious but fundamental relationship best: 'the loyalties which centre on number one are enormous. If he trips he must be sustained. If he makes mistakes they must be covered. If he sleeps he must not be wantonly disturbed. If he is no good, he must be pole axed.'[56]

Notes

1. J. Ramsden, *The Age of Churchill and Eden 1940–1957* (London: Longman, 1995), p. 93.
2. A. Seldon also uses this term in the title of his 1981 book *Churchill's Indian Summer: The Conservative Government 1951–55* (London: Hodder & Stoughton, 1981), which remains the best and most detailed account of Churchill's peacetime administration.
3. See, for example, T. Heppell's collections *Choosing the Tory Leader: Conservative Party Leadership Elections from Heath to Cameron* (London and New York: I. B. Tauris, 2008) and *Choosing the Labour Leader: Labour Party Leadership Elections from Wilson to Brown* (London: I. B. Tauris, 2010).
4. For an analysis of the fall of twentieth-century Conservative Party leaders and the Party's leadership characteristics during that period, see H. Kumarasingham, 'For the Good of the Party': An Analysis of the Fall of Conservative Party Prime Ministers from Chamberlain to Thatcher. *Political Science*, vol. 58, no. 2 (December 2006), pp. 43–62.
5. R. Jenkins, *Churchill* (London: Macmillan, 2001), p. 845.
6. See G. Stewart, *Burying Caesar: Churchill, Chamberlain and the Battle for the Tory Party* (London: Weidenfeld & Nicolson, 1999) and more generally R. Crowcroft, *The End Is Nigh: British Politics, Power, and the Road to the Second World War* (Oxford: Oxford University Press, 2019).
7. A. Roberts, *Churchill: Walking with Destiny* (London: Penguin, 2019), p. 949.
8. Seldon, *Churchill's Indian Summer*, p. 34.
9. P. Goodhart, *1922: The Story of the 1922 Committee* (London: Macmillan, 1973), pp. 159–60.
10. Seldon, *Churchill's Indian Summer*, pp. 38–9.
11. Seldon, *Churchill's Indian Summer*, pp. 38–9.
12. Seldon, *Churchill's Indian Summer*, pp. 38–9.
13. P. Addison, *Churchill on the Home Front 1900–1955* (London: Jonathan Cape, 1992), pp. 386–7.
14. Harold Macmillan diary entry, 10 August 1954, in P. Catterall (ed.), *The Macmillan Diaries: The Cabinet Years 1950–1957* (London: Macmillan, 2003), p. 345.
15. Seldon, *Indian Summer*, p. 80.
16. Roberts, *Churchill*, p. 922.
17. J. Colville, *The Fringes of Power: Downing Street Diaries 1939–1955* (London: Hodder and Stoughton, 1985), p. 642.
18. H. Pelling, *Churchill's Peacetime Ministry, 1951–1955* (London: Macmillan, 1997), p. 97.
19. M. Gilbert, *Churchill: A Life* (London: Pimlico, 2000), p. 934.
20. Ramsden, *The Age of Churchill and Eden 1940–1957*, p. 247.
21. P. Hennessy, *The Prime Minister: The Office and Its Holders since 1945* (London: Penguin, 2000), p. 197.
22. R. Jenkins, Churchill: The Government of 1951–1955. In R. Blake and W. Roger Louis (eds.), *Churchill: A Major New Assessment of His Life in Peace and War* (London: Oxford, 1993), p. 493.
23. Gilbert, *Churchill: A Life*, p. 925.
24. R. Walsha, The One Nation Group: A Tory Approach to Backbench Politics and Organisation, 1950–55. *Twentieth Century British History*, vol. 11, no. 2 (2000), p. 188.
25. Walsha, The One Nation Group, p. 203.
26. J. Bew, *Citizen Clem: A Biography of Attlee* (London: Riverrun, 2016), p. 521.

27. Pelling, *Churchill's Peacetime Ministry*, p. 104.
28. S. Onslow, *Backbench Debate within the Conservative Party and Its Influence on British Foreign Policy, 1948–57* (London: Macmillan, 1997), pp. 27–40.
29. Pelling, *Churchill's Peacetime Ministry*, pp. 126–8.
30. Roberts, *Churchill*, pp. 942–3.
31. Ramsden, *The Age of Churchill and Eden 1940–1957*, p. 264.
32. Onslow, *Backbench Debate within the Conservative Party*, p. 184.
33. Onslow, *Backbench Debate within the Conservative Party*, p. 108.
34. Harold Macmillan diary entry, 10 October 1954, in Peter Catterall (ed.), *The Macmillan Diaries*, p. 359.
35. D. R. Thorpe, *Eden: The Life and Times of Anthony Eden First Earl of Avon, 1897–1977* (London: Chatto & Windus, 2003), pp. 347–8, 350–1.
36. Macmillan diary entries, 24 and 27 August 1954, in Catterall, *The Macmillan Diaries*, vol. 1, p. 355.
37. Seldon, *Churchill's Indian Summer*, p. 43.
38. Seldon, *Churchill's Indian Summer*, p. 43.
39. E. Shuckburgh, *Descent to Suez: Diaries 1951–1956* (London: Weidenfeld & Nicolson, 1986), p. 47.
40. Thorpe, *Eden*, p. 384.
41. Roberts, *Churchill*, pp. 938–40.
42. Jenkins, Churchill: The Government of 1951–1955, p. 495.
43. Seldon, *Churchill's Indian Summer*, p. 44.
44. Seldon, *Churchill's Indian Summer*, p. 44.
45. Ramsden, *The Age of Churchill and Eden 1940–1957*, p. 273.
46. Pelling, *Churchill's Peacetime Ministry, 1951–1955*, p. 168.
47. Macmillan diary entry, 22 September 1954, in Catterall, *The Macmillan Diaries*, p. 355.
48. Seldon, *Churchill's Indian Summer*, p. 50.
49. *The Times*, 18 October 1954.
50. Seldon, *Churchill's Indian Summer*, p. 51.
51. Ramsden, *The Age of Churchill and Eden 1940–1957*, p. 273.
52. Jenkins, *Churchill*, pp. 891–2.
53. Thorpe, *Eden*, p. 425.
54. Thorpe, *Eden*, p. 428.
55. Seldon, *Churchill's Indian Summer*, p. 53.
56. P. Norton, The Party Leader. In Philip Norton (ed.), *The Conservative Party* (Hemel Hempstead: Prentice Hall/Harvester Wheatsheaf, 1996), p. 142.

Further Reading

P. Addison, *Churchill on the Home Front 1900–1955* (London: Jonathan Cape, 1992)
J. Colville, *The Fringes of Power: Downing Street Diaries 1939–1955* (London: Hodder and Stoughton, 1985)
H. Pelling, *Churchill's Peacetime Ministry, 1951–1955* (London: Macmillan, 1997)
J. Ramsden, *The Age of Churchill and Eden 1940–1957* (London: Longman, 1995)
A. Seldon, *Churchill's Indian Summer: The Conservative Government 1951–55* (London: Hodder & Stoughton, 1981)

Conclusion
Where Next for Winston Churchill?

This is not the end. It is not even the beginning of the end. But it is, perhaps, the end of the beginning.

Winston Churchill, 10 November 1942, Mansion House, London

So, Who Was Winston Churchill?

The figure who emerges from these pages is a product of his class and age, but one who was intensely driven, hardworking and unafraid to court fame or controversy, who led from the front and relied on his own eloquence to sustain his career, fund his lifestyle and shape his legacy. He embraced technological change but there were always clear limits to his radicalism, even in the early Edwardian period, and like many he seems to have become more conservative as he got older, reacting to perceived threats to the world of his youth from socialism, communism and independence movements throughout the British Empire. The aftermath of the First World War had a profound impact, challenging many of Churchill's certainties about British power and stability. His opposition to Indian autonomy and German expansionism shared some common roots, and both brought him much criticism at the time.

His natural reaction to conflict was to throw everything into the fight, a trait that made him an effective war leader but an often-difficult political colleague and a natural magnet for media attention. He liked to lead major campaigns, whether on social reform, opposition to Indian independence, British rearmament or European unity. These would become temporarily all-consuming and could dominate his writing or rhetoric, sometimes to the detriment of his political position.

It is notable that he was not a party man, only assuming the leadership of the Conservative Party after Chamberlain's death, and that he never really led a political grouping in the Commons, preferring to work alone or with an inner circle of close friends, family and advisors. And yet the fact that he was promoted to high Cabinet rank at such a young age, and then brought back into government by Lloyd George in 1917, Baldwin in 1924 and Chamberlain in 1939, shows that he was clearly seen as an effective and often inspiring politician and administrator. He had a fertile mind and was not shy of bombarding others with his views or showing his emotions, which sometimes led to question marks about his stability and judgement.

Yet, what this book has shown is that while Churchill's influence over British and imperial policy was far wider and more varied than the study of his war premiership alone would suggest, he was rarely as definitive or as singularly relevant to today as his most ardent supporters or detractors would claim. He was but one actor (albeit a consistently colourful one) on a complex and crowded national and international stage and, even as prime minister, he often had limited room to manoeuvre. His attitudes and actions, whether on social reform, aerial bombing, Ireland or European union, were often formulated in response to the perceived needs of the moment and he was prepared to adapt them in response to new realities, or to move on if they no longer seemed relevant.

It was his consistent and vocal opposition to Nazism, his assumption of the premiership in 1940 and his advocacy of a policy of continuing to wage war until victory that elevated Churchill's status above his contemporaries. His place in history was assured by British survival in 1940 and Allied victory in 1945 and secured with the help of his voice and his pen through the wide publication of his speeches and war memoirs. He believed history was made by great men and saw himself as part of a dynastic and national narrative stretching back to his ancestor John Churchill, 1st Duke of Marlborough. It is a version of history he did much to shape, and which continues to carry influence in the public sphere, but which has also always been challenged. His imperialism was driven by a desire for British power and influence but was justified by a worldview which enshrined racial hierarchies. He expressed this as supporting civilisation over barbarism and did not see it as incompatible with parliamentary democracy and social reform at home. He fought the Second World War to preserve both democracy in Britain and the Empire abroad, failing to see that the two were ultimately incompatible. His vision for the post-war world was a return to the 1930s, and by 1945 he was out of step with mainstream international and national opinion, thereby fuelling his current two-stranded and seemingly contradictory legacy of being simultaneously the saviour of democracy and a racist imperialist.

To Churchill, it was British national survival in 1940 that obviously mattered most, and the actions he took to ensure it, in courting Roosevelt and helping to draft the Atlantic Charter, and in prioritising the defence of Britain and the Mediterranean over India and the Pacific, ultimately contributed to the retreat from Empire and facilitated the liberation of western Europe and the survival of the Western democracies. Churchill had no choice but to accept the former in order to secure the latter. Criticisms can and should be made of individual decisions, and his neglect of India during the Bengal Famine has been highlighted by several authors in this book. Yet, it is generally recognised that he played his limited hand very well.

It is interesting to speculate about future research interest in Churchill. Until recently, most of those who chose to write substantively about him were White, male, from Europe or North America and preoccupied with political and military history. I hope that this volume has shown that different voices, perspectives and narratives are now emerging from a new generation of historians whose views were not formed in the immediate post-war decades. In recent years there have been important new approaches to Churchill. The interplay between his words and actions, a better understanding of his finances and their impact on his decision-making, and an appreciation of his health issues, emotions and psychology are changing our understanding of the man. The fruits of such research can be seen in several of the chapters of this volume and will continue to impact on new scholarship.

Meanwhile, the emergence of new research in the fields of gender and post-colonial studies is starting to influence the discussion of Churchill's life and legacy. That this has been a slow process is probably due in part to Churchill's iconic status in Britain and the United States and the perceived reputational risks to individuals in publicly challenging it, and to the fact that he is perhaps not seen as a natural subject choice by academics working in these areas.

Sonia Purnell (in Chapter 17) has highlighted the role of Clementine Churchill in supporting her husband, and there have been other recent works on the similar roles played by his daughters and secretaries. Niamh Gallagher's Chapter 6 on Churchill and Ireland comments on Churchill's often confrontational relationship with the women's suffrage movement. He was certainly no feminist even if he could support enfranchisement and politics remained a male space governed by masculine codes that Churchill was keen to preserve. And yet some of his social and economic policies, and his support for the mobilisation of the civilian population in two world wars, changed the nature of the society he was seeking to preserve and contributed to greater freedom for women. Despite his undoubtedly patrician outlook, his career owed much to the advice and support of his mother and Clementine. Moreover, his position on female equality seems to have moved over time away from ambiguity towards greater, if perhaps grudging, acceptance. Yet there were limits. By the 1950s, the huge technological changes which his long life had witnessed, and which in general he had embraced, were starting to sound the death knell for the world of his youth. He was not prepared to embrace the more liberal society at home and the end of empire abroad. It is not surprising therefore that his very traditional state funeral in January 1965 is often presented as a watershed moment in the history of modern Britain.

At the very beginning of this volume, Lord Boateng highlighted the role of the Sir Winston Churchill Archive Trust and the Churchill Archives Centre (home of this editor) in creating online materials. The ability to link collections and discussions will play a role in shaping future discourse about Churchill, but so will events. Brexit led to a discussion of his views on European union and the Black Lives Matter movement put the focus on his imperialism and racism, while the Russian invasion of the Ukraine in 2022 led to a renewed interest in his role in the Cold War.

Churchill is interesting, and is likely to continue to generate interest, because he sits at the crux of so many fundamental debates. How do you defend the values of liberal democracy while acknowledging the imperial exploitation that has made them possible? To what extent can you judge historic figures by the values of today? What measures are justified in war? What is Britain's place in the world? Who writes the history? To what extent can an individual impact the course of events?

Hopefully, what this book has shown is that Churchill is an excellent starting point to explore such issues.

For as he acknowledged, when paying tribute to his predecessor Neville Chamberlain on 12 November 1940, the verdict of history is not constant: 'In one phase men seem to have been right, in another they seem to have been wrong. Then again, a few years later, when the perspective of time has lengthened, all stands in a different setting. There is a new proportion. There is another scale of values.'

Appendix A

Summary of Personal, Military and Political Life, 1874–1965

1874	30 November: born, eldest son of Lord Randolph Churchill, third son of 7th Duke of Marlborough, and Jennie (née Jerome)
1888–92	Attendance at Harrow School
1893–4	Cadet at Sandhurst Royal Military Academy
1895	24 January: death of Lord Randolph Churchill
	20 February: commissioned as Second Lieutenant, 4th Hussars
	November to December: served with Spanish forces in Cuba. The trip included his first visit to the United States
1896	Posted to India with 4th Hussars
1897	September to October: served with Malakand Field Force, 31st Punjab Infantry, fighting on Indian north-west frontier
1898	August to September: served, attached 21st Lancers with Nile Expeditionary Force, present at Battle of Omdurman
1899	July: unsuccessfully contests Oldham (Conservative); appointed correspondent for *Morning Post* to South Africa to cover Second Boer War
	15 November: taken prisoner by Boers and transferred to the States Model School, Pretoria; 12 December: escapes
1900	Served as Lieutenant South African Light Horse; present at actions of Acton Homes, Venter's Spruit, Hussar Hill, Cingolo, Monte Cristo; at battles of Spion Kop, Vaal Krantz and Pieters; at engagements of Johannesburg and Diamond Hill; and at capture of Pretoria

	October: elected as MP for Oldham (Conservative, 1900–4; Liberal, 1904–6)
	December 1900 to February 1901: lecture tour of the United States and Canada
1901	28 February: delivers maiden speech in House of Commons
1904	31 May: moves from Conservative Party to Liberal Party
1905	December: appointed under secretary of state for the colonies (December 1905 to April 1908)
1906	January: elected as MP for Manchester North-West (Liberal, 1906–8)
1907	1 May: becomes privy councillor
	September 1907 to January 1908: tour of Mediterranean and East Africa
1908	April: appointed to the Cabinet as president of the Board of Trade (April 1908 to February 1910)
	April: loses seat as MP for Manchester North-West
	May: elected as MP for Dundee (Liberal, 1908–22)
	12 September: marries Clementine, daughter of Sir Henry Hozier and Lady Blanche (née Ogilvy)
1910	February: appointed as home secretary (February 1910 to October 1911)
1911	October: appointed as first lord of the admiralty (October 1911 to May 1915)
1915	May: appointed chancellor of the Duchy of Lancaster (May to November 1915)
	Takes up painting
	November: resigns from the government and takes up commission. Served Western Front with Grenadier Guards
1916	January to May: appointed as lieutenant-colonel, commanding 6th Battalion Royal Scots Fusiliers, Belgium
1917	July: appointed as minister of munitions (July 1917 to January 1919)
1919	January: appointed as secretary of state for war and air (January 1919 to February 1921, and air until April 1921)
1921	January: appointed as secretary of state for the colonies (January 1921 to October 1922)
	November: loses seat as MP for Dundee
1922	September: buys Chartwell Manor, Kent

1923	December: unsuccessfully contests seat of West Leicester (Liberal)
1924	March: unsuccessfully contests Abbey Division of Westminster (Independent)
	October: elected as MP for Epping (Independent, then returns to Conservative Party from Liberal Party and holds seat as a Conservative, 1924–45)
	November: appointed as chancellor of the exchequer (November 1924 to May 1929)
1929	August to October: lecture tour of Canada and the United States
1931–2	December 1931 to February 1932: lecture tour of the United States
1939	September: appointed as first lord of the admiralty (September 1939 to May 1940)
1940	10 May: appointed as prime minister, first lord of the Treasury and minister of defence (May 1940 to July 1945)
	May to June: repeated trips to France
1941	August: first wartime meeting with President Roosevelt off coast of Newfoundland
	December 1941 to January 1942: trip to the United States and Canada
1942	June: trip to the United States
	August: trip to Egypt and the Soviet Union
1943	January: Casablanca Conference with President Roosevelt, Morocco
	May to June: trip to the United States, Algeria and Tunisia
	August to September: trip to Canada and the United States for first Quebec Conference
	November 1943 to January 1944: trip to Malta, Iran for Tehran Conference with Stalin and Roosevelt, Tunisia and Morocco
1944	12 June: visit to beachheads in France
	August: trip to Algeria, Corsica and Italy
	September: trip to Canada and the United States for second Quebec Conference
	October: trip to the Soviet Union
	November: visit to France and return to Paris
	December: trip to Greece

1945	January to February: trip to Malta, the Crimea for Yalta Conference with Stalin and Roosevelt, Greece and Egypt
	March: trip to Germany
	July: trip to Germany for Potsdam Conference with Stalin and Truman; Conservatives lose 1945 General Election and Churchill becomes leader of the Conservative opposition (1945–51). Returned as MP for Woodford (Conservative, 1945–64)
1946	5 March: delivers 'iron curtain' speech, Fulton, Missouri
	19 September: delivers speech at University of Zurich, Switzerland
1951	October: elected as prime minister and first lord of the Treasury (October 1951 to April 1955; also minister of defence October 1951 to January 1952)
1953	Made a Knight of the Garter (henceforth styled 'Sir Winston Churchill')
	June: suffers major stroke
	October: awarded Nobel Prize for Literature
	December: attends Bermuda Conference with President Eisenhower
1954	June: visits United States and Canada
1955	5 April: resigns as prime minister
1959	May: visit to the United States as a guest of President Eisenhower
1963	9 April: made an honorary US citizen by Act of Congress
1965	24 January: dies
	30 January: state funeral and burial in Bladon churchyard, Oxfordshire

Major Literary Works by Winston S. Churchill

The Story of the Malakand Field Force (London: Longmans, Green and Co., 1898)
The River War: An Historical Account of the Reconquest of the Sudan, 2 vols. (London: Longmans, Green and Co., 1899)
Savrola (1899; London: Longmans, Green and Co., 1900)
Ian Hamilton's March (London: Longmans, Green and Co., 1900)
London to Ladysmith: Via Pretoria (London: Longmans, Green and Co., 1900)
Mr Brodrick's Army (London: A. L. Humphreys, 1903)
For Free Trade (London: A. L. Humphreys, 1906)
Lord Randolph Churchill, 2 vols. (London: Macmillan, 1906)
My African Journey (London: Hodder & Stoughton, 1908)
Liberalism and the Social Problem (London: Hodder & Stoughton, 1909)
The People's Rights (London: Hodder & Stoughton, 1909)
The World Crisis, 1911–1918, 6 vols. (London: Thornton Butterworth, 1923–31)
My Early Life: A Roving Commission (London: Thornton Butterworth, 1930)
India (London: Thornton Butterworth, 1931)
Thoughts and Adventures (London: Thornton Butterworth, 1932)
Marlborough: His Life and Times, 4 vols. (London: George Harrap Ltd, 1933–8)
Great Contemporaries (London: Thornton Butterworth, 1937)
Arms and the Covenant (London: George Harrap Ltd, 1938)
Step by Step (London: Thornton Butterworth, 1939)
Various editions of speeches published in London by Cassell & Co. Ltd, including: *Into Battle* (1941), *The Unrelenting Struggle* (1942), *The End of the Beginning* (1943), *Onwards to Victory* (1944), *The Dawn of Liberation* (1945), *Victory* (1946), *The Sinews of Peace* (1948), *Europe Unite* (1950), *In the Balance* (1951), *Stemming the Tide* (1953) and *The Unwritten Alliance* (1961)
Painting as a Pastime (London: Odhams Press, 1948)
The Second World War, 6 vols. (London: Cassell & Co. Ltd, 1948–54)
A History of the English-Speaking Peoples, 4 vols. (London: Cassell & Co. Ltd, 1956–8)
The Dream (Cambridge: International Churchill Society, 1987) – published posthumously

Index